The Ethics of Tourism

There are increasingly strident calls from many sectors of society for the tourism industry, the world's largest industry, to adopt a more ethical approach to the way it does business. In particular there has been an emphasis placed on the need for a more ethical approach to the way the tourism industry interacts with consumers, the environment, with indigenous peoples, those in poverty, and those in destinations suffering human rights abuses.

This book introduces students to the important topic of tourism ethics and illustrates how ethical principles and theory can be applied to address contemporary tourism industry issues. A critical role of the book is to highlight the ethical challenges in the tourism industry and to situate tourism ethics within wider contemporary discussions of ethics in general. Integrating theory and practice the book analyses a broad range of topical and relevant tourism ethical issues from the urgent 'big-picture' problems facing the industry as a whole (e.g. air travel and global warming) to more micro-scale everyday issues that may face individual tourism operators or, indeed, individual tourists. The book applies relevant ethical frameworks to each issue, addressing a range of ethical approaches to provide the reader with a firm grounding of applied ethics, from first principles. International case studies with reflective questions at the end are integrated throughout to provide readers with valuable insight into real world ethical dilemmas, encouraging critical analysis of tourism ethical issues as well as ethically determined decisions. Discussion questions and annotated further reading are included to aid students' understanding.

The Ethics of Tourism: Critical and Applied Perspectives is essential reading for all Tourism students globally.

Brent Lovelock is an Associate Professor in the Department of Tourism at the University of Otago, New Zealand.

Kirsten M. Lovelock is a Senior Research Fellow in the Department of Preventive and Social Medicine, University of Otago, New Zealand.

The Ethics of Tourism

Critical and applied perspectives

Brent Lovelock and
Kirsten M. Lovelock

Routledge
Taylor & Francis Group

LONDON AND NEW YORK

First published 2013
by Routledge
2 Park Square, Milton Park, Abingdon, Oxon OX14 4RN

Simultaneously published in the USA and Canada
by Routledge
711 Third Avenue, New York, NY 10017

Routledge is an imprint of the Taylor & Francis Group, an informa business

© 2013 Brent Lovelock and Kirsten M. Lovelock

The right of Brent Lovelock and Kirsten M. Lovelock to be identified as authors of this work has been asserted by them in accordance with sections 77 and 78 of the Copyright, Designs and Patents Act 1988.

All rights reserved. No part of this book may be reprinted or reproduced or utilised in any form or by any electronic, mechanical, or other means, now known or hereafter invented, including photocopying and recording, or in any information storage or retrieval system, without permission in writing from the publishers.

Trademark notice: Product or corporate names may be trademarks or registered trademarks, and are used only for identification and explanation without intent to infringe.

British Library Cataloguing in Publication Data
A catalogue record for this book is available from the British Library

Library of Congress Cataloging in Publication Data
A catalog record has been requested for this book

ISBN: 978-0-415-57557-7 (hbk)
ISBN: 978-0-415-57558-4 (pbk)
ISBN: 978-0-203-85453-2 (ebk)

Typeset in Times New Roman
by Cenveo Publisher Services

This book is dedicated to our children Millie, Oscar and Levi

Contents

Figures

Tables

Case studies

Contributors

Karla Boluk is a Lecturer in the Department of Hospitality and Tourism Management at the University of Ulster, Northern Ireland. Karla's current research interests include tourism as a potential vehicle to eradicate poverty, Fair Trade Tourism, rural development, community development/empowerment and social entrepreneurship.

John Connell is Professor of Geography at the University of Sydney. He works mainly on migration and development in the Pacific and has published various books on the migration of health workers.

Simon Darcy is an Associate Professor at the UTS Business School and Director of the Cosmopolitan Civil Societies Research Centre at the University of Technology, Sydney. He is an interdisciplinary researcher with expertise in developing inclusive organisational approaches to diversity groups. Since incurring a spinal injury in 1983 Simon is a power wheelchair user and passionately believes in the rights of all people to fully participate in all aspects of community life.

Martha Dowsley is an Associate Professor at Lakehead University in Thunder Bay, Ontario, Canada. She is cross-appointed in the departments of Anthropology and Geography. Her research focuses on cultural understandings of natural resources.

Tara Duncan is a Lecturer in the Department of Tourism at the University of Otago, New Zealand. Her background in social and cultural geography informs her current research interests in lifestyle mobilities, young budget travel (backpacking, gap years and the Overseas Experience (OE)) and everyday spaces and practices of tourism, hospitality and leisure.

Stefan Gössling is a Professor at the Department of Service Management, Lund University, and the School of Business and Economics at Linnaeus University, Kalmar, both Sweden. He is also the research co-ordinator at the Research Centre for Sustainable Tourism, Sogndal, Norway.

C. Michael Hall is a Professor in the Department of Management, University of Canterbury, New Zealand; Docent, Department of Geography, University of Oulu, Finland, and a Visiting Professor at the University of Eastern Finland, Savonlinna, and Linneaus University, Kalmar, Sweden.

Joan C. Henderson is an Associate Professor at Nanyang Business School in Singapore. Prior to this, she lectured in tourism in the United Kingdom after periods of employment in the public and private tourism sectors.

Andrew Holden is Professor of Environment and Tourism and also the Director for the Centre for Research into the Environment and Sustainable Tourism Development (CREST) at the University of Bedfordshire, England. His research focuses on the interaction between human behaviour and the natural environment within the context of tourism. Specific areas of research interest include environmental ethics, poverty and sustainable development.

Acknowledgements

A number of friends, colleagues and family members have provided support and have contributed to this book. We would like to thank all of our case study contributors for their case studies and enthusiastic support throughout the preparation of the manuscript. Thank you to: C. Michael Hall, Joan Henderson, John Connell, Simon Darcy, Andrew Holden, Martha Dowsley, Stefan Gössling, Tara Duncan and Karla Boluk. A big thanks to the commissioning editor Emma Travis for her patience and forbearance and to Carol Barber for her understanding and support throughout the process. Thank you also to Adam Doering for stirling assistance with the literature early on in the project, and to Diana Evans for dealing with our formatting woes and working so quickly to rectify them. Thank you also to Jo O'Brien for help in the initial set-up stages. Helen Dunn for final checks, and Trudie Walters for indexing. Brent would also like to thank his students for wittingly and at times unwittingly directing him toward this pathway. Thanks also to the various publishers who have allowed us to reproduce tables and figures and to draw on pivotal work in this field. Figure 8.2 reprinted with permission of the Publisher from *Critical Disability Theory*, by Dianne Pothier and Richard Devlin ©University of British Columbia Press 2005. All rights reserved by the Publisher. Figure 12.5 reprinted with permission from *Journal of Marketing*, published by the American Marketing Association, Thomas W. Dunfee, N. Craig Smith and William T. Ross, Jr., Social Contracts and Marketing Ethics *Vol. 63, No. 3 (Jul., 1999), pp. 14–32*. For photographs we would like to thank: Pin Ng, Martha Dowsley, Simon Darcy, C. Michael Hall, Andrea Farminer, Asim Tanveer and permissions from various unknown photographers. Thank you to David Fennell, C. Michael Hall, Alan Lew, Mick Smith and Rosaleen Duffy, Stroma Cole and Nigel Morgan, and Andrew Holden for inspiration and the wide range of scholars who have provided the invaluable research which informs and makes a book like this possible. Thanks also to colleagues at the University of Otago – in the Department of Tourism, David McBride in the Department of Preventive and Social Medicine, and the librarians at the Central Library. For musical inspiration: *Astro Children*, Lucinda Williams, David Kilgour, *The Clean*, Gillian Welch, Gomez and *The Civil Wars*. A number of friends and family have provided encouragement and fun evenings that allowed us to forget the book: thank you to Tina McKay, Bronwen McNoe, Hazel Tucker, Anna and Andy Thompson,

Romola McKay, Shaun Scott and Rae Hickey, Teresa La Rooy and TEU colleagues, Nicky Page and Tex Houston, Diana Saxton and James Ballard (for Naseby retreats), James Windle, Joel and Trudy Tyndall, Kathy Ferguson, Jo Preston and Marj Wright for sustenance. Finally, thanks to our children Millie, Oscar and Levi. And also, to our extended family: Fergie, Binky (for computer company), Oaky, Pecky, Betty and Hetty.

1 Introduction

'On the whole human beings want to be good, but not too good, and not quite all the time.'

George Orwell[a]

'A man without ethics is a wild beast loosed upon this world.'

Albert Camus[b]

'To educate a person in mind and not in morals is to educate a menace in society.'

Theodore Roosevelt[c]

'Ethics is a skill.'

Marianne Jennings[d]

LEARNING OBJECTIVES

After reading this chapter you will be able to:

- Understand the rationale for an 'ethics' focus on tourism.
- Define the term 'ethical tourism'.
- Understand the relationship between ethical tourism and sustainable tourism.
- Discuss the role of ethical consumption in ethical tourism.

1.1 INTRODUCTION

As recently as five years ago, one would seldom have heard the words 'ethics' and 'tourism' used together in a sentence. As recently as 10 years ago, one would seldom have heard the words 'business' and 'ethics' together – at least outside of the specific world of moral philosophy and the field of business ethics research. The Enron, WorldCom and other corporate scandals of the first decade of the twenty-first century have changed all this. The issues raised and lessons learned from these and numerous other business outrages have permeated into many aspects of our lives – to influence not only our financial concerns but also our leisure activities.

Now, some researchers and industry practitioners are starting to think, talk and write about the ethics of tourism, or, rather, about the 'ethical deficit' (Moufakkir 2012) or 'immense void' in ethics in the tourism field (Fennell 2006). Why this recent interest in ethics? What has changed about tourism? Well, of course tourism as an industry has grown, but this growth has been steady, to the point now where total global arrivals are estimated to be in the vicinity of 5 billion, with about 1 billion of these being international arrivals.[1] We acknowledge that tourism is a large industry and perhaps even the world's largest, but it is not on these grounds alone that there is a need for a text on tourism ethics. Billions of people participate in comparable leisure activities: they go to the movies, play sport, go shopping – yet there is no equivalent call for these to be placed under the same 'ethics-scope'. So what is it about tourism that would demand such consideration?

Tourism is a social practice or phenomenon that reaches into many people's lives, into communities, economies, and takes place across an incredibly diverse range of settings. It is almost ubiquitous. Despite early and optimistic hopes that tourism would be the 'smokeless' industry that could benefit communities around the world, contributing to social and economic wellbeing, it is clearly acknowledged now that tourism is linked to a range of social, economic and environmental impacts or 'tourism-related changes' as Hall and Lew (2009) describe them. These have been clearly debated and discussed in the tourism literature and by the industry for four or more decades (for a detailed coverage of tourism impacts we recommend Hall and Lew (2009) *Understanding and Managing Tourism Impacts*). Indeed, managing the impacts of tourism continues to remain a strong focus for researchers, planners and practitioners in the field today. Broadly, tourism impacts may be categorised as social–cultural, economic or environmental; however, there may be considerable overlap between these categories.

> Economic impacts encompass the monetary benefits and costs that result from the development and use of tourism facilities and services. Environmental impacts include alterations to the natural environment, including air, water, soils, vegetation and wildlife, as well as changes to the built environment.
>
> (Wall and Wright 1977 in Wall and Mathieson 2006: 38)

Social and cultural impacts of tourism include the way that tourism may 'effect changes in collective and individual value systems, behaviour patterns, community structures, lifestyle and the quality of life' (Hall and Lew 2009: 57). As Higgins-Desbiolles (2006) notes, tourism is 'more than an industry', it is a social force.

There are a number of defining characteristics of tourism as a social and physical phenomenon that, together with the sheer scale and scope of the tourism industry, require us to consider alternative approaches to 'the tourism question':

- Tourism involves (often complex) social, cultural, economic and ecological interactions.
- These interactions take place en route to and in a 'destination' which is also someone's 'place' (house, village, town, city, nation, mountain, jungle, beach, backyard).
- The visitor (and industry providers) may value this 'place' and their 'host' less than they do their own place and community.

- These interactions often involve power differentials – often with the visitor and tourism industry expressing power in a number of ways over the host.
- These interactions may result in harms or benefits – to the host (and possibly the visitor too), to their communities, their economies and their ecologies.
- Tourists (and other stakeholders in the tourism 'exchange') are inherently selfish – each seeking to maximise their personal (or group or corporate) value.

Increasingly since the 1970s, the degree of concern about the scope and scale of tourism impacts has led to the development and promotion of approaches through which we can minimise tourism's negative impacts while still allowing the benefits of tourism to flow to communities. At the forefront of such approaches has been sustainable tourism development. But can sustainable approaches address ethical concerns and ensure ethical practice? Modelled on sustainable development, which emerged from the work of the World Commission for the Environment and Development (1987) (the 'Brundtland Report' (see United Nations 2012)), sustainable tourism development involves taking 'full account of its current and future economic, social and environmental impacts, addressing the needs of visitors, the industry, the environment and host communities' (UNWTO 2012a). Sustainable tourism has been the guiding principle of the tourism industry since the late 1980s. However, critics point to the ongoing impacts of tourism, and argue that sustainable tourism is simply rhetoric, adopted by destination planners and industry practitioners to appease the travelling public, host communities and environmentalists. Referred to variously as a 'significant policy problem', a 'policy failure' (Hall 2011) and a 'myth' (Sharpley 2010), sustainable tourism is decried as being both meaningless and meaning everything – to the extent that its operationalisation is near impossible (see Chapter 9 for a full discussion of sustainable tourism development in relation to nature).

On a more profound level, sustainable tourism emerged from a neoliberal discourse on meeting pressing global problems.[2] Subsequently, sustainable development (at least in its current forms) is largely predicated upon economic growth, and thus faces challenges not only in credibility, but in creating truly (in a holistic sense) sustainable outcomes (e.g. Duffy 2008; Higgins-Desbiolles 2008; Fletcher 2011). Sustainable *tourism*, then, could be seen as a neoliberal sop to the real problems faced by tourism. Within the existing political frameworks and ideologies of many destinations, it is difficult to see 'true' sustainability becoming the dominant paradigm. In summary, a broader, ethics approach to tourism would go beyond the 'three pillars' (environmental, economic, social–cultural) of sustainability (Weeden 2002).

As the full range of externalities and opportunities from tourism has become more apparent over recent years, a number of other approaches to tourism have emerged – arguably most (if not all) emerging from the 'mother-ship' of sustainable tourism. Notably ecotourism, a form of tourism that encompasses respect for nature, learning and the positive involvement of local communities, has become widely established. Initially ecotourism was seen predominantly as a niche form of tourism, characterised by small-scale, environmentally sensitive tourism activities. Detractors, however, raise concern about the co-option of the concept by mass tourism, corporate interests, resulting in the dilution and betrayal of the initial goals of ecotourism (e.g. Wight 1993; Honey 1999), and potentially just another example of so-called 'green-washing' in the tourism industry.

But it is not only the environmental impacts of tourism that have attracted attention. The social and cultural outcomes of tourism have also led to the promulgation of community and culture-friendly forms of tourism. Among these is 'responsible tourism', which is defined in the *Cape Town Declaration on Responsible Tourism* as having the following characteristics:

- Minimises negative economic, environmental, and social impacts;
- Generates greater economic benefits for local people and enhances the well-being of host communities, improves working conditions and access to the industry;
- Involves local people in decisions that affect their lives and life chances;
- Makes positive contributions to the conservation of natural and cultural heritage, to the maintenance of the world's diversity;
- Provides more enjoyable experiences for tourists through more meaningful connections with local people, and a greater understanding of local cultural, social and environmental issues;
- Provides access for physically challenged people; and
- Is culturally sensitive, engenders respect between tourists and hosts, and builds local pride and confidence (International Centre for Responsible Tourism 2012; see also Goodwin 2011).

Responsible tourism is strongly linked to sustainable tourism (with a similar threefold focus on environmental, economic and social outcomes). However, responsible tourism is said to have broader outcomes, importantly, to assign responsibility for action to various stakeholders. For example, responsible tourism has also shaped Corporate Social Responsibility which emphasises the importance of corporate citizenship and corporate sustainability. Broadly, it is a company's commitment to operating in an ethical way that takes into account society and the environment. Fair Trade Tourism is also another example, which emerged in response to the problems evident with sustainable tourism – here principles of fair trade are introduced to address the social inequity and sustainability issues within the industry. Some countries have adopted responsible tourism rather than sustainable tourism in their tourism planning processes (e.g. South Africa), and there is now a 'World Responsible Tourism Day', while mega-travel agent Virgin Holidays sponsors annual Responsible Tourism Awards. Yet the sad fact is that only 2 per cent of tourism businesses globally are participating in responsible tourism or related initiatives (Frey and George 2010).

Ecotourism and responsible tourism are just two of a broad array of alternative tourism approaches that have proliferated in response to a growing awareness of the fragility of our planetary environment, and tourism's contribution to damaging (or preserving) our world. Other driving forces have been a growing awareness of social justice issues (arguably brought about through a combination of greater global connectivity and media pervasiveness, an enhanced sense of global citizenship, and (optimistically) incremental moral development). As a consequence, we now know a lot more about how tourism either exacerbates or ameliorates social problems. Such problems range from those of local wellbeing where tourism competes with host communities for access to critical resources such as land or water, to broader political issues, for example human rights repression, or dispossession of indigenous peoples.

Collectively the range of 'alternative tourisms' that offers solutions to the problems of unmitigated mass tourism now includes:

- sustainable tourism
- ecotourism
- green tourism
- soft tourism
- responsible tourism
- just tourism
- justice tourism
- pro-poor tourism
- new tourism
- voluntourism
- fair trade tourism.

1.2 DEFINING ETHICAL TOURISM

So how exactly does 'ethical tourism' fit in with the range of alternative tourisms and how do we define it? Strangely, writers in the field have tended to avoid defining ethical tourism, and perhaps this gives us an inkling of the difficulties of providing a useful description. Ethical tourism is not so different from the alternatives listed above, and in simple terms could be considered as an amalgam of the 'best features' of these alternative tourisms.

Industry and non-governmental organisations (NGOs), however, have not been deterred from describing the term:

> Ethical tourism has evolved as a term when one considers travelling to, or developing tourism in a destination where ethical issues are the key driver, e.g. social injustice, human rights, animal welfare or the environment. Ethical tourism is geared towards encouraging both the consumer and industry to avoid participation in activities that contribute or support negative ethical issues.
>
> (Travel Matters 2012)

Academics have been more cautious. Some have drawn links between ethical issues and ecotourism, and others to such types of tourism as sustainable, responsible, just, or pro-poor (Holden 2003; Hultsman 1995). Lea (1993) in an early discussion of ethical tourism development in the 'Third World' wrote that ethical tourism links the environmental concerns of ecotourism with the social consciousness of aid organisations. Ethical tourism has been referred to as a 'theme' that has emerged in the global North in response to concerns about the impact of mass tourism (Weeden 2005). It is an attempt to manage tourism for the benefit of all stakeholders, and to contribute (in a similar manner to sustainable tourism) to environmental, social and economic goals (Weeden 2005).

It is generally considered that ethical tourists will be concerned with a broader range of issues than the 'green' tourist: 'For example, they may be interested in human resource policies in the tourism industry, such as pay levels and the employment of local labour,

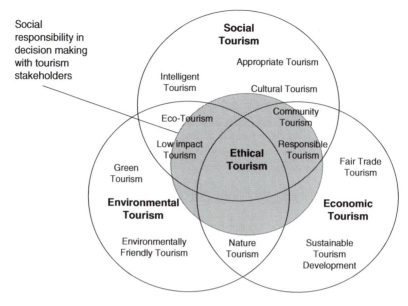

Figure 1.1 *Ethical tourism model (Speed 2008).*

as well as the way in which the economic benefits of tourism are distributed throughout the economy' (Swarbrooke and Horner 2007: 148). In a discussion of the ethicality of backpackers, Speed (2008: 61) believes that ethical backpackers would:

> respect their hosts: by treading softly on the environment; by being educated about the culture; by ensuring their stay returns fair, economic benefits, and by ensuring all decision making with all tourism's stakeholders is socially responsible.

Speed concurs with our perspective that ethical tourism is characteristic of many 'alternative' types of tourism. However, she makes the point that 'only by adopting the different values of such tourism types and ensuring that all decision making with all stakeholders, regarding environmental, social and economic issues is socially responsible, is it ethical tourism' (2008: 60). She conceptualises the relationship between ethical tourism and other forms of tourism (Figure 1.1).

The working definition in this book of ethical tourism acknowledges previous understandings of ethical tourism, and its links with sustainable tourism and other alternative tourisms:

> Ethical tourism is tourism in which all stakeholders involved apply principles of good behaviour (justice, fairness and equality), to their interactions with one another, with society, with the environment and other life forms.

1.3 THE NEED FOR AN ETHICAL APPROACH

Two questions might arise from the discussion so far: first, do we need another tourism framework? Second, what is to prevent ethical tourism becoming 'just another alternative tourism'? Will ethical tourism suffer from the credibility and implementation problems cited for some of the 'alternatives' above?

The 'failings' of sustainable tourism and concerns about some of the other alternative frameworks above are a clear indication that there is a need to reconceptualise some tourism-related problems – and indeed, tourism-related solutions. Some have pointed out that the failure of sustainable tourism lies in its disconnection from processes of governance, legislation and policy (e.g. Hall 2011; Lovelock 2011). Others argue that its multi-dimensionality and inherent contradictions have prevented sustainable tourism from reaching its full potential. Yet others attribute the blame to dominant ideologies within the political systems of destinations, arguing that while neoliberalism is the dominant discourse within globalised systems of tourism production, sustainable tourism in a holistic sense will never be realised.

Another possibility for the failing of sustainable tourism and related approaches is that they do not form a strong connection with human behaviour. They are not based upon fundamental human tenets. To illustrate: imagine that you are the owner of a company that runs tours to a remote indigenous community in the Amazon jungle. Sustainable tourism principles may tell you that you need to optimise the outcomes of your tours, in terms of the social and cultural aspects, economic benefits, and environmental impacts. In practice, 'balancing' these needs, for your current operation, for a broad range of stakeholders, while considering how your tours may also affect future generations, is difficult if not impossible. You are being asked to balance a broad range of actual and potential outcomes (or impacts). An ethical tourism approach on the other hand, while also potentially considering outcomes (consequences), may ask you to consider *how* to behave: it will ask you about your fundamental duties towards the indigenous people, towards your clients and towards yourself. In this sense, an ethics approach to tourism is more humanistic than current approaches and that is because ethics is fundamental to being human. And that is not to say that ethics approaches to tourism do not consider the non-human. In the example above, using an ethics approach, you as a tourism operator would have to consider your essential relationships and responsibilities towards non-human beings, including 'sentient' and 'non-sentient' components of the natural system (see Chapter 9).

The focus of sustainable tourism and related frameworks on the *impacts* of tourism as the traditional root of ethical issues in tourism is a fundamental failing:

> we have not yet made the leap from recognising impacts and attempting to ameliorate them beyond that which is deemed acceptable to the industry. This is very much akin to setting standards for the industry on the basis of what is deemed 'right' or 'good', without fully understanding the meaning of right or good.
>
> (Fennell 2006: 7)

Similarly tourism providers find themselves operating within legal and policy systems that only demand the minimum. While some believe that business is under no obligation 'to be moral beyond what the law requires' (Fieser 1996 in Yaman 2003: 107), from an ethical perspective, while obeying the law is necessary, it is not sufficient requirement for good conduct (Smith 2001). As Plato (427–347 BC), the classical Greek philosopher wrote, 'Good people do not need laws to tell them to act responsibly, while bad people will find a way around the laws' (in Jackson 2012: 1). Thus, for the tourism industry to become sustainable, would require the realisation that sustainable tourism is more than a process, more than impacts or outcomes and more than staying within laws and regulations. It is the recognition that sustainable tourism is also an *ethic* (Fennell 2006).

Of course, some would argue that the tourism industry is already ethical, by pointing to the raft of ethical codes that exist, from the United Nations World Tourism Organization down. For many, 'such a cookbook of guidelines is an example of the leading edge of tourism ethics' (Fennell 2006: 7). Fennell argues that identifying impacts and prescribing guidelines (e.g. codes of ethics), and rectifying the impacts 'are two very different mind-sets and actions', and believes that we have 'largely been unsuccessful' in achieving the latter (2006: 7). The ethical code approach alone is akin to a doctor prescribing the stand-ard 'two paracetamol and bed rest' for all patients – but without the patient or doctor really being aware of (or caring about) the true nature of the affliction. In other words, most codes treat the symptoms rather than the cause.

In response to the questions we raise above, ethical tourism is not just another alternative tourism. Ethical tourism is not a form of tourism – like ecotourism, pro-poor tourism or sustainable tourism. All of these forms of tourism have evolved in an era that has been dominated by neoliberal philosophy and neoliberal-informed economic policy and they have been commodified. As 'forms' they tend to be prescriptive in terms of what the tour-ist or industry can and cannot do, and this is one of the reasons why they fail – the prescrip-tions will never be able to address the wide range of social practices, events and interactions that human beings provoke and seek guidance or resolution for. Ethical tourism is a way of thinking that has applicability for all forms of tourism and for critically reflecting on behaviours in order to inform behavioural change. It is more encompassing – it is about being a moral-being rather than a 'green-being', or a 'justice-being', or an 'eco-being'.

The neoliberal hegemony, as Smith and Duffy (2003) argue, has sidelined 'ethics'. Ethics has been set aside as if unnecessary or an alternative extra. Ethics is not a thing – it is central to being human. All human societies attempt to address moral dilemmas; all make judgements about what is right or wrong. What we are proposing in this book is that there is no single answer, no single route; but we need to return ethics to its core – being human. Ethical frameworks developed by moral philosophers provide us with a range of tools that we can apply to complex situations. They allow us to ask a range of questions, allow us to critically reflect on what the implications of decisions might be and, thus, allow us to make informed critical judgements about behaviour – in this context, tourism behavior, but argu-ably all. If ethical tourism fails, it will be because we have failed to be human, failed to equip ourselves to deal with moral conduct and conflict and in the process undermined our own freedom and ultimately the freedom of others. We need to know that some 'ethical decisions' are less ethical than others; but we also need to know how to apply a range of options and then be able to weigh up and choose options that do the least harm to people and other life forms. The most important tool that the tourism industry, its practitioners and students, can employ is: critical reasoning. From this platform we explore a range of ethical frameworks in Chapter 2, and then in relation to a range of contemporary prac-tices in tourism.

DISCUSSION POINT: ETHICS AND COMPETITIVE ADVANTAGE

Apart from fundamental morality, are there other arguments that could be used to justify an ethical approach to tourism? What are the advantages of being good? Previous research has found that tourism operators that incorporate environmentally responsible behaviours can gain commercial and competitive advantage (Weeden 2002). Similarly, it is argued that tourism operators can develop ethical tourism in order to give themselves competitive advantage: within a crowded and highly competitive industry, this would 'allow companies to compete on more than just price' (Weeden 2002: 143).

Such a presumption is based upon a range of demand-side data, which suggests that the demand from consumers for more ethical products (ethical consumption), including tourism products, is increasing. Now, more than ever, greater numbers of consumers are incorporating ethical considerations into their purchase decisions (Crane 1997 in Weeden 2002). A Mintel (1999) study found that one in four consumers consider themselves to be strongly ethical, while up to three-quarters of all shoppers express concern about 'issues of conscience' when buying goods (Cleverdon and Kalisch 2000). A study of UK tourists revealed that 27 per cent felt that a company's ethical policies were 'highly important' to them when choosing a travel operator (Tearfund 2002). Over half (59 per cent) of the tourists surveyed indicated that they would be willing to pay more for a holiday if the money went to guaranteeing good wages and working conditions, to help preserve the environment, or to a local charity (Tearfund 2002). The average amount people would be prepared to pay was 5 per cent, or £25 on top of a holiday costing £500.

However, a TUI (2010) survey clearly shows that the top considerations in choosing a holiday are still price and value for money. This price sensitivity or 'low-price culture' makes commentators such as Yeoman and McMahon-Beattie (2007) pessimistic about opportunities to encourage ethical consumption. From an ethical consumption perspective, 'although surveys regularly report consumers' willingness to pay extra taxes or a premium to stay in green hotels, the magnitude of this willingness often fails to materialise into people actually paying more for the products' (2007: 4). They note that the biggest successes in ethical consumption have been products which are either marginally more expensive or the same price as the standard offerings. Ethical experiences still need to compete on price with unethical products, and while ethical 'branding' may encourage a minority of consumers to spend more, this margin may be limited (Yeoman and McMahon-Beattie 2007). Weeden also bursts the ethical demand bubble in her assertion that 'It would be inaccurate to suggest that all consumers who express an interest in ethical holidays are attracted purely because of the moral value added' (2002: 143). She believes that many may be attracted because of associated expectations of a higher quality product for the price paid – better 'value for money'.

Discussion questions

1 Are companies that simply want to gain advantage over their competitors by developing ethical policies really being ethical?
2 Similarly, are consumers who choose an ethical travel product because of the 'value proposition' rather than the 'moral proposition' ethical consumers?
3 Is simply 'paying more' the only way that we can make tourism more ethical?
4 Discuss this in relation to the neoliberal 'philosophy' identified above.

Figure 1.2 *Tourists looking at rubble of a building in Christchurch, New Zealand, from the February 2011 earthquake in which 185 people died. Is 'disaster tourism' ethical? Photo: Kirsten M. Lovelock.*

1.4 THE APPROACH AND STRUCTURE OF THIS BOOK

This book is an attempt to bring ethics to some contemporary debates in tourism, through exposing readers to the principles of morality. Forearmed with the knowledge and tools offered in this book, tourism students, researchers and practitioners alike can venture forth into the ethical minefield of tourism, better prepared to arrive at ethical options and outcomes for a range of tourism-related problems.

The book aims to cover the topic of tourism ethics through an analysis of particular topical and relevant issues, e.g. tourism air transport and global warming; tourism and human rights; tourism and poverty alleviation; sex tourism; ethical tourism marketing; tourism and the use of animals; tourism and indigenous cultures. Through the application of specific and relevant ethical frameworks of analysis for each of the above (and more) topic areas, the book addresses a range of ethical approaches, providing the reader with a grounding of applied ethics, from first principles. The primary aim of the book is to illustrate how ethical principles and theory may be applied to address and solve contemporary tourism industry issues. These range in scale from the urgent 'big-picture' problems facing the industry as a whole (e.g. air travel and global warming) to more micro-scale everyday issues that may face individual tourism operators, or indeed, individual tourists. Through discussion and case studies, readers will develop basic competencies in recognising and analysing tourism ethical issues, responsibly deliberating over ethical issues, and in making ethically determined decisions.

The first three chapters, including this introduction, set the tone for the more applied chapters – to lead the reader gently into the world of applied ethics, in such a way that they will be given a set of tools that will enable them to consider *any* tourism issue from an applied ethics perspective. The purpose of the early chapters therefore is to encourage thinking in an *ethical* way and to provide a series of usable ethical frameworks that the reader will be able to employ in the more applied chapters to follow. Chapter 3 'Mobility, borders and security' encourages the reader to consider ethical issues surrounding mobility, borders, security and associated issues of freedom of access and the right to travel.

Chapters 4 to 8 consider tourism and human rights; medical tourism; sex tourism, gender and human trafficking; tourism and indigenous peoples; tourism and disability. A focus of these chapters is upon destination communities and, as the topics listed indicate, they address issues of power and difference between tourist and host, social exclusion and disadvantage, and inequities in the sharing of the benefit (and harm) of tourism.

Chapters 9 to 11 focus upon the ethics of travel and the natural environment, progressing from macro-scale issues such as global warming to regional, ecosystem and micro-level individual species issues. Similarly, the level of tourist activity considered here progresses from the general (travel) to the specific (e.g. tourist hunting or fishing).

Chapters 12 to 14 are industry focused, considering the ethics of our relationship with the client, mainly in hospitality settings, and addressing the role and treatment of labour within the industry. A particular issue addressed is how the industry is represented and marketed. Again, the chapters here move from the general to the specific, starting with broad issues of how the industry is managed at the macro level, to specific issues relating for example to the employee. Chapter 14, on codes of ethics, outlines ethical arguments for and against these ethical 'tools'. The concluding chapter brings together and summarises some of the key arguments that have been made throughout the text and looks ahead to an ethical tourism future.

CHAPTER REVIEW

This chapter identifies that tourism is a substantial industry, with a broad range of positive and negative interactions with society and with the environment. We identify a range of alternative tourisms that have emerged in response to the impacts of tourism. Foremost among these has been sustainable tourism. However, the neoliberal context in which sustainable tourism and arguably other alternative tourisms (e.g. ecotourism, responsible tourism) have emerged and are currently situated challenge their effectiveness as solutions.

This book argues the case for the adoption of ethical frameworks to view tourism problems and challenges. We point out that ethical tourism is more than a form of tourism, rather, it provides a fundamentally humanistic perspective from which to view tourism's relationship with people and the environment and non-human forms of life. Consequently, we challenge the idea of ethics being applied for the gain of competitive advantage, and build the case for a more critical examination of how and why the tourism industry (and we as tourists) do business and engage with the world.

SUMMARY OF KEY TERMS

Competitive advantage From the work of US economist Michal Porter (1985), who argued that competitive advantage grows fundamentally out of the value a firm is able to create for its buyers, and which exceeds the firm's cost of creating it. In popular terms it is considered to be an advantage over competitors gained by offering consumers greater value, either by means of lower prices or by providing greater benefits and service that justifies higher prices.

Ethical consumption (or ethical consumerism) is the practice of purchasing products and services that actively seek to minimise social and/or environmental damage, and the avoidance of products that have a negative impact on society or the environment. It may involve 'positive buying' in which ethical products are supported, or 'negative purchasing' or boycotting of products that are deemed unethical.

Ethical tourism is tourism in which all stakeholders involved apply principles of good behaviour (justice, fairness and equality), to their interactions with one another, with society and with the environment and other life forms.

Responsible tourism emerged as an approach aimed towards enhancing the prospects of sustainable tourism. The *Cape Town Declaration* of 2002 provides a detailed definition, but broadly, responsible tourism aims to reduce impacts, contribute to conservation, involve stakeholders, improve working conditions, provide more accessible and meaningful visitor experiences, and promote community wellbeing. Responsible tourism has a focus on tourists, industry and destination stakeholders taking responsibility for their actions and outcomes.

Sustainable tourism Defined by the UNWTO (2012a) as 'Tourism that takes full account of its current and future economic, social and environmental impacts, addressing the needs of visitors, the industry, the environment and host communities.'

QUESTIONS FOR REFLECTION

1 Reflect on the last holiday that you took. Identify and list any ethical issues surrounding this holiday.
2 In what ways could YOU as the consumer have contributed to making this a more ethical holiday?
3 In what ways could some of your tourism providers have contributed to making your holiday more ethical?

EXERCISES

1 How much would you and your friends/colleagues be prepared to pay for an ethical tourism product? Conduct a mini 'survey' to determine the average 'ethical premium'?
2 What determines this 'ethical premium'?
3 Does it differ according to the type of tourism product (e.g. hospitality, transport, cultural tourism, wildlife tourism), or are there other factors, e.g. how ethical or unethical people consider a particular tourism product to be?

FURTHER READING

Fennell, D. (2006) *Tourism Ethics*, Clevedon: Channel View.
Smith, M. and Duffy, R. (2003) *The Ethics of Tourism Development*, London, New York: Routledge.

USEFUL WEBSITES

International Centre for Responsible Tourism <http://www.icrtourism.org/>
The International Ecotourism Society <http://www.ecotourism.org>
International Institute for Sustainable Development <http://www.iisd.org/>
Promoting Poor Tourism <http://www.propoortourism.info/>
Responsible Travel <http://www.responsibletravel.com>
Tourism Concern <http://www.tourismconcern.org.uk/>
UNESCO Teaching and Learning for a Sustainable Future (see Module 16 for Sustainable Tourism)
   <http://www.unesco.org/education/tlsf/TLSF/theme_c/c_mod16.htm>
United Nations World Tourism Organization (UNWTO) – Sustainable Tourism Development
   <http://sdt.unwto.org/en>
World Business Council for Sustainable Development <http://www.wbcsd.org/>

NOTES

a George Orwell (1903–50), author and essayist. From *All Art is Propaganda* (first published 1941, Boston, MA: Houghton Mifflin Harcourt, 2008.

b Albert Camus (1913–60), French novelist, essayist and playwright, 1957 Nobel Prize for Literature.

c Attributed to Theodore Roosevelt (1858–1919), American adventurer and 26th President of the USA.

d Marianne Jennings, business ethicist. From *The Board of Directors: 25 Keys to Corporate Governance* (Pocket Mba Series) (with Tom Redburn, Illustrator), New York: Lebhar-Friedman Books, 2000.

1 Tourism is an activity that involves most of the world – billions of people are tourists (estimates are that 982 million people engaged in international travel in 2011 and international tourism receipts surpassed US$ 1 trillion (UNWTO 2012b); total global arrivals (including domestic tourism) are now likely to be over 5 billion (UNWTO 2012b, estimate 2008).

2 Neoliberalism as a term was invented by German sociologist Alexander Rustow in 1938, but has undergone changes in meaning since that time, notably following the work of economists such as Milton Freidman in the 1960s. As a political movement it combines traditional liberal concerns for social justice with an emphasis on economic growth. Neoliberalism is also a philosophy 'where the operation of a market or market-like structure is seen as an ethic in itself, capable of acting as a guide for all human action, and substituting for all previously existing ethical beliefs' (Treanor 2005).

REFERENCES

Cleverdon, R. and Kalisch, A. (2000) 'Fair Trade in Tourism', *International Journal of Tourism Research,* 2: 171–87.

Duffy, R. (2008) 'Neoliberalising nature: global networks and ecotourism development in Madagascar', *Journal of Sustainable Tourism,* 16(3): 327–44.

Fletcher, R. (2011) 'Sustaining tourism, sustaining capitalism? The tourism industry's role in global capitalist expansion', *Tourism Geographies,* 13(3): 443–61.

Frey, N. and George, R. (2010) 'Responsible tourism management: the missing link between business owners' attitudes and behaviour in the Cape Town tourism industry', *Tourism Management,* 31(5): 621–8.

Goodwin, H. (2011) *Taking Responsibility for Tourism,* Oxford: Goodfellow Publishers.

Hall, C.M. (2011) 'Policy learning and policy failure in sustainable tourism governance: from first and second to third order change?', *Journal of Sustainable Tourism,* 19(4–5): 649–71.

Hall, C.M. and Lew, A. (2009) *Understanding and Managing Tourism Impacts: An Integrated Approach,* Abingdon: Routledge.

Hall, D. and Brown, F. (2006) *Tourism and Welfare: Ethics, Responsibility and Sustained Well-being,* Wallingford: CABI.

Higgins-Desbiolles, F. (2006) 'More than an industry: the forgotten power of tourism as a social force', *Tourism Management,* 27: 1192–208.

— (2008) 'Justice tourism and alternative globalisation', *Journal of Sustainable Tourism,* 16(3): 345–64.

Holden, A. (2003) 'In need of new environmental ethics for tourism?', *Annals of Tourism Research,* 30: 94–108.

Honey, M. (1999) *Ecotourism and Sustainable Development: Who Owns Paradise?* Washington, DC: Island Press.

Hudson, S. and Miller, G.A. (2005) 'The responsible marketing of tourism: the case of Canadian Mountain Holidays', *Tourism Management,* 26: 133–42.

Hultsman, J. (1995) 'Just tourism: an ethical framework', *Annals of Tourism Research,* 22: 553–67.

International Centre for Responsible Tourism (ICRT) (2012) *Responsible Tourism.* Available at <http://www.icrtourism.org/links/responsible-tourism-management-theory-and-practise/> (Accessed 14 July 2012).

Jackson, K. (2012) *Virtuosity in Business: Invisible Law Guiding the Invisible Hand,* Philadelphia: University of Pennsylvania Press.

Lea, J. (1993) 'Tourism development ethics in the third world', *Annals of Tourism Research,* 20: 701–15.

Lovelock, B.A. (2011) 'Single worthwhile policy, seeking legitimacy and implementation: sustainable tourism at the regional destination level, New Zealand', *Policy Quarterly,* 7(4): 20–6.

Mintel (1999) *The Green and Ethical Consumer.* March.

Moufakkir, O. (2012) 'Of ethics, leisure and tourism: the serious fun of doing tourism', in Moufakkir, O. and Burns, P.M. (eds) *Controversies in Tourism,* Wallingford: CABI, pp. 7–22.

Porter, M.E. (1985) *Competitive Advantage,* New York: Free Press.

Sharpley, R. (2010) *The myth of sustainable tourism.* Available at <http://www.uclan.ac.uk/schools/built_natural_environment/research/csd/files/CSD_Working_Paper_4_Sustainable_Tourism_Sharpley.pdf> (Accessed 4 July 2012).

Smith, C. (2001) 'Ethical guidelines for marketing practice: a reply to Gaski and some observations on the role of normative ethics', *Journal of Business Ethics,* 32(1): 3–18.

Speed, C. (2008) 'Are backpackers ethical tourists?', in Hannam, K. and Ateljevic, I. (eds) *Backpacker Tourism: Concepts and Profiles,* Clevedon: Channel View, pp. 54–81.

Swarbrooke, J. and Horner, S. (2007) *Consumer Behaviour in Tourism* (2nd edn), Oxford: Butterworth-Heinemann.

Tearfund (2000) *Tourism: An Ethical Issue*: Market Research Report. Available at <http://tilz.tearfund.org/webdocs/Website/Campaigning/Policy%20and%20research/Policy%20-%20Tourism%20Market%20Research%20Report.pdf> (Accessed 13 June 2011).

— (2002) *Worlds Apart: A Call to Responsible Tourism,* London: Tearfund.

Travel Matters (2012) *Ethical Tourism.* Available at <http://www.travelmatters.co.uk/ethical-tourism/> (Accessed 23 February 2012).

Treanor, P. (2005) *Neoliberalism: origins, theory, definition.* Available at <http://web.inter.nl.net/users/Paul.Treanor/neoliberalism.html.> (Accessed 3 April 2012).

TUI (2010) *TUI Travel Sustainability Survey 2010.* Available at <torc.linkbc.ca/torc/downs1/Sustainability%20Survey.pdf> (Accessed 31 March 2012).

United Nations (2012) *Report of the World Commission on Environment and Development: Our Common Future.* Available at <http://www.un-documents.net/wced-ocf.htm> (Accessed 1 May 2012).

United Nations World Tourism Organization (UNWTO) (2012a) *Sustainable Development of Tourism.* Available at <http://sdt.unwto.org/en/content/about-us-5> (Accessed 15 June 2012).

— (2012b) *Some Points on Domestic Tourism.* Available at <http://www2.unwto.org/en/agora/some-points-domestic-tourism> (Accessed 22 May 2012).

Wall, G. and Mathieson, A. (2006) *Tourism Change Impacts and Opportunities*, London: Prentice Hall.

Weeden, C. (2002) 'Ethical tourism: an opportunity for competitive advantage?', *Journal of Vacation Marketing,* 8(2): 141–53.

— (2005) 'Ethical tourism: is its future in niche tourism?', in Novelli, M. (ed.) *Niche Tourism: Contemporary Issues, Trends and Cases,* Oxford: Butterworth-Heinemann, pp. 233–45.

Wight, P.A. (1993) 'Ecotourism: ethics or eco-sell?', *Journal of Travel Research*, 31(3): 3–9.

Yaman, R.H. (2003) 'Skinner's naturalism as a paradigm for teaching business ethics: a discussion from tourism', *Teaching Business Ethics,* 7: 107–22.

Yeoman, I. and McMahon-Beattie, U. (2007) 'The UK low-cost economy', *Journal of Revenue and Pricing Management,* 6: 2–8.

2 Tourism
Ethical concepts and principles

'Never let your sense of morals get in the way of doing what's right.'

Issac Asimov[a]

'Justice will only exist where those not affected by injustice are filled with the same amount of indignation as those offended.'

Plato[b]

LEARNING OBJECTIVES

After reading this chapter you will be able to:

- Understand ethical concepts and principles and how they relate to tourism.
- Identify and discuss how these concepts and principles might shape tourist policy and practice.
- Identify and explain how ethics is situated within wider tourism industry debates.

2.1 INTRODUCTION

As the world's largest industry, tourism involves a wide range of practices, encompasses all human territories and manifests the key values and drivers of modernity. Not surprisingly ethical and moral concerns provoked by touristic practice mirror those raised in relation to modernity and modernisation. Researchers in the field have tended to emphasise, for example, the impacts that tourists and the industry that accommodates them have on our ability to sustain social life and the natural environment into the next century. Many sectors have expressed a need for the tourism industry to address the ethical and moral challenges provoked by travel and touristic practice in relation to the perpetuation of social inequality, the commodification of daily life on a global scale and the relationship between global and local environmental sustainability. This chapter introduces some of the ethical theories that are useful for an applied ethics of tourism. The literature on ethics and moral philosophy is vast and can be very daunting – the aim of this chapter is not to provide the student or industry practitioner with a comprehensive introduction to moral philosophy, but rather to provide both with a starting point to consider the wide range of touristic practices canvassed in this book. There are few books that have addressed ethics in tourism, but two that have are David Fennell's *Tourism Ethics* (2006) and Mick Smith and Rosaleen Duffy's *The Ethics of Tourism Development* (2003), both are very useful texts and provide a more in-depth coverage of, first, ethical theory and, second, ethics in relation to development.

Interest in ethics amongst tourist researchers and the industry has been relatively recent. This interest was formalised through three events in the 1990s: first, the International Association of Scientific Experts in Tourism (AIEST) congress in Paris in 1992, where it was proposed that a commission be formed to address ethical problems within the industry (Fennell 2006; Przeclawski 1996); second, the Rio Earth summit of 1992 where a commitment was made to adopting and reporting on codes of conduct addressing environmental practice and sustainability (Genot 1995: 166); and third, the internet conference on tourism in 1998 which identified key ethical issues facing the industry, from the ethics of destination promotion to cultural, religious and environmental sustainability (Fennell 2006). In general, the key issue identified at and since that time has been how the negative impacts of the industry might be mitigated and addressed by those engaged in the industry. Tourist operators, tourists, students of tourism and researchers are all moral agents, and as such are beings capable of actions that have a moral quality and actions that can be denominated as good or evil in a moral sense; as such, these 'stakeholders' have an identified role in the mitigation hoped for above.

Figure 2.1 *Ethics within reason. Cartoon: K. Lovelock.*

Central to the industry impact debate has been a focus on the environment and the implications for developing societies (Fennell 2006). The emergence of ecotourism is an example of an industry response to ethical concerns over the impact tourism is having on local environments and indeed ultimately the global environment. Ecotourism has often been showcased by those in industry as an example of ethical tourism practice, in which the 'no harm to the environment' underpinnings, the educational benefits for conservation and sustainability, and the conscious moral commitment to the importance of protecting the environment, elevated this form of tourism to one considered a 'more ethical' form of practice (Fennell and Malloy 1995, 1999; Stark 2002) (see Chapter 9).

Yet, when subject to critique, ecotourism finds itself subject to claims that it is in fact unethical – as those who accrue the greatest benefits are invariably the socially advantaged and those who reap the least reward are invariably the poor and disadvantaged (Karwacki and Boyd 1995). As an economic practice tourism can supplant agriculture and thus undermine a developing nation's ability to feed itself or sustain growth through exports; it contributes to pollution, facilitates the commodification of culture, invariably ensures the concentration and monopoly of local resources lie in the hands of already established local elites; and often involves a top-down form of management that fails to address local community concerns and needs. Ironically, as Wheeler (1994) has observed, ecotourism can in practice differ from other forms of tourism only in its claim to 'higher moral ground'. Or as others have argued, since the 1990s, the primary change in the industry has been subjective (rather than changes in practice or outcomes) where ethical and moral debates have facilitated a shift from 'fun tourism' to self-conscious 'ethical' or 'moral' tourism and where hedonistic pleasure is replaced by guilt and obligation (Butcher 2003). It might also be added that those who have expressed ethical concerns are also then cast as the 'fun police' and questions are raised about the need for ethical codes or why industry operators should be concerned about ethics at all.

More generally, the response to ethical concerns has been largely prescriptive, where various ethical codes and codes of conduct have been developed to address 'impact' outcomes (Fennell 2006; Malloy and Fennell 1998a) (see Chapter 14). Yet, little is known about the effectiveness of these codes, whether they lead to behavioural change and/or whether they can address the specificities of a range of social encounters and interactions (Malloy and Fennell 1998a). As we will see such efforts are important, but nonetheless limited, primarily because 'tourism' is conceptualised as some 'thing' that happens to people, rather than a social practice which people (here, there and everywhere) engage with and in. In addition, those who oppose engaging with ethics tend to conceptualise ethics as 'some*thing*' outside of the industry, rather than an integral part of being human and thus integral to all human behaviour and interaction.

The reification of tourism as 'thing' with impacts, serves as a diversion and prevents engagement with moral and ethical concerns connected to what is a *social practice and process, that is at once intra-societal and inter-societal*, where pathways of intersection and engagement are not always transparent, are global, with variable local manifestations. This is, as we will see, precisely why it is difficult to develop 'prescriptions for behaviour' that will successfully address ethical dilemmas for all times and in all places, and why in the field of tourism certain philosophical perspectives find favour over others.

Yet these difficulties are not insurmountable and there are implications for those who choose not to engage with ethics and touristic behaviour. The philosophical literature on ethics can be daunting and does not always address applicability for an industry such as tourism. However, as Smith and Duffy (2003: 3) observe:

> ethical frameworks offered by philosophers rarely if ever provide definitive answers to moral problems but are better treated as discursive resources that can help us to articulate and express these problems ... a knowledge of ethics is not like a knowledge of mathematics, it will not allow us to 'solve' complex social equations simply, but it might help us interpret and communicate to others what it is that we think is right or wrong about a certain situation and why ...

This is a useful perspective from which we can start to consider how those in the tourism industry might think about ethics and move toward critically applying various ethical frameworks to touristic practice.

2.2 ETHICS, CONCEPTS AND PRINCIPLES

> Ethics is the philosophical study of morality, and morality consists of beliefs concerning right and wrong, good and bad. ... doing ethics is inescapable.
>
> (Vaughn 2008: 12)

Ethics is derived from the Greek word ethos, which means 'habitual mode of conduct' and conduct that will ensure that good is being done (Fennell 2009: 213). The idea of habitual conduct is important. Habitual conduct is conduct that has emerged and been repeated over time and consequently conduct that has invited the development of rules, standards and principles – some of which are formalised in laws or codes of conduct and some of which are simply considered normative ways of behaving. In both instances, *habitual* modes of conduct are often largely unquestioned and 'taken for granted' and as such are often not reflected on. In addition, this kind of conduct is considered appropriate, authentic and for the good of members of a society, profession, or social group (Fennell and Malloy 2007 in Fennell 2009).

Morality is beliefs about right and wrong, good and bad, judgements about values, rules, principles and theories. These beliefs guide our actions, define our values and shape our behaviour (Vaughn 2008: 3). Ethics and morality are related, as ethics is concerned with moral values (Vaughn 2008: 3). Our moral values tell us what is important in life, what behaviours we should cultivate, what behaviours we should reject, the value we place on human life, what constitutes social good, justice and rights (Vaughn 2008). Or as Ray (2000: 241) states 'Ethics is the study of the rules, standards and principles that dictate right conduct among members of a society. Such rules are based on moral values.'

Can the tourism industry avoid ethics, turn a blind eye, shut out the calls and refuse to listen to the so-called 'fun police'? The answer to the last question is no, because ethics is not outside of social life, it is a fundamental aspect of living as a social being. All humans engage, wittingly or not, in debates about what they consider to be right or wrong, who is right and who has been wronged and all human societies have moral principles and codes which guide social life. In an increasingly connected world it becomes even more imperative that people are equipped to deal with moral conduct and the resolution of conflict. It is possible to ignore ethics but, as others have argued, if you do, you undermine your own personal freedom; if you fail to address ethics you may make serious mistakes and if you choose not to explore critically your learnt morality you may one day be faced with actions that seriously challenge your moral values and find yourself poorly equipped to defend them (Taylor 1975: 9–10; Vaughn 2008: 3–4).

2.3 VALUES

It is important to distinguish between values and obligations. We might be interested in judgements of value – whether someone is good, bad or an action is good, bad or otherwise. Most often these judgements of value are applied to a personality trait, motives, intentions and actions. For example, He is good; He is to blame for what happened (Vaughn 2008: 6). Value in this sense is *moral value*. There is also *non-moral value*, this is when we can speak of something being good or bad – for example, television is good, but the television *itself* can have no moral value (Vaughn 2008: 6). In addition, there are things we value in life that do not have in and of themselves any value, but they may be of value because they offer a means to something else; in this case they have *instrumental value* or *extrinsic value*. Yet, there are things that are of value in and of themselves and when this is the case they are said to have *intrinsic value*, 'they are what they are, without being a means to something else' (Vaughn 2008: 6). The concept of values is at the heart of moral systems.

Central to ethics are four key elements: the pre-eminence of reason; the universal perspective; the principle of impartiality; the dominance of moral norms (Vaughn 2008: 7).

The pre-eminence of reason

Critical reasoning is essential. This means consideration must be given to the reasons – for the action, the statement (moral or otherwise) in question. Moral judgements must be supported by sound reasoning. Central to critical reasoning is logical argument. Logical argument starts with a statement to be supported – which is the assertion that needs to be proved, the statements that support the assertion (reasons for believing the premises behind the statement and the statement). In ethics we are trying to demonstrate whether a moral judgement is sound, an action should be permissible or not, or that a moral theory is plausible. Applying logical argument helps keep feelings and irrational outbursts at bay and allows us to critically reflect on our judgements, what it is that has shaped those judgements and to focus on the moral question.

The universal perspective

This perspective asserts that a moral statement (rule, judgement, principle) must be applicable in like situations. For example: stealing from a commercial premise is wrong, stealing from a shop stall is wrong. When giving reasons for the moral statement, the reasons must also apply for the similar situations (Vaughn 2008: 8).

The principle of impartiality

Impartiality is implied in all moral statements. Equals must be treated equally. For example, those who are sick will be treated. Sometimes, however, there can be good reason for treating somebody differently; for example, in an emergency room the most critical cases will be treated first (Vaughn 2008: 8).

The dominance of moral norms

When moral norms conflict with non-moral principles or values, usually moral values override the others. For example, the justification for civil disobedience is often that laws conflict with moral norms, the laws then become invalid (Vaughn 2008: 7). An example in New Zealand would be the Springbok Tour. In 1981 the New Zealand Rugby Union invited the South African rugby team, the Springboks, to tour New Zealand. The Springboks arrived in July for a 51-day tour that generated much interest from international and domestic 'sport-tourists'. However, the tour provoked more than 100 public protests at game destinations. The tour was legal and at each protest there was a large police presence. Attempts to disrupt the games on the part of protesters were resisted by the police – as they sought to protect the players who were engaged in a lawful activity. The protesters were also largely lawful in their actions – but were often treated as though they were not. The Springbok tour illustrates what happens when moral norms conflict with non-moral principles or values. The rugby tour was within the law but many thought that it was immoral to support the tour and immoral for the games to take place. Their reasoning was it was immoral to support the tour as in doing so it was supporting a national sporting team whose membership was restricted to white players. Racial exclusion from team membership conformed to racial segregation (apartheid) and discriminatory treatment of people of colour in South Africa at that time. Thus, supporting this team was considered to be a microcosmic equivalent to supporting the wider social system that allowed coloured and black players to be excluded and racial discrimination to be practised. Civil disobedience and protest action occurred at every game throughout New Zealand and illustrates what happens when moral norms conflict with non-moral principles and values and how moral values can override the latter. While supporters argued it was legal and that politics lies outside of sport – 'It's just a game' – many challenged this non-moral value through: critical reasoning; the universal principle; the principle of impartiality and the assertion of the dominance of moral norms.

2.4 ETHICAL THEORIES

What follows is not an exhaustive coverage of ethical theories but a selection and brief appraisal of those that have relevance to critical and applied perspectives in tourism. We start with intuitionism as it is here that many of us will be familiar with responses to moral and ethical dilemmas or justifications for taking a certain stance. From here we move toward a more considered and critical approach drawing on various ethical theories, the first falling within what are called teleological theories (theories that focus on outcomes – consequences – or are end-based) and consider various theories that are deontological (theories that are non-consequentialist, theories that focus on rules, guidelines and normative behaviour). These two main bodies of theory within moral philosophy provide a starting point and useful 'tool kit' from which students and practitioners can draw when considering touristic practice. As we have already stressed there is no formula that can be applied and which will provide definitive answers to ethical dilemmas; rather, there are a range of theories that might be applied to various contexts and situations – with varying utility, some of which we explore below. As moral agents, students of tourism, tourist operators, researchers and tourists themselves need to appraise and familiarise themselves with various perspectives and frameworks that can assist in ethical decision making for touristic practices.

Intuitionism

To intuit is to know something through experience and without reference to reason or testing (Malloy et al. 2000). Intuitionism as a theory was developed by Immanuel Kant (1724–1804), a German philosopher, who argued that all humans have the ability to reason and therefore to express notions of duty and right (Fennell 2006: 66). Underpinning the theory of intuitionism is the idea that humans have an innate capacity to intuit which in turn allows them to discern whether something is moral or immoral. The problem with this theory is that people do not always share the same intuition or discernment about what is moral or immoral. That is, they have different moral intuitions and frequently disagree. In addition, even if there is a consensus, this does not mean that the intuition is correct. Feelings and sensitivities are central to intuitionism and consequent moral action (see Chapters 6 and 12).

Teleology

Teleological theories are concerned with defining and establishing the meaning of good independently from establishing rights, and where right is later defined as that which maximises good (Fennell 2006). Teleological theories are *end-based theories* with the focus being on optimal outcomes. An action is the right action when it produces an outcome that will contribute to a greater balance of good over evil (Frankena 1963: 13 in Fennell 2006: 67).

There are four main teleological theories: (i) Utilitarianism; (ii) Hedonism; (iii) Egoism; and (iv) Virtue ethics.

(i) Utilitarianism

The pursuit of happiness and avoidance of pain lies at the heart of utilitarianism, where all human decision making is underpinned by this tendency and where this theory asserts that the search for personal pleasure is morality's foundation. What makes people happy is good, what brings pain is bad (Bentham 1987: 65; Smith and Duffy 2003). Moving beyond the level of the individual to the social group, actions are good when they increase the overall pleasure of the group and actions are good when they decrease the pain experienced by a community (Smith and Duffy 2003).

Utilitarianism underpins ethical debate surrounding a number of touristic practices, including hunting, wildlife conservation policies and more generally when arguments are made in support of a practice – *because* it brings the greatest good to people (see Chapter 9). For example, the building of the new Hong Kong international airport on Lantau Island involved moving people from villages along the foreshore. These villages had been there for many generations and the contemporary villagers still relied on fishing for their livelihood. A utilitarian argument would assert that the new airport was necessary because of the increase in flights coming into Hong Kong, the revenue gained by being able to accommodate the increase in flights and people on board. The existing airport could not be supported because of the inability of the Mong Kok airport to cope with these increases and this inability over time would bring with it costs in lost opportunities for revenue. And in addition, the pollution that the airport in Mong Kok contributed to in an already densely populated urban area needed to be addressed. While some people would be inconvenienced by being moved from their villages, they were a minority and the new development was in the interest of the majority (see Chapter 3).

Utilitarianism can also be divided into *act- and rule-utilitarianism* (Fennell 2006: 69). An act is a superior act if it produces greater overall wellbeing. Moral rules can be broken, if the act brings about greater happiness. Actions can then be evaluated in terms of their own consequences, rather than being predetermined by social norms and rules. In contrast, rule utilitarianism asserts the rightness of an action is a function of adhering to rules and social norms (Fennell 2006: 70). Utilitarianism commences with the observation that seeking pleasure and avoiding pain is a universal human trait. The evaluation of an action as either good or bad is measured in terms of its utility to promote or undermine pleasure or the greatest happiness to the greatest number of people. The emphasis on the universal nature of the pursuit of happiness means that this theory can be applied in any cultural setting and offers a potential tool for considering the ethical implications of tourist practice. Further, utilitarianism offers a rational means of ascertaining whether an action is good, what some have referred to as a 'kind of moral accountancy' (Smith and Duffy 2003: 57). Utilitarianism employs an impartial stance with respect to values and therefore can be used in any number of settings. With this theory *it is the consequences that count*.

The example of zoos is often given to illustrate act utilitarianism and rule utilitarianism (Fennell 2006). It is possible to argue that caging animals is wrong but you could decide to support the establishment of a zoo in your neighbourhood (disregard the rule) because the existence of this zoo will allow people, who do not have the opportunity to see wild animals in the wild, to learn about wild animals and potentially participate in the protection and preservation of threatened species (act utilitarianism) (see Chapter 10).

Yet utilitarianism runs into trouble when we consider the case of mass tourism. A utilitarian case might be made for mass tourism, where literally masses travel to certain destinations in search of pleasure and fun and where the argument would be that it is morally right for the destination to assist in the realisation of pleasure and fun for these masses. To address this greater overall wellbeing, the destination, in this instance say a small island state undergoing the process of industrial development, removes minority populations and their dwellings from the foreshore, where they fish for a living, and relocates them into the interior in order to build a deluxe resort to externally produced specifications. Thus, the host society addresses the greater social good (the needs of the masses) and ultimately assists economic development. However, as a consequence of being moved away from the foreshore the minority populations must now walk several kilometres to reach their fishing boats and re-establish their foreshore selling away from the tourist development. This example has been made up, but there are countless real examples of tourism development and responses to mass tourism in less developed nations in the world where this has been the response to mass tourism (Mansperger 1995; Butler and Hinch 1996; Abbink 2000). While the masses are accommodated minority populations have been displaced, where these populations are often already disadvantaged economically and socially and where development through tourism has perpetuated rather than alleviated this social inequity. It is for this reason that utilitarianism has been criticised for its inability to address social justice in relation to minorities (see Chapters 3 and 8). If the happiness of the majority rules then the displacement of minorities becomes possible, relocating minorities becomes merely a means to an end. Focusing on the ends and failing to focus on the means to address the ends can lead to the unjust treatment of people (Fennell 2006) and potentially increased marginality and suffering for already marginalised groups.

(ii) Hedonism

Hedonism defines a worthwhile action as one that gives an individual pleasure. The greatest good is that connected to the pleasure experienced by the individual and that which involves the least amount of pain. Here the individual determines what is pleasurable and thus a worthwhile action (see Chapter 8).

(iii) Egoism

Egoism is self-directed action where the goals of the individual are the end in and of themselves (Fennell 2006). Therefore, helping another is only done if the individual realises some benefit in terms of their ultimate goal. Moral judgements are made in terms of the individual's goals and whether or not an action will be of benefit. Associated with egoism are debates surrounding selfishness and altruism. For some selfishness has been identified as a threat to ethical society (Blackburn 2001) while many psychologists have argued that ego-satisfaction is central to human nature and that all humans seek to satisfy their needs. However, egoism is not always the same as selfishness as it is possible to be self-directed in one's actions while not being selfish (Fennell 2006).

(iv) Virtue ethics

Virtue ethics focuses on the person, not the action. Virtues may be intrinsic to being human (Foot 1959; Fennell 2006) or human traits that have been cultivated (Cooper 1987). Some have argued that there are two central virtues held by people: one focuses on the individual and the individual's ability to be true to oneself; and the other focuses on others. Others have suggested virtue comprises three elements: (1) propriety; (2) prudence; and (3) benevolence (Smith [1759/1966] in Fennell 2006: 73). One of the strengths of virtue ethics is the acknowledgement that people have different perspectives which are shaped by different histories. The weaknesses of this approach, however, are its vagueness in relation to character traits and how one decides which traits are virtuous or not (see Chapter 12).

Deontology – non-consequentialist theories

Deontologists maintain that it is more important to uphold rules, to follow guidelines and conform to normative behaviour and duties. Codes of ethics reflect the deontological position: codes tell people what to do and what not to do, but do not explain why or what the consequences of the action may be (Malloy and Fennell 1998b; Fennell 2006) (see Chapter 14). As with teleology, deontology can be divided in terms of rule deontology and act deontology. Rule deontology is whether the rules and values have been upheld, not whether the greatest social good has been realised. Act deontology is always adhering to a rule and this rule can only be overridden by more knowledge and the formulation of a rule that is superior. There are three categories of deontological theories: (i) theology and the Golden Rule; (ii) Kantian ethics; and (iii) social contract.

(i) Theology and the Golden Rule

Codes of conduct are invariably linked to religion and religion often illustrates the ethics held in a given society (Blackburn 2001 cited in Fennell 2006: 77). The Golden Rule refers to a seemingly universal commandment found in most societies, 'do unto others as you would have them do unto you'. The Golden Rule is evident cross-culturally, in both secular and religious doctrines.

With the Golden Rule it is necessary to first recognise other people's interests and to see them as similar to your own and second to see their moral status and worth as the same or equal to your own.

(ii) Kantian ethics

The eighteenth-century philosopher Immanuel Kant argued that ethics is based on principles. Principles differ from rules: where rules are a set of guidelines which are externally imposed, principles are laws that you apply to yourself. Principles and rules can work together, where a rule over time is embraced as a principle.

Kant theorised that there was one central underlying principle which underpinned all principles – this he called the *categorical imperative* – and that this imperative could be accessed by all through *practical reason or rationality*. It is, he argued, rationality that separates humans from animals and allows humans to live a life guided by reason – an ethical life. In order to realise this ethical life humans need to balance inclination and duty. Inclinations include those actions that are habitual and feelings, but for Kant to act in accordance to inclination is to act as an animal does – without reason.

Acting from reason is what Kant called acting from motive or duty and it is this which allows action to have ethical value; it is at this point that your actions can become right or wrong. Further, Kant also argued that the ability to make rational choices gives humans control over nature (inclinations) and this he argued is freedom; the ability to make laws to live by and through laws humans achieve autonomy.

(iii) Social contract

The recognition of human rights has a long history, with claims to rights often motivating social revolutions. Inequity and social power both within societies and between societies lie at the heart of both the history of human rights and recognition of its importance (see Chapters 3, 6, 7, 8 and 13). As Smith and Duffy (2003) observe, the rights rhetoric increasingly became mainstream following the Second World War; while linked to the abuse of people during the war, it was also inextricably linked to debates over economic development. The 1948 *Universal Declaration of Human Rights* adopted by the United Nations marks formal recognition that globally equal rights for all humans provide the foundation for freedom, justice and peace in the world (Brownlie 1994 in Smith and Duffy 2003). Since then, various United Nation responses to human rights have been developed, with many having relevance to tourism (see Chapter 4).

- Universal Declaration of Human Rights, 1948;
- International Covenant on Economic, Social and Cultural Rights, 1966a;
- International Covenant on Civil and Political Rights, 1966b;
- Convention on the Rights of the Child, 1990;
- International Convention on the Protection of the Rights of all Migrant Workers and Members of Their Families, 1990;
- United Nations Convention for the Rights of Persons with Disabilities, 2006; and the
- Declaration of the Rights of Indigenous Peoples, 2007.

With respect to tourism, human rights were initially expressed through the adoption of the *Tourism Bill of Rights and Tourist Code* at the World Tourism Organization (UNWTO) meeting in Sofia in 1985 (Smith and Duffy 2003). The focus at this time was on human rights to rest, leisure and travel (Handszuh 1998 in Smith and Duffy 2003). The idea of the individual having the right to travel and/or freedom of movement both within and outside of their own society has a long history, but notably it is only recently that the rights of host communities have been considered. Central to the ethical debates surrounding the ethics of tourism development is the impact that the right to rest, leisure and travel has on host communities (Butler and Hinch 2007).

Rights rhetoric has also changed over time; for example, American and French expressions in the eighteenth century addressed both individualistic concerns and egalitarianism. Here an individual had rights *a priori* – prior to and independent of social existence and the development of societal rules and controls. These are referred to as 'natural rights' and considered essentially connected to being human but existing prior to social existence. This idea has been contested over time, countered primarily by the argument that rights are made, not natural outcomes, and it is impossible to establish whether rights exist prior to human existence, not to mention difficult to evidence their existence. Thus, increasingly it has been argued that rights are an outcome of human action, often the actions of governments, and as human constructs are subsequently subject to change (Bentham 1907 in Smith and Duffy 2003: 76).

Contemporary rights theorists have largely abandoned the idea of natural rights and consider rights to be both socially and politically created. Since the Second World War there has been an increasing focus on rights internationally – what some have described as the emergence of a 'human rights culture' (Smith and Duffy 2003: 76) – and this in turn has been subject to interpretation and critique. While on the one hand it may appear to be 'progress' in a moral sense, on the other hand it has also been argued that the institutional embracing of 'rights' by agencies such as the United Nations needs to be critically evaluated as too does the idea that 'more' necessarily means 'progress'.

We might ask the following questions: What understanding of 'rights' is being embraced? Are these understandings culturally universal? Or do they represent understandings typical of dominant and wealthy nations? The rights rhetoric and engagement is often linked to arguments that justify capitalist expansion, industrial and economic development and culturally defined understandings which suggest that these processes constitute progress. Further, some have argued that the rights culture as embraced by global agencies is emblematic of a move toward global governance (Chandler 2002; Smith and Duffy 2003) which potentially is about consolidating power for wealthy developed nations (see Chapter 4).

Within tourism, the *Tourism Bill of Rights, Tourist Code* and the *Global Code of Ethics* adopt a universalistic approach to the debate surrounding tourism and rights (Smith and Duffy 2003) and this universalistic approach has been adopted by the United Nations World Tourism Organization – an institution of global governance. Smith and Duffy (2003) point out that the move toward embracing the socially constructed nature of rights has also coincided with the co-option of rights discourse by those in power. Yet, while it appears that more agencies are embracing human rights, rights are not always applied with impartiality, and subsequently rights and or abuses of rights are frequently socially contested.

The underlying point here is that despite the emergence of this so-called rights culture, how rights are implemented, addressed and ensured continues to be shaped by unequal power relationships, and the rights rhetoric continues to be an unreliable measure of whether human rights are being addressed in practice. Thus, nations might deplore and speak out against atrocities and human rights abuses committed under some regimes, while remaining silent and continuing to support other regimes with equally poor human rights records – because it suits their own political agendas, economic objectives and/or might compromise internal political objectives. As others have observed there is often 'a gap between political rhetoric and moral reality' (Smith and Duffy 2003: 79). This does not mean that human rights treaties are value-less, rather it signals the need to critically appraise what is happening in practice. However, it does challenge universalistic positions (Kant) – where it is argued that rights can be applied equally. Clearly there are situations where rights clash with other rights and this is why it is difficult to establish universalist rules and rights that will be applicable for all people, at all times, in all places.

In tourism, it has been argued that tourism development is inherently culturally biased and subsequently so too are rights discourses. In addition some observe that different rights agendas are products of different levels of economic development (Donnelley 1999 in Smith and Duffy 2003).

With respect to tourism development and the rights debate it is acknowledged that there is a need not just to focus on the ethical conduct of individual tourists but also the industry and the role played particularly by multinational corporations. With ownership and control resting in the hands of mainly wealthy industrialised nations and within these nations in the hands of privileged minorities, the rights of those in poor destination communities are not only physically remote, but potentially and demonstrably too remote for a moral compass to offer effective guidance for some. Indeed, research suggests that the rights of clients (tourists) are prioritised by the tourism industry (George 2007; Lovelock 2007) over those of destination communities. While many emphasise the role tourism can play in alleviating poverty and addressing social inequality, and it is clear the rights and development rhetoric are closely intertwined (Smith and Duffy 2003), it is important to constantly question whether or not development through tourism is addressing local need.

The language of rights has been widely employed in various codes of ethics, for example: *The Tourism Code* and the *World Tourism Organization Global Code of Ethics* (1999) (see Chapter 14).

2.5 SOCIAL JUSTICE, CULTURAL RELATIVISM AND ETHICS OF CARE

Prompted by the understanding that the tourism industry generates and sustains many injustices, tourism and justice has become an area of debate. There are also calls for the industry to embrace justice and serve as a vehicle for social change (Higgins-Desbiolles 2006). What is social justice? American philosopher John Rawls (1921–2002) defined social justice as:

> Justice is the first virtue of social institutions, as truth is of systems of thought ... Each person possesses an inviolability founded on justice that even the welfare of society as a whole cannot override ... Therefore in a just society the liberties of equal citizenship are taken as settled; the rights secured by justice are not subject to political bargaining or to the calculus of social interests ... truth and justice are uncompromising.
>
> (Rawls 1971: 3–4).

Here justice is based on fairness – the fair and equitable distribution of goods and individual freedom. Justice theory stands in contrast to utilitarianism (it is about all, not about the majority) and stresses the importance of rights and drawing, on virtue theory, addresses what is right for the individual *and* what is right for the social group. This is premised on the idea that an absence of justice threatens the social group or community. For Rawls (1971) it was important for people to set aside their own social position and defining statuses (class, race, gender, wealth) and to embrace what he called *a veil of ignorance* – only then can we make fair decisions and avoid self serving interest in decision making. Here, the veil of ignorance is possible when people imagine what kind of society they would like to live in without knowing their class, race, gender or ability. Rawls (1971) argued that most people adopting the veil of ignorance would be self-interested (i.e. ensure against being a member of a disadvantaged group) and desiring and seeking of a society that was fair to those who were less well off or disadvantaged.

If justice is about fairness and equity, then it is clearly an issue in tourism. Some forms of tourism are inherently unjust and inequitable (Higgins-Desbiolles 2010). Medical tourism, and in particular the associated sale of organs, and sex tourism provide examples of unjust and inequitable relationships central to these touristic practices. These examples are discussed more fully in later chapters. Early work in the area of tourism and justice stressed the need to develop ethical models that would address the tourist's experience and stressed the need for tourists to be able to adopt principled practice (Hultsman 1995 in Higgins-Desbiolles 2010). However, this early work neglected the need to also consider the destination and the fairness of relationships between tourists and locals. Connected to concerns about social justice within communities is international justice and its significance to international tourism. Considerations of justice have tended to involve focusing on nation states and what is occurring within their borders. While this is important, often justice or injustice is shaped by practices and events outside of those borders (Higgins-Desbiolles 2010). An understanding of international justice is important as it addresses inequitable distribution of resources and wealth globally and highlights the need to consider distributive justice at a global level.

While Rawls (1971) advocates adopting a veil of ignorance to prevent self-serving interest in decision making (unfair decision making), Lawrence Kohlberg (1981) advocates 'walking a mile in another man's shoes', which is an equivalent to the Golden Rule. Adopting this position facilitates what he calls 'justice as reversibility'. For tourists from More Economically Developed Countries (MEDC) travelling to Less Economically Developed Countries (LEDC) this would involve, for example, considering whether having to sell their body for sex to survive economically was a reversibility they would be comfortable with. The idea of distributive justice addresses the huge inequity in wealth globally and questions whether the wealthy have the right to indulge in luxuries well beyond human need, while others in the world live in abject poverty and in the face of ongoing famines. Redistributive measures are in this context considered a moral duty (see Chapter 3, 7 and 8).

Taking this position further, some have argued that those in the affluent countries of the world are responsible for life-threatening poverty in other areas of the world (Pogge 1994; Higgins-Desbiolles 2010). Tourists in this sense then are partaking in what Crick (1989) has called 'leisure imperialism', where tourism is the 'hedonistic face of neo-colonialism', a pursuit enabled by colonialism and consequent global inequity. The key issue is that tourism does not stand outside of the processes that contribute to global poverty – it also contributes to it. While some will argue that it provides employment and foreign exchange and opportunity of economic growth to developing countries, this position can be very quickly undermined when the global trading system is considered and where it is clear Less Economically Developed Countries engage in and with this system on a very unequal footing.

Responding to those who advocate for justice in tourism a number of alternative forms of tourism have been developed where responsibility and justice become central and where the industry aims for equity, solidarity and mutual understanding (Pearce 1992). So what can justice through tourism actually entail? With redistributive measures the greater the

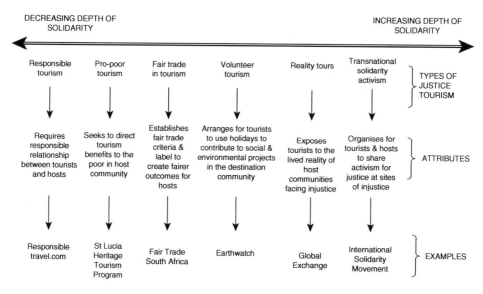

Figure 2.2 *Continuum of Justice Tourism.*
Source: Higgins-Desbiolles (2009).

depth of solidarity generated by the type of Justice Tourism the more successful the measure is likely to be in terms of bringing about social change. The various types of Justice
Tourism include: responsible tourism, pro-poor tourism, fair trade tourism, volunteer tourism, reality tours and transnational solidarity activism. All of these forms of tourism are
interested in addressing global inequity and see tourism as a vehicle for social change.
Figure 2.2 outlines a Continuum of Justice Tourism developed by Higgins-Desbiolles
(2009: 338).

Cultural relativism

How can I tell what is right or wrong or even whether my values are the same as theirs?
There are many perspectives on morality. A *cultural relativist* argument asserts that if
something that is done is in line with the cultural rules and norms of the social group the
person belongs to then it is not for others from different social groups with different values

See the following websites for the examples given in Figure 2.2:
Responsible travel: www.responsibletourism.com
St Lucia Heritage Tourism Program: www.propoortourism.org.uk
Fair Trade South Africa: www.fairtrade.org.za
Earthwatch: www.earthwatch.org
Global Exchange: www.globalexchange.org
International Solidarity Movement: www.palsolidarity.org

to judge. In part this idea comes from a desire to grant legitimacy to cultural diversity, to say, these people are merely different from us and we should not judge or measure them by our own yardstick. The problem is that this argument can be used to legitimate injustices, murders, wars, and a wide range of inhumane actions and unsustainable practices (see examples in Chapter 6 and Chapter 9). If somebody kills another and says this is acceptable under these conditions in my culture – is it? An *objectivist* would argue that just because a response is culturally appropriate it does not mean that it is morally defensible. Underpinning the objectivist stance is the idea that there are some moral norms or principles that are valid for all, any time, any place. It is important when confronted with a cultural relativist stance to ask a range of critical questions and not to leap to a position of agreement or disagreement – to for example say "oh no I do not think this is morally ok" with no supportive rationale. To respond in this way is to be *emotive*. *Emotivism* is when people simply express their preference based on how they feel about an issue, they also often hope to influence how others behave and make no effort to develop a critically informed moral position (Vaughn 2008).

Ethics of care

Ethics of care is about addressing the absence of partiality in ethics of justice. Ethics of care does not aim to establish generalised laws and emphasises the importance of considering the context within which the interaction takes place. The *care* in this ethics is literal – it is about developing an understanding and concern for those involved (Smith and Duffy 2003). The emphasis is on the relational nature of identity and requires us to be aware of the needs of others and to act on this awareness.

2.6 ETHICAL DECISION MAKING

This chapter has canvassed a wide range of theoretical perspectives and raises more questions than it answers. How can we begin then to apply these various perspectives and how can we solve some of the ethical dilemmas that touristic practice provokes? In this section we provide some road maps – where the destination is largely unknown. At the heart of ethical decision making is the ability to think critically – to resist responding on the basis of intuition, or on the basis of what Uncle John had to say or Aunty May believed.

Five steps and four key elements in the process of ethical decision making

There are various approaches to the process of ethical decision making. Here we list five steps which are useful when addressing issues in touristic practice that require ethical decision making.

1 Recognise the problem
2 Analyse the problem and clarify facts and uncertainties
3 Identify the ethical issues and values central to the decision making
4 If the values conflict you have an ethical dilemma
5 Prioritise the values in conflict. Here consider how you can prioritise in terms of what end is sought, what the means to the end is, and authenticity.

These five steps are then used in conjunction with the following four key elements (Vaughn 2008: 7):

1 The pre-eminence of reason
2 The universal perspective
3 The principle of impartiality
4 The dominance of moral norms.

Employing the five steps in conjunction with the four key elements identified above will ensure that you are working toward ethical decision making by critically evaluating the issue through identifying facts and uncertainties, reflecting on the implications for all (not just the majority), identifying where values conflict and addressing how this conflict can be resolved ethically.

Given the wide range of social practices and contexts within which tourism takes place it is not possible for one perspective to work in all situations. An eclectic approach to theory and its application offers the opportunity to address the shortcomings of the various theories canvassed in this chapter and also the ability to address a range of issues provoked through touristic practice. Schumann's (2001) Moral Principles Framework provides a useful eclectic tool to assist in ethical decision making and draws from five main ethical theories: utilitarianism, rights, distributive justice, the ethics of care, and virtue theory (Table 2.1). Schumann (2001) also advocates for the search for universal moral principles and the abandonment of ethical relativism.

The questions that each theoretical position provoke ensure that it is possible to work through a wide range of situations and although it is still the case that the framework does not cover all situations and is not necessarily exhaustive, it offers a very good starting point for those who want to engage in ethical decision making.

Table 2.1 Schumann's Moral Principles Framework

Theory	Questions
Utilitarianism	What actions will do the most good and the least harm for everyone who is affected?
	a Who are the stakeholders?
	b What are the alternative courses of action?
	c For each alternative, what are the benefits and costs?
	d Which alternative creates the most benefits and least costs?
Rights	What action do you have the moral right to take, that protects the rights of others, and that furthers the rights of others?
	a Do you have a moral right to take the action in question? Consider:
	• Are you willing to have the action in question done to you?
	• Are you willing to live in a world where everyone did the action in question?
	• Are you treating people with respect?
	b What moral rights do other stakeholders have?
	c Are there conflicts between your moral rights and others? Which takes precedence?

Continued

Table 2.1 Continued

Theory	Questions
Distributive justice	What actions produce a fair distribution of benefits and costs for all of the stakeholders? a Egalitarianism: What action produces a fair distribution of benefits and costs? b Capitalism: What actions produce costs/benefits based on the contributions of actors? c Socialism: What action distributes the benefits based on need and costs based on abilities? d Libertarianism: What action has been freely chosen by the stakeholders? e Rawls's principles: What action provides all with equal liberties and opportunities while helping those in need to the greatest extent possible?
Ethic of care	What action cares for those people with whom you have special relationships? a What action cares for your own needs? b What action cares for the needs of the others you have a relationship with (e.g. family, friends, co-workers, competitors)?
Virtue	What action displays virtuous character traits? a Does the action display virtues such as benevolence, civility, compassion, courage, fairness, conscientiousness, cooperativeness, generosity, honesty, industriousness, loyalty, moderation, self-control, self-reliance, or tolerance? b Or does the action display vices such as cowardice, deceit, laziness, neglect, or selfishness? c Take the action that displays the virtues not the vices.
Resolve the conflict	Do all five moral principles reach the same conclusion, or do they reach conflicting conclusions? a If in conflict, then, examine the nature of the conflict to see if it can be resolved by choosing a previously unconsidered course of action. b If 'a' is not possible, then collectively decide which principle(s) should take precedence in light of your values.

Source: Schumann (2001) (The table is reproduced as it appears in Fennell 2006: 272).

CHAPTER REVIEW

This chapter has explored various ethical concepts and principles and demonstrated their applicability in relation to a number of touristic examples. We have considered the concept of values, which are central to moral systems. In addition to this we have considered four key elements central to ethics, the pre-eminence of reason, the universal perspective, the principle of impartiality, and the dominance of moral norms. Critical reasoning is central to ethical decision making. We have briefly canvassed a range of ethical theories: intuitionism; the four main teleological theories – utilitarianism, hedonism, egoism and virtue ethics; and the deontological non-consequentialist theories – the Golden Rule, Kantian ethics, social contract, social justice and ethics of care. There is no formulaic solution to ethical decision making, however, a number of models have been developed by various academics interested in applied ethical decision making. This chapter concluded with a summary of a number of steps that can be taken to ensure that your approach involves critical reasoning and provides a framework that employs a range of ethical theories and provides specific questions that can be asked when you are working toward making ethical decisions about touristic practice. As moral agents, students of tourism, researchers, tourist operators and tourists themselves are engaged in practices that are intrinsically about ethics and morality. Being equipped to ask the right questions about touristic practices and developing skills that will facilitate ethical decision making in relation to touristic practices is imperative in the contemporary world.

SUMMARY OF KEY TERMS

Ethics is the philosophical study of morality, the science of what constitutes right or wrong conduct.

Morality is about patterns of conduct and rules of action based on beliefs about what is right or wrong.

Hedonism The idea that the greatest good is connected to the pleasure experienced by an individual, what is good is pleasurable.

Egoism The goals of the individual are the end in and of themselves. The individual assists only those who are of benefit to the realisation of their goals.

Intuitionism To know something through experience, without any reference to reason.

Emotivism Feelings and sensitivities inform moral action.

Instrumentalism Where assistance and inclusion is provided to others on the basis of whether they are of use to the individuals' own aims and goals.

Utilitarianism The pursuit of happiness and avoidance of pain forms the foundation for morality. Actions that bring about happiness are good and those that bring about pain are bad. Actions are good if they increase the overall pleasure of the group.

Justice Is based on fairness – the fair and equitable distribution of goods and individual freedom. Justice theory stands in contrast to utilitarianism (it is about all, not about the majority) and stresses the importance of rights. Drawing on virtue theory, justice theory addresses what is right for the individual *and* what is right for the social group. This is premised on the idea that an absence of justice threatens the social group or community.

Distributive and commutative justice Aristotle distinguished between 'distributive' and 'commutative' justice; the former is concerned with the distribution of things (goods, services, rights, etc.) and how they should be distributed among people. A central idea here is 'treating equals equally'. The latter, commutative justice, is about how an individual is treated in a specific transaction – have they been treated as they should be? Have they been accorded their rights? For Plato, this was about giving people 'their due'. Thus, retributive justice is about redressing when a person has not been treated as they should be or have not been accorded their rights.

Ethics of care Is about addressing the absence of partiality in ethics of justice. Ethics of care does not aim to establish generalised laws and emphasises the importance of considering the context within which the interaction takes place. The *care* in this ethics is literal – it is about developing an understanding and concern for those involved (Smith and Duffy 2003).

QUESTIONS FOR REFLECTION

1 How do we make ethical judgements about what is right or wrong in a culturally diverse world where diverse moral values are held?
2 What is the relationship between ethical and moral conduct and human rights and notions of justice?
3 How can the tourism industry address questions surrounding social justice and the perpetuation of global inequality – and why should it?

EXERCISE

Scenario

You are approached by a tourist operator who is having difficulty gaining the appropriate consents that will enable him to establish his tourist business. His business plan is to build and operate a hotel and bar on the foreshore of a tropical island. He is not a local inhabitant, he is an expatriate who has taken up residence on a nearby island which is more developed and offers a range of tourist amenities. His business will be financed through foreign capital and his company shareholders are primarily based in the United Kingdom. His business will be the first of its kind on this largely undeveloped island. The local inhabitants on this island are descendants of the first settlers, dating back to 1500. They rely heavily on fishing and subsistence agriculture and for many of the island's inhabitants day-to-day survival is a struggle. A large number of the island's young people migrate to larger islands to find work and remit money back home. The foreshore is considered sacred and the site where the development would take place encompasses an area where the locals believe their ancestors depart to the heavens. The locals are divided over whether the development should take place, with some in favour because of the opportunities it might provide for their children and others against because they see it as a threat to their autonomy and way of life. Tourism development in the region has led to the developed islands becoming a sought-after destination for sex tourism.

Apply Schumann's framework and as you do identify the gaps in knowledge about this context that need to be addressed before an ethical decision can be made.

FURTHER READING

Fennell, D.A. (2006) *Tourism Ethics,* Bristol: Channel View Publications.

Fennell, D.A. (2009) 'Ethics and tourism', in Tribe, J. (ed.) *Philosophical Issues in Tourism*, Bristol: Channel View Publications, pp. 211–26.

Smith, M. and Duffy, R. (2003) *The Ethics of Tourism Development*, London: Routledge.

NOTES

a Isaac Asimov (1920–92), American science and science-fiction author. In *Foundation*, 1951.

b Plato (*c*.427–347 BC), Classical Greek philosopher, mathematician, student of Socrates.

REFERENCES

Abbink, J. (2000) 'Tourism and its discontents: Suri-tourist encounters in southern Ethiopia', *Social Anthropology*, 8: 1–17.

Bentham, J. (1987) 'Introduction to the Principles of Morals and Legislation', in A. Ryan (ed.) *Utilitarianism and Other Essays: J.S. Mill and Jeremy Bentham*, Harmondsworth, UK: Penguin.

Blackburn, S. (2001) *Being Good: A Short Introduction to Ethics,* Oxford: Oxford University Press.

Butcher, J. (2003) *The Moralisation of Tourism: Sun, Sand ... And Saving the World?,* London: Routledge.

Butler, R. and Hinch, T. (eds) (1996) *Tourism and Indigenous Peoples*, London: International Thomson Business Press.

Butler, R. and Hinch, T. (eds) (2007) *Tourism and Indigenous Peoples: Issues and Implications*, revised edn, Oxford: Elsevier.

Chandler, D. (2002) *From Kosovo to Kabul: Human Rights and International Invention*, London: Pluto Press.

Cooper, T.L. (1987) 'Hierarchy, virtue, and the practice of public administration: a perspective for normative ethics', *Public Administration Review*, 47: 320–8.

Crick, M. (1989) 'Representations of international tourism in the social sciences: sun, sex, sights, savings, and servility', *Annual Review of Anthropology*, 18: 307–44.

Fennell, D.A. and Malloy, D.C. (1995) 'Ethics and ecotourism: a comprehensive ethical model', *Journal of Applied Recreation Research,* 20(3): 163–83.

Fennell, D.A. and Malloy, D.C. (1999) 'Measuring the ethical nature of tourism operators', *Annals of Tourism Research,* 26(4): 928–43.

Foot, P. (1959) 'Moral belief', *Proceedings of the Aristotelian Society,* 59: 83–104.

Genot, H. (1995) 'Voluntary environmental codes of conduct in the tourism sector', *Journal of Sustainable Tourism,* 3(3): 166–72.

George, B. (2007) 'Human rights in tourism conceptualization and stakeholder perspectives', *Electronic Journal of Business Ethics and Organization Studies,* 12: 2.

Higgins-Desbiolles, F. (2006) 'More than just an industry: the forgotten power of tourism as a social force', *Tourism Management,* 27: 1192–208.

—— (2009) 'International solidarity movement: a case study in volunteer tourism for justice', *Annals of Leisure Research,* 12: 333–49.

—— (2010) 'Justifying tourism: justice through tourism', in Cole, S. and Morgan, N. (eds) *Tourism and Inequality: Problems and Prospects,* Wallingford: CABI, pp. 194–210.

Karwacki, J. and Boyd, C. (1995) 'Ethics and ecotourism', *A European Review,* 4: 225–32.

Kohlberg, L. (1981) *The Philosophy of Moral Development (Vol.1.),* Essays on Moral Development Series, San Francisco, CA: Harper and Row.

Lovelock, B. (2007) 'Ethical travel decisions. Travel agents and human rights', *Annals of Tourism Research,* 35: 338–58.

Malloy, D.C. and Fennell, D.A. (1998a) 'Codes of ethics and tourism: an exploratory content analysis', *Tourism Management,* 19(5): 453–61.

Malloy, D.C. and Fennell, D.A. (1998b) 'Ecotourism and ethics: moral development and organizational cultures', *Journal of Travel Research,* 36: 47–56.

Malloy, D.C., Ross, S. and Zakus, D.H. (2000) *Sport Ethics:Concepts and Cases in Sport and Recreation,* Buffalo, NY: Thompson Educational Publishing.

Mansperger, M.C. (1995) 'Tourism and cultural change in small-scale societies', *Human Organizations,* 54: 87–94.

Pearce, D.G. (1992) 'Alternative tourism: concepts, classifications and questions', in Smith, V.L. and Eadington, W.R. (eds) *Tourism Alternatives,* Chichester: John Wiley, pp. 15–30.

Pogge, T.W. (1994) 'An egalitarian law of peoples', *Philosophy and Public Affairs,* 23(3): 195–224.

Przeclawski, K. (1996) 'Deontology of tourism', *Progress in Tourism and Hospitality Research,* 2: 239–45.

Rawls, J. (1971) *A Theory of Justice,* Cambridge, MA: Belknap Press.

Ray, R. (2000) *Management Strategies in Athletic Training,* 2nd edn, Champaign, IL: Human Kinetics.

Schumann, P.L. (2001) 'A moral principles framework for human resource management ethics', *Human Resource Management Review,* 11: 93–111.

Smith, M. and Duffy, R. (2003) *The Ethics of Tourism Development,* London: Routledge.

Stark, J.C. (2002) 'Ethics and ecotourism: connection and conflicts', *Philosophy and Geography,* 5(1): 101–13.

Taylor, P.W. (1975) *Principles of Ethics: An Introduction,* Belmont, CA: Dickenson.

Vaughn, L. (2008) *Ethics: Moral Reasoning and Contemporary Issues,* New York: W.W. Norton.

Wheeler, B. (1994) 'Egotourism, sustainable tourism and the environment: a symbiotic, symbolic or shambolic relationship', in Seaton, A.V. (ed.) *Tourism: The State of the Art,* Chichester: John Wiley, pp. 647–54.

3 Mobility, borders and security

'I like to go a wandering.'

Ridge and Moller[a]

'Halt, who goes there?'

Robert Howard[b]

'When in Rome, do as the Romans do.'

St Ambrose[c]

LEARNING OBJECTIVES

After reading this chapter you will be able to:

- Critically reflect on what is known as the 'new mobility paradigm'.
- Identify the key ethical issues surrounding mobility, borders, security and the institutions that they protect.
- Critically reflect on freedom of access and the right to travel.
- Understand the relevance of justice to mobility.

3.1 INTRODUCTION

The movement of people from one place to another – mobility – is enshrined in the *Universal Declaration of Human Rights*, but it is not necessarily a right shared by all. Mobility as Blomley (1994) and others have observed is intrinsically geographic and political. Mobility rights are not only about the right to move, but also the right to stay.

Mobility has become a fashionable term in social science circles over the last 30 years. In part this is an outcome of developed nation states moving into late capitalism and the recognition that there has been an intensification of interconnectedness globally. Referred to as globalisation, it is variously observed that there is increasing movement of goods, capital and people and that, in relation particularly to goods and capital, borders have become more porous (Hannerz 1997; Cunningham 2004: 329; Friedman and Randeria 2004).

The recent interest in mobility has also been triggered by the recognition that what is happening between spaces, on the way to places and while in transit, are areas of social life that have been historically ignored, both theoretically and empirically. While various disciplines have their own twists on the importance of understanding places and non-places, all share the central critique that it is necessary to move beyond the idea of social life as fixed – where everything has its place and space. All agree that it is necessary to understand the spaces and places between and beyond, as these shape our very ability to recognise boundaries and to ultimately understand how all localities are globally interconnected (Clifford 1997; Urry 2000).

While migration studies have a long history, historically, temporary mobility and the temporarily mobile – including tourists – did not attract a great deal of research attention. In contrast, those who settled were subject to a great deal of research attention. This is in part because social theory in the pre-and post-Second World War period also favoured a focus on the sedentary. It has since been recognised by a range of theorists that mobility is a manifestation of modernity that has been overlooked and which is worthy of study. In the field of tourism, researchers have focused on various mobile groups: holiday tourists, business tourists and return tourism (and the relationship between tourism and migration for permanent settlement) (Cresswell 2006: 738).

While the mobility turn offers new insights, there has also been a tendency amongst some researchers to overemphasise freedom of movement and to fail to recognise that the 'new' theoretical insights offer explanations of a social existence only relevant to a small global elite. The world may be more porous for some and a new skilled elite may well be contributing to new 'cultural' flows across numerous borders; but social inequality is produced and reproduced within and alongside these flows (Castells 1996). Central to any understanding of mobility is the need to explore not only the mobile, but the immobile and how mobility is produced, reproduced and sustained in the contemporary social world. Global interconnectedness is uneven and there are issues of exclusion and access. Flows of goods, commodities and capital can tell us about access and inclusion in global networks (Castells 1996; Susser 1996) and governance over the flow of these various entities remains central to the politics of modern nation states (Castells 1996). While there have been dramatic increases in the number of people who are globally mobile, these numbers still only represent a very small percentage of the world's population, where the majority are not mobile and where poverty ensures these people remain involuntarily and permanently sedentary (Cunningham and Heyman 2004; Hall 2010). (See Chapter 8 for a discussion of social tourism.)

While tourism is often portrayed as a fun activity which involves enacting freedom of access and the right to roam, for many this fun, this access or these rights do not exist. Tourism is a commodity available to a very small percentage of the world's population. The movement of people – mobility – is produced and its production is shaped by gender, ethnicity, class, the level of development (of one's home and or destination country) and relations with other nations. The right to roam, the right to travel are very much about inequitable spatial rights globally. Mobility is prohibited, enabled, allowed and or encouraged and legitimised through both national and international legislative frameworks which inscribe and proscribe the 'limits' of movement. The establishment of borders and issues connected to international and national security provide the clearest markers of what might be called the 'politics of mobility' and at the heart of this politic are ethical and moral concerns.

Others have observed that the way we think about geographic mobility needs to be critically appraised in terms of equity, fairness, justice and rights (Pirie 2009: 21). We need to consider also: those who cannot afford to travel (Hall 2005a); those who are compelled to travel because of war, persecution, natural and or human-made disasters; and those who are in these circumstances compelled to stay (Massey 1997; Cresswell 2001; Verstraete 2001).

Mobility studies tend to assume the mobility of the tourist is a given and typically social inequality is usually taken to reside in the destination country. The focus is on where the tourists are going, rather than what the tourists and their host society might be bringing with them, brought previously or be unwittingly contributing too, through their nation's relations with others. Tourist mobility is shaped, constrained and directed by geopolitical trends and national and international bureaucratic responses to ongoing and developing conflicts and alliances. Geopolitical networks are shaped by the flow of people, capital, goods and consumptive practices and disparate levels of control over all of these processes and associated outcomes. Understanding the micro processes of control over mobility and the macro political context within which they take place allows for a consideration of the ethics and moral issues pertinent to the study of mobility.

This chapter commences with a number of questions in mind: What determines the ability to travel internationally? Who in the main are our international travellers? How free is this international traveller? What constraints on freedom apply to various categories of international travellers? What can the governance of mobility tell us about the contemporary social world? Do the aforementioned questions also have relevance for domestic travellers? How can the moral framework of distributive justice help us understand the key ethical issues?

3.2 INVOLUNTARY IMMOBILITY AND THE INVOLUNTARY MOBILE

Involuntary immobility is a term increasingly used to refer to those who want to be mobile but for various reasons cannot be. A major reason for mobility is labour migration and globally there have been periods when labour migratory flows have been prevalent, particularly between the 1950s and 1970s, and then restricted, particularly in the 1980s and 1990s, by various countries of emigration. When entry is restricted this not only has implications for those who want to migrate to work, but also for their own countries which have usually relied on remittances to aid development at home (Carling 2002). The inability to be mobile has meant for many they have lost a strategy that previous generations had relied on to create a better life (Carling 2002). Yet while some have become involuntarily immobile others have enjoyed increased mobility and continue to sustain links transnationally. Known as transnational migration, these flows of people typically provoke social connections and networks that link their old and new societies and allow migrants to take advantage of geographical differences (Basch et al. 1994; Portes et al. 1999). Those who remain mobile contrast with those at home who cannot be mobile – and as Carling (2002) observes, mobility then serves domestically as an important social marker of status or as Bauman notes 'mobility has become the most powerful and most coveted stratifying factor' (Bauman 1998: 9). Poverty, illiteracy and poor education levels are major determinants of involuntary mobility. In addition to entry being denied on these grounds, other obstacles include a lack of social connection and family ties with the new society, prohibitive costs, dangers of travelling as an undocumented migrant and the risk of repatriation (Carling 2002: 30).

It has been observed that in contrast to the flow of humanitarian aid, the flow of refugees is comparatively more restricted, that borders are more porous to capital than to displaced people (Hyndman 1997: 149). As Hyndman (1997: 153) observes:

> 'Travelling culture' might better be described as a relationship of power which is inherently political because it is predicated upon a hierarchy of cultures which articulate unequal positions of authority and mobility.

3.3 MIGRATION AND TOURISM – A SYMBIOTIC RELATIONSHIP

What are the differences between migrants and tourists? A migrant or immigrant is usually defined as a person who travels to another country and settles for some time in that country (Lahav 2004: 33 in Wonders 2006: 67). Further, migrants move for a variety of reasons, including: escaping poverty and a desire to improve their economic status and wellbeing; escaping dangerous home societies; fleeing natural disasters; or to reunite with family who have migrated – amongst many reasons. As Wonders (2006: 69) observes, migrants are increasingly popularly perceived as people of colour, women and the poor. In contrast, tourists are typically perceived as border crossers who are wealthy, white, male (Urry 1990) and who move for pleasure and leisure (Wonders 2006: 69). Yet while these mobile are conceptualised as separate entities, they have a symbiotic relationship – where tourism as an industry generates employment that relies on cheap labour, often migrant labour, for the construction, maintenance and reproduction of a service sector that provides for the tourist.

> The dependence of the tourism industry on immigrant labour is significant in virtually all industrialised nations. This dependence is also fuelled by racist, classist and sexist stereotypes about who 'ought' perform unskilled and low wage labour.
>
> (Sole and Parella 2003 in Wonders 2006: 71)

Who builds the hotels, makes the beds and cleans the rooms, provides entertainment, provides emotional and sexual services – is all shaped by the aforementioned prejudices and resultant structured inequities. The relationship between the immigrant and the tourist is a dependent one yet the conditions on arrival, at borders and once 'settled' experienced by these two types of mobility can be very different. At the border the immigrant is potentially a threat, in contrast the tourist a welcome consumer.

3.4 CITIZENSHIP, BORDERS AND SECURITY

> Whether it is the shipment of parts for assembly across borders, the profit in petty commodity trade, the migration of people and the policing of it, or defence against feared

penetrations (of human 'enemies' or nature species and flows), borders permit, monitor, and halt movement.

(Cunningham and Heyman 2004: 293)

There are limits to mobility and nowhere is this more evident than at border crossings. International travel necessarily involves crossing borders – demarcation lines that mark out territories, territorial governance and peoples as different entities with different rules, different practices and their own geopolitical alliances (which may or not differ from the travellers' own). In the contemporary social world these borders are more often than not an outcome of the development of the modern nation state. Borders as politically inscribed boundaries (Vila 2000; Cunningham and Heyman 2004: 289) are spaces that offer the potential for understanding a range of processes related to trade, political relationships, power and social inequality as it is manifest in differential access to mobility and how macro geopolitical concerns are ultimately inscribed in, produced and reproduced through interconnected micro processes governing territorial demarcation.

For the purposes of this chapter we will be focusing on borders as the main mechanisms of control adopted by modern nation states in protecting, securing and delineating their territory from other territories and the main mechanisms employed to govern mobility. The function of an international border undoubtedly shapes tourist experience (Timothy and Tosun 2003) and for some determines that the experience will never be possible.

Figure 3.1 *UK Border: Borders are mechanisms of control and govern mobility.*
Photo: Brent Lovelock.

Border control reflects a central tension faced by modern nation states: the desire to protect and the desire to facilitate mobility – where mobility is necessary for trade and tourism, diplomacy, meeting human rights and the sharing of information, yet can potentially threaten domestic security. When security is an issue, mobility can be constrained or halted and it is here that we see a challenge to the notion that freedom to travel should be an inalienable human right. When a modern nation state considers domestic security is threatened freedom of movement is invariably curtailed – both for international travellers and domestic residents. Exceptions to freedom are enshrined in the *European Convention on Establishment* and the *United Nations Covenant on Civil and Political Rights* where national security, public order, public health or morality can be employed as a legitimate rationale for restrictions on mobility (Turack 1972: 3–4 in Salter 2004: 72).

Fears about security are not new and tourism and the tourist industry are vulnerable to changes in the global security environment (Hall et al. 2003: 2). Events in one part of the world can trigger responses elsewhere as countries move to protect their borders. The Severe Acute Respiratory Syndrome (SARS) outbreak was spread through aviation services and not surprisingly prompted travel warnings and health security or surveillance measures to be introduced at some borders (Hall et al. 2003). Security is not just about the safety of passengers, insecurity provoked by wars presents a very real economic threat to

Figure 3.2 Sign at UK border: Security concerns further support politically inscribed boundaries. Photo: Brent Lovelock.

tourism as an industry. While security is not a new concern, the nature of security has changed in the post-Cold War world. As Boulding (1991) observes:

> Environmental, social and economic issues, as well as the system of international governance by which such concerns are governed, now clearly lie within contemporary understandings of security.

> (Boulding 1991 in Hall et al. 2003: 4)

Policing borders – at internal points of entry including railway stations, roads, sea ports and airports – is about protecting the physical limits of the state. The function of policing is to discern who is desirable or undesirable and who offers the greatest threat (or enhancement) to the state's objectives. Protecting borders is about having and maintaining enough bureaucratic and physical power to exclude those who are a threat and to prevent those who have been deemed 'undesirable' from entering (Torpey 2000). The extent of permeability at the border is very much determined by the extent of socio-cultural similarity on either side (Donnan and Wilson 1999). With greater difference, very often the physical marking of the border is more extreme. For example, the Berlin Wall constructed in 1949 established a 1,393-km un-passable border consisting of metal fences, minefields, trenches, dogs, observation posts, floodlighting and concrete walls (Ritter and Hajdu 1989 in Timothy and Tosun 2003: 412).

Borders post-9/11

The freeing up of some borders in the 1990s gave rise to suggestions that we were moving toward a 'borderless world' and it was assumed by some to be connected to the demise of the nation state (Cunningham 2009). Yet despite the increase in the movement of people, greater intensification of international trade and associated flows of capital, there has been a proliferation of new borders. For example, in the former Soviet Bloc 15 new states emerged, East Timor gained independence from Indonesia, Eritrea separated from Ethiopia and there is a continued presence of independence movements (Cunningham 2009). The desire for increased trade has led to changes at some borders, enabling some to move more freely, but after 9/11 many states embracing anti-terrorism measures sought to secure their borders, some literally through fencing, at times electrified (e.g. Botswana and Zimbabwe) (Cunningham 2009).

In this period, most of the world's population is 'immobilised' and most nation state borders have remained remarkably resilient (Bauman 2002; Cunningham 2009). Borders have been re-spatialised in relation to economic regionalism or geopolitics and for some this means 'flows' and for others 'enclosures' (Cunningham 2009: 152). Many countries restrict the travel opportunities of their citizens, either not issuing exit visas, imposing high exit taxes or having currency exchange controls (Timothy and Tosun 2003), creating genuine barriers to travel and mobility. In addition, perceptions of borders and border control can also inhibit or encourage travel (Timothy 2001) and borders themselves can become tourist attractions (Timothy 1995), while for some the process of crossing a border is stressful and even frightening, with people feeling nervous despite having nothing to hide (Timothy and Tosun 2003).

Figure 3.3 *US–Mexico border: We are not a borderless world.*
Photo: Dallen Timothy.

DISCUSSION QUESTIONS

1 Social justice and distributive justice emphasise fairness, with the stress on *all*, not the majority. What are the ethical implications of inequitable rights to mobility?
2 Do open borders guarantee justice? Or should redistributive justice involve taking the resources to people rather than relying on people to move to the resources (resource-rich countries)?

3.5 MECHANISMS OF CONTROL – PASSPORTS

Passports and visas are necessary travel documents for all travellers, yet global conformity for the need for such documentation has a recent history and coincides with the consolidation of industrial capitalism, the rise of mass tourism and war (O'Byrne 2001). Historically passport and visa systems sought to ensure safe travel to the holder, often during wartime. The routine issuing of passports by some states (France, Italy and Turkey) occurred in the nineteenth century, but Britain and the United States did not issue passports until after the First World War (O'Byrne 2001). Obtaining a British passport was difficult and procurement was usually only achieved by the wealthy (Pemble 1988 in O'Byrne 2001). By 1915 the *Defence of the Realm Act* required British citizens to hold passports when they travelled abroad and by 1958 in the United States the right to hold a passport had become a constitutional right for an American citizen. Interestingly, today, British citizens do not have the right to a passport (Nichol 1993 in O'Byrne 2001). While passports are defined variously, they have three key functions: (1) to provide proof of citizenship; (2) proof of identity; (3) and provide currency for border crossing – and some assurance of protection from diplomatic services once the border has been crossed. Implicitly, the passport also indicates that the visitor will return to the country that issued it – their home country. As O'Byrne (2001: 403) observes:

> the passport is, perhaps, the most important symbol of the *nation-state system*. ... [it] is a political tool because it allows an administrative body to discriminate in terms of who can and who cannot travel in its name.

It is, however, not just a symbol of the nation state, but a mechanism which allows for inclusion or exclusion in or from a territory. In addition, the passport is not just a travel document, but also a means to identify – and therefore a surveillance tool. The ethical issues here then centre on power and control, rights and justice (fairness).

Passports serve as the primary form of identifying a person's nationality – which in turn aligns the traveller with their nation's foreign policy, identifies the traveller as friend or foe with respect to the former – and consequently allows a state to classify the traveller as safe or dangerous, high risk or low risk, desirable or undesirable (Salter 2004). The importance of passports for mobility is best illustrated by those who do not have them. Undocumented migrants may be economic migrants seeking entry to work, or refugees seeking a safe place to be (political asylum). Undocumented migrants are those who do not have passports or appropriate travel documentation and consequently have no official national affiliation or protection. They are considered 'high risk' and undesirable in contrast to those who are desirable (Salter 2004). Cunningham (2009) has referred to the two groupings as 'wanted moveables' (traders and permanent immigrants) and 'unwanted mobilities' (undocumented workers and terrorists) (Cunningham 2009: 148). Tourists arguably are also wanted moveables. Border crossings can be a very different experience depending on what kind of 'flow' you are perceived to be a part of. As Cunningham (2004: 345) observes:

> [Borders] are places where you might just be the wrong sort of flow: where your documents might be viewed as inadequate, where you might be pulled aside for a profile check, where you might be incarcerated and fingerprinted or apprehended and deported – a place where you might be denied mobility to the world's centres of capital and safety.

Freedom of movement over borders is invariably shaped by geopolitical and economic relationships. For example, the European Union passport is not standardised and some have argued that the reason behind this is that it allows member nations to maintain their various national identities (O'Byrne 2001: 414). The European Union is cited by some as an example of the demise of state sovereignty – but as Rudolph (2005: 8) argues, authority and choice are central elements of sovereignty. Integration allowed collective security and the possibility of pooling endowments and allowing trade to flow more freely. Thus, rather than diminishing state sovereignty, it is a compromise position that will ultimately increase national prosperity (Mattli 2000:150 cited in Rudolph 2005: 8) and ultimately the defence of sovereignty.

DISCUSSION QUESTIONS

Ethical issue: border restrictions and the protection of sovereignty.

1 Does the desire to protect national identity justify the exclusion of people at the border?
2 Is the flow of capital restricted in the same way?
3 With respect to human rights, are human rights being addressed in relation to mobility? Can rights be applied equally?

3.6 SURVEILLANCE – LEGITIMATE AND ILLEGITIMATE MOBILITY

As we have seen, not all nations grant passports as a right of citizenship. The modern passport document usually links the photograph of the individual with a unique code. A passport is for one person, includes biometric information and should allow the identification of the bearer through date of birth, place of birth, signature, security features, and space for visas and permits. The document also ensures that the bearer is a citizen of the state that issued the passport and is able to return there. The passport is often supplemented with a visa – which usually focuses on the reasons for the visit and allows the destination country to exert control before the border is approached and to set basic requirements for entry.

In 1985 the machine-readable passport (MRP) was introduced by the International Civil Aviation Organisation (ICAO) allowing correlation of passport information with other records (Salter 2004). It is widely used in developed countries, but many developing countries do not use it. Users of the MRP exchange information about stolen passports and the identity of 'known dangerous travellers'. Detecting dangerous travellers is not always possible using solely documented means – border control officials also employ profiling to identify those who might be 'high risk'. This procedure has been criticised not just because of failures – the examination procedure failed with two of the pilots responsible for the 9/11 attacks – but also because of assumptions made about individuals on the basis of these profiles. Fraudulent passports present a real challenge for border control. While all states regulate their borders, they are permeable and this permeability raises questions about human rights and freedom. Those that seek to make borders impenetrable for some, risk the rights of others.

9/11 – a shift from examination at the border to surveillance

The 9/11 terrorism act has had implications for all travellers with many states strengthening enforcement measures at their borders and increasing levels of securitisation (Cunningham 2009). In the United States, the Department of Homeland Security was created to address the poor coordination of intelligence concerned with domestic security. In addition, the *Enhanced Border Security and Visa Reform Act* of 2002 has served to delocalise the border (Bigo 2002); here identification and policing can now occur before the person gets to the border and can continue once the person is in the United States (Salter 2004).

The process of delocalisation has been paralleled with a shift away from the examination of the traveller toward surveillance of the mobile population (Salter 2004). Under the Bush administration, establishing a 'Smart Border' became the goal – a Smart Border is one where border security has access to a coordinated database and the use of new technologies to enhance security. With respect to the passport this has involved the introduction of a new digitised image that replaces the traditional photograph which was previously covered over with laminate (Salter 2004). The use of this imaging technology has meant that the American passport is more secure, but cannot be issued outside of the United States (Reeker 2002 in Salter 2004). Visas have also been made more tamper-resistant and the agent at the border can check the digitised image with the visa with the person in front of them. Yet, while this addresses fraud, the 9/11 terrorists entered the United States on valid passports. The issue here then is intelligence, and it is with respect to improving intelligence that concerns have been raised over freedom, privacy and mobility. Here, however, national security takes precedence over the right to travel or privacy.

Integration of information into one database system by Homeland Security was mandated with the system known as Chimera. In terms of the examination of travellers, the US Visitor and Immigrant Status Indication Technology System (US-VISIT) allows for greater examination of those considered 'high risk'. Intelligence criteria informs who these high risk people might be (when they conform to a profile) and finger prints of 'high risk' travellers are taken and matched against a database of known criminals and terrorists. There are a number of identified categories of risk, including national categories which are linked to foreign policy and domestic borders (Salter 2004). At first, high risk countries included: Iran, Iraq, Libya, Sudan, Syria and Yemen; the list has since been extended to include: Bangladesh, Egypt, Indonesia, Jordan or Kuwait, Pakistan, Saudi Arabia, Afghanistan, Algeria, Bahrain, Eritrea, Lebanon, Morocco, North Korea, Oman, Qatar, Somalia, Tunisia, United Arab Emirates (Salter 2004: 77–8). Particular attention is paid to men born before 1987 and those with a travel history to the United States. Those who match the criteria undergo extensive examination and are treated as dangerous. If granted entry the surveillance continues for those who are considered 'high risk', and they are required to report changes of address, education, employment and report in person to a Bureau of Security and Investigative Services (BSIS) official after one month and one year when at this time they are interviewed and checked against initial finger printing and photograph (Salter 2004: 78–9).

These measures mark an increase in examination for some – but as importantly, there has been an increase in surveillance *for all*, as these measures are no longer located at the border, but within the territory too. Profiling relies on suspicion, which in turn is based on statistical profiles of nationals, sociological work and unsubstantiated assumptions. Profiles are broad and lack precision (Salter 2004). These kinds of measures post-9/11 have created what has been called a 'cycle of insecurity' (Bigo 2002; Salter 2004) not just in the United States but also in Europe and arguably other developed nations. Importantly this cycle of insecurity leads to increased police powers, greater surveillance within the territory and the introduction of more layers of bureaucratic control (Salter 2004: 78); where ultimately the mobile are not only under surveillance by the agents of government but where they also learn to police themselves (Lyon 2001, 2003; Bigo 2002; Salter 2004). Further, the surveillance responsibility is passed to the citizen who is then expected to report 'illegal migrants' or those who appear suspicious. In the United States community surveillance is about 'joining the war on terror' and the Head of the Homeland Security has prepared a Citizens' Preparedness Guide which encourages citizens to do their own screening and profiling (Salter 2004: 79).

Since 9/11 the politics of control at airports has intensified, challenging popular conceptualisations of airports as fun and free places that simply facilitate travel. Securing these departure and arrival places in the post-9/11 era has challenged earlier conceptualisations that airports are 'non-spaces', somehow socially meaningless, vacuous, placeless, or spaces of flows (Auge 1995; Adey 2004). Indeed, surveillance practices control and ensure uneven flows.

Figure 3.4 LAX customer satisfaction survey device: Security as an acknowledged tourist experience. Photo: Brent Lovelock.

3.7 THE MOBILE BODY – BORDERS, BIOMETRICS AND SECURITY

Since the development of mass air transportation in the late 1960s a range of techniques has been employed on the part of airports to understand passenger mobility, with contemporary practices becoming increasingly automated and concerned with not only efficient management but also security. Early attempts to monitor passenger walking times between different facilities involved the use of punch cards as various points allowing for the tracking of passenger mobility within and between terminals. Known as critical path management, this method allowed engineers to focus on those areas in airport processing that needed attention and facilitated more efficient management. The passenger, under this form of surveillance, is a moving body – depersonalised and generalised. Yet while this early technology *dis-appears the body* – or at very least makes it one of many – more recent surveillance technologies *bring the body back*. Aviation terrorism has ensured that forms of identification beyond paper evidence have increasingly been sought and developed. The body has 'become the stable token of identity' (Adey 2004: 1369). Technologies that capture the human body are known as biometrics – capable of scanning eyes, hands and faces and the whole body thus uncovering an individual's identity (Adey 2004). These technologies allow the documentation of the body as it appears and for the comparison of this data with data on secure computer systems, and thus confirmation of authenticity and the legitimacy of travel.

These technologies are not neutral but technologies of social control, capable of determining whether the body can or cannot legitimately travel. Biometric technologies are employed to regulate mobility and address security – both in terms of terrorism but also in terms of the spread of disease. As Amoore (2006) observes, the war on terror prompted by 9/11 has spawned a range of surveillance strategies where border management has increasingly turned to digital technologies and data sharing and the human body becomes a 'biometric border' which can be read in terms of who is safe and who is unsafe. Business travellers, leisure travellers are safe, those who may be terrorists, traffickers, immigrants, or who are sick are unsafe.

> In effect, the biometric border is the portable border par excellence, carried by mobile bodies at the very same time as it is deployed to divide bodies at international boundaries, airports, railway stations, on subways or city streets, in the office or the neighbourhood.
>
> (Amoore 2006: 339).

Thermo-imaging technologies were employed at Singapore airport during the SARS outbreak, scanning body temperatures for signs of acute respiratory syndrome. These technologies are usually justified in terms of facilitating safer travel for the majority of travellers – utilitarian ethics – yet such justifications often conceal broader ethical and moral issues surrounding the control of mobility, and who and how somebody is determined as a 'good' or 'bad' traveller, where for the 'good' mobility is sped up, and for the 'bad' mobility is slowed down (Adey 2004) or halted altogether.

Adey (2004) highlights the neoliberal underpinnings of the development of these technologies and their implementation. Using the example of the Privium biometric scheme, a technology that allows retina scanning for 'known travellers' at Schiphol (in Amsterdam) airport he demonstrates how the use of these technologies can serve as a social marker. Known travellers are frequent travellers and the biometric used in this example is marketed as a tool that can address travel frustrations (delays, waiting, parking, etc.). With Privium, the 'known traveller' becomes a Privium member – pays a small fee and has a short interview; allows the scanning and then in return can check in late, park close, occupy VIP lounges, experience faster processing through immigration and security and can take close exits directly to the aeroplane. That is, this membership and allowing this form of bodily technological identification facilitates becoming a privileged traveller – or becoming a member of the 'kinetic elite' (Wolf 2000, Graham and Marvin 2004, both cited in Adey 2004: 1371). The privileged elite then move quickly through the airport, while non-members – unknown travellers – the 'others' – are given the full and slower attention of the airport staff with respect to screening and pre-departure processes.

Although there are border variations on the biometric theme, biometric marking does not end with a membership and fast tracking for those who regularly cross the US–Mexico border; it may go well beyond this if the trial for a smart card becomes routine. These cards have radio frequency identification and the holder can be tracked within the United States (Amoore 2006). Biometric borders vary, but they all depend on the idea that biometric technologies offer a means of providing infallible scientific proof of a person's identity. Interestingly though, the bio-data is always married to other data, which is assumed to have parallel legitimacy and the categories of who is desired and who is not remain the same – with many disparate social groupings being lumped together. As Amoore (2006: 345) observes of the US-VISIT programme of border controls, some become the 'trusted traveller' while some people are marked irredeemably 'Other'.

The challenges of conducting effective surveillance at airports where there are growing numbers of travellers have been met through technological innovation and the management of flows. In many airports the flow of passengers is directed, where passengers are forced to take two journeys, one of which is overt, 'the sunlit strip', and the other which is covert, an odyssey controlled by the authorities through categories and definitions and foreign languages (Pascoe 2001: 202 in Adey 2004: 1372). When passengers walk through the covert strip they are being profiled. It is the ease with which personal information can be shared that has raised ethical and moral concerns and most often these are expressed in terms of human rights. How various profiles are constructed has been subject to questioning, for example: Do these profiles discriminate against particular passengers? Or: Do these profiles discriminate against particular nationalities? The rhetoric that supports profiling and the use of technology to achieve it, emphasises that it is 'technological' rather than human judgement, but of course these technologies are not outside of the social, nor are the programmes that facilitate the profiling – they are what we might call simply *extensions of the human hand*.

Profiling has been advocated and defended in a very similar way to biometric surveillance. Bodies are treated differently, the kinetic elite move through quickly – they are embodied; those who are unknowns, the kinetic underclasses, are disembodied, move slowly and eventually sit in a smaller seat (Adey 2004). Speed becomes a new measure of access, for those that cannot afford the memberships, mobility is slowed down (Adey 2004).

Profiling is about assessing risk and increasingly simulation models are being used to design the processing facilities at airports. And while this is about facilitating flows and preventing queues, it is also about facilitating shopping in the retail outlets (Lemos 1997 cited in Adey 2004). 'Surveillance simulations are clearly also good for airport economics' (Adey 2004: 1375). Airports are clearly not places of equal flow: passengers are subject to power and control, multiple forms of surveillance that are linked to a wider web of technologies, in order that travellers be classified as either high or low risk. And in these spaces, it is important to present oneself in a docile manner, or as Salman Rushdie describes of his own border crossing:

> At the frontier our liberty is stripped away – we hope temporarily – and we enter the universe of control … These people, guarding these lines must tell us who we are. We must be passive, docile … This is where we must present ourselves as simple, as obvious: I am coming home. I am on a business trip. I am visiting my girlfriend … I am one dimensional. Truly. I am simple. Let me pass.

(Rushdie 2002: 412 cited in Adey 2004: 1377)

Those who create the profiles are not subject to scrutiny – nor are the profiles they construct for the categorising of others – only the traveller is scrutinised and either they conform or they do not.

CASE STUDY: TOURISM, VISAS AND THE GEOPOLITICS OF MOBILITY: 'WE ARE ALL TERROR SUSPECTS NOW' – *C. MICHAEL HALL*

… the one thing the 9/11 attacks have achieved, for those of us who spend too much time in airports, is to make suspicion universal; fear and discomfort are equal-opportunity employers now. The world is flat in ways the high-flying global theoreticians don't always acknowledge; these days, even someone from the materially fortunate parts of the world – a man with a ruddy complexion, a woman in a Prada suit – is pulled aside for what is quixotically known as 'random screening' (The Guardian 2011).

It used to be that the rich corners of the world seemed relatively safe, protected, and the poor ones too dangerous to enter. Now, the logic of the terrorist attacks on New York and Washington has reversed all that. If anything, it's the rich places that feel unsettled. It used to be that officials would alight on people who look like me – from nations of need, in worn jeans, bearing the passports of more prosperous countries – as likely troublemakers; now they realise that even the well-born and well-dressed may not always be well-intentioned (Iyer 2011).

Despite the portrayal of international travel as a form of 'freedom' the reality is that there is no international right to travel to another country. In some states citizens have rights to travel and hence depart but they may not have rights to enter their proposed destination (Coles and Hall 2011). Rights of travellers have been declared in some jurisdictions, although there is very little articulation of the rights of movement under international law. Although many nation states have entered into bilateral and multilateral agreements that facilitate mobility between parties the prerogative to control entry remains with the nation state (Hall 2008a). Indeed, under international covenants, such as the *Universal Declaration of Human Rights*, the rights to enter another country do not exist. Even the advisory *Universal Declaration of Human Rights* only postulates a right of exit and entry to one's own country and freedom of mobility within a citizen's own country. Article 13 states:

1 Everyone has the right to freedom of movement and residence within the borders of each state.
2 Everyone has the right to leave any country, including his own, and to return to his country (United Nations 1948).

Declarations of organisations such as the United Nations World Tourism Organization (UNWTO) with respect to a *Global Code of Ethics for Tourism* or the *Tourism Bill of Rights and Tourist Code,* carry little weight in international law and they are generally characterised as non-binding 'soft law' (Hall 2008a, 2008b).

Citizenship also does not automatically entitle rights of departure or access. Indeed, citizenship is a concept that has been largely taken for granted in studies of travel and tourism (Coles 2008a, 2008b; Coles and Hall 2011). Orthodox interpretations, especially those used in public policy, focus on the duality of rights and responsibilities bestowed on each citizen. Rights and responsibilities are both granted to, and expected by, social groups and citizen members. In exchange for discharging their responsibilities to a group, citizens have rights to conduct certain activities. This state-based view forms the basis for understanding most individual movements across territorial borders. At its simplest, without a passport or identity card, travel is not sanctioned. The nature of the passport or identity card determines what other permissions are necessary (such as visas, entry permits, fees) for entry or departure, or not as the case may be (Coles 2008a). As such, the complex geographies of regulation and rights of entry play significant roles in determining global patterns of travel and tourism (Coles and Hall 2011). There is, as Neumayer (2006) describes it, 'unequal access to foreign spaces'. Arguably, this situation has become even more unequal in a post-9/11 world in which there are increasing concerns by many states over security as well as unwanted migrants and persons. However, this situation actually raises a range of paradoxes and issues because at the same time as there has been within contemporary globalisation an increase in the free flow of goods and services via free trade agreements so there has been a desire by states to maintain or increase their ability and capacity to exercise stringent controls over who enters their national borders. Indeed, by the mid-1990s Sassen

(1996) had already raised concerns that stringent border controls ran counter to the expansion of human and civil rights to resident immigrants. More recently, Clemens (2011a, 2011b) has argued that even a modest relaxation of barriers to international human mobility:

> would provide more global economic prosperity than the total elimination of all remaining policy barriers to goods trade – every tariff, every quota – plus the elimination of every last restriction on the free movement of capital. ... Large numbers of people wish to move permanently to another country – more than 40% of adults in the poorest quarter of nations. But most of them are either ineligible for any form of legal movement or face waiting lists of a decade or more. Those giant walls are a human creation, but cause more than just human harm: they hobble the global economy, costing the world roughly half its potential economic product.
>
> (Clemens 2011b)

The restriction of access of individuals from one state to another can occur for various reasons including (Neumayer 2006; Coles and Hall 2011; Hall 2011; Hall and James 2011):

- security, including the restriction of criminal and terrorist activity
- diplomatic policy, i.e. using visa restrictions and costs to send diplomatic messages
- immigration policy, i.e. seeking to ensure that individuals seek to migrate through official channels and meet desired criteria. This may be because of economic reasons or concerns over social and ethno-cultural stability
- fundraising – visa costs can be used as a fundraising measure
- health and environmental reasons, i.e. concerns over the spread of disease or pathogens.

Even in the case of the European Union the development of the Schengen agreement which allowed greater ease of international travel within the EU was arguably at the cost of increased visa restrictions on access to Europe. With an original list of 73 countries, the number of countries facing common visa restrictions to all Schengen countries increased to 108 in the 1995 regulation and to 132 in the 2001 regulation (Neumayer 2006). Former Ukrainian President Leonid Kuchma warned that the Schengen visa rules would 'replace the Iron Curtain with a different, more humane but no less dangerous Paper Curtain' (Lavenex and Uçarer 2004: 433f. in Neumayer 2006). Indeed, in Europe greater and easier freedom of movement for 'insiders' was achieved at the expense of decreased mobility for those 'outsiders' from countries included on the list of those that require a visa for entry. A situation prompting critics to speak of efforts to create a 'fortress Europe' (Gordon 1989; Ireland 1991; Richmond 1993; Mitchell and Russell 1994). However, such a description is just as apt with respect to perceptions of the USA post-9/11.

In 2009 there were 2.4 million fewer international tourists visiting the USA than in 2000. According to a senior vice-president of the US Travel Association,

Geoff Freeman, 'The perception of "fortress America" has taken hold, partly because we haven't gone out and told people we want their business … And so we've had fewer overseas travellers every year since 9/11' (quoted in Mann 2010). In order to increase the number of international tourists coming to the USA President Obama signed the *Travel Promotion Act* into law in 2010. The Act added a fee to the US 'visa waiver' program (VWP) that is mainly used by tourists and short-stay business travellers from 36 countries (as of September 2011) for the purposes of raising funds for the 'Come to America' tourism campaign. To be eligible for a visa waiver travellers seeking admission to the USA must be a citizen of a country that has been designated by the US Secretary of Homeland Security, in consultation with the Secretary of State, as a 'program country'. The criteria for designation as program countries stress passport security and a very low non-immigrant visa refusal rate, as well as ongoing compliance with the immigration law of the United States. Two countries, Argentina and Uruguay, were removed from the program in 2002 and 2003 respectively because economic instability raised concerns in the USA that there may be more immigration over-stayers from those countries. All participating nations in the program must provide reciprocal visa-free travel for US citizens.

However, travellers wanting to participate in the VWP face a further number of requirements, including:

- All travellers must have individual passports. Children cannot be included on a parent's passport for the program.
- Passports issued or renewed after 26 October 2006 must be biometric machine-readable passports.
- Incoming travellers who intend to use the VWP are required to complete the I-94W form online (known as the Electronic System for Travel Authorisation (ESTA)) before departure to the USA, but preferably at least 72 hours in advance. This is mandatory for passengers on incoming flights and without it passengers are not allowed to board planes or ships that have a US port of entry.

However, even if an ESTA has been approved this is not a guarantee of admissibility to the United States at a port of entry. Instead, ESTA approval only authorises a traveller to board a carrier for travel to the USA under the VWP. It is up to the customs and border protection staff to determine admissibility. Indeed, arrival at the US border control raises a whole new raft of questions and issues not only with respect to entry, but also with the material preconditions for access in terms of Internet access and cost.

The USA introduced new screening rules for passengers arriving by air from 14 nations which the authorities deem to be a security risk in January 2010. This focused on flights from Cuba, Iran, Sudan and Syria (countries classified by the USA as state sponsors of terror) as well as from Afghanistan, Algeria,

Iraq, Lebanon, Libya, Nigeria, Pakistan, Saudi Arabia, Somalia and Yemen which were to receive enhanced screening. According to Nawar Shora of the American–Arab Anti-Discrimination Committee, 'This is extreme and very dangerous. All of a sudden people are labelled as related to terrorism just because of the nation they are from' (quoted in BBC News 2010). However, the situation arguably also reflects some of the wider issues facing immigrant Muslims and Arab-Americans post-9/11 (The Guardian 2011). Furthermore, as part of the new guidelines, passengers travelling from any other foreign country may also be checked at random.

We are therefore in a new geopolitics of mobility in which the regulation of mobility, of which tourism is an important part, has fundamentally become a geopolitical exercise, involving the formulation of spatial strategies and territorial arrangements to preserve the integrity of borders and to contain perceived external threats (Collinson 1996; Nagel 2002). In the case of tourism this applies at both state and individual scales. However, its application is uneven and raises fundamental questions of identity, transnationalism, citizenship and rights. The end result being a diverse geography of tourist experiences of constraints on mobility both pre, at and post the border that contrasts with the homogeneous representations of tourist freedom and accessibility found in dominant societal discourses of travel.

Reflection questions

1 Do people have a right to travel to another country as a tourist?
2 Is it right that security profiling of international tourists is undertaken on the basis of their nationality, religion and language?

Resources

Coles, T.E. (2008a) 'Citizenship and the state: hidden features in the internationalisation of tourism', in Coles, T.E. and Hall, C.M. (eds.) *International Business and Tourism: Global Issues, Contemporary Interactions*, London: Routledge, pp. 55–69.
Coles, T.E. and Hall, C.M. (2011) 'Rights and regulation of travel and tourism mobility', *Journal of Policy Research in Tourism, Leisure and Events*, 3(3): 209–23.
Hall, C.M. (2008a) 'Regulating the international trade in tourism services', in Coles, T.E. and Hall, C.M. (eds.) *International Business and Tourism: Global Issues, Contemporary Interactions*, London: Routledge, pp. 33–54.

References

BBC News (2010) Tougher US air screening for 'security-risk' countries. 4 January, Online. Available at <http://news.bbc.co.uk/2/hi/8438803.stm> (Accessed 3 September 2011).
Clemens, M.A. (2011a) 'Economics and emigration: Trillion-dollar bills on the sidewalk?', *Journal of Economic Perspectives*, 25(3): 83–106.

— (2011b) 'A world without borders makes economic sense. Allowing workers to change location significantly enriches the world economy. So why do we erect barriers to human mobility?' Povertymatters blog, guardian.co.uk, 5 September 2011, Online. Available at <http://www.guardian.co.uk/global-development/poverty-matters/2011/sep/05/migration-increase-global-economy> (Accessed 5 September 2011).

Coles, T.E. (2008b) 'Telling tales of tourism, mobility and citizenship in the 2004 EU Enlargement', in Burns, P.M. and Novelli, M. (eds) *Tourism and Mobilities: Local-Global Connections,* Wallingford: CABI, pp. 65–80.

Collinson, S. (1996) 'Visa requirements, carrier sanctions, "safe third countries" and "readmission": the development of an asylum "buffer zone" in Europe', *Transactions of the Institute of British Geographers*, 21: 76–90.

Gordon, P. (1989) *Fortress Europe? The meaning of 1992*, London: Runnymede Trust.

Hall, C.M. (2008b) *Tourism Planning: Policies, Processes and Relationships* (2nd edn), Harlow: Prentice Hall.

— (2011) 'Biosecurity, tourism and mobility: Institutional arrangements for managing biological invasions', *Journal of Policy Research in Tourism, Leisure and Events*, 3(3): 256–80.

Hall, C.M. and James, M. (2011) 'Medical tourism: emerging biosecurity and nosocomial issues', *Tourism Review*, 66(1/2): 118–26.

Ireland, P. (1991) 'Facing the true fortress Europe: immigrants and politics in the EC', *Journal of Common Market Studies*, 24: 457–79.

Iyer, P. (2011) 'We're all terror suspects now', *The Guardian*, 28 August. Online. Available at <http://www.guardian.co.uk/world/2011/aug/28/we-all-terror-suspects-now> (Accessed 29 August 2011).

Lavenex, S. and Uçarer, E.M. (2004) 'The external dimension of Europeanization – the case of immigration policies', *Cooperation and Conflict*, 39: 417–43.

Mann, S. (2010) 'US kicks off tourist drive with entry fee', *The Age*, March 9.

Mitchell, M. and Russell, D. (1994) 'Race, citizenship and "fortress Europe"', in Brown, P. and Crompton, R. (eds) *Economic Restructuring and Social Exclusion,* London: Routledge, pp. 136–56.

Nagel, C.R. (2002) 'Geopolitics by another name: immigration and the politics of assimilation', *Political Geography*, 21: 971–87.

Neumayer, E. (2006) 'Unequal access to foreign spaces: How states use visa restrictions to regulate mobility in a globalised world', *Transactions of the British Institute of Geographers*, 31(1): 72–84.

Richmond, A. (1993) 'Open and closed borders: Is the new world order creating a system of global apartheid?' *Refuge*, 13(1): 6–10.

Sassen, S. (1996) *Losing Control? Sovereignty in an Age of Globalization*, New York: Columbia University Press.

The Guardian (2011) 'After 9/11: "You no longer have rights" – extract' *The Guardian*, 2 September. Available at <http://www.guardian.co.uk/world/2011/sep/02/after-9-11-muslim-arab-american-stories> (Accessed 3 September 2011).

United Nations (1948) *Universal Declaration of Human Rights*, Adopted and proclaimed by General Assembly resolution 217 A (III) of 10 December 1948. New York: United Nations. Available at <http://daccessdds.un.org/doc/RESOLUTION/GEN/NR0/043/88/IMG/NR004388.pdf?OpenElement> (Accessed 3 September 2011).

CHAPTER REVIEW

This chapter has explored the study of mobility. Tourism is often portrayed as a fun activity that involves enacting freedom of access and the right to roam. Clearly, mobility is not an option for many; significant global inequity ensures that many are immobile and that as a consequence of famine, war and inhumane acts many people are involuntarily mobile. Security in the post-9/11 era involves significant ethical issues, including: the increasing surveillance of all – not just travellers; increased blurring of personal boundaries as surveillance technologies screen the body to establish identity; profiling that relies on cultural and racial stereotypes which can and do contribute to the reproduction of inequity and erosion of human rights for some. Invariably protecting borders, and employing various technologies to do so, is justified in terms of the interests of the majority (a utilitarian ethics framework).

SUMMARY OF KEY TERMS

Biometric technologies Technologies that allow for the human body to be screened – capable of screening eyes, hands and faces. These technologies allow states to document bodies and to call upon this documentation at border control posts. Increasingly they are assumed to provide identification that is 'authentic' and 'absolute'. These technologies can also be employed to detect disease, e.g. thermo-imaging technologies used during the SARS outbreak.

Biosecurity is about protecting the country's, region's or location's economic, environmental and or/human health from harmful organisms (Hall 2005b). Managing these threats at borders and once people are within borders is a significant issue for the tourism industry.

Machine-Readable Passport (MRP) A passport developed post-9/11 introduced by the International Civil Aviation Organisation (ICAO) which allows passport information to be correlated with other intelligence records.

Chimera A database system established by the Department of Homeland Security in the USA. This system allowed for the integration of a number of intelligence databases into one system.

QUESTION FOR REFLECTION

1 How do controls on mobility contribute to inequitable global relationships?
2 Increasing surveillance at borders is justified in terms of the end justifies the means. Does it?
3 Whose 'intelligence' is being relied on? Is it available at all borders?

4 How much freedom are people prepared to give up to gain security?

5 How are Human Rights ultimately protected?

6 What are the consequences of adopting a utilitarian ethics framework in relation to mobility and border security?

EXERCISE

Scenarios

1 The tourist travels to a location that lacks adequate sewerage facilities and may circumvent this by buying bottled water – while the communities surrounding the resort have polluted wells, unsafe beaches and declining fish resources because of pollution.
2 The tourist travels to their location, vaccinated and carrying prescription medicines that will protect them from local ills – while children and adults in the villages nearby die from inadequate medical care and diseases that vaccination would protect them from.
3 A tourist is at the border and notices his fellow traveller and friend has been taken aside. They are holidaying together, both hold American passports, both work for the same organisation and both are spending the same amount of time in the tourist location. His friend's first name is of Arabic origin, he was born in the United States and is an American citizen. His friend is detained and then deported under special provisions made to prevent the entry of terrorists.

Apply Schumann's framework (Chapter 2) to each of these situations and identify the key ethical issues.

NOTES

a Words by Antonia Ridge and Music by Friedrich W. Moller.
b 'Halt! Who Goes There?' by Robert Ervin Howard, first published in *The Yellow Jacket*, 24 September 1924.
c A saying attributed to Saint Ambrose (*c.*330–397), who was archbishop of Milan and became one of the most influential ecclesiastical figures of the fourth century.

REFERENCES

Adey, P. (2004) 'Surveillance at the airport: surveilling mobility/mobilising surveillance', *Environment and Planning,* 36: 1365–80.

Amoore, L. (2006) 'Biometric borders: governing mobilities in the war on terror', *Political Geography,* 25: 336–51.

Auge, M. (1995) *Non-Places: Introduction to an Anthropology of Supermodernity,* London: Verso.

Basch, L., Schiller, N.G. and Blanc, C.S. (1994) *Nations Unbound: Transnational Projects, Postcolonial Predicaments and Deterritorialized Nation States,* Amsterdam: Gordon and Breach.

Bauman, Z. (1998) *Globalization: The Human Consequences,* Cambridge: Polity Press.

— (2002) *Society Under Siege,* Cambridge: Polity Press.

Bigo, D. (2002) 'Security and immigration: toward a critique of the governmentality of unease', *Alternatives,* 27: 63–92.

Blomley, N.K. (1994) 'Mobility, empowerment and the rights revolution', *Political Geography,* 13(5): 407–22.

Carling, J. (2002) 'Migration in the age of involuntary immobility: theoretical reflections and Cape Verdean experiences', *Journal of Ethnic and Migration Studies,* 28(1): 5–42.

Castells, M. (1996) *The Rise of the Network Society: The Information Age: Economy, Society and Culture,* Hoboken, NJ: John Wiley.

Clifford, J. (1997) *Routes: Travel and Translation in the late 20th Century,* Cambridge, MA: Harvard University Press.

Cresswell, T. (2001) 'The production of mobilities', *New Formations,* 43: 3–25.

— (2006) *On the Move: Mobility in the Western World,* London: Routledge.

Cunningham, H. (2004) 'Nations rebound? Crossing borders in a gated globe', *Identities: Global Studies in Culture and Power,* 11: 329–50.

— (2009) 'Mobilities and enclosures after Seattle: politicizing borders in a "Borderless" world', *Dialectical Anthropology,* 33: 143–56.

Cunningham, H. and Heyman, J. (2004) 'Introduction: mobilities and enclosures at borders', *Identities: Global Studies in Culture and Power,* 11: 289–302.

Donnan, H., and Wilson, T.M. (1999) *Borders: Frontiers of Identity, Nation and State,* Oxford: Berg.

Friedman, J. and Randeria, S. (eds) (2004) *Worlds on the Move: Globalisation, Migration and Cultural Security,* London: Tauris.

Hall, C.M. (2005a) *Tourism: Rethinking the Social Science of Mobility,* Harlow: Pearson.

— (2005b) 'Biosecurity and wine tourism', *Tourism Management,* 26: 931–8.

— (2010) 'Equal access for all? Regulative mechanisms, inequality and tourism mobility', in Stroma Cole and Nigel Morgan (eds) *Tourism and Inequality: Problems and Prospects,* Wallingford: CABI.

Hall, C.M., Dallen, J.T. and Duval, D.T. (2003) 'Security and tourism: towards a new understanding?', *Journal of Travel and Tourism Marketing,* 15(2&3): 1–18.

Hannerz, U. (1997) 'Borders', *International Social Science Journal,* 49(154): 537–548.

Hyndman, J. (1997) 'Border crossings', *Antipode,* 29(2): 149–76.

Lahav, G. (2004) *Immigration and Politics in the New Europe,* Cambridge: Cambridge University Press.

Lyon, D. (2001) *Surveillance Society: Monitoring Everyday Life,* New York: Routledge.

— (2003) *Surveillance After Sept. 11,* Malden, MA: Polity.

Massey, D. (1997) 'A global sense of place', in Barnes, T. and Gregory, D. (eds) *Reading Human Geography,* London: Arnold, pp. 315–23.

O'Byrne, D. (2001) 'On passports and border controls', *Annals of Tourism,* 28(2): 399–416.

Pirie, G.H. (2009) 'Virtuous mobility: moralising vs measuring geographic mobility in Africa', *Afrika Focus,* 22: 21–35.

Portes, A., Guarnizo, L.E. and Landolt, P. (1999) 'The study of transnationalism: pitfalls and promise of an emergent research field', *Ethnic and Racial Studies,* 22(2): 217–37.

Rudolph, C. (2005) 'Sovereignty and territorial borders in a global age', *International Studies Review,* 7: 1–20.

Salter, M. (2004) 'Passports, mobility, and security: how smart can the border be?', *International Studies Perspectives,* 5(1): 71–91.

Sole, C., and Parella, S. (2003) 'The labor market and racial discrimination in Spain', *Journal of Ethnic and Migrant Studies*, 29(1): 121–41.

Susser, I. (1996) 'The construction of poverty and homelessness in US cities', *Annual Review of Anthropology,* 25: 411–35.

Timothy, D.J. (1995) 'Political boundaries and tourism: borders as tourist attractions', *Tourism Management,* 16(7): 525–32.

— (2001) *Tourism and Political Boundaries,* London: Routledge.

Timothy, D.J. and Tosun, C. (2003) 'Tourists' perceptions of the Canada–USA border as a barrier to tourism at the International Peace Garden', *Tourism Management,* 24: 411–21.

Torpey, J. (2000) *The Invention of the Passport: Surveillance, Citizenship and the State,* Cambridge: Cambridge University Press.

Urry, J. (1990) *The Tourist Gaze: Leisure and Travel in Contemporary Society,* London: Sage.

— (2000) 'Mobile sociology', *British Journal of Sociology,* 51(1): 185–203.

Verstraete, G. (2001) 'Technological frontiers and the politics of mobility in the European Union', *New Formations,* 43: 26–43.

Vila, P. (2000) *Crossing Borders, Reinforcing Borders: Social Categories, Metaphors, and Narrative Identities on the US–Mexico Frontier,* Austin: University of Texas Press.

Wonders, N.A. (2006) 'Global flows, semi-permeable borders and new channels of inequality', in Pickering, S. and Weber, L. (eds) *Borders, Mobility and Technologies of Control,* Netherlands: Springer, pp. 63–86.

4 | Human rights

'The rights of every man are diminished when the rights of one man are threatened.'

John F. Kennedy[a]

'It is time in the West to defend not so much human rights as human obligations.'

Alexander Solzhenitsyn[b]

'It is the inherent nature of all human beings to yearn for freedom, equality and dignity, and they have an equal right to achieve that.'

Dalai Lama[c]

'Travel is fatal to prejudice, bigotry, and narrow-mindedness.'

Mark Twain[d]

LEARNING OBJECTIVES

After reading this chapter you will be able to:

- Define human rights and discuss their relevance to tourism.
- Describe major human rights policy and legislation and how they impact the tourism industry.
- Critically discuss alternative forms of tourism (e.g. responsible tourism) in relation to human rights.
- Understand how tourism may improve or detract from the human rights of people living in destination communities.
- Consider key ethical approaches to the question of human rights.

4.1 INTRODUCTION

Usually we tend to think of human rights as being linked to the 'big' issues involving war, refugees and racial or ethnic discrimination. It may be surprising to learn that tourism is positioned by many as a human rights issue – or, more accurately, that tourism may contribute to the deterioration of the human rights of individuals living in destination communities.

Rather than alleviating poverty, tourism can exacerbate existing unequal, exploitative relationships and the poorest members of communities often feel the burdens hardest, frequently at the expense of their human rights.

(Cole and Eriksson 2010: 109)

In fact it is suggested that sustainable tourism is not possible until human rights as a relevant criterion has been recognised by all stakeholders (George 2008). Rarely has 'sustainability' or sustainable tourism been employed in holistic terms (Hall and Brown 2006), nor has much attention been given to issues of politics and power in relation to sustainable tourism (Coles and Church 2007; Mowforth and Munt 2009). This absence is important, considering debate around the role that tourism may play in supporting political regimes in destinations where there are known and significant human rights abuses. Alternatively, there is an argument for travel to politically repressed destinations, where tourism may contribute to political change, peace and reconciliation and an improvement in the human rights situation of citizens (e.g. Butler and Suntikul 2010).

This chapter discusses the complex relationship between tourism and human rights, and introduces some ethical frameworks for considering the rights of different tourism stakeholders. The chapter begins by outlining what human rights are, and the ethical basis for such rights. We then discuss the tourism industry's response to the human rights question, illustrating with cases of human rights breaches, as well as examples of good practice, along with new approaches to human rights, including Responsible Tourism. In the chapter we consider human rights on different scales – from the national to the local. Beyond the bigger questions of the state's abuses of its citizens' rights at a national scale, there are also more localised, destination-level human rights issues, often linked to specific local tourism developments. Some tourism researchers discuss the latter under the banner of 'welfare' (e.g. Hall and Brown 2006), and we acknowledge that there is considerable intersection between human rights and welfare. The chapter also considers the 'micro' or personal-level roles of stakeholders within the tourism industry, with respect to human rights. What products are ethical to sell, what are ethical to purchase, and how do we define 'ethical decision making'?

4.2 THE ORIGIN OF HUMAN RIGHTS

At the beginning of the twenty-first century, governments' disrespect for human rights is still evident in all regions of the world, and 'human rights violations continue to be the norm rather than the exception' (Dreher et al. 2010: 4). According to the NGO Amnesty International, millions of people are still denied fundamental human rights (Amnesty International 2012). For authoritarian governments, human rights repression is a tool to solve conflicts, 'if a government is threatened it reacts by repressing human rights' (Dreher et al. 2010: 4).

Chapter 2 provides an overview of ethical approaches to rights, and should be read in conjunction with this section. It is generally accepted that human rights derive from the inherent dignity of the human person (United Nations International Covenant on Civil and Political Rights 1966). Therefore one has human rights as moral rights simply because one is human, and no conditions apply (Lau 2008). While human rights may be defined legally (see below), it is relevant to consider the ethical foundations for human rights, which may be useful to help us obtain an understanding of the different types of rights and their relative importance.

While moral philosophy addresses issues of justice quite well (e.g. Rawls and distributive justice – see Chapters 2 and 8) (and we note that tourism is very much a justice issue (D'Sa 1999)), the ethical foundations for human rights are more debatable. Langlois (2009) provides a comprehensive overview of the ethical origins of contemporary human rights. He explains that prior to the enlightenment, values were spoken of in relation to an objective moral order that stood over and above all people. This order was conceptualised as the natural law, which, after the rise of Christianity, became associated with the Church. Under the natural law, rights were derived from the duties owed to one another under God. Growing clamour for individual liberty and political freedom from oppressive monarchies in the sixteenth century led to the 'rights of man' developed under natural law, being used for revolutionary purposes (Langlois 2009). The most famous example of this is the US Declaration of Independence of 1776. Central to such declarations is the idea of natural rights:

> We hold these truths to be self-evident, that all men are created equal, that they are endowed by their creator with certain unalienable Rights, that among these are Life, Liberty and the pursuit of Happiness.
>
> (US Declaration of Independence 1776)

However, by the time of such rights declarations, philosophers were attacking the idea of natural rights (Langlois 2009). Conservatives, liberals and radicals all voiced their opinion against natural rights. Burke (1729–97) argued that man had rights because of the organic traditions of his society, while utilitarian philosopher Jeremy Bentham referred to natural rights as 'nonsense upon stilts', while Marx wrote of such rights being only available for 'bourgeois man' (Langlois 2009).

Such criticisms were put aside, however, after the horrors of the Second World War, when the atrocities of the Jewish Holocaust 'outraged the conscience of mankind' (Universal Declaration of Human Rights (UDHR) 1948 in Langlois 2009). After the war, natural rights triumphed and re-emerged as human rights (Haule 2006). The return to natural law is evident within the 1948 UDHR, the first article of which declares that 'all human beings are born free and equal in dignity and rights'. Importantly, no philosophical justification was given for the UDHR, mainly because of the desire for its acceptance across a range of human belief systems (Socialist collective, Western liberal, Christian, Islamic, Confucian, etc.). Some argue that the UDHR and other human rights treaties are problematic because of this lack of foundation in moral philosophy – resulting in difficulties such as states disagreeing about which rights are human rights, and which rights should have priority (Posner 2008). Others go so far as to question whether human rights may be a fashionable contemporary alternative for true morality (Haule 2006).

One key difficulty for the UDHR – indeed, any set of human rights – is its claim to have universal application. Cultural relativists would claim that norms are only appropriate for the cultures out of which they emerge; therefore the norms of human rights that originate from the West only apply in the West (Langlois 2009; note that Langlois claims that relativists are refuted by their own doctrine: by claiming that all truths are relative, they proclaim the relativism of their own truths, and incoherence of their position (2009: 20)). Conversely, human rights universalists are accused of being imperialistic, and that human rights are a political tool to advance the interests of the West. These challenges, along with others from feminists, religious and special interest groups alert us to the political nature of human rights, and that they emerged from a tradition of political liberalism with which not all identify (Langlois 2009).

The philosophic literature around human rights now focuses on contractarian and welfarist approaches (Posner 2008). Contractarians derive human rights from a Rawlsian 'original position' argument, where a 'veil of ignorance' deprives people of knowledge of their nationality. Not knowing which nation they belong to, people in the original position would choose international institutions that protect the human rights of all human beings. Welfarists argue that everyone has moral worth, and that just international institutions would maximise a social welfare function that included the utilities of all people in the world (Posner 2008: 8). Rights are presented as either positive (the rights to receive benefits from governments), or negative (the rights to be free from interference from other people and the government) (Posner 2008). Under international law, the primary responsibility for the realisation of human rights rests with the state, which has three sets of obligations (Eide 2004: 7 in Cole and Eriksson 2010: 110):

1 To respect the freedom and dignity of the individual.
2 To protect them against third parties.
3 To provide access to welfare covering basic needs such as food, shelter, education and health.

Within the tourism industry, there is little guidance, however, as to the role of the private sector – individual businesses or industry bodies – even though the private sector has been implicated strongly in the abuse or decline of human rights, of workers and members of destination communities. The commonly accepted understanding of the respective responsibilities of business and government in the modern industrialised world can be traced back to a tacit 'social contract' that emerged following the Second World War (Cragg 2000). The effect of this contract was to assign responsibility for generating wealth to business, and responsibility for ensuring the equitable sharing of wealth to the state. Cragg argues, however, that with the advance of economic globalisation and the growing power and influence of multinational corporations, this division of responsibilities is no longer 'viable or defensible' (2000: 1).

> What is needed, fifty years after the United Nations Declaration of Human Rights, is a new social contract that shares responsibilities for human rights and related ethical responsibilities in a manner more in keeping with the vision captured by the post war Declaration.
>
> (Cragg 2000: 1)

The next section discusses the raft of mechanisms for addressing human rights, and considers the extent to which industry codes may provide some guidance to the tourism industry.

4.3 TOURISM AND HUMAN RIGHTS TREATIES AND CODES

In 1993, every country endorsed the 1948 International Declaration of Human Rights at the Vienna World Conference on Human Rights, and reaffirmed it in 2005 at the UN World Summit in New York. However, since 1993, we have seen an increase in violations of human rights (e.g. genocide, increased use of torture) (Donnelly 2008).

While the *Universal Declaration of Human Rights* (UNDHR) (1948) has a broad agenda, it does address aspects of tourism, for example through Article 13(2): *Everyone has the right to leave any country, including his own, and to return to his* country; and Article 24: *Everyone has the right to rest and leisure, including reasonable limitation of working hours and periodic holidays with pay.*

The UNDHR itself has no legal standing, but forms the overarching framework for an enforceable human rights treaty system, that encompasses nine major UN-endorsed treaties:

Convention on the Elimination of All Forms of Racial Discrimination (1969)
International Covenant on Civil and Political Rights (1976)
International Covenant on Economic, Social and Cultural Rights (1976)
Convention on the Elimination of All Forms of Discrimination Against Women (1981)
Convention Against Torture, and Other Cruel, Inhuman or Degrading Treatment or Punishment (1987)
Convention on the Rights of the Child (1990)
International Convention on the Protection of the Rights of All Migrant Workers and Members of Their Families (2003)
Convention on the Rights of Persons with Disabilities (2008)
International Convention for the Protection of All Persons from Enforced Disappearance (2010).

Many of these are related to tourism in some way, e.g. the *Convention on the Rights of the Child* relates in part to child sex tourism. In addition, there are regional treaties, such as the *European Convention on Human Rights* (1998), the *American Convention on Human Rights* (1978) and the *African Charter on Human and People's Rights* (1986).

The tourism industry itself also addresses human rights, through the UNWTO's 1999 *Global Code of Ethics for Tourism*. But, as indicated in Chapter 2 and covered more thoroughly below, there are problems when there are potential conflicts between the allocation and prioritisation of rights for different parties within the tourism system.

According to the UNWTO, its *Global Code of Ethics for Tourism* is 'anchored to the same standards for integrity, mutual respect and dignity enshrined in the *Universal Declaration of Human Rights*' (Rifai 2012 in Martin 2012). Rifai, Secretary General of the UNWTO, claims that 'the promotion of human rights through the Code of Ethics is fundamental to the work of the Organization', but acknowledges that the code is not legally binding: 'We advise our Member States as to the respect for human rights in tourism through encouraging States to put into practice, and include in their legislation, the principles of the Code within their respective territories' (Rifai in Martín 2012) (see Chapter 14 for discussion of codes of ethics).

In 2006 the UNWTO announced a tourism and human rights initiative to 'Create a Framework to assist the tourism industry to address human rights within their own business operations and to develop and adopt a specific set of human rights principles for the industry' (IBLF 2006 in Cole and Eriksson 2010: 121). More recently the UNWTO announced an initiative to fight exploitation and human trafficking in tourism:

> Victims of trafficking are most often enslaved for sexual purposes, but they might also be found in kitchens or cleaning guesthouses, restaurants and bars. Tourism infrastructure can, in turn, create markets for forced and exploitative begging and street hawking. Even organs from victims of trafficking are used today to attract people who need a transplant.

(UNWTO 2012)

However, the UNWTO's credibility as a human rights champion was recently tarnished by its invitation to Robert Mugabe, President of Zimbabwe, to act as a 'leader for tourism' to champion efforts to boost global tourism. Critics angrily pointed to Mugabe's history of ethnic cleansing, rigging elections, terrorising opposition, controlling media and presiding over a collapsed economy (Smith 2012). The UNWTO has said it had not appointed Mugabe to any *formal* position but acknowledged he would receive an open letter like some other selected heads of state who have joined its leaders for tourism campaign. Ironically, Mugabe himself is under an EU travel ban because of suspected crimes against humanity.

DISCUSSION POINT: *GLOBAL CODE OF ETHICS FOR TOURISM –* A CONTRADICTION IN PRACTICE?

As Payne and Dimanche note, 'society at large is often not recognized as being impacted by tourism, therefore is forgotten in codes of ethics' (1996: 1003). An exception is the UN World Tourism Organization's 'Global Code of Ethics for Tourism' (see also Chapter 14).

Article 2 of the code states that tourism activities 'should promote human rights and more particularly, the individual rights of the most vulnerable groups' (UNWTO 1999: 2). However, in practice, it is arguable whether or not many tourism practitioners, especially in such a sector as travel agencies, would have even heard of the UNWTO, let alone have knowledge of, or feel any obeisance to, its global code.

Furthermore, Article 2 could be seen to be in conflict with Article 7 of that code, which stresses the individual's rights to freedom of travel. This article would thus appear to preclude any option of travel bans or boycotts for destinations suffering human rights abuses (at least in the mass or organised sense of the term boycott).

Article 7 is reflective of, and offers further support to, the commonly held view in society at large (at least in liberal democracies) that consumers should have freedom of choice – and by association, freedom of travel.

Discussion question

How would you rewrite the UNWTO Global Code of Ethics to address this apparent inconsistency and potential conflict between the traveller and the destination community within the code?

Sources

UNWTO (1999) *Global Code of Ethics for Tourism*. Available at <http://ethics.unwto. org/en/content/global-code-ethics-tourism> (Accessed 10 June 2010).
Lovelock, B.A. (2008) 'Ethical travel decisions: travel agents and human rights', *Annals of Tourism Research,* 35(2): 338–58.

4.4 PRIORITISING RIGHTS AND ETHICAL DECISION MAKING

A critical issue in addressing the human rights of people within destination communities is to prioritise their rights over those of the tourist and the tourist industry. However, this is problematic within a highly competitive tourism industry setting, when tourism service providers and intermediaries face narrow margins and increasing competition, and do not have the luxury of selecting or presenting products that have a 'human-rights stamp of approval'. Achieving this is also increasingly challenged by the changing nature of travel planning and of purchasing travel products, in a Web-enabled world – where intermediaries play less of a role than previously – and ethical decision making is more in the hands of a potentially less well-informed travelling public.

In the conventional practice of tourism, the motto is, 'Customer is the King' (Branson and Craven 2002 in George and Varghese 2007). It is argued that because of this, the human rights of tourists are over-stressed and that those of the other significant stakeholders are under-stressed (George and Varghese 2007). This is at odds with a human rights mantra that may claim to distribute the benefits of human rights universally.

Tourism has been presented as 'the gratification of the "self" at the expense of the "other": in that process … residents at the destination areas find their human rights being violated by the visitors and *their* [our emphasis] industry' (George and Varghese 2007). It is interesting to note the separation of the host community from the tourism industry in the above statement, as often the host community is conceptualised as being an integral part of the tourism system and industry. Yet tourism does violate human rights, especially of local people at the destination (Dann and Seaton 2001), and perhaps the disparity in human rights between tourist, industry and destination community is great enough to warrant this conceptual separation especially in the case of the poorer and more vulnerable groups (Hemingway 2004).

DISCUSSION POINT: TOURISM'S USE OF WATER – A HUMAN RIGHTS ISSUE?

NGO Tourism Concern notes that tourism can impact communities' rights, including their rights to water (2007). The United Nations (2006) reports on local women having to compete with the tourism sector over access, allocation and use of water for their personal and domestic needs. Tourism places a substantial strain on water supplies and can also contribute to water pollution (Cole and Eriksson 2010). Tourists in the Mediterranean use between 300 and 850 litres per day. Landscaping, water parks, swimming pools, especially in naturally arid regions, can usurp limited water supplies that have traditionally been used for local consumption. Just one golf course can use one million cubic metres of water in a year – the equivalent of a city of 12,000 inhabitants (De Stefano 2004). Due to the water shortage caused by tourism, the coastal communities are forced to produce drinking water out of seawater or to import expensive drinking water from elsewhere (Visser 1999 in Cole and Eriksson 2010: 117). Similarly, Hemingway (2004) writes of the problems arising for women in South East Asia as a result of tourism development. These include loss of access to clean, potable water, when water resources get diverted or polluted by tourism resort development. Mowforth and Munt (2003 in Lansing and De Vries 2007) describe how the InterContinental Hotel Group's luxury swimming pool at its property in Managua, Nicaragua, is replenished regularly, while water conditions in nearby slums are very poor.

There can exist a variety of water-related human rights impacts from tourism, evident, for example, from houseboat tourism in Allepey, Kerala, India (George and Varghese 2007). This is a seemingly benign tourism activity where tourists stay overnight on houseboats floating on the waterways of the region. However, water-related human rights issues in Allepey include:

- Sewage pumped out of the houseboats renders the waters unhealthy for human consumption – the locals use to utilise these waters for virtually everything in their daily lives, but now there is a shortage of potable water.
- An impact on the harvesting of fish, for sustenance.
- Tourism property developers have land-grabbed, and there have been forceful evictions from farmland along the waterfront, which is desirable for resort construction.

Discussion questions

1. Why is access to potable water a 'human right'?
2. How does it compare with other rights such as freedom of speech?
3. Identify the key stakeholders for the issue of tourism and water use, and outline their ethical duties/responsibilities.

Figure 4.1 *Water is a human rights issue: Is this luxury resort swimming pool (located in an arid region of the Mediterranean) the best use of scarce water resources? Photo: Brent Lovelock.*

Resources

Tourism Concern (2012) *Water Equity in Tourism: A Human Right – A Global Responsibility*. Available at <http://www.tourismconcern.org/wet.html>

De Stefano, L. (2004) *Fresh Water and Tourism in the Mediterranean WWF*. Available at <http://assets.panda.org/downloads/medpotourismreportfinal_ofnc.pdf>

United Nations (2006) *Human Development Report Beyond Scarcity: Power, Poverty and the Global Water Crisis*. Available at <http://hdr.undp.org/en/reports/global/hdr2006>

As pointed out by Scheyvens (2011) many of the human rights problems in destinations arise from power differentials across different stakeholders within the tourism 'system'. But such problems also arise because of a conscious (or subconscious/ignorant) privileging of the human rights and wellbeing of certain tourism stakeholders over others. Typically the privileged are the tourists, and those who provide immediate pecuniary services to them. Such privileging also arises because, intuitively, people tend to be more concerned about moral issues that affect those close to them, rather than those with whom they have little contact, as in a distant country (Jones 1991). As noted by Cole and Eriksson (2010: 107) 'Frequently, however, the right of freedom to travel for the rich impacts negatively on the rights of people in destination communities', and the rights of local people 'take second place' to the needs and expectations of foreign tourists and the profits of tourism businesses (Mowforth et al. 2008; George and Varghese 2007). At this point it is useful to consider how this prioritising of needs (versus rights) takes place, and the factors that affect ethical decision making.

Ethical decision making

Lovelock (2008) explores this aspect in his study of the ethical decision making of travel agents, in relation to selling tourism products for destinations that have known human rights abuses. His study uses the 'moral intensity framework' to help explain why travel agents may, for example, continue to sell travel to clients who wish to travel to destinations that have blatant human rights abuses, or even to clients who they suspect may be travelling for child sex.

The selling of travel products by intermediaries such as travel agents is an ethical issue: an ethical issue is said to be present 'when a person's actions when freely performed, may harm or benefit others' (Velasquz and Rostanskowski 1985 in Jones 1991: 376). Travel agents are important in human rights discussions because they provide expert advice on topics as diverse as politics and weather, and consequently have the power to both create and limit opportunities for tourists (Cheong and Miller 2000). Not only are agents important in destination choice, they also act as moral mediators when faced with a number of alternative choices that benefit or harm various stakeholders. They may make a booking, refuse a booking or pass on information that will make the client choose an alternative destination – each with different consequences for tourists, host communities, travel agencies and the agents themselves. Importantly, *even if unaware that moral issues are at stake*, intermediaries remain 'moral mediators' (Jones 1991). Although the client has ultimate responsibility for deciding where to visit, a travel agent has what is termed 'associational responsibility' (Heider 1958 in Jones 1991: 382) for the outcome of that decision.

Jones's (1991) Ethical Decision Making model rests on 'moral agents' making decisions based upon six dimensions of the moral issue:

Magnitude of consequences (the sum of the harms (or benefits) to victims – or beneficiaries – of the moral act in question).

Social consensus (the degree of social agreement that a proposed act is evil or good).

Probability of effect (a joint function of the probability that the act in question will actually take place and this will actually cause the harm or benefit predicted).

Temporal immediacy (the length of time between the present and the onset of consequences of the moral act in question; shorter length of time implies greater immediacy).

Proximity (the feeling of nearness – social, cultural, psychological, physical – that the moral agent has for victims or beneficiaries of the evil or beneficial act in question).

Concentration of effect (an inverse function of the number of people affected by an act of given magnitude).

Lovelock's (2007) study of travel agents revealed that all of the components of the moral intensity framework were evident. The travel agents in the study continued to sell travel products for destinations, even when they were aware of human rights problems in those destinations (e.g. Zimbabwe), or if their clients were travelling for nefarious purposes (e.g. sex tourism in Thailand).

The notion of proximity was dominant, shaping travel agents' evaluations of the issue and ultimately their ethical retail behaviour Lovelock (2008). Jones argues that moral intensity is related to the social, cultural, physical and psychological distance from the moral agent to the affected stakeholders. In Lovelock's study, the client and the travel agency assumed

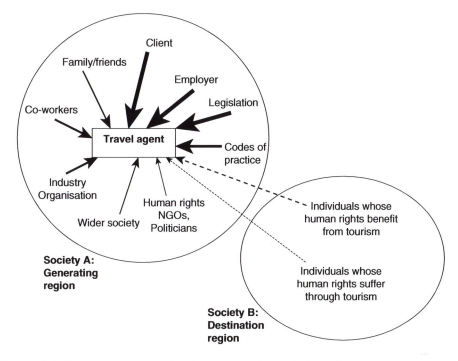

Figure 4.2 *Travel agents' stakeholders and ethical relationships.*
Source: Lovelock (2007).

the *proximate* position while the host community remained *distant*. Figure 4.2 illustrates the stakeholders both influencing and impacted by the ethical decision making of travel agents – in the proximate generating region and the distant destination region. Tourism, through its training programmes, organisational cultures and industry codes of practice, strongly favours the rights of the client, reinforcing the position of the proximate stakeholder.

CASE STUDY: FIJI 'BEFORE AND AFTER' THE COUP

Fiji has traditionally been a destination of choice for many, but the 'innocence' of this friendly isle has been tarnished since the coups d'état of 1987, 2000 and 2006, and the subsequent failure of Fiji to return to a democratically elected government.

While most Australians and New Zealanders may not think twice before purchasing a package holiday to Fiji, there are many who do. Furthermore, human rights organisations, trade unions and journalists have called for a boycott of the Fiji tourism industry due to ongoing human rights abuses in Fiji on the grounds that Fiji remains a military dictatorship which:

> denies its citizens the right to take part in self-government through free and fair elections, as well as the freedoms of speech, press, assembly, and religion ...

> Four people have died in military or police custody and dozens of people have been intimidated, beaten, sexually assaulted, or subjected to degrading treatment.
>
> (Human Rights Watch 2009)

In a survey of New Zealand travel agents Lovelock (2007) asked about their selling behaviour with respect to Fiji, following the coup in 2000. Just over half (52 per cent) of travel agents continued to sell Fiji products over this time, and of those who stopped, the main reasons given were safety concerns for clients, and lack of demand. Only 1 per cent of agents stopped selling Fiji products because of ethical concerns about what was happening in Fiji.

In 2001, to reassure the market, a series of commercials promoting holidays in Fiji were shown on New Zealand television – known as the 'Before and After' commercials. They depicted an idyllic palm-lined beach, asked the viewer what has changed since the coup, and then showed the exact scene again – indicating that nothing had changed in Fiji and that it was 'business as usual' as far as tourism goes. The commercials appalled human rights activists and many ex-pat Fijians living in New Zealand, who complained to the New Zealand Advertising Standards Authority, which subsequently ruled that the commercials be changed. The truth was that human rights had indeed deteriorated after the coup, and indeed, still remain under threat in Fiji.

Discussion questions

1 If you were a travel agent with Fiji in your portfolio of products, would you continue to sell travel there or not? Justify your answer.
2 Identify the ethical agent, and associated stakeholders in this case.
3 To whom do travel agents have the greatest ethical responsibility?

Source

Lovelock, B.A. (2007) 'Obstacles to ethical travel: attitudes and behaviours of New Zealand travel agents with respect to politically repressed destinations', *Tourism Review International,* 11(4): 329–48.

Further reading

Harrison, D. and Pratt, S. (2010) 'Political change and tourism: Coups in Fiji', in Butler, R. and Suntikul, W. (eds) *Tourism and Political Change*, Oxford: Goodfellow, pp. 160–74.

4.5 TRAVEL SANCTIONS OR BOYCOTTS FOR HUMAN RIGHTS?

Codes of ethics that assert a right to travel may be counteractive to the use of tourism to enhance human rights in destinations, for example, through the use of travel sanctions or boycotts. As recently as 2010, ethical tourism NGO, Tourism Concern, was calling for a total travel ban on Myanmar (see Case Study below). Tony Blair, former UK prime minister urged Britons not to visit Myanmar, as part of a drive to end 'appalling human rights violations' by the Myanmar authorities. Similarly, in Nepal, during the civil war (1996–2006), Maoist fighters asked tourists to 'think twice' before patronising certain tourism businesses, especially the big hotels, which are mostly controlled by the ruling Shah-Rana families (Grandon 2007 in Upadhayaya et al. 2010).

While the above calls for travel boycotts of destinations or certain tourism products are motivated by longstanding human rights issues, sometimes such calls emerge in response to critical human-rights incidents within destinations that have gained media attention (see Table 4.1). For example, following intense media coverage and public reaction to the Tiananmen Square massacre in Beijing in 1989, many travel agents in the USA chose not to book clients to China on the grounds that continued tourism would implicitly support the violent actions of a non-democratic regime (Roehl 1990)

But despite the rhetoric and initial enthusiasm surrounding travel boycotts few appear to be consistently *and* persistently applied. Like wider trade embargoes and sanctions, travel boycotts have strong supporters and opponents and there is neither strong evidence for or against them as a political tool to bring about positive change in terms of human rights within destinations (Kulessa 2000). While Tourism Concern and some other organisations are strong supporters of travel boycotts, other NGOs such as Amnesty International and Human Rights Watch acknowledge that tourism boycotts are unlikely to cause a nation to change its politics, and encourage what some have termed 'informed visiting'.

Table 4.1 Calls for travel boycotts

Boycott destination/date	Reason for boycott	Origin of boycott
Arizona 2010	Immigration laws	National Council of La Raza
Australia 2008	Aboriginal rights	Human rights NGOs
Botswana 2002	Treatment of indigenous communities	Survival International
China 2008	Tibet issue, general human rights	Reporters Without Borders
France 2008	Protests against China re Tibet	Grass roots
Israel 2008	Invasion of Lebanon, siege of Gaza	The Coalition to Boycott World Pride Jerusalem
Jamaica 2012	GLBT human rights	Boycott Jamaica
Thailand* 1990s	Government inaction against sex tourism	Human rights NGOs
Utah 2008	Mormon Church role against gay marriage in California	Gay rights activists
Zimbabwe* ongoing	Human rights abuses	Human rights NGOs

* from Glaesser (2006).

Travel sanctions

Travel sanctions are legally enforced bans on travel to certain destinations, by traveller-generating regions. These may be a part of a package of wider economic sanctions – a term used for a range of laws or regulations that restrict or prohibit the export and import of weapons and goods, and freeze assets abroad belonging to targeted countries or their elites. They may be applied for a range of purposes, including changing a country's basic political system and improving the human rights of citizens within the targeted country. International tourism plays an important role in economic sanctions and is typically discouraged along with other forms of trade (Kim et al. 2007b). Travel sanctions therefore have significant implications for human rights.

Sanctions include the ban on travel to Cuba for most Americans – part of an economic embargo dating from 1962. The US government in recent years has also restricted travel to Libya, Iraq and North Korea. Similarly, in some Arab states it is a crime for their citizens to enter Israel, and some Arab and Islamic countries deny entry to any person that has been to Israel. South Korean citizens have been restricted in their visits to North Korea, and only as recently as January 2010 did North Korea lift restrictions on American visitors. China operates an 'Approved Destination Status' for their citizens, in effect restricting mass outbound tourism to selected countries.

Methods of restricting travel may include requiring a licence to travel to a specified country, limiting or prohibiting transactions in which a traveller may engage while in a targeted country, prohibiting the use of a nation's passports to travel to or through a targeted country, or limiting the means of transportation to a targeted country (Epstein and Rennack 2003).

However, a common criticism of travel sanctions is their subjectivity – how it is decided which destinations deserve to have sanctions applied against them (Lovelock 2008). In 2002, when the US House of Representatives voted to lift the ban on US citizens travelling to Cuba (later rejected under threat of veto from President Bush), the lack of consistency in applying travel bans was one aspect of the debate; as US Representative Delahunt noted, 'Americans can travel to North Korea and Iran, two-thirds of the axis of evil, but not to Cuba' (Milligan 2002: 1).

Sanctions may also result in severe social consequences and humanitarian impacts, disrupting humanitarian relief operations, delivery of medicines, and prevent individuals travelling for specialised medical care (Cortright et al. 2000). And, of course, there is a direct impact on would-be inbound travellers. Strug and Lemkau (2008) describe the effects of US travel policies on Cuban-Americans who have relatives in Cuba, identifying travel-related psychological distress in response to restrictions to their travel.

Inbound travel sanctions against 'rogue' states are seldom applied; there have only been four cases where UN Security Council Resolutions have led to prohibition of commercial flights to countries: Iraq 1990, Libya 1992, Yugoslavia 1992 and Angola 1997, with sanctions virtually shutting down air passenger travel to those countries (Conroy 2000). And while it is argued that travel sanctions have been used to good effect, for example in

Figure 4.3 *Can tourism contribute to political change and the toppling of totalitarian regimes? Photo: Brent Lovelock.*

Libya – when a ban on commercial passenger flights after the bombing of Pan Am flight 103 over Lockerbie, Scotland, led Libya to denounce terrorism – it is more difficult to judge the effectiveness of such sanctions in terms of broader human rights gains (e.g. 50 years of such sanctions against Cuba have led to little change).

CASE STUDY: TOURISM BOYCOTTS: THE CASE OF MYANMAR – *JOAN C. HENDERSON*

Myanmar politics

The armed forces staged a coup in Burma in 1962 and seized power, initially pursuing policies of isolation and economic centralisation. Former place names were abandoned and Burma and its capital of Rangoon became Myanmar and Yangon respectively. Myanmar citizens were denied freedom of political association and expression by a military dictatorship which continuously and consistently suppressed political opposition.

The National League for Democracy (NLD), headed by Aung San Suu Kyi, won over 80 per cent of the vote in elections held in 1990. It was prevented from taking office, prompting domestic discontent and strong condemnation overseas. Discontent erupted again in 2007 when there were mass demonstrations against the government, followed by arrests and imprisonments. Aung San Suu Kyi, awarded the Nobel Peace Prize in 1991, spent over 11 years under house arrest. Other human rights abuses and unacceptable practices have been documented by bodies such as Amnesty International and the International Labour Organization with reports of the displacement of people, intimidation, violence, forced labour, torture, eviction and land confiscation by officials. The country's 100 or so ethnic minority communities have been particularly adversely affected.

Myanmar's politics have damaged its relations with parts of the outside world, especially in the West, and selected sanctions were imposed by European and American governments. In contrast, the Association of South East Asian Nations (ASEAN), of which Myanmar is a member, advocated constructive engagement as the region is an important trading partner alongside China and Japan.

On 30 March 2011, military leaders formally handed over power to a civilian President. Aung San Suu Kyi was freed from house arrest and large numbers of political prisoners were released. There were also new labour laws allowing trade unions and moves to relax restrictions on press freedom. Parliamentary by-elections in April 2012 were judged relatively free and fair by foreign observers. NLD candidates, amongst them Aung San Suu Kyi, won 43 out of the contested 44 seats and it seemed indeed that a new era had begun.

To boycott or not to boycott?

Myanmar possesses many outstanding natural and cultural resources, but political circumstances have undermined its performance as a destination. The regime originally rejected overseas tourists as a pernicious external influence, but had revised this position by the mid-1990s in acknowledgement of tourism's economic and other rewards. After the launch of Visit Myanmar Year in 1996, the National Coalition Government of the Union of Burma (NCGUB) asked tourists to boycott the country until democratic change was evident. The NLD maintained that it was too early to receive tourists and tourism investment, flows of which should depend on progress towards democratisation. Aung San Suu Kyi requested potential visitors not to 'buy their pleasure at the expense of the ordinary people' who had suffered to facilitate tourism (1997: 168). Various Burmese and non-Burmese individuals and groups backed this stance, amongst them Burma Campaign and Tourism Concern. Tourism was thus used as a weapon with which to attack the authorities and exert pressure for political change. Proponents believed that a travel ban would deny the government the income and respectability attendant on acceptance as an international tourist destination.

Tourism in Myanmar has also been linked to breaches of human rights in a manner illustrated by allegations that children, pregnant women and the elderly were commandeered as labourers for infrastructure projects. There are also suspicions that workers were coerced into heritage site restoration and that redevelopment as a whole has required massive resettlement. Further concerns are that the army leadership gained personally from the tourism industry because individuals and their families and associates had a financial stake in some lucrative enterprises.

The accession of a purportedly civilian government has been an opportunity to review stances and the NLD decided to move from backing an outright ban to a targeted boycott of large-scale package tourism. An NLD leader spoke of wanting 'people to come to Burma, not to help the junta, but to help the people by understanding the situation: political, economic, moral – everything' (Burma Campaign UK 2010).

A number of foreign tour operators stopped selling Myanmar in the decades after the military coup for reasons including uncertain security, falling demand and Aung San Suu Kyi's pleas. However, the Burma Campaign named over 50 tourism-related enterprises in its 'dirty list' and operators based in the UK accounted for almost half the total. Representatives of some opined that the politics of a destination was largely irrelevant and countries around the world were guilty of abuses so Myanmar did not deserve to be singled out. Others openly recognised the brutality of the regime and resultant dilemmas for would-be travellers, but proclaimed the right of tourists to see for themselves and make up their own minds. Tourism was hailed for its ability to foster communication and understanding and accelerate economic advance, improving everyday life for locals.

Guidebook publishers too were divided and Lonely Planet was condemned for its Myanmar edition, although this did address issues of politics. Their 2011 website included a 14-page 'chapter' which summarised contrary points of view. It suggested that those who elected to visit spent at local and not state-sponsored suppliers as far as possible and avoided package tours. On their return home, visitors should complain directly to the government about its record and share information and their experiences with other travellers (Lonely Planet 2011).

Discussion questions

1 How appropriate and effective were calls for a tourist boycott of Myanmar prior to 2012?
2 Should the boycott be lifted in light of events since 2011?
3 Should tourists have visited Myanmar in the past when it was under direct military rule? Would you have visited Myanmar?

4 Was it ethical for tour operators based overseas to sell Myanmar as a destination prior to 2011–12?

5 Was it ethical for foreign companies such as hotel groups and airlines to invest in Myanmar in the same period?

6 Are there likely to have been differences between Eastern and Western tourists in their perceptions of the boycott debate?

References

Aung Sang Suu Kyi (1997) *The Voice of Hope*, London: Penguin Books.

Burma Campaign UK (2010) *Burma tourism*. Available at <http://www.burmacampaign.org.uk/index> (Accessed 4 October 2011).

Lonely Planet (2011) *Should you go?* Available at <http://www.lonelyplanet.com/myanmar-burma> (Accessed 5 October 2011).

Sources and further reading

Amnesty International (2012) *Myanmar*. Available at <http://www.amnesty.org./en/library/info/ASA16/001/2012/en> (Accessed 24 February 2012).

Free Burma Coalition (2010) *Towards an open society in Burma/Myanmar through interactions and integration*. Available at <http://www.freeburmacoalition.org/> (Accessed 31 July 2010).

Henderson, J.C. (2003) 'The politics of tourism in Myanmar', *Current Issues in Tourism*, 6(2): 97–118.

Hudson, S. (2007) 'To go or not to go? Ethical perspectives on tourism in an "outpost of tyranny"', *Journal of Business Ethics*, 76: 385–96.

Lonely Planet (2012) *Travelling responsibly to Burma*. Available at <http://www.lonelyplanet.com/myanmar-burma/travel-tips-and-articles/76954.> (Accessed 24 February 2012).

Tourism Concern (2012) *Burma*. Available at <http//:www.tourismconcern.org.uk/Burma> (Accessed 24 February 2012).

Tourism Transparency (2012) Available at <http://www.tourismtransparency.org> (Accessed 13 March 2012).

Voices for Burma (2010) *Our policy on tourism*. Available at <http://www.voicesforburma.org/aboutus> (Accessed 31 July 2010).

DISCUSSION POINT: MODELLING AN ETHICAL TRAVEL WORLD

Lovelock (2012) models how travel sanctions could impact global travel if they were consistently and objectively applied to destinations with serious human rights abuses. Scenarios of ethical travel are developed, based upon UNWTO international arrival data, together with human rights indices (using NGO Freedom House's *World Freedom Survey*) for over 200 destinations. The 'extreme' scenarios illustrated (Figure 4.4) involve substantial numbers

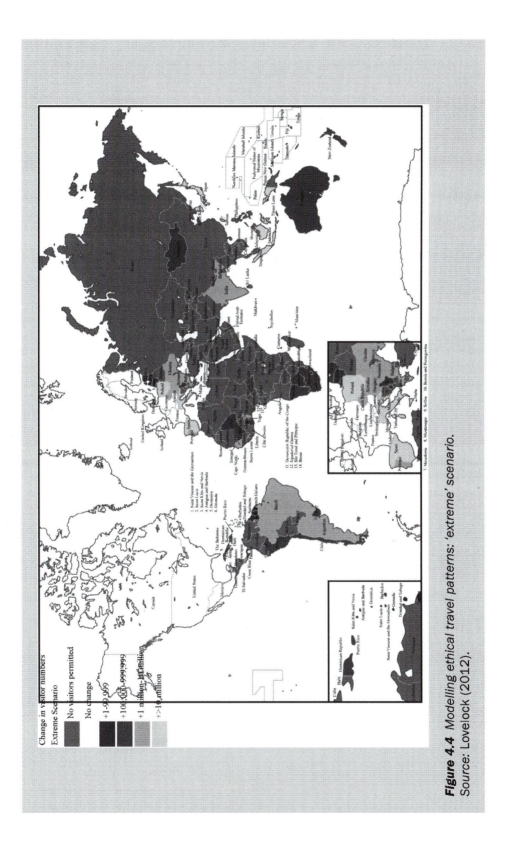

Figure 4.4 *Modelling ethical travel patterns: 'extreme' scenario.*
Source: Lovelock (2012).

of visitors being 'redirected' from those destinations with human rights abuses ('Partly Free' or 'Not Free') to destinations classified as 'Free'. In this scenario, nearly 350 million international visitors would be affected, and 104 destinations with human rights abuses.

Discussion questions

1 Are there ethical problems with classifying destinations by their human rights records into those that are 'Free' or 'Not Free'?
2 Could the redirection of 350 million international travellers (in terms of human rights) to 'Free' destinations result in other ethical problems?

Sources

Freedom House (2012) *World Freedom Survey*. Available at <http://www.freedom-house.org>
Lovelock (2012) 'Human rights and human travel: Modelling global travel patterns under an ethical tourism regime', *Tourism Review International*, 16(3).

4.6 TOURISM AND PEACE

Peace and human rights are inextricably linked. Tourism has been recognised as a major force for influencing political policies, international relations and world peace (Butler and Suntikul 2010; Sarkar and George 2010; Rabu 2003 and D'Amore 2002 in Sarkar and George 2010). Tourism has even been referred to as the world's 'biggest peace industry' (Malley 2002 in Sarkar and George 2010). Some destinations host 'political tours', to deliberately use tourism as a strategy for peace and social justice. Such tours aim to expose visitors to the complexities associated with conflict zones, and to convince visitors to advocate for repressed peoples and for social justice, upon their return home (Chaitlin 2011). In this way, such political tourism can help grow an international constituency of support for a particular cause. Political tourism has its roots in the 1960s when US President John F. Kennedy described travel as 'one the great forces for peace and under-standing in our time' (Kennedy 1961 in D'Amore 2007).

The 1980 World Tourism Organization's *Manila Declaration* in a sense validated the role that tourism may play for peace. In 1986, the International Institute for Peace Through Tourism (IIPT) (<http://www.iipt.org>) was founded, with a vision of travel and tourism becoming the world's first 'global peace industry', an industry that promotes and supports the belief that every traveller is potentially an 'ambassador for peace' (D'Amore 2007). Such initiatives have been underlined more recently by the UNWTO, which in its *Global Code of Ethics* recognises the role of tourism in contributing to international understanding and peace (1999).

In a practical sense, political tourism as an experience and a 'product' has emerged in former and ongoing conflict zones, including Cuba, Northern Ireland, South Africa, Egypt,

Israel, North and South Korea and Cyprus (Chaitlin 2011). Sometimes peace tourism is referred to as 'justice tourism' (see later in this chapter), although this term is more broadly applied to tourism and a range of human rights issues.

Isaac and Hodge (2011: 107) present a case study of justice tourism in Palestine. There, a number of tour organisations operate with the goal of 'transforming tourists into "advocates of just causes" for the Palestinian people'. Some of the statements from their study respondents who had participated on the tours reflect this:

> Of course, [my impression] changed, deepened and broadened my grasp of the situation.

> Knowledge commitment to be an advocate in the US for peace and justice in the Middle East.

> On-the-ground experience launched my activism on the issue. It was a huge step forward in my life and career.

> > Tourist participants in Isaac and Hodge (2011: 106)

Isaac and Hodge argue that tourists who engage in such activities can 'become holders of the knowledge that will one day lead to equality, democracy and human rights for all' (2011: 104).

But while there is an intuitive belief that tourism can contribute to peace, apart from visitor affirmations such as those above, there is very little empirical research to support the contribution that tourism can make. Var and Ap (1998) acknowledge that tourism can promote cross-cultural exchange and understanding, but point to a lack of evidence that tourism unequivocally encourages world peace. Similarly, Salazar (2006) attributes peace gains to higher level political activity rather than civil society's efforts.

Cho's (2007) study of cross-border tourism between South and North Korea is one of the few studies that does attempt to provide empirical data on this issue, but is pessimistic about the role of tourism. Cho analysed the peace tourism role of the Mt Kumgang resort, a showpiece of the 'Sunshine' policy, developed in North Korea, with South Korean investment, and open to South Korean visitors (until the shooting of a female South Korean tourist by North Korean soldiers in 2010). The study revealed 'at best a weak and

Figure 4.5 *A conceptual framework for the interrelationship of peace, conflict and tourism.*
Source: Upadhayaya et al. (2010).

slow contribution to peaceful relations' (Lee et al. 2012: 72) (see also Kim et al. 2007a for a discussion of the role of tourism in promoting peace on the Korean peninsula).

While tourism may not always be successful in winning over hearts and minds, few question that tourism does have an economic impact, which may be linked to overcoming conflict and improving human rights. In Nepal, a country which was racked by civil war for over 10 years (1996–2006) the economic impact of tourism has been seen as a critical pathway for peace. In their research on the Maoist-government conflict in Nepal, Upadhayaya et al. conclude that tourism can be 'an agent for peace by assisting in the development of a supportive environment' (2010: 35) (Figure 4.5). Upadhayaya et al.'s (2010) model of the interrelationships of peace, conflict and tourism shows that peace 'accelerates' tourism, and conflict has the opposite effect. Their argument is that poverty is a root cause of conflict in Nepal, and that tourism development programmes have helped to institutionalise sustainable and participatory tourism practices, contributing to equity, equality and social justice.

4.7 MEGA TOURISM EVENTS AND HUMAN RIGHTS

In a similar way to tourism, sport has been advocated as a means of achieving global peace and understanding. Mega sports events are among the major processes through which the rhetoric of global peace and understanding runs. However, such events have also been linked to negative outcomes for human rights, including: the forcible relocation of communities in order to meet the physical and infrastructural development requirements for new stadia and facilities (Matheson and Finkel 2011); and human trafficking for sexual purposes (Hennig et al. 2007; Future Group 2007) (The 2010 Vancouver Winter Olympics was found to be tenuously linked to human trafficking for sexual purposes (Matheson and Finkel 2011).)

On a political level, granting the hosting rights of mega events to repressive regimes is seen as tantamount to supporting their political doctrines, and human rights practices. Hollinshead writes of the 'worldmaking' power of tourism, which he describes as a 'strong and pervasive producer of political meanings (or contested versions) of locality' (2009: 139). While this power of tourism can be used positively, it can also be used for darker political purposes. The Beijing Olympics for example were an opportunity for China to win over the hearts and minds of foreigners (Hollinshead 2011). While such processes often take place in subtle ways, the human rights of vulnerable groups are often violated in much more tangible ways.

It is not just the economic expectations from increased tourism that drive nations in the super-competitive process to win hosting rights for the Games. Hosting the Games can potentially provide a great amount of prestige by giving the host country a unique opportunity to convey to the world favourable impressions of its tourism, economic offerings and system of government (Mastrocola 1995). The use of sport as an instrument of propaganda in modern times began with Hitler and Nazi Germany, with the Berlin Olympics of 1936. The award of the 1936 Olympics to Berlin helped to confirm Germany's re-entry into the mainstream of international relations after the First World War. Furthermore Hitler used the Berlin Games not only to increase national prestige, but also for the promotion of Nazi ideology (Nafziger and Strenk 1978).

When Beijing first bid for the 2000 Olympics, back in the early 1990s, it was inevitable that human rights would be brought into consideration. Indeed, Beijing's bid was opposed by a number of organisations and countries (including the USA) on human rights grounds.

China's motives for hosting the Olympic Games were based on the typical goal of exhibiting its culture on the world stage, and as a means of gaining international prestige. They also envisioned hosting the Olympics as a way to improve the country's image after the 1989 Tiananmen Square massacre (Mastrocola 1995).

Despite opposition to the bid, some argued that holding the Games in a country known for human rights abuses would be one way to accelerate China's respect for human rights – the so-called 'Olympic constructive engagement' approach. The proponents of this approach acknowledged the human rights abuses but concluded that it was worth taking a chance that the prospect of praise for a successful Olympics would encourage the regime to improve human rights conditions (Mastrocola 1995). Using this argument to justify China's hosting of the 2008 Games, Liu (2007) points to the 1988 Seoul Olympic Games as an example of the Games as a positive force for human rights reform. The 1988 Seoul Olympics were a transition point for South Korea 'from dictatorship to democracy' through international visibility and increased pressure for reform. Notably, the human rights NGO Human Rights Watch did not oppose Beijing as an Olympic host city because they felt that allowing the Games to proceed in Beijing would focus attention on China's human rights violations on the world stage (Jones 2001 in Liu 2007). Mastrocola (1995) argues, though, that the Olympic constructive engagement approach fails under scrutiny because even if awarding the Games to Beijing promoted greater economic openness, it would also have provided a stamp of approval for China's 'offensive' human rights policies.

Historically, hosting of such mega events in the past has led to little in the way of human rights improvements. In Mexico City, over 500 demonstrators were murdered by Mexican 'security' forces 10 days before the city was permitted to host the 1968 Olympic Games. In 1978 FIFA (International Federation of Association Football) granted the World Cup finals to the junta that ruled Argentina, the junta accused of murdering 30,000 people and detaining and torturing tens of thousands more between 1976 and 1983. Nor are developed nations free from critical scrutiny: prior to the 1982 Commonwealth Games in Brisbane, Australia, the state of Queensland legislature passed an Act that 'effectively cleared aboriginals from the streets' (Giulianotti 2004: 359). These examples paint a picture of ongoing failure of international sports movements to critically appraise and avoid states that have systematically impugned the human rights of their citizens (Giulianotti 2004). It could be argued that due to the strong mutual association between these mega events and tourism, that the tourism industry is also implicit in this failure.

Dislocation of citizens by Games development

Several studies of destination communities have noted the infringement of human rights through the forcible relocation of locals to free up land for tourism development (e.g. George and Varghese 2007; Mowforth et al. 2008; Hemingway 2004). But mega events have been noted as being particularly responsible for major human relocations (Table 4.2).

Table 4.2 *Residents displaced by Olympic Games*

Olympic Games	Residents Displaced
Seoul (1988)	720,000
Barcelona (1992)	2,500
Atlanta (1996)	30,000
Sydney (2000)	0*
Athens (2004)	2,700
Beijing (2008)	1,500,000
London (2012)	1,000

*While there were no reported forced evictions in preparation for the 2000 Olympics in Sydney, housing in the city became much less accessible and affordable for lower-income residents of the area.

Sources: Battan (2008); Advocates for Human Dignity (2012 <http://advocatedignity.com/archives/1284/>).

The forced eviction of citizens from their homes within areas tagged for Olympic Games-related development is a directly observable and tangible human rights infringement. Prior to the 2008 Beijing Olympics, human rights advocates estimated that from hundreds of thousands to over one million Chinese were made homeless as a result of such forced evictions (Anderson 2005 in Liu 2007). This dislocation included the 'floating population', as well as homeowners and tenants, and was fuelled by urban development in preparation for the Games. In China, demolition of private property usually happens with minimal notice, if any; a Chinese character *chai* meaning 'demolish' is simply painted on the front door to notify residents of upcoming demolition (Anderson 2005 in Liu 2007). In protest over these forced evictions, people held non-violent protests, created Internet petitions and, at the extreme, some engaged in self-immolation at Tiananmen Square (Anderson 2005 in Liu 2007).

4.8 ALTERNATIVE AND RESPONSIBLE TOURISM

Closely linked to the incorporation of human rights within tourism are the concepts of 'alternative tourism' and 'responsible tourism'. Alternative tourism is said to have its origins in the 1960s counterculture movement: 'Alternative tourism in rejecting mass tourism is a similar radical attempt to transform social relations' (Higgins-Desbiolles 2008: 346). While alternative tourism did not really find a voice until the 1990s (e.g. in Lanfant and Graburn's note that alternative tourism 'aspires to become the tourism in the promotion of a new order' (1992: 92)), it is now being reconceptualised as a non-mass form of tourism with a human (rather than business) face, aimed at addressing human rights violations at the destination level.

While peace through tourism and responsible tourism are both facets of alternative tourism, some writers are critical of alternative tourism, believing it to be co-opted by a 'threatened tourism industry' (Higgins-Desbiolles 2008: 347). Of all the forms of alternative tourism, only justice tourism stands out in its 'unwavering commitment to overturning inequitable tourism and capitalist globalisation' (Higgins-Desbiolles 2008: 347). The purported neoliberal 'capture' of alternative tourism and the lip-service paid by industry to tourism and human rights, is aptly illustrated by the tourism industry's rejection of a proposed 'poverty-alleviation tax' on international airline tickets. A $1 tax per ticket was advocated to raise funds for poverty-alleviation projects, and was projected to raise $10 billion (Bianchi 2005 and Smith 2005 in Higgins-Desbiolles 2008). Yet the proposal was rejected by industry organisations (e.g. peak body, the World Travel and Tourism Council), on the grounds that it would harm a struggling aviation industry. (Note: the global aviation industry is *only* expecting a $3 billion profit for 2012 (IATA 2012)).

Higgins-Desbiolles (2008) identifies a number of forms of justice tourism, including hosts telling stories of past oppression and tourists learning about poverty issues. She notes that the *World Social Forum* held in Mumbai in 2004 formed a Tourism Interventions Group that highlighted tourism connections across a range of human rights issues, including those related to women, children, dalits ('untouchables'), indigenous people, migrants and unorganised labour. However, Higgins-Desbiolles doubts the will of the tourism industry to address these rights issues, citing the powerful economic forces of globalisation as contributing to ongoing human rights problems (an issue also raised by Cole and Eriksson 2010).

While justice tourism advocates such as Higgins-Desbiolles link the processes of globalisation with declines in the human rights of destination communities, there are mixed views on this. Law (2008: 1282), for example, argues that globalisation will promote the protection of human rights, as countries compete on a global market for labour by offering 'bundles of human and economic rights that are attractive to investors and [mobile] elite workers'. Consider the case of Singapore, where same-sex sexual relationships are a criminal activity: Lau (2008: 2022) observes arguments for liberalisation of sex laws there 'that say nothing about the humanity of sexual orientation rights but focus on how legal reform can enhance a jurisdiction's attractiveness as a tourist and investment destination'. Similarly, in California in 2008, when the state was considering granting marriage licences to same-sex couples, human rights advocates argued that California could capture a monopoly on the same-sex marriage industry, related tourism and other economic benefits. Lau argues that such an approach to human rights is at odds with human rights derived from normative principles concerning human dignity.

Globalisation is multidimensional, and there is some evidence that the social dimension of globalisation, which includes tourism, may be linked to enhanced human rights outcomes. Dreher (2006) developed an Index of Globalisation which is based on the different dimensions of globalisation – economic, political and social. The social globalisation dimension has three categories: information flow; cultural proximity; and personal contacts. The latter includes the 'degree of tourism (incoming and outgoing) a country's population is exposed to' (Dreher et al. 2010: 20). When the authors considered the relationship between human rights and the degree of globalisation across 106 countries, they found that human rights *increase* with globalisation and economic freedom. However, this finding is restricted to 'physical integrity' rights (e.g. absence of torture, extrajudicial killings, political imprisonments and disappearances); 'empowerment' rights (e.g. freedom of movement, freedom of speech, workers' rights, political participation and freedom of religion) are *not* affected by the degree of globalisation (Dreher et al. 2010). Social globalisation produces internationally recognised social norms that give governments and politicians an incentive to follow. If a country is highly dependent on tourism, social globalisation offers a chance to attract tourists, but at the same time the country risks losing them due to the negative publicity of human rights abuses (Dreher et al. 2010).

USEFUL SOURCES: TOURISM HUMAN RIGHTS NON-GOVERNMENTAL ORGANISATIONS

Tourism NGOs play an important role in promoting alternative modes of tourism – alternative, ethical and responsible. Below are listed some of the key tourism NGOs. Note that other human rights NGOs such as **Amnesty International** (www.amnesty.org) and **Human Rights Watch** (www.hrw.org) play a broader human rights advocacy role that does, however, also include tourism-related issues.

ECOT Ecumenical Coalition on Tourism (www.ecotonline.org)

ECPAT International End Child Prostitution, Child Pornography and Trafficking of Children for Sexual Purposes (www.ecpat.net)

Equitable Tourism Options (EQUATIONS) (www.equitabletourism.org)

Tourism Concern (www.tourismconcern.org.uk)

Tourism Transparency (www.tourismtransparency.org)

CHAPTER REVIEW

This chapter has outlined some of the key challenges for the tourism industry in addressing human rights issues. There are varying approaches to recognising and assigning rights, and although the 'natural rights' argument has been increasingly challenged by moral philosophers, this approach forms the basis of our current international treaty system beneath the UNDHR which emerged after the Second World War. We note that the relativist/universalist dilemma poses challenges to the enforcement of a global human rights. While the state is recognised as the main actor in ensuring human rights, this is increasingly challenged, with an enhanced role for the private sector now being advocated.

Human rights issues that arise within destination communities are primarily the product of power differentials between tourism stakeholders within generating regions and destinations. On an individual basis, tourism practitioners face challenges in meeting the human rights needs of those people in distant communities, as ethical decision making within the industry tends to prioritise the client at all costs.

We discuss tourism as a political act and how tourism may either exacerbate or alleviate human rights problems in repressive countries. It is noted that tourism boycotts and/or sanctions, as a part of wider economic sanctions, may have a positive influence. Peace, politics and human rights are all inextricably linked, and the role of tourism as a peacemaker is discussed. While appearing to have great potential, empirical evidence would suggest that this is mainly at the personal level. We discussed alternative, responsible and justice tourism as ways of better incorporating human rights thinking in the tourism industry. Tourism as a part of the process of globalisation is addressed and the challenges of enhancing human rights in the face of economic globalisation acknowledged.

On economic grounds alone there are arguments for the tourism industry to improve its performance with respect to human rights. As noted by Cole and Eriksson (2010), increasingly the liberal middle classes do not want to travel to destinations where people are having their rights violated to cater for their holidays. We do caution, however, about human rights being conditional on economic 'success' at either the individual business level or the destination level. Such an approach, while appealing to tourism industry operators, perhaps, is not based within normative ethics, nor upon the inherent right to freedom and dignity of the individual.

SUMMARY OF KEY TERMS

Alternative tourism A non-mass form of tourism with social responsibilities, may be aimed at addressing human rights violations in destinations.

Associational responsibility occurs when a person may be held accountable for an ethical decision, even though he or she is not causally involved.

Ethical decision making A multi-staged process that involves: recognising an issue as moral; making a moral judgement; establishing moral intent; and engaging in moral behaviour.

Ethical issue is said to be present when a person's actions when freely performed may harm or benefit others.

Human rights The basic rights and freedoms to which all humans are entitled, often held to include the right to life and liberty, freedom of thought and expression, and equality before the law. Such rights are considered universal to humanity, regardless of citizenship, residency status, ethnicity, gender or other considerations.

Justice tourism A just form of travel between members of different communities which seeks to achieve mutual understanding, solidarity and equality amongst participants.

Moral agent A being who is capable of acting with reference to right and wrong.

Natural rights The theory that human rights derive from the inherent dignity of the human person. Therefore one has human rights as moral rights simply because one is human, with no conditions applying.

Political tourism Travel with a political purpose, politically arranged journeys and journeys to political destinations. May involve travel to areas of conflict to experience the circumstances on the ground, and to develop an understanding of the local political situation.

Responsible tourism Tourism that improves the conditions for host communities, and contributes to better places to visit for tourists.

Travel boycott A group's refusal to have tourism dealings with some organisation or destination in protest against its policies.

Travel sanction A legally enforced ban on travel to certain destinations, by traveller-generating regions.

QUESTIONS FOR REFLECTION

1 Some commentators advocate a business approach to human rights, i.e. that human rights be reflected in Corporate Social Responsibility policies and initiatives. Is such an approach, resting on the basis that human rights is 'good business', the best and most ethical approach?
2 When we purchase a pair of running shoes it may be difficult for us to have a full knowledge of the human rights implications of that purchase. Similarly, for a tourist, it may be difficult for them to ascertain the human rights implications of their tourism product purchase. Should tourists be concerned about this and, if so, how could they 'track and trace' the human rights implications of their purchase?

EXERCISE

Hemingway (2004) in her study of how tourism impacts upon communities in South East Asia proposes a number of actions by which tourism could be encouraged or induced to contribute to the recognition of human rights. These include:

- Meaningful community consultation in destination regions.
- Legal enforcement of the principles contained in codes of behaviour for tourist organisations.
- Destination-state regulation of tourism operators and tourist activities.
- Tourist-generating state regulation of tourism operators and tourist activities.
- Transparency in contracts between developing states and the private sector.

- Assistance by generating states in establishing industry regulation in destination states.
- An international law enforcement agency to oversee tourism.
- Recognition of human rights as an element of ecotourism.
- Traveller education.
- Encouragement of responsible tourism.

Discussion questions

1 Looking at the list above, what do you think are the most important or urgent actions to be taken and why?
2 There are inherent challenges in putting into practice some of the above actions – identify some of the challenges (including ethical challenges) in making these 'happen'.

Source

Hemingway, S. (2004) 'The impact of tourism on the human rights of women in South East Asia', *International Journal of Human Rights*, 8(3): 275–304.

NOTES

a John F. Kennedy (1917–63) US President. Civil Rights Announcement, 11 June 1963. Available at <http://www.pbs.org/wgbh/americanexperience/features/primary-resources/jfk-civilrights/> (Accessed 10 September 2012).
b Alexander Solzhenitsyn (1918–2008), Russian author and dissident. From Commencement speech, Harvard University, 8 June 1978.
c Dalai Lama (Spiritual leader of Tibetan people). From a speech given by His Holiness the Dalai Lama to the United Nations World Conference on Human Rights, Vienna, Austria, June 1993. Available at <http://www.freetibet.org/about/dalai5> (Accessed 10 September 2012).
d Mark Twain (1835–1910), author. From *Innocents Abroad* (first published 1869). Available at <http://www.gutenberg.org/ebooks/3176> (Accessed 10 September 2012).

REFERENCES

Battan, C. (2008) 'The Beijing Olympics by the numbers', *Dollars and Sense: Real World Economics*. Available at <http://www.dollarsandsense.org/archives/2008/0808battan.html> (Accessed 20 April 2012).

Butler, R. and Suntikul, W. (eds) (2010) *Tourism and Political Change*, Oxford: Goodfellow Publishers.

Chaitlin, J. (2011) '"Here's the Separation Wall": Political tourism in the Holy Land', *Conflict Resolution Quarterly*, 29(1): 39–63.

Cheong, S., and Miller, M. (2000) 'Power and tourism: a Foucauldian observation', *Annals of Tourism Research*, 27: 371–90.

Cho, M. (2007) 'A re-examination of tourism and peace: the case of the Mt. Gumgang tourism development on the Korean Peninsula', *Tourism Management*, 28(2): 556–69.

Cole, S. and Eriksson, J. (2010) 'Tourism and human rights', in Cole, S. and Morgan, N. (eds) *Tourism and Inequality: Problems and Prospects,* Wallingford: CABI, pp. 107–25.

Coles, T. and Church, A. (2007) 'Tourism, politics and the forgotten entanglements of power', in Church, A. and Coles, T. (eds) *Tourism, Power and Space*, London: Routledge, pp. 1–42.

Conroy, R. (2000) 'Implementation problems of travel bans: practical and legal aspects', *First Expert Seminar: Smart sanctions: the next step: Arms embargoes and travel sanctions*, Bonn: Bonn International Centre for Conversion.

Cortright, D., Lopex, G., and Conroy R. (2000) 'Are travel sanctions "smart?" A review of theory and practice', *First Expert Seminar, Smart sanctions: the next step: Arms embargoes and travel sanctions*, Bonn: Bonn International Centre for Conversion.

Cragg, W. (2000) 'Human rights and business ethics: fashioning a new social contract', *Journal of Business Ethics*, 27(1–2): 205–14.

D'Amore, L. (2007) 'Tourism: the global peace industry', *World & I,* Summer, pp. 66–76.

D'Sa, E. (1999) 'Wanted: tourists with a social conscience', *International Journal of Contemporary Hospitality Management,* 11(2/3): 64–8.

Dann, G.M.S. and Seaton, A.V. (2001) 'Slavery, contested heritage, and thanatourism', *International Journal of Hospitality and Tourism Administration*, 2(3/4): 1–29.

Donnelly, P. (2008) 'Sport and human rights', *Sport in Society: Cultures, Commerce, Media, Politics*, 11(4): 381–94.

Dreher, A. (2006) 'Does globalization affect growth? Evidence from a new index of globalization', *Applied Economics,* 38(10): 1091–110.

Dreher, A., Gassebner, M. and Siemers, L.H.R. (2010) *Globalization, Economic Freedom and Human Rights*. Discussion Paper Number 115, October. Gottingen: Center for European Governance and Economic Development Research.

Epstein, S. and Rennack, D. (2003) *Travel Restrictions: U.S. Government Limits on American Citizens' Travel Abroad. Congressional Research Service*. The Library of Congress. Available at <http://assets.opencrs.com/rpts/RS21003_20030128.pdf> (Accessed October 16th 2009).

Future Group (2007) *Faster, Higher, Stronger: Preventing Human Trafficking at the 2010 Olympics*, Calgary: Future Group.

George, B.P. (2008) 'Towards an inclusive framework to assess human rights in tourism: a review of major stakeholder perspectives'. Available at SSRN: http://ssrn.com/abstract=1275352

George, B.P. and Varghese, V. (2007) 'Human rights in tourism: Conceptualization and stakeholder perspectives', *EJBO Electronic Journal of Business Ethics and Organization Studies,* 12(2): 40–8.

Giulianotti, R. (2004) 'Human rights, globalization and sentimental education: The case of sport', *Sport in Society: Cultures, Commerce, Media, Politics*, 7(3): 355–69.

Glaesser, D. (2006) *Crisis Management in the Tourism Industry*, Oxford: Butterworth-Heinemann.

Hall, C.M. (2003) 'Politics and place: an analysis of power in tourism communities', in Singh, S., Timothy, D.J. and Dowling, R.K. (eds) *Tourism in Destination Communities,* Wallingford: CABI, pp. 99–113.

Hall, D. and Brown, F. (2006) *Tourism and Welfare: Ethics, Responsibility and Sustained Well-being,* Wallingford: CABI.

Haule, R. (2006) 'Some reflections on the foundations of human rights – are human rights an alternative to moral values?', *Max Planck Yearbook of United Nations Law* 10: 367–95. Available at <http://www.mpil.de/shared/data/pdf/pdfmpunyb/08_romuald.pdf> (Accessed 3 June 2012).

Hemingway, S. (2004) 'The impact of tourism on the human rights of women in South East Asia', *International Journal of Human Rights*, 8(3): 275–304.

Hennig, J., Craggs, S., Laczko, F. and Larsson, F. (2007) *Trafficking in Human Beings and the 2006 World Cup in Germany*, Geneva: International Organization for Migration.

Higgins-Desbiolles, F. (2008) 'Justice tourism: a pathway to alternative globalisation', *Journal of Sustainable Tourism,* 16(3): 345–64.

Hollinshead, K. (2009) 'The "worldmaking" prodigy of tourism: The reach and power of tourism in the dynamics of change and transformation', *Tourism Analysis,* 14(1): 139–52.

— (2011) '"Soft Power" in action: The new – or old? – declarative and diplomatic function of tourism', in *Proceedings CAUTHE National Conference 8–11 February 2011,* University of South Australia, Adelaide, pp. 1113–16.

Hudson, S. (2007) 'To go or not to go? Ethical perspectives on tourism in an "outpost of tyranny"', *Journal of Business Ethics,* 76: 385–96.

Human Rights Watch (2009) 'Universal periodic review of Fiji', August 26. Available at http://www.hrw.org/news/2010/02/09/universal-periodic-review-fiji

IATA (2012) 'Highlight quotes from the remarks of Tony Tyler Director General and CEO International Air Transport Association (IATA)', *State of the Air Transport Industry IATA 68th Annual General Meeting and World Air Transport Summit 11 June 2012, Beijing, China.* Available at <http://www.iata.org/events/agm/2012/Documents/state-industry-video-highlight-quotes.pdf> (Accessed 17 August 2012).

Isaac, R.K. and Hodge, D. (2011) 'An exploratory study: justice tourism in controversial areas: the case of Palestine', *Tourism Planning & Development,* 8(1): 101–8.

Jones, T. (1991) 'Ethical decision making by individuals in organizations: an issue-contingent model', *Academy of Management Review,* 16: 366–95.

Kim, S., Prideaux, B. and Prideaux, J. (2007a) 'Using tourism to promote peace on the Korean Peninsula', *Annals of Tourism Research,* 34(2): 291–309.

Kim, S., Timothy, D. and Han, H. (2007b) 'Tourism and political ideologies: a case of tourism in North Korea', *Tourism Management,* 28: 1031–43.

Kulessa, M. (2000) 'Potentials, problems and prospects of various types of travel sanctions', in *Smart sanctions: the next step: Arms embargoes and travel sanctions,* First Expert Seminar, Bonn: Bonn International Center for Conversion, pp. 1–7.

Lanfant, M.F. and Graburn, N.H.H. (1992) 'International tourism reconsidered: the principle of the alternative', in V.L. Smith and W.R. Eadington (eds) *Tourism Alternatives,* Chichester: Wiley.

Langlois, A.J. (2009) 'Normative and theoretical foundations of human rights', in Goodhart, M. (ed.) *Human Rights Politics and Practice,* Oxford: Oxford University Press, pp. 11–25.

Lansing, P. and De Vries, P. (2007) 'Sustainable tourism: ethical alternative or marketing ploy?', *Journal of Business Ethics,* 72(1): 77–85.

Lau, H. (2008) 'Human rights and globalization: putting the race to the top into perspective', *Northwestern University Law Review,* 102(4): 2021–33.

Law, D.S. (2008) 'Globalization and the future of constitutional rights', *Northwestern University Law Review,* 102(3): 1–89.

Lee, C., Bendle, L. J., Yoon, Y. and Kim, M. (2012) 'Thanatourism or peace Tturism: perceived value at a North Korean resort from an indigenous perspective', *International Journal of Tourism Research,* 14: 71–90.

Liu, J.H. (2007) 'Lighting the torch of human rights: the Olympic Games as a vehicle for human rights reform', *Northwestern Journal of International Human Rights,* 5(2): 213–35.

Lovelock, B.A. (2007) 'Obstacles to ethical travel: attitudes and behaviours of New Zealand travel agents with respect to politically repressed destinations', *Tourism Review International,* 11(4): 329–48.

Lovelock, B.A. (2008) 'Ethical travel decisions: travel agents and human rights', *Annals of Tourism Research,* 35(2): 338–58.

Martín, J.L. (2012) 'Sustainability is the key to protecting natural, cultural and historical assets – Taleb Rifai' 21 February. Available at <http://trumanfactor.com/2012/taleb-rifai-interview/> (Accessed 30 June 2012).

Mastrocola, P. (1995) 'The Lords of the Rings: the role of Olympic site selection as a weapon against human rights abuses: China's bid for the 2000 Olympics', *Third World Law Journal,* 15(7): 141–70.

Matheson, C. and Finkel, R. (2011) 'The relationship between human rights and mega sporting events: a case study of the Vancouver Winter Olympics and the spectre of human trafficking', in *Book of Proceedings Vol II International Conference on Tourism and Management Studies, Algarve,* pp. 1051–3.

Milligan, S. (2002) 'House votes to lift ban on Cuba travel, White House sought to keep the sanctions', *Boston Globe,* 24 July. Available at <http://www.commondreams.org/headlines02/0724–08. htm> (Accessed 16 October 2009).

Mowforth,M. and Munt, I. (2009) *Tourism and Sustainability: New Tourism in the Third World,* London: Routledge.

Mowforth, M., Charlton, C. and Munt, I. (2008) *Tourism Responsibility: Perspectives from Latin America and the Caribbean,* London: Routledge.

Nafziger, J.A.R. and Strenk, A. (1978) 'the political uses and abuses of sports', *Connecticut Law Review,* 10(2): 259–89.

Payne, D. and Dimanche, F. (1996) 'Towards a code of conduct for the tourism industry: an ethics model', *Journal of Business Ethics,* 15: 997–1007.

Posner, E.A. (2008) 'Human welfare, not human rights', *John M. Olin Law and Economic Working Paper No. 394,* The Law School, University of Chicago. Available at <http://www.law.uchicago. edu/Lawecon/index.html> (Accessed 20 April 2012).

Rabu (2003) 'Building a culture of peace through tourism', *Pacific Link.* Available at <http://kolom. pacific.net.id/ind> (Accessed 18 October 2009).

Rest, J. (1986) *Moral Development: Advances in Research and Theory,* New York: Praeger.

Roehl, W. (1990) 'Travel agent attitudes toward China after Tiananmen Square', *Journal of Travel Research,* 29(2): 16–22.

Salazar, N.B. (2006) 'Building a "Culture of Peace" through tourism: reflexive and analytical notes and queries', *Universitas Hunistica,* 62: 319–33.

Sarkar, S.K. and George, B.P. (2010) 'Peace through alternative tourism: case studies from Bengal, India', *Journal of Tourism and Peace Research,* 1(1): 27–41.

Scheyvens, R. (2011) 'The challenge of sustainable tourism development in the Maldives: understanding the social and political dimensions of sustainability', *Asia Pacific Viewpoint,* 52(2): 148–64.

Smith, D. (2012) 'Robert Mugabe asked to be UN "leader for tourism"', *Guardian online,* 29 May. Available at <http://www.guardian.co.uk/world/2012/may/29/robert-mugabe-un-internationalenvoy-tourism> (Accessed 1 August 2012).

Strug, D. and Lemkau, J. (2008) 'Psychological distress of Cuban Americans affected by restrictive U.S. travel policies', *Journal of Progressive Human Services,* 19(1): 1–18.

Tourism Concern (2012) *Water Equity in Tourism: A Human Right, A Global Responsibility* (edited by Rachel Noble, Paul Smith, Polly Pattullo), London: Tourism Concern.

UNWTO (2012) 'We must act together to fight exploitation and human trafficking in tourism, say UN and international partners'. Available at <http://media.unwto.org/en/press-release/2012-04-24/> (Accessed 27 June 2012).

Upadhayaya, P.K., Müller-Böker, U. and Sharma, S.R. (2010) 'Tourism amidst armed conflict: consequences, copings, and creativity for peace-building through tourism in Nepal', *Journal of Tourism and Peace Research,* 1(2): 22–40.

Var, T. and Ap, J. (1998) 'Tourism and world peace', in Theobald, W.F. (ed.) *Global Tourism* (2nd edn), Portsmouth, NH: Butterworth-Heinemann, pp. 44–57.

Weber, J. (1990) 'Managers' moral reasoning: assessing their responses to three moral dilemmas', *Human Relations,* 43: 687–702.

5 Medical tourism

Primum non nocere: 'Above all do no harm.'[a]

LEARNING OBJECTIVES

After reading this chapter you will be able to:

- Identify and discuss the key ethical issues that medical tourism provokes.
- Understand how medical tourism differs from other forms of health care trade.
- Describe the processes involved and identify the key inequities produced by this trade.
- Understand the effect of medical tourism on provider and departure societies.
- Understand how medical tourism aids further privatisation of health care provision, the commodification of health care and the perception of the patient as a consumer.
- Discuss the implications for access to medical care for locals and the nature of health system development in provider countries.
- Understand the risks for patients and the costs of follow-up care for home health systems.

5.1 INTRODUCTION

Medical tourism is practice, whereby individuals travel across national borders with the intention of receiving medical care.

(Snyder et al. 2011a)

Medical tourism is:

The intentional pursuit of non-emergency medical treatment outside of a patient's home country that is likely to include a pre or post-operative stay abroad during which some tourist activities may be undertaken.

(Johnston et al. 2010: 3)

Medical tourism:

> constitutes an individual solution to what is traditionally considered a public (government) concern, health for its citizens.
>
> (Pocock and Phua 2011: 2)

Medical tourism is differentiated from cross-border care primarily because the individual initiates and covers all of the expenses associated with the treatment they are seeking abroad. Medical tourists can also be domestic tourists, citizens seeking treatment within developing countries and within the developed world. Medical tourists are motivated by a range of factors including long waiting lists for treatment in their own country, expensive treatment costs in their own country, a lack of providers at home and treatment not on offer at home – either because it is new or because it is illegal. In addition, the Internet has ensured people can more easily learn of treatments offered abroad, cheaper air travel can be procured and with the emergence of brokers connections can easily be established with other hospital systems (Connell 2006, 2011; Johnston et al. 2010). Medical tourism is a distinct niche within health tourism; it can be differentiated from other forms of health tourism on the basis that it involves medical interventions (Connell 2006). The marketing efforts of health care providers in destination countries involve making a deliberate link between medical care and tourism, emphasising the potential for pre-operative tourist activity (for patients and their travelling companions) and post-operative recovery in an exotic location (Connell 2006; Hopkins et al. 2010). Together, all of these interrelated factors have ensured that medical tourism has developed into a multi-billion dollar industry (Pennings 2007; Pocock and Phua 2011).

The trend of people travelling for treatment tends to be one where those in high income developed countries seek treatment in low income developing countries (Connell 2006; Crooks et al. 2010: 1). Most of the medical tourists are North American, Western European and Middle Eastern in origin, and in India the medical tourists are typically expatriates or descendants of expatriates from Britain and the United States (Connell, 2006: 1096). There also appear to be patterns of mobility, where patients from the dominant departing countries seek treatment in 'preferred' destinations. Preference is shaped variously by targeted marketing by the destination country, price, proximity, the treatment sought and religious observations. Thus, Europeans seek treatment in Asia, specifically Thailand and Malaysia. Malaysia is a destination for patients from the Middle East. However, the majority from the United Arab Emirates seek treatment in Singapore; and Omanis prefer treatment in India. Thailand competes with Singapore for the Japanese medical tourist (Connell 2006: 1096) and destinations variously become known as the place for heart surgery, dental treatments, transplants, reproductive assistance and cosmetic surgery.

While there is potentially an endless list of treatments sought, the most common include: hip replacements, heart surgery, transplant surgery, cosmetic surgery, reproductive treatments and experimental treatments. With respect to ethical issues, transplant tourism and reproductive tourism raise a range of ethical issues and concerns that differ from some of the aforementioned procedures because of the implications they have for the commodification of the (donor) body, gender discrimination and understandings of health care rights (Pennings 2007; Budiani-Saberi and Delmonico 2008; Snyder et al. 2012). Yet this flow of people seeking treatment abroad is not just driven by individual motivations, rather this flow, as with many others, is enmeshed in the neoliberal informed shift toward the liberalisation of all services. Health care, as with other forms of care, has become a tradable commodity (Hermans 2000). Medical tourism stands alongside other forms of health care trade: the trade of health services, foreign investment in health care and health insurance; and telemedicine (direct cross-border trade) (Pennings 2007; Cortez 2008).

It is asserted that medical tourism now involves significant flows of people seeking treatment abroad. However, actual figures are difficult to establish as the various facilitators of this niche tourism typically do not keep reliable records. For example, the reasons for departure taken at most international borders may not allow identification that medical tourism is the motivation for travel (Johnston et al. 2010; Snyder et al. 2011a). Further, most health systems in departure countries have no means to or do not record either the number of patients in their jurisdiction going abroad for treatment or whether medical tourism is a reason for the need for health care on return. While insurance companies would have records of claims for treatments received abroad, commercial sensitivity often precludes full disclosure (Hopkins et al. 2010). Nonetheless, despite the aforementioned problems, it is forecast that by 2017 the number of medical tourists seeking treatment abroad will have reached approximately 23.2 million people (Hopkins et al. 2010: 188).

Medical tourism has only recently attracted research attention, with most empirical research being conducted since the early 2000s. Until this time most of the commentary has been generated by journalists and is observational commentary rather than empirically based exploration. There is still no hard and reliable data on the size of this industry, patient flows, the scale of revenue generated, and limited research documenting the outcomes for destination and departing health systems (Hopkins et al. 2010). There is an emerging body of research that addresses medical tourism in specific regions (Connell 2006, 2008; Chee 2007) and the movement and experiences of medical tourists (Snyder et al. 2011a). With respect to the implications for departing health systems and health care less is known; however, there is research currently underway in the United Kingdom (Lunt, pers. com.) and preliminary research in New Zealand (Lovelock and Lovelock 2013) and doubtless other research projects underway, but yet to be published. Yet the paucity of reliable research does not undermine the fact that medical tourism is now considered a significant form of touristic practice with wide-ranging implications for individuals, health systems and health care, specific localities, and global health inequity.

In this chapter we will explore a range of ethical issues provoked by the practice of medical tourism, including:

- The effect of medical tourism on provider and departure societies.
- How medical tourism aids further privatisation of health care provision, the commodification of health care and the perception of the patient as a consumer.
- The implications for access to medical care for locals and the nature of health system development in provider countries.
- The role medical tourists play in the spread of infectious disease and the implications for public health in departure countries and globally.
- The risks for patients.

- The costs of follow-up care for home health care systems.
- Ethical issues and decision-making processes in relation to medical tourism as a practice.

5.2 THE EFFECT OF MEDICAL TOURISM ON DESTINATION AND DEPARTURE COUNTRIES

Medical tourism is part of the wider and more encompassing sub-industry of health tourism, but differs as it is does not involve a formal cross-border arrangement between countries and is initiated by the patient rather than the patient's home country health service or system. While medical tourists will travel within their own countries for treatment, the most significant flow is from high income countries to medium or low income countries. The major medical tourism destinations are in lower and middle income countries, where the competitive advantage rests with lower exchange rates (Johnston et al. 2010) lower labour costs, inexpensive pharmaceuticals, low-cost or absent malpractice insurance; all of these factors allow cheaper treatment costs for a range of medical conditions (Hopkins et al. 2010).

The tourism side of medical tourism emerges in relation to those who establish the connection between would-be patient traveller, the destination provider, the accommodation, the mode of travel, and the pre-operative and recovery experience. In contrast to say poverty tourism, the medical tourism industry has invested in promoting a more positive image of third world destinations, emphasising the credentials of those who will perform the medical service and the safety accreditations of the destination health services, while simultaneously promoting the destination as the ideal place to recover from surgery and/or other treatments (Johnston et al. 2010; Hopkins et al. 2010; Connell 2006). Market promotion stressing reliability, safety and quality care has also been assisted through

Figure 5.1 *Medical tourism. Cartoon: K. Lovelock.*

partnerships with international medical facilities with international reputations for high quality service and care, e.g. the Dubai Healthcare City is partnered with the Mayo Clinic, and the Wockhardt Group Medical Facility (a chain of health care facilities in India) is affiliated with Harvard Medical International (Hopkins et al. 2010: 187).

There is no regulatory framework for medical tourism and in the absence of regulation it becomes possible for already existent health inequities to become perpetuated and entrenched. Internationally health equity and in particular the provision of universally available care has been promoted as a means to address significant gaps in health outcomes for marginal populations in high, middle and low income countries. Medical tourism hinges on the development of private provision of care, for profit, for those who can afford it. Thus, it contributes to the trade of health care, the commodification of health care, can undermine efforts to address structural inequity in health care provision in the medical tourist's own country and the destination country, and ultimately contributes to the perpetuation of global health inequalities.

The key ethical dilemma provoked by medical tourism (and its many manifestations) is the issue of distributive justice and the challenge it presents to notions of social good and universal public provision of health care. Recall in Chapter 2 the calls for the tourism industry to address justice and to serve as a vehicle for social change. Social justice is about fairness and equity. Medical tourism throws into relief a range of issues surrounding *just* distribution of health care and raises many issues about how a would-be medical tourist might adopt principled practice when considering seeking treatment abroad. Medical tourism immediately demands that distributive justice must also be considered in terms of how this practice impacts on the distribution of health resources internationally and what redistributive measures are necessary to ensure more equitable health outcomes globally.

5.3 UNDERMINING HEALTH SERVICES AT HOME

All high income countries are experiencing considerable pressure on their health care systems, with ageing populations, increases in the number of people with chronic conditions and increasing costs associated with treatment and care (WHO 2008). Medical tourism seemingly offers a panacea to the pressure within high income countries to deliver certain kinds of surgery and care whilst simultaneously providing a cheaper option for those prepared to pay for their health care (Turner 2007, 2008). Some may perceive the exchange that is taking place as one of 'mutual' benefit, where low income countries can attract foreign exchange and improve their health infrastructure and high income countries can address increased need and constrained health budgets. But while we might be able to identify 'mutuality' it does not necessarily mean that an *equal exchange* is taking place or that the outcomes will be mutually beneficial for *all or even the majority* of members of either departure or destination countries.

When the medical tourist steps out of their own health system because they cannot procure a service, or the waiting lists are long, they simultaneously (and quite possibly unwittingly) undermine domestic lobbying for improved health services in their own country (Snyder et al. 2012: 3). Ultimately, the more who opt out and choose medical tourism as a solution, the smaller the lobby group domestically and potentially too the greater likelihood that the local health care provision budget will be reduced with further publicly funded health care provisions ultimately being compromised. This argument is informed by understandings of what happens when private provision of health care competes with public in high income countries. But with respect to medical tourism it largely remains an untested hypothesis, as research in this area is limited. However, a recent qualitative study conducted by Snyder and colleagues (2011a) suggests that for some medical tourists in Canada, having treatment abroad has thrown into relief what they perceive is missing at home, suggesting that the experience might for some Canadian medical tourists inform resistance to inadequate service and health care in their own society. This is a little like the awareness arguments that are made in favour of poverty tourism (but reverses the wealth/poverty experience). Having health care abroad in a private facility heightens awareness of what is missing at home, the patient becomes more informed, possibly a little more annoyed about perceived inadequacies of their own health system and then more likely to voice this concern. Yet, the same study also suggests that the contrasts being made by the Canadian medical tourists about care abroad and care at home, hinge on service, the provision of coffee (patient as customer and consumer) and the aesthetics of their health care environment abroad. What is being appreciated then is not necessarily the treatment, but the conditions within which the treatment is being provided (packaged). This tends to support the argument that medical tourism encourages commodification of health care (private, consumer-focused service) and suggests that commoditised and private provision of care could become a preference that could ultimately undermine public provision of care in their home society. While more research is needed in this area, it is clear that this gives rise to a range of ethical issues connected to private and public provision of health care and who can and cannot afford to access the former and what happens when the latter is ultimately eroded.

Medical tourism provokes other potential issues for publicly funded health services in the medical tourist's home country. If the medical tourist experiences complications upon return their home health system must address their health care needs and carry the costs associated with this. In addition to this, there are a number of risks associated with travelling for treatment, including: embarking on long flights after surgery and the risk of embolisms (Carabello 2008); disruption of care when the patient travels home (Jesitus 2006); and the inability to address malpractice in the destination country (Burkett 2007). A recent review of literature did not locate statistical data on complication rates for medical tourists, but there were many anecdotal accounts of medical misadventure, with some authors arguing that the costs for public health systems in home countries is extensive (Hopkins et al. 2010: 191). In addition, as brokers often facilitate the link between the patient and hospital abroad, brokers can make ill-informed judgements about the nature of care needed, direct patients to seek treatments that stand in opposition to advice provided by the patients' home physician and/or facilitate treatments abroad that are un-approved at home because they are considered 'too risky' (Turner 2007; Snyder et al. 2011b). Further, patients may not be provided with adequate information and the accepted Western medical norm of 'informed consent' may be compromised through this process (Snyder et al. 2011b). Snyder et al.'s (2011b: 531) study of medical tourism facilitators revealed that they considered their role as akin to being 'that patient's physician one-step removed' while they also acknowledged the tensions provoked by the business side of the relationship. The problem with this is that most brokers or facilitators are not physicians; they are then in fact a broker one-step removed from the physician and lacking physician knowledge.

International travel for medical care can also expose medical tourists to infectious diseases which in turn becomes a public health issue when they return home. The NDM-1 drug-resistant enzyme was thought to have been spread to Canada, the USA and the UK by medical tourists who had been in India for health care (Kumarasamy et al. 2010; Snyder et al. 2011a). The risk of spreading infectious diseases is high because of the largely unregulated nature of this industry. Specifically, the inability for local or national health authorities to monitor or predict what may or may not be coming in across the borders (Crooks et al. 2010).

Further reading

Birch, Daniel, W., Lan Vu, Karmali, S., Stoklossa, C.J. and Sharma, A.M. (2010) 'Medical tourism in bariatric surgery', *American Journal of Surgery,* 199: 604–8.
Newman, M.I., Camberos, A.E. and Ascherman, J. (2005) 'Mycobacteria abscessus outbreak in US patients linked to offshore surgicenter', *Annals of Plastic Surgery,* 55(1): 107–10.

In addition, the unregulated nature of this industry ensures that it is difficult if not impossible to track within health system jurisdictions patients who have opted to seek treatment abroad. Ultimately this has implications for how health systems manage and target their budgets and service delivery for local populations (Cortez 2008; Wolff 2007).

DISCUSSION QUESTIONS

1 If these are issues in high income countries, what are the issues for middle and low income countries providing the services? How does medical tourism impact on local populations in low to medium income destinations? How does medical tourism shape the development of health services and systems in low to medium income destinations? Does medical tourism offer more than it can deliver?

2 Utilitarianism would have us ask: What actions will do the most good and the least harm for everyone who is affected? We need to know: Who are the stakeholders? What are the alternative courses of action? For each alternative what are the benefits and costs? And, which alternative creates the most benefits and costs? (See Schumann's framework in Chapter 2.)

3 And from Rawls's principles: What action provides all with equal liberties and opportunities while helping those in need to the greatest extent possible?

5.4 HEALTH SERVICE AND CARE PROVISION ABROAD – TOURISTS VERSUS LOCALS

Medical tourism has been variously positioned as a means of addressing service problems faced by patients in departing countries and providing countries. With respect to the latter it is argued that the industry brings in revenue that can be employed to improve health infrastructure and that these improvements do and will continue to benefit the local population (Mudur 2003; Chee 2007; Connell 2008). As with tourism more generally medical tourism in developing countries provides an important source of foreign revenue. Yet, as a practice, medical tourism has been criticised for ultimately draining public resources in destination countries, undermining the equitable distribution of funds in destination countries, encouraging the inequitable distribution and provision of skill – where skilled health professionals are addressing the needs of paying foreign tourists in private facilities over and above the needs of locals. Further, medical tourism encourages an internal migration where skilled health professionals migrate from rural to urban areas to work in the new private facilities and to serve foreigners, leaving rural areas with recruitment and retention challenges (Pachanee and Wibulpolprasert 2006; Wibulpolprasert and Pengbaibon 2003). For example, in Thailand there is a health professional shortage in the public sector. In 2005, 6,000 positions remained unfilled as health professionals increasingly sought higher paid work in the private sector (Hopkins et al. 2010). Similar impacts in countries such as South Africa, Ghana and Pakistan are anticipated. This will serve to compound existing health professional shortages where in these countries nearly half of their medical graduates migrate abroad for work (Saniotis 2007 in Hopkins et al. 2010).

Of course developing countries have been experiencing skill shortages for years, where health professionals migrate abroad and join what has been called the 'global health conveyor belt' (Schrecker and Labonte 2004; Pennings 2007), yet while medical tourism potentially offers a means to stem this flow, stemming the flow does not always mean benefits for the majority local population. Rather, it can contribute to the development of a two-tiered system that facilitates the flow of wealthy patients into private hospitals and the local poor into hospitals for locals or without adequate care (Chanda 2002). Such two-tiered systems are evident in Israel (Even and Zinshtein in Snyder et al. 2012), India (Gupta 2007), and Malaysia (Leng 2007; Chee 2007) and ultimately contribute to poor access to health care for locals and poorer health outcomes. In those destination countries where health professional training is publicly funded, ethical issues emerge in relation to those professionals who then engage in providing services for wealthy tourists rather than addressing preventive medicine or public health concerns amongst their own population (Gupta 2007; Pennings 2007; Snyder et al. 2012). Additionally, in these countries, developers are often offered tax incentives to develop private hospitals in return for providing health care for locals, yet once the concessions have been made some developers do not deliver on the promise of health care for locals (Snyder et al. 2012). This might be described as the generation of a *double burden* for the local population, with a loss of taxes that might have assisted with health service delivery locally and no provision of improved health service delivery in return for tax concessions. Most low income countries have insufficient if no regulatory measures in place to ensure that the taxes claimed through medical tourism are channelled back into public health care

(Gupta 2007; Hopkins et al. 2010; Pocock and Phua 2011). All of these movements – poor to rich, rural to urban, public to private – are not only happening in developing countries, they are also evident in developed countries, and are a problem for distributive justice (Bauer 2003; Pennings 2007). While two-tier systems are not problematic in and of themselves, it is when one tier is compromised by the other, specifically when the public provision of care is compromised by the private sector, that questions of inequity emerge and the fundamental right to care is undermined. Here the key ethical issue is that the ability to pay becomes more important than health care provision on the basis of need (Pennings 2007: 506).

CASE STUDY: MEDICAL TOURIST FLOWS AND UNEVEN REGIONAL HEALTHCARE CAPACITY – *JOHN CONNELL*

Medical tourism raises various ethical questions centred on issues of accreditation, the quality of care (and after-care), the validity of particular 'extreme' procedures, such as transplant tourism (often not undertaken in the patients' home countries) and possible biosecurity risks from the spread of infections and pandemics by returning medical tourists (Hall and James 2011). The ethics of media depictions of body shapes, involving the pathologising of (usually) women's bodies and invocations to change have also been questioned (Sarwer and Crerand 2004; Buote et al. 2011). Inherent inequality has posed multiple ethical questions, especially for new and experimental procedures where a variety of unusual practices are subordinated to the 'logic of the market' (Parry 2008) in contexts where regulation is weak.

A constantly recurring ethical question concerns the impact of medical tourism on the health care of nationals in destination countries. Obviously medical tourism takes patients across international borders, beyond the perhaps comfortable and familiar cultural relationships between health care providers, doctors and patients, to places that may be culturally, climatically and linguistically distinct and unfamiliar. The main destinations are Mexico and the Asian 'big four': Singapore, Thailand, Malaysia and India (Connell 2011). For decades health systems, in countries such as India, have been conventionally regarded in the West as inadequate, with deficient facilities, practices and personnel. Cautionary notes have frequently come from professional bodies in source countries, whose members may have to remedy botched procedures and complications. However, the professional bodies, who record misadventure, have obvious vested interests. Real rates of success and failure are immeasurable: there is no means of recording this, and no guidelines against which to measure success rates, especially in such areas as cosmetic surgery where disappointments and failures may be more frequent.

Nonetheless to remedy some real deficiencies but particularly perceptions of inadequacies, countries and hospitals seeking to become medical tourism destinations have had to invest considerable resources in developing health care systems that meet the needs of relatively wealthy visitors from more developed countries, and in promoting those services in those source countries. This investment has substantially raised the standards of care in some key hospitals, most notably Bumrungrad International Hospital in Bangkok – perhaps the single largest destination for medical tourists. Such large hospitals oriented to medical tourism have amenities that have resulted in their being described as 'hospitels'. Investment in such hospitals and in related infrastructure – such as transport, sewerage, water and electricity supplies – is usually concentrated in the capital cities where most medical tourism facilities are located and since expenditure is finite this may be at the cost of investment in rural and regional areas. This is precisely where, in most countries, health care needs are greatest but least well served.

Health care systems in developing countries, including the main destinations of medical tourists, are notoriously uneven, and often becoming more so, in circumstances where both urban bias and the decay of remote and regional facilities have long occurred. Such centralisation has been hastened by privatisation, stagnant budgets for health expenditure and, probably, by medical tourism (Connell 2011).

There is a considerable disjuncture between the branded corporate images of medical tourism and the sometimes harsh reality of majority health care in particular countries. This is particularly evident in India where the divide between the public sector and the expanding private sector is epitomised in medical tourism and the emergence of corporate medical chains, such as Apollo Hospitals. While India's public-sector health care and sanitation systems are detached and distinct from medical tourism they are all part of a national political economy. Expansion of the private sector is at some cost to the public sector, where patients have very limited ability to pay, especially if skilled workers move away from that sector. The recent growth of medical tourism in India has occurred in a context where, despite rapid national economic growth, some 40 per cent of India's population live below the poverty line and have minimal access to basic health care so that infant and maternal mortality rates are high (Connell 2011).

The rapid expansion of a private health sector has resulted in the movement of health workers into that urban, private sector, where salaries and working conditions are usually superior. That sometimes involves migration from rural areas, further emphasising existing regional inequalities in access to health care. As the Secretary General of the Thai Holistic Health Foundation has pointed out, 'In the past we had a brain drain; doctors wanted to work outside the country to make more money. Now they don't have to leave the country, the brain drain is another part of our own society' (quoted in Connell 2011).

Five years later medical tourism was regarded by the Secretary General of the National Health Commission of Thailand as 'the accelerator causing the brain-drain of doctors, super-specialists and other medical workers to private hospitals' (quoted in Connell 2011).

Many medical tourism destinations, notably India, have a shortage of doctors (and other health professionals). India has just four doctors per 10,000 people whereas the United States has 27, and accelerated international migration of health workers has meant that these numerical disparities are steadily increasing (Connell 2011). There is a serious shortage of doctors in many parts of Thailand, alongside continued migration, an 'internal brain drain', from the peripheries and from primary and preventive health care (Wibulpolprasert and Pengbaibon 2003; Wibulpolprasert and Pachanee 2008). Ironically part of medical tourism is a response to long waiting lists in developed countries, hence demand and waiting lists are transferred to relatively poor or middle income countries. The flow of medical tourists away from still better served countries emphasises that medical tourism is a perverse flow in terms of overall national health system capacities (Connell 2011).

Despite considerable concern, most of the literature on the broad socio-economic impact of medical tourism is based on assumptions that rarely address such wider questions. In some part that may be because the questions that medical tourism raises are not easily answerable. However in some contexts 'a dual medical system has emerged in which specialisation in cardiology, ophthalmology and plastic surgery serves the foreign and wealthy domestic patients while the [majority of the] local populations lack basics such as sanitation, clean water and regular deworming' (Bookman and Bookman 2007: 7, Connell 2011). Such situations characterise India and occur less dramatically in Thailand, Malaysia and elsewhere (NaRanong and NaRanong 2011) and are accentuated by the rural–urban migration of skilled health workers from rural and regional areas and from the public sector into the private sector. Medical tourism has thus been described as an 'elite private space ... inextricably linked to a beleaguered national medical program' and a 'reverse subsidy for the elite' (Ackerman 2010: 403; Sengupta 2011: 312). In South Africa it has also emphasised the 'racialized inequality in health care' (Mazzaschi 2011).

Market mechanisms have become increasingly important in health care. With privatisation and growing international competition for markets, that medical care is increasingly global rather than local, and traded rather than perceived as a right. The outsourcing of medical care, through medical tourism, shows that even the most seemingly location-specific activity is mobile. Tensions between national policies of promotion of health care within states and international strategies to generate income through promoting mobility between states have emerged raising new ethical issues. All forms of medical tourism raise questions about the appropriate use of skilled health workers, the allocation of financial resources and the distribution of health care (Connell 2011).

References

Ackerman, S. (2010) 'Plastic paradise: Transforming bodies and selves in Costa Rica's cosmetic surgery tourism industry', *Medical Anthropology*, 29: 403–23.

Bookman, M. and Bookman, K. (2007) *Medical Tourism in Developing Countries*, Basingstoke: Palgrave Macmillan.

Buote, M., Wilson, A., Strahan, E., Gazzola, S. and Papps, F. (2011) 'Setting the bar: Divergent sociocultural norms for women's and men's ideal appearance in real-world contexts', *Body Image*, 8: 322–34.

Connell, J. (2011) *Medical Tourism*, Wallingford: CABI.

Hall,C.M. and James, M. (2011) 'Medical tourism: emerging biosecurity and nosocomial issues', *Tourism Review*, 66: 118–26.

Mazzaschi, A. (2011) 'Surgeon and safari: Producing valuable bodies in Johannesburg', *Signs*, 36: 303–12.

NaRanong, A. and NaRanong, V. (2011) 'The effects of medical tourism: Thailand's experience', *Bulletin of the World Health Organization*, 89: 336–44.

Parry, B. (2008) 'Entangled exchange: Reconceptualising the characterisation and practice of bodily commodification', *Geoforum*, 39: 1133–44.

Sarwer, D. and Crerand, C. (2004) 'Body image and cosmetic medical treatments', *Body Image*, 1: 99–111.

Sengupta, A. (2011) 'Medical tourism: Reverse subsidy for the elite', *Signs*, 36: 312–19.

DISCUSSION POINT

With respect to medical tourism distributive justice might involve some of the following:

1 Closer regulation, involving: redistributive financing mechanisms through taxing medical tourists where the taxes are reinvested in the public health system.
2 Ensuring that access for locals is not tied to ability to pay (social insurance).
3 Ensuring that private providers are required to provide coverage for locals.

Discussion question

What actions produce a fair distribution of benefits and costs for all of the stakeholders?

5.4 PRIVATISATION AND GLOBALISATION OF HEALTH CARE

Wealthy elites travelling abroad for treatment and surgery is not new; historically many state leaders and members of elite groups have travelled for specialist treatment abroad (Kangas 2002; Connell 2006). However, medical tourism in its current form is relatively recent. While still dominated by wealthy elites, increasingly it is within the grasp of middle income earners in developed and developing countries – this shift has been aided by the globalisation and liberalisation of the health services industry. Specifically, medical tourism is an outcome of the privatisation of medical care and the growth of the health care market globally (Hopkins et al. 2010) . For example, India, Thailand, Indonesia and Nepal have relaxed restrictions on foreign direct investment with the aim of encouraging growth in the commercial health sector (Hopkins et al. 2010: 192). Underpinning this development has been the widespread adoption of neoliberal economic policies in many developed nations. These policies have led to the withdrawal of the welfare state and subsequently a wide range of 'care' and/or 'responsibility' provisions for their citizens have been devolved to the individual. While historically health care for the majority has been typically addressed within borders, increasingly pressure on health systems within these borders and relaxations with respect to trade have ensured that health care services are tradable commodities and health care professionals are no longer locked into serving in the locality within which they were trained or trained for.

These changes locally and globally have ensured that therapeutic itineraries are more than ever shaped by a web of interconnected processes involving people *and* technology, capital, images and ideologies (Kangas 2002: 44). And with respect to medical tourism these itineraries remain largely unregulated, lucrative for some and disenfranchising for others. In the United States various tasks are now outsourced, such as insurance claim processing and diagnostic test interpretations, but by far the most significant shift is the globalisation of the market for patients (Cortez 2008: 76). The Internet has been a major facilitator of medical tourism. Patients can research their medical conditions, search for providers, products and treatment options on line (Cortez 2008: 85) and brokerages who can link patients to facilities (Hopkins et al. 2010). One of the most popular uses of the Internet is searching for health information, coming only second to using email and standing alongside searching for other consumer products and services (Cortez 2008: 76).

Websites

A simple search demonstrates how websites facilitate this industry, see for example:

http://www.apollohospitals.com;
http://www.bumrungrad.com;
http://www.wockhardthospitals.net

Increasing privatisation of health care services in provider and departure countries has also facilitated the global nature of this industry. With governments seeking to play a reduced role in health care delivery, provisions are made to attract foreign investment in health care delivery. This has ensured that health care is now one of the most significant markets in the world (Cortez 2008: 88).

Until recently most of the trade in health services has involved the movement of health professionals, but increasingly with relaxation of foreign investment laws in many destinations there is the emergence of a global hospital industry, with companies acquiring hospitals in multiple locations across regions. This has occurred alongside the globalisation of associated industries, for example, the pharmaceutical industry, health insurance markets, telemedicine and the biotechnology industry (Cortez 2008: 89), where increasingly clinical trials, testing, providers and producers are globally located.

At a global level, the General Agreement on Trade and Services (GATS) represents the liberalisation of all services and optimises the neoliberal legacy. This is well illustrated by the Indian state response to GATS and the provisions made for private hospitals and the intention to expand medical tourism for foreign currency earnings (Hopkins et al. 2010: 193). Under GATS countries could make binding liberalisation commitments in relation to four areas: (1) cross-border supply (telehealth or laboratory services), (2) consumption abroad (medical tourism), (3) commercial presence (foreign investment in health facilities), and (4) natural persons (temporary migration of health workers abroad) (Hopkins et al. 2010: 193). There is now pressure from medical tourism destination providers, through GATS negotiations, to ensure that insurance companies will cover services provided abroad. Those that have committed to foreign investment in health facilities (35 countries so far) will contribute to the growth of medical tourism, but it is uncertain that this will lead to better health care for locals (Hopkins et al. 2010). It is also not clear whether the associated economic benefits generated by medical tourism, for a range of tourist players, including travel agents, airlines, hotels, taxis and local vendors, will be enough to offset the long-term implications of the rise of two-tier health systems and inadequate public provision of health care for the poor in destination countries.

DISCUSSION POINT

It is argued by many that medically essential services need to be controlled and provided by public health care if equitable access to quality health care, a fundamental human right, is to be maintained (Pennings 2007: 505). With medical tourism, once a significant number of people in a given society grow accustomed to purchasing health care, care will increasingly be perceived as a purchasable commodity and this practice will be embraced as normative. This shift in perception and practice in turn undermines the observance of health care as a fundamental human right that the public provision of health care attempts to address (Snyder et al. 2011a).

Discussion questions

1 What are the ethical implications of the privatisation of health care?
2 How does privatisation impact on access for those most in need?

We will now consider two forms of medical tourism: transplant tourism and reproductive tourism. In terms of the ethical issues they appear to be immediately obvious and the practices problematic, but as Hopkins et al. (2010: 190), observe, they may not be the most troubling global health inequity concern.

DISCUSSION POINT: TRANSPLANT TOURISM – MEDICAL TOURISM

Transplant tourism is where a person undergoes a transplant abroad and is the recipient of an organ purchased through the illicit organ trade (Shimanzo 2007 in Evans 2008). Transplant tourism also involves intermediaries – agents and health care providers who arrange the recruitment of donors and travel for the transplant. The shortage of organ donors has led to trafficking in organs and the emergence of transplant tourism. Transplant tourism accounts for approximately 10 per cent of global transplants (WHO 2007). In 2005, 66,000 kidneys were transplanted from 98 countries, yet this only addressed 10 per cent of the need (Kokubo 2009). Transplant tourism has raised concerns about the nature of the procurement of organs and the conditions within which procurement is made. China and the Philippines have been significant suppliers of organs for transplant. A number of countries advertise transplantation tourism, including Columbia, Pakistan, India, China, the Philippines, Bolivia, Brazil, Iraq, Israel, Moldova, Peru, South Africa and Turkey; all export commercially donated organs (Shimazono 2007; Turner 2008). Organ trafficking and transplantation tourism is illegal in these countries, the harvesting of organs from executed prisoners in China has been outlawed, yet the trade continues and it appears little is done to sanction those who break the laws in relation to this industry (Turner 2008). While there is trade in the North and some includes cadaver organs, most involves organs taken from live people in the South transplanted into unrelated people. The organ trade can also take other forms, for example a live donor and recipient from different countries will move to a third country for the transplant. Those providing the organs are motivated by financial incentives, invariably live in extreme poverty and are providing organs for people from high income countries. Brokers have emerged in relation to this trade and central to this is the ethical concern about informed consent and the potential coercive nature of the relationship between the broker and the organ provider. While the financial incentives motivate people in poverty to provide organs, many of these people experience deteriorating health status after the procedure, which in turn can compound their impoverished living conditions when they are unable to work, have to pay for health care and/or are ostracised from their communities (Scheper-Hughes 2002).

The buying and selling of organs is a major ethical issue for commercial living organ donors, clinicians and recipients. While all countries are trying to address the shortage of organs for transplantation, all are not addressing the exploitative practices of organ trafficking.

United Nations definition of organ trafficking

Organ trafficking entails the recruitment, transport, transfer, harbouring or receipt of persons, by means of the threat or use of force or other forms of coercion, of abduction, of fraud, of deception, of the abuse of power, of a position of vulnerability, of the giving or receiving of payments or benefits to achieve the consent of a person having control over another person, for the purpose of exploitation by the removal of organs, tissues or cells for transplantation. The reason to oppose organ trafficking is the global injustice of using a vulnerable segment of a country or population as a source of organs (vulnerable defined by social status, ethnicity, gender or age) (Budiani-Saberi and Delmonico 2008: 925).

For those who undergo transplants from an unknown vendor risks include transmitted infection such as hepatitis or tuberculosis or a donor transmitted malignancy. Transplant tourists have a more complex post-transplantation course and have a higher incidence of acute rejection and severe infection complications (Gill et al. 2008). For those who sell their organs they seldom have adequate medical follow-up, experience poor health, suffer depression, regret and often experience discrimination in their communities (Zargooshi 2001).

Some argue that a person has the right to decide to sell one of their organs – that this is simply the expression of autonomy and the exercise of their moral autonomy. The notion of autonomy derives from liberal moral and political traditions and means free from external constraint, with the presence of all critical mental capacities, the individual acts in accordance with their self-chosen path (Beauchamp 2007: 4). Yet with respect to the organ trade focusing on the idea of autonomy obscures the fact that most people who sell organs in the developing world live in abject poverty – choice in this context is to a large extent determined by the role of others and here not simply limited to the brokers who set out to procure the organs, but to the governments that fail to address this poverty and the desperate circumstances of these peoples' lives.

Discussion questions

1 Who are the world's organ donors?
2 What are the health implications for donors in developing countries?
3 Does a one-off payment for a kidney morally recompense the vendor?

Resources

Bramstedt, K.A. and Xu, J. (2007) 'Checklist: Passport, plane ticket, organ transplant', *American Journal of Transplantation*, 7: 1698–1701.
Biggins, S.W., Bambha, K., Terrault, N., Inadomi, J., Roberts, J.O. and Bass, N. (2009) 'Transplant tourism to China: the impact on domestic patient-care decisions', *Clinical Transplantation*, 23: 831–38.

5.5 ETHICAL DECISION MAKING

'It's really unfair. … I'm just lucky … to be able to do this, like it sucks for other people that don't get to do this, and I feel for them.'

(A Canadian medical tourist, Snyder et al., 2011a)

With respect to individual responsibility, Snyder et al. (2012: 8) have developed a decision-making model with the aim of assisting patients to engage in the ethics of medical tourism (Figure 5.3).

The model allows the would-be medical tourist to consider how they contribute to systems of trade in health services and what the impact of their choices might be on other people. Responding to this ethical process is, however, currently constrained by the absence of reliable empirical data on the effects of medical tourism long term. Despite being hamstrung in this way, there is sufficient information available for people to adopt a politically

Figure 5.2 *Kidney trade – men bearing their scars. Photo: Asim Tanveer.*

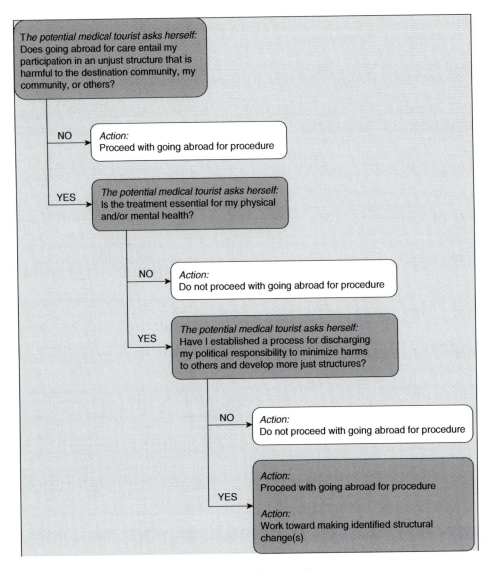

Figure 5.3 *Decision-making process of medical tourist*
Source: Snyder et al. (2012).

responsible approach to medical tourism and if medical tourists engage in this process it is arguably the case that those supplying these services abroad will be more responsive to local responsibilities. In addition, Snyder et al. (2011a) suggest health equity impact ratings for medical tourism providers and facilitators – thus compelling providers to move beyond accreditation that assists in their marketing, toward addressing the impacts of the industry on local health care and outcomes.

Figure 5.4 Dentist, border town, Mexico: Many thousands of 'dental tourists' travel internationally for cheaper dental treatment. Photo: Brent Lovelock.

DISCUSSION POINT: PROCREATIVE TOURISM – REPRODUCTIVE TOURISM

The term procreative tourism was coined by Knoppers and Lebris (1991) and describes the practice of citizens exercising their personal reproductive choices by travelling to states that will provide services or treatments that are not available at home (Cohen 2006). Reproductive tourism is defined as 'the travelling by candidate service recipients from one institution, jurisdiction or country where treatment is not available in another institution, jurisdiction or country where they can obtain the kind of medically assisted reproduction they desire' (Pennings 2002: 337). In addition to services not being available, the high cost of fertility treatments is also another reason why people seek treatment in other countries. In addition, in many countries where fertility treatment is provided through the public health system the waiting lists are long. Waiting is not an option for some, particularly when age is a significant factor in the success rates for in vitro fertilisation. Procreative tourism in Europe is driven by all of these factors, but arguably the most compelling is that certain treatments are prohibited in some European countries. For example, Belgium and Italy are destination countries for a range of reproductive procedures, in particular in vitro fertilisation (IVF), as both of these countries have very little legislative or regulatory processes surrounding medically assisted reproduction. Procreative tourists from Germany and France, where legislation prohibits certain procedures, travel to Belgium and Italy for assistance they cannot procure at home (Cortez 2008: 77). Sometimes certain treatments are not available because they have not been approved by regulators and this has ensured flows from Europe, in particular Western Europe to the Middle East where more experimental technologies are used and not subject to regulatory control.

Others have observed that various forms of medical tourism are pursued because of the anonymity that distance accords the patient. For example, sex-change surgery and cosmetic surgery are often sought abroad for this reason (Connell 2006: 1097). This is also the case with reproductive tourism; where there is a cultural taboo associated with infertility people will travel for treatment and the motivation for travel can easily be concealed. For example, in New Zealand, tourists from Asia will seek treatment for infertility, not simply because the treatment is cheaper than it is at home, but also because the reasons for travel can be packaged as a honeymoon or holiday, and upon return the couple can be expecting their first child. The cultural shame of infertility ensures these tourists seek assisted conception away from home, where they can be anonymous and assistance can remain invisible (Lovelock pers. com).

Much of the ethical debate surrounding procreative tourism hinges on the notion of rights and in particular moral autonomy. Through this lens, procreative tourism allows people to avert moral conflict within their own society and to express their moral autonomy in another who allows the procedure they seek. Acceptance of procreative tourism is the expression of recognition of another's moral autonomy (Pennings 2002, 2004).

Sources

Pennings, G. (2002) 'Reproductive tourism as moral pluralism in motion', *Journal of Medical Ethics*, 28: 337–41.
— (2004) 'Legal harmonization and reproductive tourism in Europe', *Human Reproduction,* 19(12): 2689–94.

Assisted conception

Yet, moral autonomy has also been challenged by those who, as with organ trafficking, highlight the commodification of body parts that is associated with assisted conception, the potential for the exploitation of the poor and the gendered nature of exploitation where brokers secure commercial donors amongst the world's female poor. Here the commercial procurement of egg donors, sperm donors, gestational surrogates and access to sex-selection technology where selection is invariably in favour of male children are all practices that raise ethical concern. Sometimes referred to as 'third party reproduction', donation and surrogacy raise questions and ethical concerns about parental rights, the commodification of bodies, body parts, and babies (Martin 2009). More recently there is the emergent category of the 'travelling foreign egg donor', where young women seek economic mobility through the sale of eggs (body parts) (Heng 2007) or surrogacy (Malhotra and Malhotra 2009). Reproductive tourism highlights the uneven nature of globalisation, where the wealthy can access assistance internationally and the poor often play a role as 'third parties'. There is a large body of literature addressing the social, political and cultural implications of reproductive technologies and the ethical debate surrounding assisted conception. There is now also an emerging literature addressing reproductive tourism.

Further sources

Donchin, A. (2010) 'Reproductive tourism and the quest for global gender justice', *Bioethics*, 24(7): 323–32.
Inhorn, M.C. (2011) 'Globalization and gametes: reproductive "tourism", Islamic bioethics, and Middle Eastern modernity', *Anthropology and Medicine*, 18(1): 87–103.
Martin, L.J. (2009) 'Reproductive tourism in the age of globalization', *Globalizations*, 6(2): 249–63.

Discussion questions

1 Are there limits to procreative liberty?
2 Does the phrase reproductive tourism adequately convey this mobility and treatment?

CHAPTER REVIEW

This chapter has explored the complex issues and ethical dilemmas that arise from medical tourism. Various researchers and commentators have explored the key issues connected to this niche form of tourism, including: the implications for destination and departure health systems and health care services; the inequitable use of health care resources; the emergence of two-tiered health systems in destination countries which are already struggling to provide adequate public health care for the majority of their populations; increased investment in private care facilitated by public funding (tax incentives, cheap land); non-compliance of foreign investors and developers to agreed health care provisions of local populations; health risks for patients, public health risks posed by the spread of infectious disease; erosion of public health care for citizens in departure countries; hidden costs to health systems in departure countries arising from addressing post-operative complications of returning medical tourists; and issues connected to liability and malpractice. Medical tourism provokes a range of ethical concerns and complexities and underpinning these is the dominant concern that this form of tourism will contribute to or at the very least perpetuate existing global health inequities, both between departing and destination countries and within countries. There is also concern that this form of medical care, private care, will ultimately erode the provision of public health care within countries and impact persuasively on health outcomes for the vulnerable.

SUMMARY OF KEY TERMS

Medical tourism is variously defined as:

[a] practice, whereby individuals travel across national borders with the intention of receiving medical care.

(Snyder et al. 2011a).

The intentional pursuit of non-emergency medical treatment outside of a patient's home country that is likely to include a pre or post-operative stay abroad during which some tourist activities may be undertaken.

(Johnston et al. 2010: 3)

Transplant tourism is where a person undergoes a transplant abroad and is the recipient of an organ purchased through the illicit organ trade (Shimazono 2007). The buying and selling of organs and the associated transplant tourism is a major ethical issue for commercial living organ donors, clinicians and recipients.

Procreative tourism – reproductive tourism The practice of citizens exercising their personal reproductive choices by travelling to states that will provide reproductive treatments which are not available at home (Cohen 2006). Reproductive tourism is defined as 'the travelling by candidate service recipients from one institution, jurisdiction or country where treatment is not available in another institution, jurisdiction or country where they can obtain the kind of medically assisted reproduction they desire' (Pennings 2002: 337).

QUESTIONS FOR REFLECTION

1 What might the long-term implications of medical tourism be for developing countries?

2 If tourists apply Snyder et al.'s (2012) model, will this impact on some of the unethical practices in medical tourism?

3 What are the ethical implications of the world's poor being the dominant donors – for reproduction and organs? What conclusions would you draw after applying Schumann's framework (in Chapter 2)?

EXERCISE

Using Snyder et al.'s (2011a) ethical decision-making process, imagine that you are a medical tourist seeking abroad:

- Cosmetic surgery
- Bariatric surgery
- An organ transplant
- Reproductive treatment to assist conception
- Heart surgery
- Dental treatment
- A hip replacement.

With regard to all of these treatments what do you conclude with respect to your travel plans?

FURTHER READING

Connell, J. (2011) *Medical Tourism*, Wallingford: CABI.

Healy, C. (2009) 'Surgical tourism and the globalisation of healthcare', *Irish Journal of Medical Science*, 178(2): 125–7.

Jeevan, R. and Armstrong, A. (2008) 'Cosmetic tourism and the burden on the NHS', *Journal of Plastic, Reconstructive & Aesthetic Surgery*, 61(12): 1423–4.

NOTE

a The expression is attributed to Thomas Sydenham (1624–89) who was cited in a book by Thomas Inman (1860), *The Foundation for a New Theory and Practice of Medicine,* London: Reed and Pardon Printers.

REFERENCES

Bauer, K. (2003) 'Distributive justice and rural healthcare: a case for e-health', *International Journal of Applied Philosophy*, 17: 241–52.

Beauchamp, T.L. (2007) 'The "Four Principles" approach to health care ethics', in Ashcroft, R.E., Dawson, M.A., Draper, H. and McMillan J.R. (eds) *Principles of Health Care Ethics* (2nd edn), Chichester: John Wiley.

Biggins, S.W., Bambha, K., Terrault, N., Inadomi, J., Roberts, J.O. and Bass, N. (2009) 'Transplant tourism to China: the impact on domestic patient-care decisions', *Clinical Transplantation,* 23: 831–8.

Birch, D.W., Lan Vu, Karmali, S., Stoklossa, C.J. and Sharma, A.M. (2010) 'Medical tourism in bariatric surgery', *American Journal of Surgery,* 199: 604–8.

Bramstedt, K.A. and Xu, J. (2007) 'Checklist: passport, plane ticket, organ transplant', *American Journal of Transplantation,* 7: 1698–701.

Budiani-Saberi, D.A. and Delmonico, F.L. (2008) 'Organ trafficking and transplant tourism: a commentary on the global realities', *American Journal of Transplantation,* 8: 925–9.

Burkett, L. (2007) 'Medical tourism. Concerns, benefits, and the American legal perspective', *Journal of Legal Medicine,* 28: 223–45.

Carabello, L. (2008) 'A medical tourism primer for U.S. Physicians', *Journal of Medical Practice Management,* 23(5): 291–4.

Chanda, R. (2002) 'Trade in health services', *Bulletin World Health Organization,* 80: 158–63.

Chee, H.L. (2007) *Medical Tourism in Malaysia: International Movement of Healthcare Consumers and the Commodification of Healthcare,* Singapore: Asia Research Institute.

Cohen, J. (2006) 'Procreative tourism and reproductive freedom', *Reproductive Biomedicine Online,* 13(1): 145–6.

Connell, J. (2006) 'Medical tourism: sea, sun, sand and … surgery', *Tourism Management,* 27: 1093–100.

— (2008) 'Tummy tucks and the Taj Mahal? Medical tourism and the globalization of health care', in Woodside, A.G. and Wallingford, M.D. (eds) *Tourism Management: Analysis, Behaviour and Strategy,* Wallingford: CABI, pp. 232–44.

— (2011) *Medical Tourism,* Wallingford: CABI.

Cortez, N. (2008) 'Patient without borders: the emerging global market for patients and the evolution of modern health care', *Indiana Law Journal,* 83: 71.

Crooks, V., Kingsbury, P., Snyder, J. and Johnston, R. (2010) 'What is known about the patient's experience of medical tourism? A scoping review', *BMC Health Services Research,* 10: 266–77.

Donchin, A. (2010) 'Reproductive tourism and the quest for global gender justice', *Bioethics,* 24(7): 323–32.

Evans, R.W. (2008) 'Ethnocentrism is an unacceptable rationale for health care policy: a critique of transplant tourism position statements', *American Journal of Transplantation,* 8: 1089–95.

Gill, J., Madhira, B.R., Gjertson, D., Lipshutz, G., Cecka, J.M., Pham, P.T., et al. (2008) 'Transplant tourism in the United States: a single-center experience', *Clinical Journal of the American Society of Nephrology,* 3: 1820–8.

Gupta, Amit Sen (2007) 'Medical tourism in India: winners and losers. Editorial', *Indian Journal of Medical Ethics,* 5(1).

Healy, C. (2009) 'Surgical tourism and the globalisation of healthcare', *Irish Journal of Medical Science,* 178(2): 125–7.

Heng, B.C. (2007) 'Regulatory safeguards needed for the travelling foreign egg donor', *Human Reproduction,* 3571–2.

Hermans, H. (2000) 'Cross-border health care in the European Union, recent legal implications of Decker and Kohll', *Journal of Evaluation in Clinical Practice,* 6: 431–9.

Hopkins, L., Labonte, R., Runnels, V. and Packer, C. (2010) 'Medical tourism today: What is the state of existing knowledge?', *Journal of Public Health Policy,* 31(2): 185–98.

Inhorn, M.C. (2011) 'Globalization and gametes: reproductive "tourism", Islamic bioethics, and Middle Eastern modernity', *Anthropology and Medicine,* 18(1): 87–103.

Jeevan, R. and Armstrong, A. (2008) 'Cosmetic tourism and the burden on the NHS', *Journal of Plastic, Reconstructive & Aesthetic Surgery,* 61(12): 1423–4.

Jesitus, J. (2006) 'Safari surgery', *Cosmetic Surgical Times,* 9: 1–14.

Johnston, R., Crooks, V.A., Snyder, J. and Kingsbury, P. (2010) 'What is known about the effects of medical tourism in destination and departure countries? A scoping review', *International Journal for Equity in Health,* 9(24).

Kangas, B. (2002) 'Therapeutic itineraries in a global world: Yemenis and their search for biomedical treatment abroad', *Medical Anthropology,* 21: 35–78.

Knoppers, B.M. and Lebris, S. (1991) 'Recent advances in medically assisted conception: legal, ethical and social issues', *American Journal of Law and Medicine,* 329.

Kokubo, A. (2009) 'The interaction of the international society concerning kidney transplants – A consideration of diseased kidney transplants in Japan and transplant tourism over the world', *Legal Medicine,* 11: S393–S395.

Kumarasamy, K.K., Toleman, M.A., Walsh, T.R. *et al.* (2010) 'Emergence of a new antibiotic resistance mechanism in India, Pakistan, and the UK: a molecular, biological and epidemiological study', *The Lancet Infectious Diseases,* 10: 597–602.

Leng, C. (2007) *Medical Tourism in Malaysia: International Movement of Healthcare Consumers and the Commodification of Healthcare,* Asia Research Institute, Working Paper Series No. 83. National University of Singapore. Available at <http:/ssrn.com/abstract = 1317163> (Accessed 13 August 2012).

Malhotra, A. and Malhotra, R. (2009) 'Commercial surrogacy in India', *International Family Law,* March: 9–11.

Martin, L.J. (2009) 'Reproductive tourism in the age of globalization', *Globalizations,* 6(2): 249–63.

Mudur, G. (2003) 'India plans to expand private sector in healthcare review', *British Medical Journal,* 326: 520–5.

Newman, M.I., Camberos, A.E. and Ascherman, J. (2005) 'Mycobacteria abscessus outbreak in US patients linked to offshore surgicenter', *Annals of Plastic Surgery,* 55(1): 107–10.

Pachanee, C. and Wibulpolprasert, S. (2006) 'Incoherent policies on universal coverage of health insurance and promotion of international trade in health services in Thailand', *Health Policy Plan,* 21: 310–18.

Pennings, G. (2007) 'Ethics without boundaries: medical tourism', in R.E. Ashcroft, A. Dawson, H. Draper and J.R. McMillan (eds) *Principles of Health Care Ethics,* 2nd edn, Chichester: John Wiley.

Pocock, N.S. and Kai Hong Phua. (2011) 'Medical tourism and policy implications for health systems: a conceptual framework from a comparative study of Thailand, Singapore and Malaysia', *Globalization and Health,* 7: 12.

Scheper-Hughes, N. (2002) 'The ends of the body – commodity fetishism and the global traffic in organs', *School of Advanced International Studies Review,* 22(1): 61–80.

Schrecker, T. and Labonte, R. (2004) 'Training the brain drain: a challenge to public health systems in Southern Africa', *International Journal of Occupational and Environmental Health,* 10: 409–15.

Shimazono, Y. (2007) 'The state of the international organ trade: a provisional picture based on integration of available information', *Bulletin of the World Health Organization,* 85(12): 955–62.

Snyder, J., Crooks, V., and Johnston, R. (2011a) 'Perceptions of the ethics of medical tourism: comparing patient and academic perspectives', *Public Health Ethics,* 11 December, 1–9. Oxford University Press.

Snyder, J., Crooks, V., Adams, K., Kingsbury, P., and Johnston, R. (2011b) ' "The patient's physician one-step removed": the evolving roles of medical tourism facilitators'. *Journal of Medical Ethics,* 37: 530–4.

Snyder, J., Crooks, V., Johnson, R., and Kingsbury, P. (2012) 'Beyond sun, sand, and stitches: assigning responsibility for the harms of medical tourism', *Bioethics* online, Blackwell publishing: Wiley OnLine Publishing.

Turner, L. (2007) 'First world health care at third world prices: globalization, bioethics and medical tourism', *Biosocieties,* 2: 303–25.

— (2008) 'Medical Tourism' initiatives should exclude commercial organ transplantation', *Journal of the Royal Society of Medicine,* 101(8): 391–4.

Wibulpolprasert, S. and Pengbaibon, P. (2003) 'Integrated strategies to tackle the inequitable distribution of doctors in Thailand: four decades of experience', *Human Resources for Health,* 1(12).

Available at <http:// www.human-resources-health.com/content/1/1/12> (Accessed 12 May 2012).

Wibulpolprasert, S. and Pachanee, C.A. (2008) 'Trade in health services in the ASEAN context', in C. Blouin, J. Heymann and L. Drager (eds) *Trade and Health: Seeking Common Ground,* Quebec: McGill-Queens Open University Press.

Wolff, J. (2007) 'Passport to cheaper health care?', *Good Housekeeping,* 245: 190.

World Health Organisation (WHO) (2007) The social determinants of health, report (Kelly, M.P., Morgan, A., Bonnetoy, J., Butt, J. and Bergman, V.), Geneva: WHO.

— (2008) *Closing the Gap in a Generation: Health Equity through action on the Social Determinants of Health*, Final Report of the Commission on Social Determinants of Health, Geneva: WHO.

Zargooshi, J. (2001) 'Quality of life of Iranian kidney "donors"', *Journal Urology*, 166: 1790–9.

6 | Sex tourism

'Sex tourism at its most crass or romanticised is literally a classic moment in international relations. Pleasure and danger come together with transgressions across the borders of power along First World–Third World, Rich–Poor, Male–Female (often), old–young (often) in a peculiar and unstable combination of sexuality, nationalism and economic power.'[a]

LEARNING OBJECTIVES

After reading this chapter you will be able to:

- Critically appraise the ethical and moral issues surrounding sex tourism.
- Understand the relationship between sex, tourism, sex tourism and child sex tourism.
- Understand why some regions in the world have become dominant destinations for sex tourists.
- Apply a number of ethical frameworks to sex tourism.

6.1 INTRODUCTION

Romance and sexual opportunity lie at the heart of many advertisements for travel, with people clad in scanty beach attire locked in embraces on beaches at sunset frequently used to promote the 'tour' product and the possibilities of this form of consumption in this destination. Yet sexual encounters are not necessarily always happenstance and the tourism industry has also exploited and relied on a more direct form of delivery, via prostitution. In terms of morals and ethics, sex tourism like no other area in tourism invites considerable controversy, outrage and moral condemnation. However, this outrage can obscure our ability to critically consider the nature of sex tourism and to explore why, how and in what contexts sex is transformed into such a lucrative product for the tourist market. Emotivism and intuitionism offer a poor starting place for the consideration of the ethics of sex tourism; what is necessary is to apply critically various ethical frameworks and to address systematically the fundamental inequities that underpin sex tourism, child sex tourism and the trafficking of women and children for prostitution.

This chapter introduces some of the key issues in sex tourism and emergent ethical and moral concerns. We will consider the socio-economic underpinnings that serve as determinants for the growth of sex tourism markets, the links between the trafficking of women and children domestically and internationally, and prostitution. We will explore how various ethical frameworks can help facilitate critical reflection on this growing sector within the tourism industry and how global inequality sustains, perpetuates and enables the growth of the sex tourism industry.

6.2 TOURISM AND SEX

> Sex tourism may be defined as tourism where the main purpose or motivation of at least part of the trip is to consummate sexual relations.
>
> (Ryan and Hall 2001: ix)

Sex tourism in tourism studies did not attract serious research attention until the 1970s. The industry comprises different sectors, from the formally organised supply of sexual services that can be pre-arranged before travel to informal supply where the tourist makes their own arrangements on arrival. While bodies are for sale, other sex commodities usually meet voyeuristic and or vicarious requirements. The sex market can be differentiated in this way domestically and internationally. There is formalised work for some and casualised work for others. The sex worker labour market is supplied locally and comprises significant numbers of migrant workers – some voluntary, and others 'trafficked'. The migrant and trafficked workers are also invariably women and children. Trafficked workers are involuntarily mobile, sold and coerced and often bonded into working in the sex industry. Depending on location, prostitution is legal or illegal and in both contexts there are often significant health issues, for both the sex worker and client. In developing countries, the sex workers are invariably poor and have had limited access, if any, to education, health services or adequate housing.

With the spread of HIV/AIDS, research interest increased in this field during the 1980s and 1990s, with some arguing that this interest was an outcome of the serious health implications posed by HIV for the male tourist or that at least HIV/AIDS served as a catalyst for thinking about sex tourism (Ryan and Hall 2001: 48). However, HIV/AIDS also presented a significant economic threat for those countries whose development had become increasingly linked to sex tourism – to warn of HIV/AIDS could also mean to scare off customers and lose revenue (see Cohen 1988 for a fuller discussion of the impact in Thailand). Sexually transmitted disease has always been a risk for those purchasing sex in tourist destinations. While sex tourism is usually understood to involve male tourists seeking sexual services from women in the destination country, it can also involve male prostitution, where women tourists seek services from men, men from men, and men from children of either sex (Ryan and Hall 2001: xii).

There is now a large literature addressing sex tourism, encompassing: the issue of human rights and sex tourism, justice and sex tourism, the trafficking of women and children, sex

Figure 6.1 *Billboard advocating awareness of sexually transmitted diseases in Africa. Photo: Brent Lovelock.*

tourism and public health, sex tourism and social inequality, sex tourism and romance, the political economy of sex tourism, sex tourism and development, sex tourism-criminality and other illicit trade. It is beyond the scope of this chapter to address all of these areas in any detail – however, there is considerable overlap between each of these areas with respect to emergent ethical and moral debate.

'Sex tourism' can be defined as varieties of leisure travel where part of the purpose is to procure sexual services (Wonders and Michalowski 2001: 545). It involves: a convergence of prostitution and tourism and the production and consumption of sexual services which are locally and globally sustained. As Wonders and Michalowski (2001: 546) observe, sex tourism is a transnational business, like any other. Increasing mobility is also central to sex tourism where suppliers and consumers are mobile, but often for different reasons. The tourist may seek new experiences, including sex while abroad, but in contrast the sex worker may be providing this service because it is the only form of work she or he can procure. Migration has become increasingly feminised and with this feminisation it is not only the factors that push women to be mobile (poverty, deteriorating socio-economic conditions in developing countries and barriers to employment at home and in countries they migrate to) but also the pull of the tourism industry which is a major employer of women in various service roles – from hotel cleaners to prostitutes – and where the production and consumption of sexual services is a significant and growing component of the tourism industry.

Sex tourism is a multimillion dollar industry, estimated to be worth 'at least $20 billion a year' (Herman 1995: 5 in Wonders and Michalowski 2001: 549). Sex tourists are predominantly men and sex workers are overwhelmingly poor women and poor children. Sex tourism is not just gendered it is also racialised. Sex tourism does not differ greatly from tourism more generally, if tourism involves experiencing that which the tourist's country of origin has promoted as being on offer for consumption in the destination country – and the destination attempts to provide that which they think will be consumed. Sex simply becomes yet another tourist product. And while the objectification of the 'other' is often central to the tourist experience, in sex tourism the objectification of the other and others' *bodies* – in particular the bodies of women and children and to a lesser extent men – is central to the process of commodification and ultimately consumption.

> Whether prostitutes are displayed in windows (like clothes on mannequins) or appear in hotel lobbies (as though they are complementary beverages), bodies increasingly are used as simulacra to represent 'something else' to the leisure tourist; prostitutes appear as 'minor wives', 'girl-friends', 'exotic others' or 'sex toys'.
>
> (Wonders and Michalowski 2001: 551)

With sex tourism the destination becomes the body of 'the other'. While many people have moral issues about the sale of sex, as Hall (1996) has argued the key ethical issues with sex tourism are the gendered and economic inequalities that enable and reproduce exploitative relationships and the facilitation of an industry that relies on inequity. For women and children born into poverty, their body may be the only 'asset' they can offer for sale in a marketplace that either does not value highly other forms of labour or where potential for the sale of their labour is either limited or not available. The relationship between the client and the person providing sexual services often mirrors in microcosm the power differential between developing and developed nations (Hall 1996: 119; Smith and Duffy 2003: 92). The excessive global inequalities generated by capitalism and the associated objectification of a range of bodies into a racial and gendered hierarchy underpin the sex tourism industry. If the sex tourist is searching for difference the destination is the body of the 'exotic other' and this 'other' is invariably hierarchically disadvantaged, locally and globally (Wonders and Michalowski 2001: 551; Rojec and Urry 1997: 17). The privileged tourist can afford to seek encounters abroad and realise their 'fantasies' – although, as O'Connell-Davidson (2004: 40) observes, encounters with those who are structurally less advantaged could equally be sought at home, and yet

> we rarely see ordinary, middle-aged men and women flirting with homeless teenagers who sit on the pavements begging for spare change, or inviting them out to dinner and then back home to bed ... [this disparity ensures that we are then required] to think about the connections between travel, sex and race, and to consider what is being consumed within tourism more generally.

Ethical issue: When a monetary value is placed on the human body the person's moral identity is compromised as they are reduced to an object – which can be bought and sold and thereby become subject to control, exploitation and violence.

6.3 SOCIAL INEQUALITY: THE POLITICAL ECONOMY OF SEX TOURISM

"The economic and political position of tourists could not be more different from that of locals they come in contact with in developing countries. Even the working-class, budget tourist from Britain or Germany, for instance, is in a position to spend about as much on a package holiday in Thailand or the Caribbean as most ordinary local and marginal people working in the formal or informal tourism economy will earn in a year. This means that tourists, as well as being able to afford to consume sexual services if they so choose, are in a position to freely dispense gifts and sums of money which, though negligible to them, represent significant benefits to the average local person… Small wonder then, that many locals, both adult and child, seek to befriend tourists and/or to enter into sexual relationships with them".

(O'Connell-Davidson 2004: 39)

Sex tourism occurs in all countries in the world and while Asia is generally acknowledged as a region and major destination for those seeking sex, the selling of women and children into prostitution is a global phenomenon. Research on sex tourism and child sexual exploitation has tended to focus on South East Asia, in particular Thailand and the Philippines and more recently Vietnam and Cambodia; also South Asia, in particular India, Nepal and Sri Lanka; and in North Asia, particularly China. In the West, research has also documented sex trade in Australia, Canada, the United States and Western Europe. Research in other parts of the world is less common, but there is a significant sex trade industry in Eastern Europe, Latin America and Africa (Flowers 2001: 148) with the trafficking of women and children linked to this industry. Very often sex tourism destinations in poorer countries and regions offer the tourist something they cannot have at home and at a cheaper rate. Tourists availing themselves of these sexual experiences describe these destinations as a 'Sexual Paradise' or 'Disneyland' – yet as O'Connell-Davidson and Sánchez Taylor (1999) also observe these sexual lands/heavens have been created and these creations are invariably linked to global economic relations, international debt, economic development policy (local and international) and the structural adjustments many developing countries have to make when shifting from subsistence economies to fully industrialised economies. Invariably these shifts have resulted in significant urban migration, high unemployment, insufficient or non-existent welfare provisions, currency depreciation and a surplus of cheap labour. All of these conditions impact negatively on the poor, many of whom are in a position of having to address their low-waged employment (or lack of) through opportunities in the informal economic sector, of which the informal tourism economy plays an increasingly important role (Beddoe 1998; O'Connell-Davidson 2004: 38).

Sex tourism is also not a new phenomenon; while the contemporary scale of the industry has undoubtedly been facilitated by mass communication and commercial air travel the industry arguably predates these developments in most regions in the world. Research on sex tourism in Thailand provides an illustration and challenges the notion that it is a recent industry and an outcome of increasing numbers of foreigners visiting Thailand. As Montgomery (2008) and others observe, sex tourism in Thailand has a much longer history and is associated with the trafficking of women and slavery in the region more generally, not only between countries but also within (Truong 1990; Leheny 1995). If anything the industry became more formalised and visible internationally during and following the Vietnam War. The Vietnam War brought with it an influx of American servicemen on leave which enabled the growth and formalisation of the provision of sexual services to foreigners (Taylor 2010). After the end of the war and the departure of the servicemen the infrastructure remained in place and enabled the continuation of the industry which provided (as it always had) for both locals and foreigners but arguably on a bigger scale. In addition, Thai women were now internationally stereotypically recognised as docile, compliant and beautiful and these characteristics defined the sex product available for consumption in Thailand (Montgomery 2008). By the 1980s tourism revenues became increasingly important to development initiatives in Thailand and there was implicit support for sex tourism and child sex tourism from the government. The sex tourism industry in Thailand provides an insight into the gendered nature of the industry and a particular view of female sexuality that pivots on compliance and docility and childlike innocence, and for the foreigner this is combined with understandings of the 'exotic other' informed by orientalism (Said 1978). This feminised stereotype also ensures that child sex tourism both complements adult sex tourism and does not appear as an anomaly in the 'market' place. In addition, prostitution in Thailand is well established in relation to the domestic market, where it has been estimated 75 per cent of Thai men have had sex with a prostitute (Sachs 1994). It is also the case that those that consume are not always paedophiles, but rather prostitute users in general (Glover 2006).

More generally, the rest and recuperation (R & R) form of entertainment facilitated by war in South East Asia provided the foundations for contemporary sex tourism in this region. As Taylor (2010: 50) observes:

> Entry into the tourist market for many South-east Asian countries rested on exploiting the existing entertainment infrastructure created by the US military for quick foreign exchange. Generous incentives were given to foreign investors which resulted in many of the girlie bars, go-go bars and sex floor shows being foreign owned and run. The red light areas and brothel districts that became most famous among tourists were those developed by this kind of 'sexpatriate' involvement and investment.

DISCUSSION POINT: SEX TOURISM AND RIGHTS

What are the consequences of sex tourism? What are the costs? Are there any benefits? Sex tourism facilitates economic development through increases in foreign exchange. However, it does so at the cost of human dignity, health and wellbeing and as an industry underpins the majority of human trafficking in the world and therefore modern forms of slavery.

Sex tourism and tourism's relationship with prostitution has generated increasing research attention over the last two decades. In many respects the bodies of women and children providing sexual services to tourists for payment can also be thought about in terms of the politics of the body, where

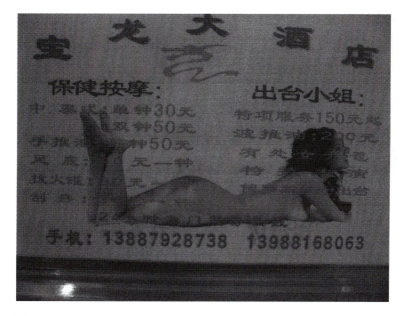

Figure 6.2 *Sex menu in a hotel in Myanmar catering to cross-border Chinese sex tourists. Photo: Brent Lovelock.*

the body becomes a site where the international and the personal converge – at times painfully (Pettman 1997: 93).

The ethics of sex tourism has received relatively little direct attention but is addressed more obliquely through considerations of the morality of prostitution and the parallel issues that emerge in relation to selling sex, i.e. whether this is simply another form of labour or an abuse of human rights. As Pettman (1997: 01) observes:

> Arguments have long raged over whether the prostitute – or the institution of prostitution is immoral; whether prostitution is an example, or emblematic, of women's oppression; whether it is a form of economic exploitation, or necessity, or opportunity; whether the state should criminalise, regulate or remove itself from prostitution.

But how do these debates relate to women, children, boys and men who provide sexual services for payment to tourists? Much of the debate has tended to hinge on women's rights/human rights/children's rights – but as Truong (1990) argues the rights rhetoric does not address the complex issues involved in sex tourism (in Thailand and elsewhere) as it often neglects the specificities of the full range of cultural, economic, social and political issues and fails to address differences within and between localities.

Ethical thinking needs to recognise 'that the particular dwells within a shifting universal' (Plummer 2010: 238). Western thought and modern economic philosophy emphasises an individualist ideology where individuals are conceived of as living in a world of infinite choices. The women, children, boys and men who provide sexual services to sex tourists often do not come from societies that subscribe to individualism, rather they live in societies where choice is recognised as 'rightly' collectively determined and constrained. However, we need to ask what differences matter and what happens if we let difference become more important than seeking universal justice?

Human dignity is at the core of modern liberal democratic thought and it is usually taken to involve the idea of equal worth between: rich and poor, rural and urban, female and male, where all are taken to be equally deserving of respect, by simply being human (Plummer 2010). With respect to sex tourism how can social justice and ethics of care frameworks help us address ethical dilemmas?

Discussion questions

1 Does sex tourism involve the violation of anybody's rights?
2 Does engaging in sex tourism infringe on other people's rights?
3 Does engaging in sex tourism further the rights of others?
4 In terms of justice ethics, are the benefits and costs shared equally between all parties?

There are two dominant moral positions with respect to prostitution (which have been applied to human trafficking):

The moral view of the abolitionists is one where prostitution is considered inherently violative of the human body, regardless of choice or consent. It is taken to be inherently violent and exploitative. Thus, commercial sex of any variety violates the condition that to be moral, sex must be non-instrumental and non-harmful (Peach 2005: 115). Abolitionists stress prostitution violates human rights and should not be distinguished from trafficking. The abolitionists also contend it should be illegal.

The moral view of the reformists contends that prostitution should be defined as 'sex work' and that in defining it in this way the work of prostitutes can be visible and recognised in law, both with respect to labour law and human rights. Most reformists distinguish between trafficking and prostitution, but some are more cautious about emphasising that those in one group have no choice and those in the other have choices. Reformists oppose moralistic approaches as they contend this simply divides people and allows people to justify punishing those in prostitution without impunity (Peach 2005). Most reformists hold the liberal view that prostitution is not inherently immoral.

Further reading

Peach, L. (2005) '"Sex slaves" or "sex workers"? Cross-cultural and comparative religious perspectives on sexuality, subjectivity, and moral identity in anti-sex trafficking discourse', *Culture and Religion: An Interdisciplinary Journal*, 6(1): 107–34.

6.4 CHILD PROSTITUTION – CHILD SEX TOURISM

Child sex tourism is defined as the sexual abuse and exploitation of children through their involvement in (a) prostitution and sex tourism, (b) paedophilia-related child abuse, (c) pornography (Beddoe et al. 2001: 11).

In 1996, the *First World Congress Against the Commercial Sexual Exploitation of Children* was held in Stockholm, where the resulting declaration and proposed action stressed the following:

> The commercial sexual exploitation of children is a fundamental violation of children's rights. It comprises sexual abuse by the adult and remuneration in cash or kind to the child or third person or persons. The child is treated as a sexual object and as a commercial object. The commercial sexual exploitation of children constitutes a form of coercion and violence against children, and amounts to forced labour and a contemporary form of slavery.

(cited in Beddoe et al. 2001: 17)

And from the *Code of Ethical Conduct* (World Tourism Organization 1999):

> The exploitation of human beings in any form, particularly sexual, especially when applied to children, conflicts with the fundamental aims of tourism and is the negation of tourism; as such, in accordance with international law, it should be energetically combatted with the cooperation of all the States concerned and penalised without concession by the national legislation of both the countries visited and the countries of the perpetrators of these acts, even when they are carried out abroad.

The child sex tourism industry involves domestic and international tourists and foreigners who have temporary residence; it often operates in conjunction with the local sex industry and can be supported and patronised by locals (Beddoe et al. 2001). Contact with this industry can be arranged formally, but increasingly it is arranged informally and takes place in restaurants, bars, hotels, guesthouses and other places of accommodation for tourists. The commercial sexual exploitation of children is associated with poverty and child sex tourism and trafficking often takes place in conjunction with other criminal social practices. Children of poverty, children from rural backgrounds where rural labour no longer offers employment opportunities, children who are marginal because of their gender (in particular girls in societies where boys are more highly valued), children who are disabled, orphaned children or children from families who can no longer support them are particularly vulnerable to trafficking and being lured or sold into the sex industry. While men are the primary consumers, not all are tourists. The consumers are heterogeneous and include: paedophiles, sex tourists and locals, and prostitute users (Beddoe et al. 2001).

Early research in the 1980s, in Thailand, the Philippines, Sri Lanka and Taiwan, documented increasing numbers of children in tourism-related prostitution. The link between child sex tourism and sex tourism has meant that those who seek to abolish child sex tourism need to engage with those in the sex tourism industry. It is estimated that children forced into sexual exploitation in Asia number at least 1 million (note data collection methods are controversial; De Cock 2007).

There have been a number of international campaigns to prevent child sex tourism with the NGO End Child Prostitution and Trafficking (ECPAT) playing a key role in raising consciousness internationally about child sex tourism. Throughout the 1980s and 1990s ECPAT campaigned to raise consciousness in destination countries and increasingly applied pressure on various foreign governments to introduce extraterritorial laws for child sex offences committed abroad (O'Connell-Davidson 2004). By the late 1990s, 20 countries had introduced extraterritorial laws for child sex offences committed abroad, yet under these laws very few offenders have been prosecuted. Campaigns also focused on those who arranged formal child sex tours and profited from doing so. These campaigns resulted in Britain passing the 1996 *Sexual Offences (Conspiracy and Incitement)* legislation which addressed those who organised sex tours, and in Australia the 1994 *Crimes (Child Sex Tourism) Amendment Act* was passed which addressed those who were responsible for organising sex tours where the purpose was to engage with minors while abroad (O'Connell-Davidson 2004; Ryan and Hall 2001).

However, it has been observed that these pieces of legislation suffer from poor or insufficiently defined understandings of what constitutes sex tourism or child sex tourism (O'Connell-Davidson 2004; Ryan and Hall 2001). As O'Connell-Davidson (2004: 35) observes, there are no 'paedophile package tour operators' and there is not necessarily a clear line between child sex tourism and sex tourism or tourism more generally. Campaigners tend to separate out child sex tourism from other forms of sex tourism (within which it is often embedded) while also divorcing the practice from the social and economic and political conditions within which it thrives. Ultimately, failing to address the considerable overlap between sex tourism, tourism and child sex tourism and the fundamental economic inequalities that underpin the industry, means that these campaigns will have limited effectiveness (O'Connell-Davidson 2004). Legislation alone cannot determine ethical tourism; as Smith and Duffy (2003) argue more fruitful outcomes might result from a move toward the idea of a *responsive ethics*, where tourists learn to empathise with 'the other' and engage in an ethical relationships with 'the other'.

6.5 GUIDELINES AND DECLARATIONS

The industry has responded with guidelines for travel operators and declarations condemning child sex tourism (Beddoe et al. 2001). The UN World Tourism Organization (UNWTO) has held two Congresses against the commercial sexual exploitation of children, in 1996 and 2001. In 1996, the UNWTO set up a task force to address the sexual exploitation of children in tourism and has engaged in a number of projects since 2000. There are a range of issues: (1) addressing the sexual exploitation of children means addressing heterogeneous manifestations – with those who offend also comprising a heterogeneous grouping: diverse ethnicities, men and women (although men remain dominant), domestic and international tourists, locals, those who are part of paedophile rings, those on organised tours for sex and those who are operating seemingly independently; (2) some legitimate tourist businesses serve as fronts for child sex tourism; (3) child sex tourism it is often associated with organised crime; and, (4) these children are vulnerable to sexually transmitted disease, including HIV (Beddoe et al. 2001: 26; O'Connell-Davidson 2004; Montgomery 2008: 910; Tepelus 2008).

Industry schemes and initiatives

There have been a range of industry initiatives which include schemes that focus on youth training and international hotels, where training is provided for high school graduates from poor backgrounds (Tepelus 2008). For example, the Youth Challenge International (YCI) scheme is a programme run by London-based international business leaders in conjunction with international tourism partners and currently operates in eight countries including: Brazil, Ethiopia, Thailand, Philippines, Indonesia, Australia, Romania and Poland. Programmes such as this offer an alternative route into the tourism industry for young people at risk. ChildWise is another example of a non-governmental organisation which focuses on eliminating child sex tourism (CST) through focusing on the destinations to which Australians travel. In conjunction with ECPAT International they are working toward the elimination of the sexual exploitation of children. ECPAT began in Thailand and now has 62 countries involved in the campaign against child prostitution. ChildWise works on the assumption that CST for Australians often occurs outside of formalised tourist structures in destination countries and thus is beyond most Codes of Practice. An education-based programme, it targets those working in the industry, allowing them to readily identify children at risk of sexual exploitation. World Vision also runs a deterrent campaign which raises awareness and stresses the legal implications for those who engage in child sex tourism. Industry has also developed a multi-sector code: the Code of Conduct for the Protection of Children from Sexual Exploitation in Travel and Tourism. Those that endorse this Code make a commitment to educating their staff about CST, incorporating joint repudiation clauses into their contracts with suppliers, working with key persons to prevent CST and reporting on the measures they have implemented annually (Tepelus 2008: 106).

In addition there have been a number of government-led campaigns against CST. UNICEF continues to play a role as the UN agency responsible for advocating the protection of children's rights. The Organisation for Security and Cooperation in Europe (OSCE) works from the premise that the tourism industry is uniquely placed to play an instrumental role in raising awareness and combating both trafficking and the sexual exploitation of children (Tepelus 2008). A range of international organisations have documented child sex tourism and generated guidelines and educational materials, including the International Labour Organization (ILO), the UN Office on Drugs and Crime (UNODC) and the International Organization for Migration (IOM). The wide range of organisations points to the interconnection linking migration, trafficking, criminal activity, labour supply and exploitation with child sex tourism and sex tourism more generally and the global nature of the problem.

Child sex tourism does not occur in a vacuum. Montgomery's (2008) ethnographic research in Thailand demonstrates that the child prostitutes turned to prostitution because they had very little choice. They are invariably economically marginal and seek work in the growing tourism sector only to find that prostitution pays better than any other form of labour. She observes:

> Much of the Thai sex tourism industry is concerned with selling juvenility, encouraging men to think their sexual partners are young, innocent and childlike … there is a very thin

line between those men who hate paedophiles and those who are prepared to have sex with children.

(Montgomery 2008: 914)

Thai women are often contrasted as the opposite to Western women, the 'othering' involves a claim that unlike Western women they are innocent, pliable, faithful, beautiful, little – and childlike. As Montgomery (2008: 914) observes:

> What many sex tourists fail to realise is that the artlessness, 'freshness' and childlike innocence that they most admire in Thai prostitutes are entirely commercialised. These women are fulfilling a fantasy and doing what is expected of them, and it is for that, as much as for sex, that they get paid.

These issues are not just specific to Thailand; other destinations in Asia and other regions in the world also have significant numbers of children in prostitution serving the tourist sector. All of these destinations seek to meet tourist expectations with respect to the sex products on offer and all are able to meet the demands because of the systemic issue of poverty and the limited opportunities for the average family to meet their daily needs.

Useful websites

ECPAT: A global network of organisations and individuals for the elimination of child prostitution, child pornography and the trafficking of children for sexual exploitation. www.ecpat.net.ei

ChildWise's primary purpose is to prevent the abuse of children before it happens. www.childwise.net/

United Nations Children's Fund. www.unicef.org/

International Labour Organization. www.ilo.org/

International Organization for Migration. www.iom.int/

United Nations Office on Drugs and Crime. www.unodc.org/

The Code of Conduct for the Protection of Children from Sexual Exploitation in Travel and Tourism can be found at: www.thecode.org/

6.6 TRAFFICKING OF WOMEN AND CHILDREN

The trafficking of women and children has been recognised as a global concern since the late nineteenth century. Trafficking invariably involves traffickers tricking or coercing women and children into travelling either to another region or country – they are invariably offered a better life but this promise is never realised. For those who are trafficked they often experience rape, beatings, intimidation and debt bondage which keeps them bound to their trafficker, sometimes for years.

Trafficking is defined by the United Nations General Assembly (2000) as:

> The recruitment, transportation, transfer, harbouring or receipt of persons, by means of the threat or use of force or tougher forms of coercion, of abduction, of fraud, or deception, or the abuse of power or of a position of vulnerability or of the giving or receiving of payments or benefits to achieve the consent of a person, for the purpose of exploitation. Exploitation

includes, at a minimum, the exploitation of the prostitution of others or other forms of sexual exploitation, forced labour or services, slavery or practices similar to slavery, servitude or the removal of organs.

(UNODC 2006: 7)

Trafficking and child sex tourism are linked, where tourism businesses can be used, intentionally or not, to facilitate both trafficking and host sites for child sex tourism. Trafficking can involve crossing domestic and international borders. International legal frameworks state that children under the age of 18 years cannot give valid consent – any recruitment, transportation or receiving of children for the purpose of exploitation is trafficking (UNODC 2007; Tepelus 2008). It is estimated that approximately 1.2 million children are trafficked every year (UNICEF 2007); child prostitution is estimated to involve 2 million children and Asia is the centre for child prostitution with most of the prostitutes girls under the age of 16 (Glover 2006; UNICEF 2007). Children become particularly vulnerable during times of natural disaster or political unrest; for example the tsunami which hit South Asia in 2005 resulted in many children being orphaned and subsequently trafficked and sold into the child sex industry (Cotter 2009: 494). In post-earthquake Haiti, the trafficking of children for prostitution and illegal adoption also took place, and the war in Bosnia and Herzegovina in the late 1990s also led to thousands of women and children being trafficked from Eastern Europe and to Bosnia for bonded prostitution (Ryan and Hall 2001: 126).

DISCUSSION POINT

Human trafficking has an estimated value of over US$32 billion a year (ILO) and is thought to be the second biggest industry in the world.

- 80 per cent of those trafficked are women and girls
- 50 per cent of those trafficked are minors
- 42 per cent of those recruiting victims for trafficking are women
- The average age of entry into prostitution or sexual exploitation is 12 years of age.

Useful website

http://www.humantrafficking.org

A web resource for combating human trafficking.

Why does this multimillion dollar industry continue to prosper when there has been a range of international conventions and treaties which condemn this practice and the associated forms of exploitation and slavery?

Most of the ethical arguments against the trafficking of children and women for prostitution (and those who end up working in the sex tourism industry) are rights-based arguments and arguments that stress justice and responsible tourism. Less sustainable are ethical arguments based on hedonism (where a worthwhile action is one that gives pleasure and the greatest good is connected to the pleasure experienced by the individual); or egoism (where helping another is only embarked on if it is of some benefit to the individual's ultimate goal).

Sex trafficking is prohibited under both international law and human rights law. People are trafficked to meet a variety of ends, including:

1 Forced labour in sweat shops
2 To provide agricultural labour
3 For use in armed conflict; and last, and most significantly
4 For commercial sexual exploitation – as this is the motivation behind the greatest proportion of all trafficking (Todres 2006: 887).

At the heart of trafficking are three key systemic problems: racism, sexism and poverty. Todres (2006: 888) argues that if prevention is to work these systemic issues must be addressed simultaneously and these issues are usually explicated in terms of a range of rights, which includes:

• The right to be free from gender-based violence and discrimination;
• The right to be free from other forms of discrimination, including discrimination on the basis of race, religion and class;
• The right to birth registration (undocumented women and children are more vulnerable to traffickers and can more easily become invisible to protective agencies);
• The right to health care; and finally,
• The right to education.

Trafficking violates civil and political rights, equality rights and the right to be free from slavery – all of these rights are enshrined in various international treaties and UN resolutions, with the first being passed in 1904 and variously amended and built on since then.

There are four central human rights treaties which have relevance to sex trafficking:

(a) The International Covenant on Civil and Political Rights (ICCPR);
(b) The Convention on the Elimination of Discrimination Against Women (CEDAW);
(c) The International Covenant on Economic, Social and Cultural Rights; and
(d) The Convention on the Rights of the Child.

For a detailed discussion see: Farrior, S. (2006) 'The international law on trafficking in women and children for prostitution: Making it live up to its potential', *Harvard Human Rights Journal,* 10: 213–55.

Questions for reflection

1 The international community is in general agreement that sex tourism and sex trafficking involving children is morally wrong – why does this trade and industry persist?

2 What ethical reasoning seems to apply to the tourist who procures sex from a child while travelling?

3 If you were to apply the universal perspective what issues would be revealed? For example: How would you respond if somebody argued that child prostitution was not alright in New Zealand, but it was alright in Asia? The person might add: because it was culturally acceptable over there. How would you respond?

4 How would the principle of impartiality help you here?

5 What are the central problems with cultural relativism?

6 If discrimination and poverty are at the heart of the persistence of this trade and industry, how can the dominance of moral norms assist those who seek to prevent the sexual exploitation of children globally?

6.7 SEX TOURISM WITHOUT SEX TOURISTS – A MATTER OF DEFINITION?

When 'Western' women tourists engage in commercial sex with third world men, this is often referred to as 'romance tourism' rather than 'sex tourism' (Pruitt and LaFont 1995; Dahles and Bras 1999; Herold et al. 2001). Is it simply a matter of semantics?

As Taylor (2001: 750) observes:

> The behaviour of 'First World' women who travel to poor countries for sex with local men is generally interpreted in a very different way from that of First World men who engage in the same practices. The tourist woman who buys meals and gifts for her local sexual partner is enjoying a 'romance', not using a prostitute. In addition these women are also often portrayed as lonely and vulnerable to the advances of beach boys and vulnerable to being used.
>
> (Momsen 1994: 116)

Female sex tourism becomes 'romance tourism' with potentially positive outcomes. Here romance tourism is contrasted with sex tourism, where it is argued sex tourism perpetuates patriarchal dominance and romance tourism provokes new understandings of gendered relationships (Pruitt and LaFont 1995: 423).

However, this redefinition – 'romance tourism' – obscures the sexual–economic exchanges which do take place when women travel and procure sex from locals while abroad. Questioning this gendered definition of sex tourism when it involves First World women, Taylor's (2001: 757) research amongst tourist women in Jamaica and the Dominican Republic, who had sex with local men, revealed various forms of economic exchanges took place. Some of these economic exchanges took place after the women had returned home – and took the form of monthly remittances. Sometimes the women were 'tricked' for payment, where the beach boy took her to bars or restaurants owned by friends and where the woman is overcharged and the beach boy and friend split the overcharging later. Taylor (2001) and O'Connell-Davidson (2001) observe payment can be as simple as a shower in the tourist's hotel room and while these women tourists do not necessarily recognise this as a payment this is largely an outcome of a lack of understanding about the level of poverty these men live with. While these women may not view these encounters as prostitution – and many of these local men do not either – the redefinition from sex tourism to romance tourism conforms to commonly accepted understandings of gendered relationships, where women cannot be predators and men cannot be preyed upon (Taylor 2001: 758).

Within this frame of reference only women and homosexual men can be prostitutes and only men can be clients. But the question remains, because these women and men do not define their relationship in terms of sex tourism or prostitution – and underplay the sexual–economic exchange – does it mean that it is not? And what are the ethical implications of this gendered redefinition? Does it absolve women tourists who have sex with local men and provide some form of economic recompense from considering what other wider social inequalities they are helping perpetuate? Does it mean that these women tourists are precluded from pondering the ethical and moral issues that these interactions and transactions provoke?

As Taylor (2001) and others (O'Connell-Davidson 2001; Garrick 2005) observe, there are a number of problems with the differentiation between (female) romance tourism and male sex tourism. Males also engage in a wide range of sexual–economic relationships with local women, men and children; with many prostitutes acting as the tourist's 'girlfriend' while they stay in the area – accepting not cash payments but gifts 'for their kindnesses'. Many men also do not see themselves as prostitute users or sex tourists – even if this is the reason why they have travelled to this destination (Cohen 1988). Many men say they are looking for love, many have had failed marriages in the West, many are lonely and alienated from their own societies and their desire for sex and engagement with the sex industry is in part about seeking reinforcement of their attractiveness and repositioning themselves as a potential mate (Cohen 1993; Garrick 2005: 506).

In contrast, there are also men who can be defined as 'hard core' sex tourists, men who seek to reclaim a form of domination that relies on the sexual objectification of others – where 'the others' are racially different and who occupy a less privileged place economically in the contemporary world (O'Connell-Davidson 2001: 21). While we might be reluctant to class these men as 'romance tourists', would we entertain defining men, who are seeking love and belonging through prostitution, as 'romance tourists'?

Women can be sexually predatory, do enter into explicitly commercial sexual relationships, do pay others to procure men or boys of a particular age, shape and even smell (Taylor 2001: 759), albeit in much smaller numbers than their male counterparts. The essentialisation of sexual difference between men and women underpins the idea that women are vulnerable and that men, even if prostitutes, are getting benefit beyond the payment, through accessing the female body. As Taylor (2001: 760) also observes, playing up so-called 'gendered difference' downplays the racialised nature of the interaction where the female tourist seeks the 'other' while abroad. These female tourists, just as with male tourists, also hold racist ideas about sexuality. Here racist stereotypes ensure that black men are perceived as 'overly sexual' – and ironically and inadvertently this explains why they want to have sex with often overweight and older white women tourists. What is also underplayed is the very often significant economic differential between the woman tourist and the local man.

Like male sex tourists, being able to command 'fit' and sexually desirable bodies which would otherwise be denied to them reaffirms female tourists' sense of their own privilege as 'First World' citizens ... Most, however, tap into exoticising rather than denigrating racisms and use their economic power to control the relationship in ways in which they could never do with men back home.

(Taylor 2001: 760)

The subjective payoff these women experience is not very different from those that men attribute to their sexual relationships with prostitutes while abroad.

Yet while there are similarities, there are also differences. Notably there are differences in the markets for men and women: where formal commercial sexual markets exist for male tourists they seldom do for female tourists who rely more heavily on the informal commercial sex market. Men also remain the dominant group of tourists seeking commercial sex. There are also differences with respect to violence, where female tourists are less likely to inflict violence on their beach boy, and the local police are less likely to harass the beach boy than they are the local female prostitute (Taylor 2001: 761). There are, nonetheless, many similarities; as Taylor (2001: 761–2) observes it is important to remain cognisant that:

Gender is not a unitary category undifferentiated by class or race, and the power relations involved in heterosexual encounters are therefore not always identical, even if discourses of heterosexual romance construct them as such. Sexual relationships between local men and tourist women are typically relationships between individuals who are massively unequal in terms of economic and political power, usually also unequal in terms of racialised power. Very often there is also a large age gap between the tourist woman and the local man.

Yet, as Jeffreys (2003) argues, it would be a mistake to see this power differential as static – it can change and in some situations is completely redressed if the women tourist takes on a more permanent relationship and permanent settlement with the local male. Taylor (2001 in Jeffreys 2003) notes that women who took on these more permanent relationships jeopardised their outsider status and many found themselves, once locally ensconced, in abusive relationships. Unlike men who can become *sexpatriates*, it appears that it is not possible for women to sustain their race and economic privilege if they decide to make the holiday more permanent. At this point the gender hierarchy assumes dominance, and foreignness and economic strength become secondary to the nature of the relationship. The white woman is localised – and then subject to the local norms of violence against women.

Jeffreys's (2003) phrase 'women do it too' is a useful starting point for thinking about whether or not this means what they do *is sex tourism*. It is clear there are power differentials between men that do and women that do, just as there are between those they do it with. In all of the current research there are central issues that emerge surrounding intention, the idea that a sexual encounter can be happenstance (while the tourist is there on business, or was out taking a walk); the notion of choice and the important questions surrounding what shapes the range of choices available (to the local and the tourist) and how the nature of economic exchanges for sex can obscure intention. What is clear is that more often than not the participants in research on sex tourism seldom classify themselves as paedophiles, sex tourists or habitual prostitute users; but does their subjective take on the experience and self-definition provide an accurate or objective take on what is actually taking place? Or is subjectivity being used here to obscure and make more morally palatable a consumption practice that might be 'frowned on' back home? If subjectivity is stressed is this simply a means of camouflaging the instrumentality and utilitarian nature of the exchange that is taking place (Padilla 2007b)? It is interesting that the sexpatriates in Montgomery's (2008) research, who regularly had sex with local children, did not wish to meet her or to be participants in the research project.

DISCUSSION QUESTIONS

1 When 'women do it to' is this sex tourism?
2 Why is intention important?
3 How does self-definition obscure the ethical issues surrounding sex tourism?

Further reading

On sex tourism and romance tourism:

Jacobs, J. (2009) 'Have sex will travel: romantic "sex tourism" and women negotiating modernity in the Sinai', *Gender, Place & Culture*, 16(1): 43–61.
Herold, E., Garcia, R. and De Moya, T. (2001) 'Female tourists and beach boys: Romance or sex tourism', *Annals of Tourism Research*, 28(4): 978–97.

Selling ethical travel:

Lovelock, B.A. (2007) 'Ethical travel decisions: Travel agents and human rights', *Annals of Tourism Research*, 35: 338–58.

6.8 SEXUALITY AND SEX TOURISM

Gay sex tourism is also often conceptualised in terms of 'romance tourism'. This is in part because it has been argued that gay tourists experience a variety of discriminations as tourists, from destinations not accommodating them and adding to their marginality to homophobia informing stereotypical ideas that all gay tourism must necessarily be sex tourism (Ryan and Hall 2001). The gay and lesbian travel sector is estimated to be worth US$43.3 billion, and gays and lesbians are more likely to travel than are their heterosexual counterparts (Ryan and Hall 2001: 104).

Padilla's (2007a) ethnographic research focuses on male sex workers in the tourism economy, in Santo Domingo and Boc Chica in the Dominican Republic. Sexual–economic exchanges with gay tourists are less researched than same-sex relationships, and this in part has been attributed to the often clandestine nature of the gay sex industry. The Western Union daddies of Padilla's (2007b) research are the older men who pay remittances back to the younger men they have procured sex from while on tour. For these sex workers there is a preference for foreign customers because they are more likely to pay remittances. The importance of remittances must be understood in terms of the precarious nature of surviving economically on intermittent wages and the significant place that remittances, primarily from foreign family members, play generally in the Dominican economy. As Padilla (2007b) writes:

> Regular clients, whether foreign or local, often provide a safety net for men who have no steady wage or whose income does not meet their basic needs. Sex workers often explained to me that these longer-term relationships are more reliable than simple one-night stands. ... While frequently including cash or regular monthly remittances, support from Western Union daddies is often oriented toward assisting sex workers with regular household and living expenses including items such as construction materials, automobiles or motorcycles, clothes and supplies for children, household furniture, university tuition and fees, cellular phones, and food. It also is noteworthy that sex workers often emphasise support for children in their descriptions of regular clients' forms of assistance, a pattern that parallels statements by Dominican female sex workers.

(Padilla 2007b: 256)

Those who provide remittances back for *same*-sex encounters often describe the relationships as long term and with emotional connectedness (O'Connell-Davidson and Sánchez Taylor 1999). This is also the case with the gay sex tourists in Padilla's research. Yet, as Padilla emphasises, there remains a central tension that hinges on the overt economic inequities between the tourist and the sex worker.

> As O'Connell-Davidson and Sánchez Taylor (1999) argue, in global sex tourism, the commercial nature of the sex worker–client exchange essentially strips all mutuality from sexual relations and 'provides a conveniently ready-dehumanized sexual object for the client' (p. 40). Yet, in the context of 'romance tourism' – or the longer-term, more intimate relationships typical of Western Union daddies – this tendency toward dehumanisation must be resolved, insofar as it is understood to be antithetical to true intimacy and emotional mutuality. Thus, while sex tourism in places such as the Dominican Republic opens certain avenues by which Westerners can rework their identities vis-à-vis the 'Other,' it also can create dilemmas for them as they struggle to imagine themselves as worthy beings amidst the inequalities that can never be entirely erased from consciousness.

(Padilla 2007b: 256)

CHAPTER REVIEW

This chapter has explored some of the key issues in sex tourism and the socio-economic factors that underpin the growth and reproduction of sex tourism markets. We have considered how it is often difficult to draw a clear line between tourism and sex tourism and that often too there are definitional problems surrounding sex and romance tourism as researchers have struggled with the heterogeneous population and various subjective experiences of both clients and providers. But conceptual problems do not alter the fact that tourism markets, sex tourism markets, the trafficking of women and children for prostitution and sexual servitude are all interconnected. It is not simply a coincidence that some of the major sex tourist destinations are societies that are less developed and where poverty is a significant issue for the majority of the population. Nor is it happenstance that women and children predominate as trafficked subjects, as prostitutes, as economically marginal citizens in the contemporary world, and connected to the aforementioned are more likely to be mobile. Class, race and sexuality inform the gendered and sexual hierarchies evident in the sex tourism industry and economic global inequity is at the heart of sex tourism and the sex product in tourism.

SUMMARY OF KEY TERMS

Sex tourism May be defined as tourism where the main purpose or motivation of at least part of the trip is to consummate sexual relations (Ryan & Hall 2001: ix).

Child sex tourism (CST) is the commercial sexual exploitation of children by foreigners, including paedophiles, businessmen and tourists. It usually refers to either persons who travel from their own country to another to engage in sexual acts with children, or foreigners who engage in sexual activity with a child while overseas. Child sex tourism often involves a third party who procures a child from local communities (trafficking).

Sex trafficking is a modern-day form of slavery in which a commercial sex act is induced by force, fraud, or coercion, or in which the person induced to perform such an act is under the age of 18 years.

Trafficking of women and children The United Nations General Assembly (2000) defines trafficking as follows: 'the recruitment, transportation, transfer, harbouring or receipt of persons, by means of the threat or use of force or tougher forms of coercion, of abduction, of fraud, or deception, or the abuse of power or of a position of vulnerability or of the giving or receiving of payments or benefits to achieve the consent of a person, for the purpose of exploitation. Exploitation includes, at a minimum, the exploitation of the prostitution of others or other forms of sexual exploitation, forced labour or services, slavery or practices similar to slavery, servitude or the removal of organs' (UNODC 2006: 7).

Sexpatriates Former sex tourists who take up residence in the destination so they can avail themselves of commercial sexual relationships (often with minors) they would have difficulty securing at home.

QUESTIONS FOR REFLECTION

1 What factors underpin the development of sex tourism?
2 What is meant when people say that poverty, race and gender are systemic to sex trafficking and sex tourism?
3 Is cultural relativism used to justify sex tourism? And if so, what are the ethical implications?
4 A utilitarian approach would stress social good for the majority. What are the problems with this approach in relation to sex tourism?
5 Does intention matter? If it is a chance encounter with a prostitute – with whom the tourist got on really well – is that sex tourism?
6 Why is it argued that there is very little difference between tourism and sex tourism?
7 Why is it important to recognise how blurred the categories of sex tourism and child sex tourism are?
8 Does a person's sexuality change the ethics and morality of sex tourism?

EXERCISES

1 Choose three known sex tourist destinations and search on the Internet to see how the destination is promoted. Is sex as a product used to enhance the desirability of the location?
2 What laws exist in your country that allow for extraterritorial prosecution for sex acts with minors while abroad.

FURTHER READING

O'Connell-Davidson, J. (2001) 'The sex tourist, the expatriate, his ex-wife and her "other": the politics of loss, difference and desire', *Sexualities,* 4(5): 5–24.

Shen, H. (2008) 'The purchase of transnational intimacy: women's bodies, transnational masculine privileges in Chinese Economic Zones', *Asian Studies Review*, (32): 57–75.

Padilla, M.B. (2007a) *Caribbean Pleasure Industry: Tourism, Sexuality and Aids in the Dominican Republic,* Chicago, IL: University of Chicago Press.

— (2007b) '"Western Union Daddies" and their quest for authenticity: An ethnographic study of the Dominican gay sex tourism industry', *Journal of Homosexuality*, 53(1–2): 241–75.

NOTE

Pettman, J.J. (1997) 'Body politics: international sex tourism', *Third World Quarterly*, 18(1): 93–108.

REFERENCES

Beddoe, C. (1998) 'Beachboys and tourists: links in the chain of child prostitution in Sri Lanka', in M. Opperman, M. (ed.) *Sex Tourism and Prostitution: Aspects of Leisure*, Recreation and Work, New York: Cognizant Communications, pp. 45–59.

Beddoe, C., Hall, C.M. and Ryan, C. (2001) *Incidence of Sexual Exploitation of Children in Tourism*. A report commissioned by the World Tourism Organization, Madrid: World Tourism Organization.

Cohen, E. (1988) 'Tourism and Aids in Thailand', *Annals of Tourism Research*, 15: 467–86.

—— (1993) 'Lovelorn farangs: the correspondence between foreign men and Thai girls', *Anthropological Quarterly,* 59(3): 115–27.

Cotter, K.M. (2009) 'Combating child sex tourism in South East Asia', *Denver Journal of International Law and Policy,* 37(3): 493–512.

Dahles, H. and Bras, B. (1999) 'Entrepreneurs in romance: tourism in Indonesia', *Annals of Tourism Research,* 26: 267–93.

De Cock, M. (2007) *Directions for National and International Data Collection on Forced Labour*, Geneva: International Labour Organization.

Flowers, R. (2001) 'The sex trade industry', *Annals of the American Academy of Political and Social Science,* 575(1): 147–57.

Garrick, D. (2005) 'Excuses, excuses: rationalisations of Western sex tourists in Thailand', *Current Issues in Tourism*, 8(6): 497–509.

Glover, K. (2006) 'Human trafficking and the sex tourism industry', *Crime & Justice International*, 22(92): 4–10.

Hall, C.M. (1996) 'Gender and economic interests in tourism prostitution', in Y. Apostolopoulos, S. Leivadi and A. Yiannakis (eds) *The Sociology of Tourism: Theoretical and Empirical Investigations,* New York: Routledge.

Jeffreys, S. (2003) 'Sex tourism: do women do it too?', *Leisure Studies*, 22: 223–38.

Leheny, D. (1995) 'A political economy of Asian sex tourism', *Annals of Tourism Research*, 22(2): 367–84.

Momsen, J. (1994) 'Tourism, gender and development in the Caribbean', in Kinnaird, V. and Hall. D. (eds) *Tourism: A Gender Analysis,* Chichester: Wiley, pp. 106–20.

Montgomery, H. (2008) 'Buying innocence: child-sex tourists in Thailand', *Third World Quarterly*, 29(5): 903–17.

O'Connell-Davidson, J. (2004) 'Child sex tourism: an anomalous form of movement?', *Journal of Contemporary European Studies*, 12(1): 31–46.

O'Connell-Davidson, J. and Sanchez Taylor, J. (1998) 'Fantasy islands: exploring the demand for sex tourism', in K. Kempadoo (ed.) *Sun, Sex, and Gold: Tourism and Sex Work in the Caribbean*, Lanham, MD: Rowman and Littlefield.

Peach, L.J. (2005) '"Sex slaves" or "sex workers"? Cross-cultural and comparative religious perspectives on sexuality, subjectivity, and moral identity in anti-sex trafficking discourse', *Culture and Religion: An Interdisciplinary Journal*, 6(1): 107–34.

Pettman, J.J. (1997) 'Body politics: international sex tourism', *Third World Quartlerly,* 18(1): 93–108.

Plummer, K. (2010) 'The square of intimate citizenship: some preliminary proposals', *Citizenship Studies*, 5(3): 237–53.

Pruitt, D. and LaFont, S. (1995) 'For love and money: romance tourism in Jamaica', *Annals of Tourism Research,* 22: 422–40.

Rojec, C. and Urry, J. (1997) *Touring Cultures: Transformations of Travel and Theory,* London: Routledge.

Ryan, C. and Hall, C.M. (2001) *Sex Tourism: Marginal People and Liminalities*, London: Routledge.

Sachs, A. (1994) 'The last commodity: child prostitution in the developing world', *World Watch*, 7(4): 24–30.

Said, E. (1978) *Orientalism,* London: Penguin.

Sánchez Taylor, J.S. (2001) 'Dollars are a girl's best friend? Female tourists' sexual behaviour in the Caribbean', *Sociology,* 35(3): 749–64.

Smith, M. and Duffy, R. (2003) *The Ethics of Tourism Development,* London: Routledge.

— (2010) 'Sex tourism and inequalities', in Cole, S. and Morgan, N. (eds) *Tourism and Inequality: Problems and Prospects,* Wallingford: CABI, pp. 49–66.

Tepelus, C.M. (2008) 'Social responsibility and innovation on trafficking and child sex tourism: morphing of practice into sustainable tourism policies?', *Tourism and Hospitality Research,* 8(2): 98–115.

Todres, J. (2006) *The Importance of Realizing 'Other Rights' to Prevent Sex Trafficking*, New York University Public Law and Legal Theory Working Papers. Paper 32. Available at <http://lsr.nellco.org/nyu_plltwp/32> (Accessed 13 June 2012).

Truong, T. (1990) *Sex, Money and Morality: Prostitution and Tourism in Southeast Asia*, London: Zed Books.

UNICEF (2007) 'Poverty reduction – the pro-growth and pro-poor strategy', *International Journal of Development Studies,* 2(3): 73–8.

UNODC (United Nations Office on Drugs and Crime) (2006) *World Drug Report, Vol. 2: Statistics.* Available at <http://www.unodc.org/pdf/WDR_2006/wdr2006_volume2.pdf> (Accessed 4 August 2011).

— (2007) *Annual Report*. Available at <http://www.unodc.org/pdf/annual_report_2007/AR06_full-report.pdf> (Accessed 10 August 2011).

Wonders, N. and Michalowski, R. (2001) 'Bodies, borders, and sex tourism in a globalized world: a tale of two cities – Amsterdam and Havana', *Social Problems,* 48(4): 545–71.

Tourism and indigenous peoples

7

'Home is not where you live, but where they understand you.'

Christian Morganstern[a]

'Tourists came around and looked into our tipis. That those were the homes we choose to live in didn't bother them at all. They untied the door, opened the flap, and barged right in, touching our things, poking through our bedrolls, inspecting everything. It boggles my mind that tourists feel they have the god-given right to intrude everywhere.'

Russell Means[b]

'It seemed like many other travel destinations in the world, where many people starved and the tourists ate well and were fussed over.'

Paul Theroux[c]

LEARNING OBJECTIVES

After reading this chapter you will be able to:

- Identify a range of ethical issues in relation to tourism and indigenous peoples.
- Identify and discuss ethical issues relating to the commodification of culture and the implications for indigenous populations.
- Define 'pro-poor' tourism and explain why this concept and practice has emerged.
- Describe the changing roles and responsibilities of the post-colonial states towards indigenous populations and the ethical issues that emerge in tourism as a consequence.
- Describe why justice tourism and its key aspirations are useful for critically evaluating various alternative forms of tourism.

7.1 INTRODUCTION

[Indigenous] [t]ourism is increasingly viewed not simply as a force for the creation of a stereotypical image of a marginalised people, but as a means by which those peoples aspire to economic and political power for self-advancement, and as a place of dialogue between and within differing world views.

(Ryan 2005: 4)

In the 1970s scholars highlighted the importance of understanding the role that tourism plays in relation to indigenous populations, stressing the potential of tourism to both exploit and potentially assist indigenous populations. Issues central to the research that followed were the implications of the commodification of culture, cultural change imposed by tourists and the industry on indigenous culture(s), specifically, the erosion of cultural value – or authenticity – and the potential for further marginalisation for indigenous populations (Smith 1977, Altman 1989 and Johnston 1990 in Hinch and Butler 1996: 6). More recently tourism has been embraced as a development strategy in developing societies and research has focused on the tension provoked when indigenous populations are expected to present an authentic past whilst simultaneously transitioning into a more prosperous present and future. While some stress the potential for tourism to generate greater understanding of indigenous populations, most are now addressing how indigenous populations have or might engage in tourist enterprises and what processes and factors are necessary for realising more *just* socio-economic and political outcomes for indigenous communities in the post-colonial era.

In this chapter we will explore a number of emergent issues in relation to indigenous tourism specifically and more generally the assumed role that tourism can play in development and alleviation of poverty. Central to this chapter is a critical reflection on the ethical implications of various social groups (localised tourist operators, multinational industry operators and shareholders, governments) engaging in indigenous tourism and the implications for indigenous operators and indigenous populations. Indigenous populations comprise 5 per cent of the world's population and occupy about half of the world's land area, with presence in 70 countries. To varying extents, tourism has impacted on indigenous peoples and indigenous peoples have increasingly engaged in indigenous tourism enterprises (Weaver 2010: 43).

The indigenous tourist system is multifaceted and comprises a number of components and relationships, as schematised in Figure 7.1 Framework for Indigenous Tourism (Butler and Hinch 2007: 7).

The model highlights the flow of tourists to destinations and the flow of capital (financial resources), information and ideas. These flows are not necessarily equal, particularly with respect to capital, and it is the unequal nature of exchanges that generate controversy and raise ethical flags. While other tourism systems are similar to the one diagrammatically represented here, central to the indigenous tourism system is the emphasis placed on 'culture' and the commodification of difference or 'otherness' that often lies at the heart of the host's enterprise to attract visitors (Butler and Hinch 2007: 8).

However, in any indigenous tourist destination there is no one 'culture', rather there are always a multitude of ideas, beliefs and practices that underpin (enable, obstruct, embed) how the enterprise commenced, evolved and what it entails. Overarching this diversity, however, is a dominant cultural perspective and it is the dominant cultural perspective that shapes the nature of the institutions, laws and the national political system that the

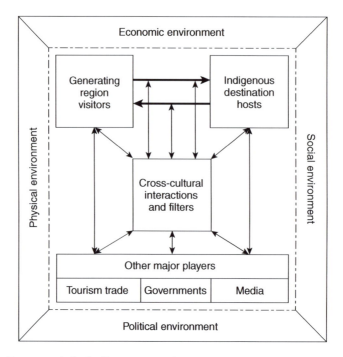

Figure 7.1 *Framework for indigenous tourism.*
Source: Butler and Hinch (2007).

indigenous tourism operator must engage with. Ultimately, too, how their nation stands in relation to others and how the global tourism industry shapes indigenous enterprises are also contended with, at times in overt ways and at other times implicitly (Butler and Hinch 2007: 8). In addition to these relationships, which can be characterised as culturally heterogeneous, there are a number of influential groups and operators integral to the indigenous tourism industry. These include: (1) travel agents in the country of origin (tourists' country); (2) transportation companies that facilitate the physical travel of the tourist; and (3) outbound and inbound tour operators who develop the range of tour packages available (Butler and Hinch 2007: 8–9). Less visible are the shareholders of the companies that operate all of these services and provide these functional prerequisites in this industry. Yet, while these players are less visible, their demands, perspectives and financial investments ensure the globally located nature of the industry, the multifaceted nature of social connections and a complex web of interests are involved.

Indigenous tourist operators work within and in response to this range of relationships and often in societies where there has been significant government support for developing an indigenous tourist industry as a means of addressing socio-economic deprivation amongst indigenous populations. As with any other tourist system, the indigenous tourism system is not a closed system and is subject to all of these relationships and responsive to a range of opportunities and constraints at a range of levels, including between and within levels.

Figure 7.2 *Mesa Verde, Colorado, where an ancient indigenous site is being inter-preted to visitors by park serivce rangers. Photo: Brent Lovelock.*

7.2 'INDIGENOUS' AND 'CULTURE'

As Weaver (2010: 43) observes there is no official definition of indigenous, it is a term:

> applied by the United Nations to people on the collective basis of self-identification, historical continuity with pre-settler societies, close links with particular territories and their natural resources, distinct socio-economic systems and cultures, non-dominant status within a society and resolution to maintain and perpetuate aspects of ancestral culture and lifestyle as distinctive communities.
>
> (Xanthaki 2009)

Internationally there have been social movements that have provoked debate about the role the tourism industry plays in either addressing or disregarding indigenous peoples' rights. The International Labour Organization's 1989 Convention No. 169 – *Indigenous and Tribal Peoples Convention* – provided a minimum standard for the protection of indigenous peoples. This convention was followed in 1999 by the United Nations *Draft Declaration on the Rights of Indigenous Peoples* which illustrates the increasing importance placed on indigenous peoples' rights and which will ultimately impact on how the industry, governments and indigenous communities interact with one another and what outcomes will emerge as a consequence of this interaction (United Nations General Assembly 2007; Higgins-Desbiolles 2008). Indigenous rights emerged alongside the human rights movement of the twentieth century, but differ as they concern themselves with communal rights rather than individual rights (Higgins-Desbiolles 2007: 87). One of the most contentious components of this Declaration has been the principle that asserts the right to self-determination (Article 3), and which underpins all of the other principles of this Declaration.

Higgins-Desbiolles (2007: 89–90) outlines some of the principles that have relevance to the tourism industry. These include:

(i) Cordoning off indigenous culture from economic exploitation by outsiders without permission.

(ii) The demand for restitution for improper usurpation of indigenous culture and knowledge.

(iii) Blocked access to and protection of indigenous sacred sites from non-indigenous people.

(iv) The right to demand access to sacred sites that are under the ownership of others.

(v) Banning or restricting the use of indigenous words and names by non-indigenous people.

(vi) Advocates for the provision of public education and the provision of information to non-indigenous people about the 'dignity and diversity of their (indigenous peoples') cultures, traditions, histories and aspirations'.

(vii) Indigenous participation in decision making at all levels in decisions that affect them.

(viii) Advocates for the indigenous right to maintain and manage their own development and subsistence and calls for compensation when this right is impinged upon.

(ix) Statement of the right to ownership and control of their total environment (land, water, air, coastal seas, sea ice, flora and fauna).

(x) It provides for the right to conservation, restoration and protection of their total environment (hence, could prevent development projects).

(xi) Describes the right to 'full ownership and control and protection of … cultural and intellectual property'.

(xii) The right to determination of development strategies and that states must secure their consent for development projects which affect their lands and resources. Compensation rights if these are not addressed.

(xiii) Indigenous peoples have the right to self-determination, through their own institutions and structures equating to autonomy or self-government in all matters – culture, religion, society, economy and resources.

Further reading

Johnston, A. (2000) 'Indigenous peoples and ecotourism: bringing indigenous knowledge and rights into the sustainability equation', *Tourism Recreation Research*, 25(2): 89–96.

Johnston, A.M. (2003) 'Self-determination: exercising indigenous rights in tourism', in Singh, S., Timothy, D.J. and Dowling, R.K. (eds) *Tourism in Destination Communities,* Wallingford: CABI, pp. 115–34.

Higgins-Desbiolles, F. (2003) 'Reconciliation tourism: tourism healing divided societies', *Tourism Recreation Research*, 28(3): 35–44.

— (2004) 'Reconciliation tourism: challenging the constraints of economic rationalism', in Ryan, C. and Aicken, M. (eds) *Indigenous Tourism: The Commodification and Management of Culture,* Amsterdam: Elsevier, pp. 223–45.

Humans are curious about other humans. Curiosity, however, is not a benign state of being – it is embedded within power relations that are in turn the drivers and shapers of historical notions of the 'other'. In turn, these notions are not simply ideas, but are part and parcel of humans seeking to discover, conquer and invariably acquire territories globally. It is this history and these notions that underpin contemporary tourism and its territories and what it is that people seek to see or view and experience. These notions and practices also underpin the position many indigenous communities find themselves in with respect to access to economic and social resources. A 'culture of poverty' is common to many indigenous communities and it is an outcome of imperialism, colonialism and post-colonialism – processes through which indigenous populations became the 'other' to be discovered, conquered and civilised and ultimately socially and economically marginalised by the colonisers.

The history of tourism is enmeshed in the history of imperialism. The grand tour illustrates how the well-educated classes travelled abroad to both 'view' and learn about other 'cultures'. Since the grand tour, the tourism industry has created a range of tour options that capitalise on the myth and intrigue surrounding discovery. Increasingly contemporary tourism, in response to mass tourism, has sought destinations assumed to be still pristine and relatively 'untouched' (Hinch and Butler 1996: 3) and to find the 'other' in their natural environment – close to their 'original state'. Yet, for the latter to be possible, indigenous populations have had to repackage themselves or be repackaged – with their culture being the sought-after commodity. Consequently, tourism has been labelled the 'new colonialism', where indigenous populations are in effect 're-colonialised', by an industry which relies on their presence for the consumption of an assumed human past. Indigenous populations have not fared well from colonialism and in the post-colonial era have increasingly sought means by which they can address economic, social and cultural marginality.

The tourism industry is a dual-edged sword for indigenous populations. On the one hand it offers the potential for indigenous peoples to market themselves and take advantage of the economic gains to be made from the commodification of culture. Yet, on the other hand, there are a number of factors that mitigate against the tourism industry serving as a panacea for the challenges faced by indigenous populations. As Hinch and Butler (1996: 6) observe there are a number of assumptions made about how tourism might facilitate improved life chances and the life experiences for indigenous people, including:

- touristic practice provides an opportunity to raise awareness and facilitate understanding;
- raised awareness leads to changed behaviours which are ultimately more just;
- indigenous peoples have control over the process of marketing themselves and can govern the nature of the experience;
- engaging in indigenous tourism will assist in improving community capacity and economic independence.

Critics have rightly highlighted, however, that the tourism industry is typically dominated by 'outside interests', where ownership and control lie in the hands of those who live elsewhere and where the benefit usually goes back to this base. Additionally, raised awareness does not always translate into changed behaviours and nor do the behaviours of tourists shape in a direct or lineal way the wider economic relations within which this industry is embedded. In short, we need to question the politics of awareness, whether awareness changes behaviour, how much control indigenous communities have over indigenous tourism and whether indigenous tourism does facilitate community capacity and economic independence. This critical reflection ensures that we can explore the ethical issues surrounding indigenous tourism and here justice frameworks are particularly useful.

7.3 CULTURE – CONCEPT, PRACTICE, 'THING'

We also need to explore some of the central concepts employed in relation to indigenous tourism and arguably all touristic practices. If culture lies at the heart of indigenous tourism – what is culture? Do some people have more of 'it' than others? What ethical issues surround this concept and what ethical issues emerge when this concept is reified?

Culture is a thorny concept which needs to be clarified before we can begin to consider the ethical issues surrounding the relationship between the business of tourism and indigenous peoples. Culture is a concept that has been particularly prone to reification. When a concept is reified it is made a 'thing', e.g. John's 'culture' compelled him to act in the way that he did. As a concept, culture has been variously defined by some as a collection of ideas and beliefs that shape how a group of people behave and by others as a collection of behaviours that differentiate groups of humans from each other. These are referred to as, first, an ideational definition of culture and, second, a material definition of culture. More recently, culture has been defined in terms of both – that is a collection of beliefs and ideas and behaviours rooted in the material realities of daily life: what some people might refer to as a 'way of life'. For the purposes of this chapter it is the latter definition of culture that we will be using. Culture is not a 'thing', it is a concept that we employ to explain and understand human life in any given setting.

The commodification of culture that occurs in tourism and indigenous tourism is *literally* the reification of culture: concept becomes thing and as a thing/object that is enmeshed in a specific production process, industry and capitalist economic system, it is a thing = commodity. This objectification into commodity means it can be valued (priced) and traded for profit. Of course, all peoples produce *things* that are traded – pots, cars, boats, paper. But none of these things originated as a 'way of life' – rather they are physical objects that are an outcome of a 'way of life'. These things may well have started out as an 'idea' but they realise a physicality that is visible, tangible and crafted out of materiality and through human enterprise/labour. Here the concept of culture allows you to think about the conditions within which these things are produced how these conditions shape the subjective experience of the production and consumption of things. When the concept of culture – which represents both subjective and material realities of human life – is reified many of the previously 'intangible' values of social life become tangible (objectified) and once objectified can then be manipulated in ways that give rise to a range of ethical dilemmas. First Nations, Inuit and Native Americans resisted being photographed. It is not just the reproduction of the face or body that is of concern but the capturing (objectification) of the person's spirit and the potentiality of giving that spirit (the intangible) a materiality that can then be used – passed on, manipulated – as though independent of the person. In addition, and as importantly, the process of commodification (reification) obscures 'tangible' aspects of social life – culture *does this*, it is *because of her culture* that she does x or y. Culture becomes this all powerful *thing* (beyond explanation) *that does things*. Reification is problematic as it undoes the explanatory power of a concept by concealing the nuts and bolts of what the concept refers to: beliefs and ideas and behaviours rooted in the material realities of everyday life. The 'concept now thing' becomes the doer, the actor, the manufacturer, no longer a conceptual tool that facilitates explanation and understanding, rather a blanket term that is 'taken for granted' – and consequently devoid of its explanatory power.

With respect to peoples and their beliefs and ideas, the commodification of culture makes things of what are usually intangibles. For many human groups the intangible is powerful, valued (feared and admired) and central to the fabric of social and cultural life. It is also very often the intangible that provides meaning and conveys morality. Ironically, while making the intangible tangible, commodification also allows the tangible to become intangible. It thus potentially undermines the power of the intangible and simultaneously empowers (through concealing the dynamics and features of) the already tangible. This process is not innocent or benign, the process of commodification of culture lies at the heart of ethical concerns surrounding indigenous (and arguably all) tourism. For indigenous populations, or ethnic minority groups who are socially and economically marginal, this process is not always beneficial.

The process of the commodification of culture involves packaging culture in a way that is desirable and desirability is defined by understandings about what constitutes value. Culture as commodity becomes simplified and entails the indigenous guide/operator's collaboration in self-exoticising. As Bunten (2008: 386) observes:

> with the culture on display transformed into iconic visuals such as traditional dress, digestible sound bites such as a greeting in the Native tongue, and standardized ethnographic information presented on tour. Self-exoticizing requires the Native tour guide to present a simplified version of the self that conforms to Western concepts of the Other popularized in television, movies, books, museums, and the marketing efforts of tour operators.

Yet, as Bunten (2008) goes on to argue, indigenous tour guides do not stand outside of this process. Rather, the guide can and often does control the commodification of their persona, and this can be empowering. Consciously packaging and delivering this self-presentation, the guide is able to deliver a conscious representation of their culture – that was – and thus can assert and control the narrative of historical loss (Clifford 2004: 6; Bunten 2008: 392). However, as Notzke (2004: 47) observes in Southern Alberta: 'The aboriginal hosts who incorporate cultural elements in their tourist product are constantly faced with the challenge of sharing their culture without compromising their integrity.'

So far we have discussed the reification of the concept of culture and the commodification of culture and the implications for indigenous peoples, yet we have avoided the problematic category of indigenous tourism itself. As Hall (2007: 315) argues the category of indigenous tourism is highly problematic – largely because it has not been problematised by those who use it. As we discussed in Chapter 2, at the heart of ethical decision making is the ability to think critically. A range of issues have been addressed, including how

Figure 7.3 *Indigenous peoples' band, entertaining tourists in China. Photo: Brent Lovelock.*

indigenous populations are represented by the industry, and power relations between the indigenous population and the dominant cultural group. However, power relations and heterogeneity within indigenous groups are often not considered – nor are the macro factors (beyond the tourism industry) that shape the economic, socio-cultural and political wellbeing of indigenous populations. Hall (2007) emphasises the tourism industry does not invent interests, values and power through engagement, rather it draws on an established political economy which has ensured the marginality of indigenous populations globally. It is as a consequence of these very processes that we are able to identify indigenous groups as somehow being distinct from other social groups. We are able to do this despite significant migratory processes that have ensured that the lands they now inhabit are culturally diverse and despite the fact that indigenous populations have been intermarrying with new and not so new settlers for many generations. Yet in the process of identification we have to be careful not to cordon off indigenous populations as distinct and separate entities, because if we do, we will be engaging in what Hall (2007) warns against – thinking within a power-free vacuum and failing to consider how indigeneity and indigenous tourism is shaped in relation not only to other tourisms but in relation to a larger political economy.

Indigenous tourism shares features in common with other tourisms – in particular tourism initiatives that attempt to address socio-economic marginality and poverty for particular groups in any given society. While there are a particular set of power dynamics and historic interplays that are specific to indigenous populations, tourism as a means to address marginality is a practice increasingly engaged in by other groups who have been disenfranchised through related though slightly different processes. These forms of tourism include: poverty tourism, poorism, slumming and township tourism. Indigenous tourism also shares in common characteristics and practices with cultural or ethnic tourism (Bennett and Blundell 1995; Pitchford 2008) and heritage tourism – where the culture and the heritage is about the dominant culture, but where the experience, packaging and delivery follows a very similar format and one that is imitated in the packaging of indigeneity as commodity in indigenous tourism (Bunten 2008).

However, indigenous tourism is differentiated from other forms of tourism by Hinch and Butler (1996) who stress that this form of tourism is identifiable when indigenous peoples are directly involved either through control of the operation and/or when their culture is the attraction and it is embedded in an industry that is dominated by non-indigenous individuals and organisations (Hinch and Butler 1996: 11). We can also stress here that self-determination is key to indigenous tourism – that indigenous populations are not 'stakeholders', but holders of collective and human rights, including the right to self-determination (McLaren 2003: 3 in Higgins-Desbiolles 2007: 93–4). The historical engagement with indigenous people shapes the nature of the industry and tourist encounter and the temporal dimensions of power relationships ensure that control over indigenous tourist enterprises is not always straightforward, just or ethical. It is, however, as with all cultural politics, always contested.

As Papson (1981: 225) observed:

> Tourism depends on preconceived definitions of place and people. These definitions are created by the marketing arm of government and of private enterprise in order to induce the tourist to visit specific areas … government and private enterprises not only define social reality but also recreate it to fit those definitions. This process is both interactive and dialectical. To the extent that this process takes place, the category of everyday life is annihilated.

7.4 TOURISM AS A FACILITATOR OF ECONOMIC INDEPENDENCE

Most of the world's indigenous populations are marginal economically and while the tourism industry might assist in addressing this marginality, it can and has for some involved the commodification of marginality itself (Azarya 2004). Writing of the Maasai, Azarya (2004) explores the process of commodification and how marginality is not only a driver for the commodification of culture, but marginality itself becomes the 'commodity'. This is not necessarily an intentional outcome rather it is an outcome of marginality being the dominant feature of the contemporary culture of most if not all indigenous populations. The indigenous population in seeking economic incorporation (and when encouraged to do so) engage in a process of exhibiting their 'culture' and in order to do this in a compelling way they must be very familiar with it – they must at least in part live it. In 'Selling their own marginality' (Azarya 2004: 961) they are compelled to engage with the new economy and society yet simultaneously to continue to inhabit their cultural marginality.

The outcome of the exhibit is therefore a greater incorporation in the new economy and society, but also a continuity of cultural marginality (Azarya 2004: 962).

Figure 7.4 *Sami tent, Norway, where sami operate 'cultural immersion' tours for visitors. Photo: Brent Lovelock*

They must maintain their difference in order to sustain appeal for the tourist and commercial value. Yet indigenous populations do not engage in this process alone. Both governments and private enterprises within localities and internationally collaborate to produce indigenous *tourist exhibits*, to use Azarya's (2004) phrase. In New Zealand, Hall (1996) writes of the significant control the New Zealand tourism industry has had over the representation of Māori since the 1870s. This control has increasingly been contested, but nonetheless:

> Pakeha New Zealanders have never been slow to exploit this indigenous culture in promotion and advertising – often in ways that drew Māori disapproval. There was a time when foreigners could have been excused for thinking, by the posters and videos they saw, that New Zealand existed solely of flax-skirted Māori jumping in and out of steaming pools.

> (Barber 1992: 91 in Hall 1996: 157)

Indigenous tourism in developing countries presents a number of other issues and concerns. While tourism is embraced as a means to facilitate development, indigenous populations contribute through presenting and representing 'a disappearing world' (Azarya, 2004: 964), but this for some requires that they are never fully incorporated as they must sustain at least the outward appearance of not 'being developed'. Also writing of the Maasai of East Africa, Mowforth and Munt describe their role in development as one of 'reinforced primitivism', where if they wish to accommodate their protected lands they must pay by conforming to traditional stereotypes (1998: 273 in Azarya 2004: 964). Or as MacCannell (1992: 18) observes:

> Enacted or staged savagery is already well established as a small but stable part of the world system of social and economic exchanges. Many formerly primitive groups earn their living by

charging visitors admission to their sacred shrines, ritual performances, and displays of more or less 'ethnologized' everyday life.

Yet, while in many destinations, this ethnologised indigeneity is the attraction, there is also a move toward 'protecting' indigenous populations from touristic intrusion and again this hinges on the idea of 'preserving' what are considered 'former ways of life'. The following story appeared in the Associated Press in July 2012:

INDIA'S TOP COURT BANS TOURISM, COMMERCIAL ACTIVITY NEAR TRIBE'S HABITAT IN ADAMAN ISLANDS

NEW DELHI – India's Supreme Court has banned all commercial and tourism activity near an ancient tribe's habitat in the country's remote Andaman and Nicobar islands in the Indian Ocean.

This week's order by India's top court bars hotels and resorts from operating within a five-kilometre (three-mile) buffer zone around the Jarawa reserve, which is home to the ancient Jarawa tribal people.

The court's order means a number of resorts that had opened near the indigenous Andamanese tribe's reserve will have to close.

However, a London-based international rights group for indigenous people is urging India to also halt safari runs by buses that pass through the reserve.

The Jawara are among the world's most ancient people, with many still hunting with bows and arrows and rubbing stones together to make fire.

Available at <http://www.news1130.com/article/print/379358>
(Accessed 5 July 2012).

The tourism industry has been resisted by indigenous groups and in some instances openly and actively contested. While we have considered that many governments encourage tourism as a means to achieve their development goals, state tourism development programmes do not go uncontested. Goa provides a very good illustration of local resistance to what was considered unbridled tourism development (Lea 1993: 708). By the early 1990s Goa had become a tourist destination, with 69 hotels developed along the Goan coastline. These developments were openly opposed by a group of workers, students, professionals and individuals calling themselves the *Jagrut Goencaranchi Fauz* (JGF). Publishing a five-part declaration the group addressed the overdevelopment of Goa by five-star resorts (Lea 1993: 708). The campaign launched by the JGF in the late 1980s, ultimately disrupted the tourism development programme in the 1990s, gained international media coverage and ensured developers were subject to successful legal action for breaking local environmental law. The resistance in Goa is an illustration of anti-tourism and a shift in ethical focus where not only the social and cultural implications of mass tourism for indigenous culture are asserted as important considerations, but also the associated environmental implications of tourism, in particular the exhaustion of water and energy supplies in destinations already facing scarcity of these resources (Lea 1993: 710).

Does tourism fulfil its promise of addressing economic and social marginality for indigenous populations? It appears that while many governments have encouraged indigenous engagement with tourism as a strategy to address marginality many enterprises do not achieve longevity and many enterprises remain marginal to the industry as a whole (Butler and Hinch 2007: 324). In connection with this, education and training (capacity) have increasingly been recognised as central to the success of such enterprises, where education and training are about equipping a community to be successfully engaged in tourism operations. Yet it remains that most training and educational programmes do not anticipate an indigenous audience and typically do not tailor their programmes accordingly (Butler and Hinch 2007: 325).

As with other enterprises in the tourism industry, in order to be successful indigenous tourist operators need to be able to link to the international tourist market. This is not always an easy feat, particularly for those operators based in colonially designated territories, which are frequently geographically isolated areas with weak infrastructural features (roads, rail, air, limited accommodation). Thus, there are a number of hurdles to get past before the international tourist can 'get there', 'stay there' and 'spend there'; all of which can undermine the viability of the enterprise. Linkages in these instances often rely on intermediaries – and these intermediaries can impact both positively and negatively on indigenous operations.

Figure 7.5 *'Nice Indians' sign in Arizona: Encouraging tourists to stop to buy handicrafts. Photo: Brent Lovelock.*

What is being perpetuated?

The tourist industry has always relied on images to convey to potential tourists what they might encounter in the destination. Images of indigenous populations used for this purpose have always been part of marketing in the tourist industry. As others have noted, these images historically have typically been prepared by non-indigenous photographers, artists and marketing agents and have often reflected racist, sexist and stereotypical understandings of indigeneity generally and of specific indigenous populations (Albers and James 1988; Cohen 1993; Hollinshead 1996). Invariably, images of indigenous populations are subsumed or framed in terms of national identity and as Hall (2007) notes these images are just one product produced and enmeshed within the broader political economy of indigenous tourism.

> Decisions affecting all aspects of indigenous tourism: the nature of government involvement in indigenous tourism; the structure of public agencies responsible for indigenous tourism development; participation in policy formulation and implementation; and identification and representation of indigenous tourism resources and attractions, such as heritage, within indigenous communities all emerge from political process. This process involves the values of actors (individuals, interest groups and public and private organisations) in a struggle for power.
>
> (Hall 2007: 306)

Power is not evenly distributed in any society, community or household. Consequently, for those who are socially and economically marginal (whether indigenous or otherwise) it is unlikely they are engaging in this enterprise on a level playing field. How can distributive justice frameworks help with respect to addressing these issues in practice?

Underpinning most of the central issues in relation to indigenous tourism is inequity and invariably poverty. We will now consider some alternative forms of tourism and poverty.

DISCUSSION POINT: ALTERNATIVE FORMS OF TOURISM

Alternative forms of tourism have emerged as a response to the excesses of mass tourism and the negative impacts of the industry – they include: soft tourism, new tourism, lower impact tourism, special interest tourism, green tourism, altruistic tourism, volunteer tourism, responsible tourism, justice tourism and pro-poor tourism (Scheyvens 2007; Higgins-Desbiolles 2008) all are underpinned with a view to sustainable livelihoods (Wheeller 1991; Poon 1993; Goodwin 1998; Wearing and Neil 1999; Sharpley 2000; Douglas et al. 2001; Mowforth and Munt 2003) and with the objective of bringing about social change (Higgins-Desbiolles 2008: 347).

Many questions have been raised with respect to these aspirations. Central questions include whether or not these forms of tourism are simply a diversionary tactic by tourism authorities and that it is actually business as usual; whether the sustainability rhetoric is actually about sustaining the industry itself (Wheeller 1991) and whether or not these forms of tourism can ultimately and practicably contribute to social change and justice. For example, Whitford and Ruhanen's (2010: 491) review of the development of Australian indigenous tourism policy and sustainability issues found that most focused on economic issues at the expense of considering in any detail the socio-cultural and environmental issues. In addition there was a tendency to underappreciate diversity and complexity in indigenous cultures, and a propensity to adopt top-down approaches to indigenous tourism development. Such approaches fail to engage indigenous peoples in the development of policy; fail to address capacity building in indigenous communities; and generally fail to acknowledge that in order for sustainability to be realised indigenous peoples need to be the subjects of their own capacity development. These authors concluded:

> it is not enough for governments to simply produce and publish indigenous tourism policy. The very presence of such policy espousing the virtues of sustainability does not necessarily translate into the practical and sustainable implementation and development of indigenous tourism.
>
> (Whitford and Ruhanen 2010: 492)

In response to these questions and critical appraisals some have argued that justice tourism is less susceptible to manipulation that meets the ends of the industry rather than those it purports to assist (Scheyvens 2002; Smith and Duffy 2003; Higgins-Desbiolles 2008).

Justice tourism (as previously discussed in Chapter 4) provides a useful place to think about indigenous tourism and other alternative forms of tourism that seek to shape social change. Scheyvens (2002: 104) identifies four attributes of justice tourism:

1 Builds solidarity between visitors and those visited.
2 Promotes mutual understanding and relationships based on equity, sharing and respect.
3 Supports self-sufficiency and self-determination of local communities.
4 Maximises local economic, cultural and social benefits.

In addition, just tourism from the destination community perspective promises (Scheyvens, 2002: 104):

1 Travellers will be people who are coming to share and not to dominate their lives.
2 Local accommodation and infrastructure will be used. As far as possible the services of foreign-owned and operated companies will be avoided.
3 Tourist sites and shows that degrade or debase the culture will be avoided. Opportunity will be given for local people to develop a real presentation of their culture with pride and dignity.

4 Travellers will be required to observe standards of decency and will not be tolerated if their presence is offensive to local people.

Discussion question: applying Rawls's principles

What action provides all with equal liberties and opportunities while helping those in need to the greatest extent possible?

7.5 PRO-POOR TOURISM

Tourists learning about poverty issues has been identified as one of five forms of justice tourism (Scheyvens 2002). Pro-poor tourism (PPT) is an alternative form of tourism, influenced by sustainability arguments, that focuses on people and poverty and the environment. Can tourism alleviate poverty? Those who think that the industry can play a key role in alleviating poverty engage in what is called pro-poor tourism (PPT); yet not all agree on how alleviation of poverty can be successfully achieved (Harrison 2008; Chok et al. 2007).

The potential for tourism to assist in development was recognised in the 1970s and, following a range of initiatives in the 1990s, the Millennium Development Goals were adopted by the United Nations General Assembly in 2000. Focusing on the eradication of extreme poverty and hunger, tourism was identified as a means to alleviate poverty and assist with community-based development initiatives (Harrison 2008: 852; Scheyvens 2007: 235). In 2002 the World Tourism Organisation launched the Sustainable Tourism-Eliminating Poverty programme (ST-EP). This programme has buy-in from a range of sectors, including the World Travel and Tourism Council, which comprises 100 of the world's foremost companies (Chok et al 2007: 145). In addition, the Asian Development Bank and the World Bank also support a range of 'pro-poor growth' projects (Sofield et al. 2004 in Chok et al. 2007). A range of international development organisations play a role in pro-poor tourism, including the UK Department for International Development (DFID), the Overseas Development Institute (ODI) – which is also part of the Pro-Poor Tourism Partnership (PPT Partnership) which in turn is engaged in a collaborative research initiative with the International Centre for Responsible Tourism (ICRT), the International Institute for Environment and Development (IIED) and the ODI (Chok et al. 2007: 145; Scheyvens 2007: 236). Thus, there are a range of stakeholders engaged in pro-poor tourism, from corporations to banks, aid agencies, research institutes and governmental bureaucracies.

The pro-poor movement comprises necessarily then a range of views and positions, some of them conflicting. Pro-poor initiatives are by their very nature morally charged and provoke a range of ethical issues. The central tenets of pro-poor tourism are: (1) tourism generates net benefits for the poor (cultural, social, economic and environmental); and (2) tourism is an industry that the poor can both actively participate in and benefit from. There are a range of principles which underpin pro-poor tourism, all of which acknowledge the multifaceted nature of poverty. Table 7.1 outlines these principles.

Table 7.1 *Pro-poor tourism principles*

PPT Principles
Participation. Poor people must participate in tourism decisions if their livelihood priorities are to be reflected in the way tourism is developed.
A holistic livelihoods approach. Recognition of the range of livelihood concerns of the poor (economic, social and environmental; short term and long term). A narrow focus on cash or jobs is inadequate.
Balanced approach. Diversity of actions needed, from micro to macro level. Linkages are crucial with wider tourism systems. Complementary products and sectors (for example, transport and marketing) need to support pro-poor initiatives.
Wide application. Pro-poor principles apply to any tourism segment, though strategies may vary between them (for example between mass tourism and wildlife tourism).
Distribution. Promoting PPT requires some analysis of the distribution of both benefits and costs – and how to influence it.
Flexibility. Blue-print approaches are unlikely to maximise benefits to the poor. The pace and scale of development may need to be adapted; appropriate strategies and positive impacts will take time to develop; situations are widely divergent.
Commercial realism. PPT strategies have to work within the constraints of commercial viability.
Cross-disciplinary learning. As much is untested, learning from experience is essential. PPT also needs to draw on lessons from poverty analysis, environmental management, good governance and small enterprise development.

Source: Chok et al. 2007: 147 (sourced from Ashley et al. 2000; Roe and Urquhart 2004).

In addition to these principles there are a number of core areas involving a range of strategies. What is sought is economic and non-economic benefits and policy formation in conjunction with building capacity amongst the poor to strengthen participation in decision making (Roe and Urquhart 2004).

It is argued that tourism can help alleviate poverty as it is already a significant sector in developing countries, it offers small-scale opportunities outside of agriculture, it is a diverse industry, it is an industry that provides opportunities for women and an industry that provides opportunity in the informal sector (Chok et al. 2007: 148). PPT is not a 'product' but an approach or orientation to tourism development and management (Harrison 2008). PPT focuses on the destinations – as a component in local economies – from the household level to the national and international level. PPT identifies the *net benefits* to the poor and environmental concerns are met by maintaining this overall goal. PPT works with general tourism strategies and works towards expanding informal networks in order to meet the needs of the poor producers and residents in the destination. It is what some have called people-focused development (Haysom 2005 in Chok et al. 2007).

PPT faces a number of challenges. First there are a number of structural factors that need to be present, including: supportive policy, favourable location, attitudinal support and sufficient people who are able to engage in a labour-intensive approach (Roe and Urquhart 2004). PPT must also be commercially viable, there must be local capacity – and in the absence of commercial viability and human capacity these must be sought from elsewhere. The central tension here is that in order to be viable there are times when foreign investment in the broadest sense becomes necessary, but ultimately this investment threatens the goal of empowerment in the locality and feeds into and reproduces inequitable power relations between the collaborators. In this situation those in developing countries have comparatively weak bargaining power and potentially less control over investment decisions.

There are also a number of questions that arise over whether net benefit is enough. PPT is not underpinned by a principle of distributive justice, thus the rich can get richer, some of the poor can benefit – but not all of the poor. The poor with lower skill levels and less capacity will not benefit to the same extent as the poor who have comparatively higher skill and capacity levels. In short, the poor are not a homogeneous group any more than are PPT advocates or tourism operators. If commercial viability is a goal then other interests will come into play with respect to decision making and the heterogeneous nature of the enterprise will to a large extent determine who and why some people will benefit more than others. Thus, PPT is not politically neutral (Chok et al. 2007): competing perspectives and interpretations exist at the operational level (Scheyvens 2007).

PPT involves not just addressing the social and economic but also the environmental. PPT tends to take place in areas that are already experiencing ecological vulnerability. It has been observed: 'there is a strong convergence of endangered biodiversity hotspots, marginalised indigenous peoples, fragile economies and expanding tourism development' (Chok et al. 2007: 154).

Further, we are currently at a crossroads where threatened biodiversity, the basic survival of millions of people and the tourism industry intersect (Christ et al. 2003 in Chok et al. 2007). In tourist destinations where water is a scarce commodity, tourists exacerbate the situation. The degradation of natural resources needed by the poor is a major issue generated by tourism in poor destinations (Richter 2001: 50; Scheyvens 2007). Once environmental issues are considered in relation to the tourism industry and the poor, it becomes clear that the highly polluting and resource-intensive nature of the industry should not be considered a secondary concern in PPT debates. Further, it brings into question whether PPT as a strategy can ever be large scale and demonstrates its weak sustainability (Mastny 2002 in Chok et al. 2007).

Furthermore, relegating the environment to a secondary concern is only possible if the moral position of alleviating poverty foreshadows the reality that PPT is taking place in a 'business as usual environment' where underpinning 'business as usual' is the idea that natural resources are infinite. For PPT to meet all of its principles it would be necessary for the tourist(s) to meet the social, economic, cultural and environmental costs. As Chok et al. (2007: 155) observe: 'Successful PPT relies, to a large extent, on the altruism of non-poor tourist stakeholders to drive the industry towards increasing benefits and reducing costs for the poor.' This will require significant attitudinal change – but also behavioural change. Ecotourism studies have revealed that tourists who embark on these tours demonstrate the same range of behaviours as mass tourists – the goals of the operators thus do not always parallel the goal of the consumer (Chok et al. 2007).

It has been argued that PPT (as with tourism more generally) offers employment opportunities for the poor, but as we see in Chapter 13 there are significant issues surrounding labour, conditions of labour, employment and unemployment in this sector. Many workers remain vulnerable and without safety nets in developing countries. Sudden changes in the global market can and have led to significant unemployment amongst workers in tourism. For those who are economically marginal, insecurity of employment contributes to the erosion of their limited assets and the cycle of poverty: 'The bottom-line is that *any* industry or commercial activity that condones exploitative labour conditions and income instability cannot be considered pro-poor' (Chok et al 2007: 160).

The mutual benefit rhetoric of PPT is deeply problematic. In PPT there are winners and losers, the poor are engaged in an enterprise that is asymmetrical, politically and economically (Chok et al 2007). Chok et al (2007) argue that it might be better to have altruism as a non-negotiable principle and to abandon the pretence of mutual benefit altogether. The risk for those who are interested in the commercial enterprise will be that it will be tourism strong on moral imperatives, but weak on profit margins (Chok et al 2007). Further, PPT takes place predominantly in rural areas, yet most of the poorest nations in the world are rapidly urbanising. Of those living in urban areas in the developing world today, approximately 80 per cent live in slums and it is projected that by 2033 one in three people will live in urban slums (Chok et al 2007: 159). Given the usual draw cards for PPT in rural areas, it is difficult to see what promotional materials would look like for the urban slums of the future and what mutual benefits might be secured. PPT practitioners have raised awareness about poverty, but as Harrison (2008) argues practitioners and academics need to work more closely together if poverty is to be addressed more systematically through PPT-type development initiatives.

The tourism poverty nexus reveals parallel issues faced by indigenous tourism. As Enloe (1990: 31) observes:

> Tourism is promoted today as an industry that can turn poor countries' very poverty into a magnet for sorely needed foreign currency. *For to be a poor society in the late twentieth-century is to be 'unspoilt'* [authors' emphasis].

7.6 SLUM TOURISM

Slum tourism has emerged as an alternative form of tourism which aims to raise consciousness of urban poverty in destination countries. Tours through disadvantaged parts of large cities in the developing world began in the mid-1990s (Rolfes 2009). Such tours are operated on a reasonable scale, for example in Johannesburg, Cape Town, Rio de Janeiro, Calcutta, Mumbai and Delhi. International tourists are the main group who take these tours. Marketing such tours varies, with some emphasising the idea that such tours are 'reality' tours and others stressing 'getting off the beaten path', authenticity, referring to

Figure 7.6 *Slum tourism. Cartoon: K. Lovelock.*

this kind of tourism as ethnic tourism and stressing the educational role played by such tours (Rolfes 2009: 2). Others have traced the origins of tours that focus on viewing or interacting with the dark side of urban life. For example, *slumming,* as this form of tourism is also referred to, has been found to date back to the nineteenth century in England, when members of the Victorian middle and upper classes toured the poorer areas of London to see this 'reality' (Koven 2004). Thus, more recent slumming tours fit within an established tradition. Research in this field has tended to focus on the motivations behind taking such tours and has established that tourist motivations are mainly to understand the country's culture and residents' living conditions (Rolfes 2009: 3). Slum tourism also stands alongside favela tourism or township tourism.

DISCUSSION POINT: SLUM TOURISM

Freire-Medeiros (2009: 587) writes:

> Tourism in favelas is ... part of a global phenomenon which has been reaching unexpected proportions, and which can be used as the basis for wider discussions, such as the politics of commodification of places, cultures, and people in the context of globalisation and inequality. Capable of instilling both fear and repulsion, poverty-stricken and segregated areas are transformed around the world into attractions highly regarded by the international tourist. ... If tourism may work towards building a new politics of visibility for the favela and its inhabitants, one

that challenges the prevailing stigmas, this does not mean that economic development, for instance, is really occurring.

Slum tourism and the idea that poverty is the attraction – alongside viewing the human condition and experience of misery, hopelessness, unemployment, hunger and disease – provokes some controversy and moral outrage. This outrage pivots on the ethics of the commodification of misery and poverty (Freire-Medeiros 2009: 582) and the moral questionability of the voyeurism associated with this form of tourism.

Discussion questions

1 What ethical issues arise from the commodification of poverty?
2 What ethical issues arise from the commodification of misery and suffering?
3 Are the poor, the new 'exotic other'? And, if so, what will come from this otherness as consumer object?
4 Is the tourist dollar reinvested in the favela/slum/impoverished neighbourhood?

Useful sources

<http://www.smithsonianmag.com/people-places/10024016.html> 'Next Stop, Squalor: Is poverty tourism "poorism", they call it exploration or exploitation?'

Websites promoting reality tours

<http://globalexchange.org>
<http://realitytoursandtravel.com/history/>

Further reading

Medina, L.K. (2003) 'Commoditizing culture: tourism and Maya identity', *Annals of Tourism Research*, 30(2): 353–68.
Notzke, C. (2004) 'Indigenous tourism development in southern Alberta, Canada: tentative engagement', *Journal of Sustainable Tourism*, 12(1): 29–54.
Ruiz-Ballesteros, E. and Herandex-Ramirez, M. (2010) 'Tourism that empowers? Commodification and appropriation in Ecuador's Turismo Comunitaro', *Critique of Anthropology*, 30(2): 201–29.

CHAPTER REVIEW

This chapter has explored indigenous tourism and alternative forms of tourism including pro-poor tourism, justice tourism and slum tourism. The aim of this chapter has been to identify a range of ethical issues in relation to tourism and indigenous people and to explore the commonality between this form of tourism and other alternative forms of tourism that aim to address poverty eradication. The key issues hinge on whether or not these forms of tourism can or do address poverty and what the implications are long term for communities who are engaging in tourism as a means of addressing their social, cultural and economic marginality – locally and globally. Justice and distributive justice frameworks are useful when considering the range of issues connected to these forms of tourism.

SUMMARY OF KEY TERMS

Indigenous tourism is a term: 'applied by the United Nations to people on the collective basis of self-identification, historical continuity with pre-settler societies, close links with particular territories and their natural resources, distinct socio-economic systems and cultures, non-dominant status within a society and resolution to maintain and perpetuate aspects of ancestral culture and lifestyle as distinctive communities' (Xanthaki 2009).

Justice tourism as an alternative form of tourism aims to: (1) build solidarity between visitors and those visited; (2) promote mutual understanding and relationships based on equity, sharing and respect; (3) support self-sufficiency and self-determination of local communities; (4) maximise local economic, cultural and social benefits (Higgins-Desbiolles 2008: 362).

Pro-poor tourism (PPT) is an alternative form of tourism, influenced by sustainability arguments, that focuses on people and poverty and the environment. The central tenets of pro-poor tourism are: (1) tourism generating net benefits for the poor (cultural, social, economic and environmental); (2) tourism as an industry which the poor can both actively participate in and benefit from. The principles underpinning PPT are explained in this chapter.

Slum tourism A form of tourism where the destination and tour take place in disadvantaged places – typically in large urban centres, primarily in the developing world – and where the tourists are predominantly international. Slum tourism also stands alongside favela tourism or township tourism. Slum tourism raises ethical concern with respect to the commodification of misery and poverty and the moral implications of voyeurism associated with this form of tourism.

Questions for reflection

1 What is meant by commodified primitivism?
2 What are the implications of the commodification of culture for indigenous populations?
3 What are some of the central ethical tensions provoked by the combination of indigeneity and tourism?
4 Can tourism assist in the eradication of poverty?

> 5 What alternative forms of tourism explicitly address poverty?
> 6 What structural factors need to be present for PPT to be successful?
> 7 PPT is not underpinned by the principle of distributive justice – what are the implications of this for destination communities?
> 8 Why is it important to consider the resource-intensive nature of the industry in relation to PPT tourism?

Exercise

Visit the following website, which addresses the issue of whether or not tourists should climb Uluru (Ayers Rock), Australia: <http://www.outback-australia-travel-secrets.com/climbing-ayers-rock-uluru.html>

Apply Schumann's Moral Principles framework (Chapter 2) and address questions connected to justice tourism. Would *you* climb Uluru? Why or why not?

FURTHER READING

Butler, R. and Hinch, T. (eds) (2007) *Tourism and Indigenous Peoples: Issues and Implications*, London: International Thompson Business Press.

NOTES

a *The Gallows Songs. Christian Morgenstern's Galgenlieder*, translated by Max Knight, Berkeley: University of California Press, 1964.
b Russell Means (1939–2012), Russell Means was an Oglala Sioux activist for The rights of Native American people. From *Where White Men Fear to Tread: The Autobiography of Russell Means*, New York: St Martin's Press, 1995.
c Paul Theroux (1941–), American travel writer and novelist. From *The Lower River*, New York: Houghton Mifflin Harcourt, 2012.

REFERENCES

Albers, P. and James, W. (1988) 'Travel photography: a methodological approach', *Annals of Tourism Research*, 15(1): 1134–58.
Ashley, C., Boyd, C. and Goodwin, H. (2000) 'Pro-poor tourism: putting poverty at the heart of the tourism agenda', *Natural Resource Perspectives*, 51 (March).
Azarya, V. (2004) 'Globalization and international tourism in developing countries: marginality as a commercial commodity', *Current Sociology*, 52: 949–67.
Bennett, T. and Blundell, V. (1995) 'Introduction: first peoples', *Cultural Studies*, 9(1): 1–10.
Bunten, A.C. (2008) 'Sharing culture or selling out? Developing the commodified persona in the heritage industry', *American Ethnologist*, 35(3): 380–95.

Butler, R. and Hinch, T. (eds) (2007) *Tourism and Indigenous Peoples: Issues and Implications,* Amsterdam: Butterworth-Heinemann.

Chok, S., Macbeth, J. and Warren, C. (2007) 'Tourism as a tool for poverty alleviation: a critical analysis of "Pro-Poor Tourism" and implications for sustainability', *Current Issues in Tourism,* 10(2&3): 144–65.

Clifford, J. (2004) 'Looking several ways, anthropology and native heritage in Alaska', *Current Anthropology,* 45(1): 5–30.

Cohen, E. (1993) 'The study of touristic images of native people: mitigating the stereotype of the stereotype', in Pearce, D. and Butler, R.W. (eds) *Tourism Research: Critiques and Challenges,* London: Routledge, pp. 36–69.

Douglas, N., Douglas, N. and Derrett, R. (eds) (2001) *Special Interest Tourism,* Brisbane: Wiley.

Enloe, C. (1990) *Bananas, Beaches and Bases: Making Feminist Sense of International Politics,* Berkeley: University of California Press.

Freire-Medeiros, B. (2009) 'The favela and its touristic transits', *Geoforum,* 40(4): 580–8.

Goodwin, H. (1998) *Sustainable Tourism and Poverty Elimination.* Available at <http://www.haroldgoodwin.info/resources/dfidpaper.pdf> (Accessed 19 February 2011).

Hall, C.M. (1996) 'Gender and economic interests in tourism prostitution', in Apostolopoulos, Y., Leivadi, S. and Yiannakis, A. (eds) *The Sociology of Tourism: Theoretical and Empirical Investigations,* New York: Routledge.

— (2007) 'Politics, power and indigenous tourism', in Butler, R. and Hinch, T. (eds) *Tourism and Indigenous Peoples: Issues and Implications,* London: International Thompson Business Press, pp. 305–18.

Harrison, D. (2008) 'Pro-poor tourism: a critique', *Third World Quarterly,* 29(5): 851–68.

Higgins-Desbiolles, F. (2003) 'Reconciliation tourism: tourism healing divided societies', *Tourism Recreation Research,* 28(3): 35–44.

— (2004) 'Reconciliation tourism: challenging the constraints of economic rationalism', in Ryan, C. and Aicken, M. (eds) *Indigenous Tourism: The Commodification and Management of Culture,* Amsterdam: Elsevier, pp. 223–45.

— (2007) 'Hostile meeting grounds: encounters between the wretched of the earth and the tourist through tourism and terrorism in the 21st century', in Burns, P., and Novelli, M. (eds) *Tourism and Politics: Global Frameworks and Local Realities,* Amsterdam: Elsevier, pp. 309–32.

— (2008) 'Justice tourism: a pathway to alternative globalisation', *Journal of Sustainable Tourism,* 16(3): 345–64.

Hinch, T. and Butler, R. (1996) 'Indigenous tourism: a common ground for discussion', in Butler, R. and Hinch, T. (eds) *Tourism and Indigenous Peoples,* London: International Thompson Business Press, pp. 3–19.

Hollinshead, K. (1996) 'Marketing and metaphysical realism: the dis-identification of Aboriginal life and traditions through tourism', in Butler, R. and Hinch, T. (eds) *Tourism and Indigenous Peoples,* London: International Thompson Business Press, pp. 308–47.

Johnston, A. (2000) 'Indigenous peoples and ecotourism: bringing indigenous knowledge and rights into the sustainability equation', *Tourism Recreation Research,* 25(2): 89–96.

Johnston, A.M. (2003) 'Self-determination: exercising indigenous rights in tourism', in Singh, S., Timothy, D.J. and Dowling, R.K. (eds) *Tourism in Destination Communities,* Wallingford: CABI, pp. 115–34.

Koven, S. (2004) *Slumming: Sexual and Social Politics in Victorian London,* Princeton, NJ: Princeton University Press.

Lea, J.P. (1993) 'Tourism development ethics in the Third World', *Annals of Tourism Research,* 20: 701–15.

MacCannell, D. (1992) *Empty Meeting Grounds: The Tourist Papers,* London: Routledge.

Mowforth, M. and Munt, L. (2003) *Tourism and Sustainability: Development and New Tourism in the Third World* (2nd edn), London: Routledge.

Papson, S. (1981) 'Spuriousness and tourism: politics of two Canadian provincial governments', *Annals of Tourism Research*, 8(2): 220–35.

Pitchford, S.R. (2008) *Identity Tourism: Imaging and Imagining the Nation*, Bingley, UK: Emerald Group Publishing.

Poon, A. (1993) *Tourism, Technology and Competitive Strategies*, Wallingford: CABI.

Richter, L.K. (2001) 'Tourism challenges in developing nations: continuity and change in the millennium', in Harrison, D. (ed.) *Tourism and the Less Developed World: Issues and Case Studies,* New York: CABI, pp. 47–59.

Roe, D. and Urquhart, P. (2004) 'Pro-poor tourism: harnessing the world's largest industry for the world's poor; turning the rhetoric into action for sustainable development and poverty reduction', in Bigg, T. (ed.) *Survival for a Small Planet – The Sustainable Development Agenda,* London: Earthscan, pp. 309–25.

Rolfes, M. (2009) 'Poverty Tourism: theoretical reflections and empirical findings regarding an extraordinary form of tourism', *GeoJournal*, 26 September, pp. 421–42.

Ryan, C. (2005) 'Tourist–host nexus: research considerations', in Ryan, C. and Aicken, M. (eds) *Indigenous Tourism: The Commodification and Management of Culture*, Amsterdam: Elsevier, pp. 1–11.

Scheyvens, R. (2002) *Tourism for Development: Empowering Communities,* Harlow: Prentice Hall.

—— (2007) 'Exploring the tourism–poverty nexus', *Current Issues in Tourism*, 10(2&3): 231–54.

Sharpley, R. (2000) 'Tourism and sustainable development: exploring the theoretical divide', *Journal of Sustainable Tourism,* 8: 1–19.

Smith, M. and Duffy, R. (2003) *The Ethics of Tourism Development*, London: Routledge.

United Nations General Assembly (UNGA) (2007) *Declaration on the Rights of Indigenous Peoples*. Available at <http:www.iwgia.org/sw248.asp.> (Accessed 2 June 2012).

Wearing, S. and Neil, J. (1999) *Ecotourism: Impacts, Potentials and Possibilities,* Oxford: Butterworth-Heinemann.

Weaver, D. (2010) 'Indigenous tourism stages and their implications for sustainability', *Journal of Sustainable Tourism*, 18(1): 43–60.

Wheeler, B. (1991) 'Tourism's troubled times: responsible tourism is not the answer', *Tourism Management,* 12(2): 91–6.

Whitford, M.M. and Ruhanen, L.M. (2010) 'Australian indigenous tourism policy: practice and sustainable policies?', *Journal of Sustainable Tourism*, 18(4): 475–96.

Xanthaki, A. (2009) 'Indigenous rights in international Law over the last 10 years and future developments', *Melbourne Journal of International Law,* 10(1): 3.

8 Tourism and disability

'Until the great mass of the people shall be filled with the sense of responsibility for each other's welfare, social justice can never be attained.'

Helen Keller[a]

'The first step in the evolution of ethics is a sense of solidarity with other human beings.'

Albert Schweitzer[b]

'The moral test of government is how it treats those who are in the dawn of life ... the children; those who are in the twilight of life ... the elderly; and those who are in the shadow of life ... the sick ... the needy ... and the disabled.'

Hubert H. Humphrey[c]

LEARNING OBJECTIVES

After reading this chapter you will be able to:

- Define disability and discuss its relevance to tourism.
- Describe the policy and legal environment relevant to tourism and disability.
- Understand the nature of the tourist experience of persons with disabilities.
- Discuss the different models of disability and how they influence society's response to disability.
- Consider key ethical approaches to the question of disability.
- Describe the issues concerning 'reasonable accommodation' for the needs of persons with disabilities.

8.1 INTRODUCTION

In recent years there has been a growing interest from the tourism sector in persons with disabilities. This is evidenced by the emergent discourse around what is referred to as 'Accessible Tourism'. In part this has been motivated by an altruistic concern for providing equitable access to tourism services and products. But the industry is slowly awakening to the size of the market and the opportunities it presents to destinations and operators (Var et al. 2011). To put the scale of disability as a phenomenom into perspective: 'Every person is likely to experience disability of a permanent or transient nature in his or her own lifetime' (Green 2011: 219). Currently, there are estimated to be over 650 million disabled people in the world – comprising roughly 8 per cent of the world's population (UNWTO 2011). In America alone, there are 54 million people covered under the Americans with Disabilities Act, constituting nearly 21 per cent of the US population (Israeli 2002). Overall, the number of persons with disabilities (PWD) is projected to grow – not only with the increase in the world's population, but also with changing demographics, specifically an 'ageing' population, particularly in Western, developed countries. Increasingly older people will share many of the access barriers faced by PWD (Var et al. 2011). Thus PWD, their caregivers, families and friends, in the brutal terms of the marketplace, collectively comprise a substantial and largely untapped niche market, potentially worth 'billions of Euros for the tourism industry' (Var et al. 2011: 602). Described as 'the largest minority group in the world' (Etravelblackboard.com 2010), creating accessible tourist destinations 'is not charity. It is good business' (Rains 2007 in UNESCAP 2007).

Yet despite this enticement, few consumer groups 'are more ignored than the disabled' (Burnett and Bender Baker 2001). A growing body of tourism research points to an industry that is yet to really engage with the disabled, evidenced by the disproportionate number of PWD who do not regularly participate in tourism. This is despite PWD having 'the same needs and desires for tourism as others' (Yau et al. 2004: 946) – or perhaps even more so. The tourism experience may be particularly meaningful for the disabled in terms of providing opportunities to be freed from the role of 'objects of care', for overcoming self-doubt, building self-confidence, and developing other skills or aptitudes that can be taken back into everyday life (Blichfeldt and Nicolaisen 2010; McAvoy et al. 2006).

But when the disabled *do* travel, they get a mixed reception. A study on the French Riviera, for example, found that the services offered to tourists with disabilities are the product of a mixture of willingness and legal obligation, and that 'disabled people are not yet considered as real clients but as a separate population, not to be mixed with the able-bodied holiday clientele' (Christofle and Massiera 2009: 97). Yet researchers are pointing out the links between accessible tourism and sustainable tourism, arguing that there are triple bottom-line advantages for meeting the needs of the disabled, while also advocating for a 'whole of life' approach to tourism that will address the challenges of changing demographics (Darcy et al. 2010; Darcy and Dickson 2009).

8.2 DISABILITY

Disability is described by the World Health Organization as 'any restriction or lack (resulting from impairment) of ability to perform an activity in the manner or within the range considered normal for a human being' (WHO 1980). Similarly, the UK Disability Discrimination Act describes a disabled person as someone who 'has a physical or mental impairment which has a substantial and long-term adverse effect on his/her ability to carry out normal day-to-day activities' (United Kingdom Office of Public Sector Information 1995). (Impairments are problems in body function or structure such as a significant deviation or loss (WHO 2002: 10)).

Disability can be categorised into four types: hearing disability, sight disability, physical disability and intelligence deficiency (Daniels et al. 2005). Correspondingly, the *United Nations Convention on the Rights of Persons with Disabilities* states that persons with disabilities include those who have 'long-term physical, mental, intellectual or sensory impairments which in interaction with various barriers may hinder their full and effective participation in society on an equal basis with others' (United Nations 2006: 3, Article 1).

8.3 POLICY AND LEGISLATIVE ENVIRONMENT

As noted above, research has highlighted the benefits of travel for PWD (e.g. Daniels et al. 2005). Basic human rights aside, that travel has such potential to enhance the wellbeing of persons with disabilities points to the importance of an effective policy and legislative framework to address the travel needs of those with disabilities. Such a framework has been developed beneath the umbrella of the *Universal Declaration of Human Rights* (1948) which states that all humans are born free and equal in dignity and rights, with everyone entitled to the same rights and freedoms, without distinction of any kind. Pursuant to the *Universal Declaration* is the *United Nations Convention on the Rights of Persons with Disabilities* (2006), the purpose of which is to promote, protect and ensure the full and equal enjoyment of all human rights and fundamental freedoms by all persons with disabilities, and to promote respect for their inherent dignity.

If we consider how tourism rights in particular are addressed through these, we note that the *Universal Declaration* specifies the right to freedom of movement and the right to rest and leisure (United Nations 1948). Similarly, Article 20 of the *Convention on the Rights of Persons with Disabilities*, titled 'Personal mobility', notes that 'Parties shall take effective measures to ensure personal mobility with the greatest possible independence for persons with disabilities', by:

a) Facilitating the personal mobility of persons with disabilities in the manner and at the time of their choice, and at affordable cost;
b) Facilitating access by persons with disabilities to quality mobility aids, devices, assistive technologies and forms of live assistance and intermediaries, including by making them available at affordable cost;
c) Providing training in mobility skills to persons with disabilities and to specialist staff working with persons with disabilities;
d) Encouraging entities that produce mobility aids, devices and assistive technologies to take into account all aspects of mobility for persons with disabilities.

We take reference to 'all aspects of mobility' to include activities such as tourism. However, disability-specific policy within the tourism sector is led by the United Nations World Tourism Organization (UNWTO), which 'is convinced that the facilitation of tourist travel by persons with disabilities is a vital element of any responsible and sustainable tourism development policy' (UNWTO 2011). In 2005, the UNWTO adopted the resolution 'Accessible Tourism for All', featuring a series of recommendations to the sector, including the necessity of providing clear information on the accessibility of tourism facilities, the availability of support services in destinations for persons with disabilities, and the training of employees on the special needs of these individuals. In 2009 the

UNWTO adopted a further 'Declaration on the Facilitation of Tourist Travel'. While this too is only of a 'purely recommendatory nature', it advises that 'great efforts should be made to ensure that tourism policies and practices are inclusive of persons with disabilities' (UNWTO 2011).

The declarations and conventions cited above are examples of 'soft law' that until transformed into 'hard law' through ratification and enactment into legislation remain largely inspirational and recommendatory. But increasingly the rights of disabled persons have become mandated through legislation and policy, for example the *Americans with Disabilities Act* (1990), the *Disability Discrimination Act* (1995) in the United Kingdom, Australia's *Disability Discrimination Act* (1992) and New Zealand's *Public Health and Disability Act* (2000). Recently the European Union implemented Regulation (EC) [1107/2006] which stipulates that 'disabled people and people with reduced mobility have the same right as any other citizens to free movement' (in Richards et al. 2010).

Is legislation and policy working?

But despite a strong overarching policy and legal environment that attempts to provide for tourists (or would-be tourists) with disabilities in many destinations, evidence suggests that there is some way to go until the tourism industry is 'disability-friendly'. Miller and Kirk (2002) in their article 'The Disability Discrimination Act: Time for the Stick' discuss the effectiveness of this legislation (introduced in the UK in 1995) in promoting accessible tourism opportunities for those with disabilities. The Act makes it illegal to: refuse to serve a disabled person; provide disabled people with a lower standard of service; or provide a service on worse terms. The disabled market in the UK was estimated to be worth £6 billion (in 1996). Yet a significant proportion of the disabled population do not take holidays, despite evidence suggesting that a high percentage of disabled people feel holidays are important to them. To assess the response of the tourism industry to demands from the disabled, researchers engaged a visually impaired 'mystery shopper' with specific travel needs. Most tourism businesses were found seriously wanting, with generally an 'extremely low ability of organisations to meet the simple requests made' (Miller and Kirk 2002: 82). The researchers concluded that the 'carrot' of the £6 billion was not enough to entice tourism businesses to address the needs of those with disabilities, and that the threat of the 'stick' (the punitive aspects of the legislation) would be needed to achieve this.

CASE STUDY: AN ACT OF OMISSION, RESOURCING AND WILL: TOURISM, DISABILITY AND ACCESS WITHIN THE PUBLIC POLICY SPHERE – *SIMON DARCY*

The acting Prime Minister of Australia Wayne Swan, the opposition leader Tony Abbott, Senator Jan McLucas the Parliamentary Secretary for Disability and Carers, State Disability Ministers and a large number of VIPs welcomed home the Australian Paralympic Team from the London 2012 Paralympic Games on Thursday, 13 September 2012. The Australian Paralympic Team had done extraordinarily well and were greeted by speeches lauding their performances, their inspiration and their sportsmanship. They were told what a wonderful performance they had achieved on the world stage and how all Australians supported them. Yet, these same Australians do not have an equal opportunity when it comes to tourism within their own country or when they travel abroad unless they are part of an elite sporting team. Why is this so?

An examination of the corporate website of Tourism Australia, Australia's Commonwealth tourism marketing authority, reveals that it has no reference to disability or accessible tourism – apart from a human resources statement about recruitment where it states that:

> Tourism Australia is committed to eliminating an adverse action against a person who is an employee, or prospective employee, of the employer because of the person's sex, marital status, pregnancy, parenthood, race (including colour, national or ethnic origin), age, sexual preference, disability, religious or political conviction.

> (Tourism Australia 2011)

With regards to its consumer website, there is a single paragraph that states:

> Accessible Travel: If you have a disability and are planning to explore Australia, there is a host of services and special deals to meet your needs. Thorough preparation is essential to a successful trip, so speak to your travel agent about your specific requirements. For more information on accessible tourism in Australia go to NICAN or the AustraliaForAll websites.

> (Tourism Australia 2011)

Effectively Tourism Australia suggest that two small not-for-profit organisations can provide information on accessible tourism, whereas a very well-resourced (AU$180 million) government entity does not provide any specific programmes. The corporate site on which Tourism Australia identifies their targeted market segments (including the Australian cruise industry; the youth segment; the family segment; the holidaymaker segment; and the honeymoon segment), has no recognition that PWD could be part of all of those segments, but require specific information if they are able to participate. Currently the Australian Tourism Data Warehouse is the database that provides information on Australian tourism products and services but no detailed access information is collected (Australian Tourism Data Warehouse 2012). This overt omission by Australia's national tourism authority is a failure to be inclusive for Australians with disabilities travelling domestically or for tourists from overseas, who have disabilities. This situation is even more disappointing, considering that in 2011 NICAN (an organisation providing inclusive information for sport and tourism) together with Senator Jan McLucas, Parliamentary Secretary for Disabilities and Carers, hosted a National Tourism Dialogue at Parliament House that brought together stakeholders in disability and tourism in Australia. The outcome of the dialogue was the joint issuing of a Communiqué, where the stakeholders called for increasing access to tourism for people with disability. Senator McLucas issued a media release supporting the communiqué (McLucas 2011; NICAN 2011). But 18 months on, there has been no further commitment to increasing access to tourism for people with disability from the Commonwealth government.

The above reflects, historically, Australian approaches to disability and tourism policy, which can be characterised as a series of well-documented policy announcements (Darcy et al. 2012) that have not been resourced. This lack of leadership at the Commonwealth level can partly explain the cases of disability discrimination in tourism outlined elsewhere in this chapter. The Commonwealth, in its role as a coordination agency for tourism information, marketing and promotion, needs to lead the industry, setting the benchmark for inclusive approaches to tourism information that offers a foundation for tourism trip planning; Australia's Disability Discrimination Act applies to all services open to the public and states that service providers should offer an equality of opportunity for people with disability. However, as the disability discrimination cases highlight, even in this most basic of tourism functions (information provision) there has been an abject failure to treat people with disability equally before the law. The Australian situation is very similar to that of the UK and the United States where similar types of omission and lack of considerations or willpower for provision lead to discrimination.

The UN *Convention on the Rights of Persons with Disabilities* was adopted by over 150 nations in 2008. This presents a significant challenge to government tourism marketing authorities and the industry as Article 30 clearly identifies their responsibilities to provide equality of tourism experiences for this group. This requires more than policy rhetoric and a significant contribution towards ensuring that the travel chain offers people with disability the opportunities that the rest of the travelling population take for granted (World Health Organization and World Bank 2011: 179). The travel chain in tourism starts with information to allow tourism planning, and then goes on to include transport, accommodation, attractions and other destination experiences.

So, with the closing of the London 2012 Olympic and Paralympic Games we can take heart in the extensive programme of new offerings that Visit England has undertaken over the last three years. These include research, policy, industry collaboration, awareness workshops and a celebration that the Olympic and Paralympic Games offered an opportunity to improve accessibility for all those coming to the UK (VisitEngland 2012). We can only hope that other destination marketing authorities consider their equity responsibilities in the same way. As the world looks towards the Rio 2016 Olympic and Paralympic Games, we can hope that politicians can in the future truly welcome back our Paralympians and offer them an equality of tourism experience in the same way that they experience sport at the elite level.

Discussion questions

1 Why should the state (governments) have a special role with respect to leadership in the provision of tourism information and services for PWD?
2 If there is a cost applied to accessing tourism information, should this cost also apply to persons with disabilities accessing the same information?
3 What do you think are the biggest hurdles for governments in ensuring equality of opportunity for PWD?
4 For tourism, identify some pathways for overcoming the obstacles identified in the question above.

References

Australian Tourism Data Warehouse. (2012) *About us – a brief explanation*. Available at <http://www.atdw.com.au/aboutus.aspx> (Accessed 12 July 2012).

Darcy, S., Cameron, B., and Schweinsberg, S. (2012) 'Accessible Tourism in Australia', in Buhalis, D., Darcy, S. and Ambrose, I. (eds) *Best Practice in Accessible Tourism: Inclusion, Disability, Ageing Population and Tourism,* Bristol: Channel View, pp. 79–113.

McLucas, J. (2011) *Media release: Increasing Access to Tourism for People with a Disability*. Available at <http://www.janmclucas.fahcsia.gov.au/mediare-leases/2011/Pages/increase_access_tourism_20062011.aspx> (Accessed 25 June 2011).

NICAN (2011) *Communiqué: National Tourism Dialogue*. Available at <http://www.nican.com.au/news/communique-national-tourism-dialogue> (Accessed 1 September 2012).

Tourism Australia (2011) *HR 33 Recruitment*, Sydney: Tourism Australia.

— (2012) *Useful tips*. Available at <http://www.australia.com/plan/before-you-go/useful-tips.aspx> (Accessed 13 September 2012).

VisitEngland (2012) *Accessible Tourism*. Available at <http://www.visitengland.org/busdev/bussupport/access/index.aspx> (Accessed 11 September, 2012).

World Health Organization and World Bank (2011) *World Report on Disability*. Available at <http://www.who.int/disabilities/world_report/2011/report/en/index.html> (Accessed 12 September 2012).

8.4 TRAVEL EXPERIENCES OF THE DISABLED

Other examples abound within the tourism literature of limits placed upon disabled travellers, and the many difficulties they face (e.g. Israeli 2002; Takeda and Card 2002; Daniels et al. 2005; Shaw and Coles 2004; Poria et al. 2009, 2010; Freeman and Selmi 2010). Often, studies have found lower participation rates in tourism for those with disabilities (e.g. Packer et al. 2002). And when persons with disabilities *do* travel, their experiences are still 'highly restricted by physical accessibility barriers, such as: transportation constraints, inaccessible accommodation and tourism sites as well as information barriers' (Pühretmair and Buhalis 2008: 969).

Useful sources for travel stories of PWD

<http://www.e-bility.com/articles/index.php>
<http://www.disabledtravelers.com/articles.htm>
<http://www.d-ability.org/travel.php?subcat_id = 206>
<http://www.miusa.org/ncde/stories/blog> (includes stories from students with disabilities who travel or are on exchange programmes).

The above examples and others, demonstrate that for those with disabilites, travel is perceived to have a significant element of personal risk (Yau et al. 2004). In Yau et al.'s study, participants with spinal cord injuries worried about pragmatic issues such as bladder control, and the risk of personal embarrassment related to this. There was also worry that airlines could potentially lose their wheelchair. If the sum of these perceived risks is too high the individual will not travel (Yau et al. 2004).

Experiences for the visually impaired

Apart from the pragmatic concerns, there are social and psychological challenges with travel. Yau et al. (2004) describe how the visually impaired participants in their study felt vulnerable in new and unfamiliar surroundings, and worried about their personal safety. Packer et al. (2008) provide an interesting study of the tourist experiences of individuals with vision impairment, finding that they faced significant challenges in terms of accessing information, navigating the physical environment safely and travelling with a guide dog. They also have to cope with the insensitivity of those they may encounter during their travel. Some researchers have described the 'inhospitable tourism spaces' that the visually impaired need to negotiate (Richards et al. 2010).

Museums and galleries as significant tourist attractions in many destinations provide a good illustration of the difficulties that the visually impaired visitor faces in obtaining a satisfactory experience. The challenge of providing meaningful experiences for the visually impaired, through touch, in museums and galleries are substantial (Hetherington 2000; Hillis 2005). And while museums are now meeting the challenge of physical access, to the extent that visually impaired visitors 'will not find, as they might have found in the past, the door slammed in their face' (Hetherington 2000: 461), the transformation of these museums into user-friendly spaces for the disabled is not yet complete. Hetherington believes that the visually impaired now have an ambivalent status in museums, 'a kind of deferral of how to respond' (Hetherington 2000: 461). This deferral, he concludes, also means deferring on ethical questions around the needs of the visually impaired who want to visit museums and be given access to items on display best suited to their own needs – overcoming the 'do not touch' approach. Similarly, Poria and colleagues (2009) report on similar experiences for disabled museum visitors in Israel, who have '"major difficulties" in achieving a "full museum experience"' (2009: 117). In their study, the non-physical elements (staff and other visitors' attitudes) were at least as important as the physical aspects of the museum environment.

It is argued that the tourism industry and community should endeavour to reconceptualise the tourist experience, go beyond the 'visual gaze' and understand the multi-sensory nature of the tourist experience. In doing so the experiences of sighted as well as the visually impaired will be enhanced (Small et al. 2011).

DISCUSSION POINT: PLANES AND WHEELCHAIRS

Ryanair left a wheelchair-bound passenger on the runway at Luton Airport because 'all it was interested in was getting the plane airborne on time' according to a judge.

Jo Heath, who suffers multiple sclerosis, had to be carried on to the aircraft by her husband Paul using a fireman's lift. Northampton County Court ruled the airline broke disability discrimination laws and breached its contract with Heath after its staff refused to help the couple in June 2008. The court awarded the Heaths £1,750.

Husband Paul said: 'Ryanair tried to brush us under the carpet. They offered us more money than we eventually received but we refused it because they wanted us to sign a confidentiality clause.'

Jo Heath said: 'I'm not terribly impressed with the pay-out but it's not a question of money. It's about standing up for people with disabilities.'

Judge Paul McHale ruled: 'I find as a matter of fact that anything that interfered with the [aircraft] turnaround time was going to be ignored. All the defendant was interested in was getting the plane airborne on time.'

Ryanair said it would appeal on the grounds that Luton Airport was responsible for assisting the passengers under European Union law. The couple had submitted a special requirements request for a hydraulic Ambulift, which failed to turn up on the day.

Source

Ryanair found guilty in disability discrimination case. Available at <http://www.travelweekly.co.uk/> (15 April 2011).

Discussion question

This example demonstrates that while legislation is important in enforcing the rights of persons with disabilities, legislation as an incentive for companies to develop services for the disabled has not been entirely effective. The provider in this case is a Low Cost Carrier (LCC). A characteristic of LCCs is a lower standard of service than standard airlines, with many of the normal aspects of service requiring an additional charge on the passenger. Should the persons with disabilities in this case have expected to receive the same level of service in relation to their disability as they would have received if they had flown on a standard airline? Discuss why or why not.

Figure 8.1 Do airlines have a moral requirement to meet the needs of PWD?
Photo: Brent Lovelock.

DISCUSSION POINT: 'REASONABLE ACCOMMODATION'

In 2002 Valerie Smith complained to New Zealand's Human Rights Commission that Air New Zealand charged her extra for oxygen when she flew, and she regarded this as discriminatory. Valerie suffers a congenital respiratory disorder which means she needs extra oxygen when she travels by air. She took a case to the Human Rights Review Tribunal, stating that she had been discriminated against under the Human Rights Act and that the airline had failed to 'reasonably accommodate' her needs as stated under the act. The tribunal found that Air New Zealand had treated Valerie Smith less favourably than other passengers because of her disability, but that the airline had acted reasonably in charging for the extra oxygen.

Valerie Smith appealed the tribunal's decision that the airline had acted reasonably in charging her to the High Court, and Air New Zealand also cross-appealed the finding of discrimination. The High Court allowed Air New Zealand's appeal and concluded that the airline had not discriminated against Valerie Smith.

The case was taken to the Court of Appeal which has dismissed Valerie Smith's appeal that the airline had not acted reasonably in charging for extra oxygen, but reinstated the finding of discrimination under section 44 of the Human Rights Act. Service providers to whom the Human Rights Act applies will have to provide services to a person with a disability or treat those persons no less favourably in connection with the provision of those services – subject to a reasonableness requirement.

The New Zealand Human Rights Commission noted that, contrary to what had been thought, there is an obligation to accommodate PWD to the extent that it is unreasonable to expect a provider to do so.

Discussion questions:

1 What is meant by the 'reasonableness requirement'?
2 From whose perspective is this defined?
3 When would it become 'unreasonable' to expect a tourism provider to accommodate the needs of PWD?
4 What are some examples from the airline and other sectors of the tourism industry where it may be 'reasonable' or 'unreasonable' to accommodate the needs of PWD?

Source

New Zealand Human Rights Commission. Available at <http://www.hrc.co.nz/2011/human-rights-case-update> (Accessed 12 February 2012).

While access, involving a range of barriers, is shown to be an issue for the disabled, physical access is but one issue, with other constraints often being more significant to this group:

> there is an important segment of disabled people for whom removing the barriers of physical access is only part of the problem. For this group, holidays are not possible because of financial restrictions. These are clearly associated with disabilities in that these restrict access to the world of work.

> (Shaw and Coles 2004: 402)

It is argued that the disabled are a marginal group, and that the tourism industry's boosterism of the economic opportunities represented by the disabled market does not align with the realities of this group of marginal tourists (Shaw and Coles 2004; Shaw 2007). So, addressing the structural denial of access for the disabled to 'loot and clout' is more fundamental than merely dismantling barriers to physical access (Shelton and Tucker 2005). Ultimately, becoming 'travel active' involves more than just overcoming physical barriers (Yau et al. 2004).

As noted by Shaw (2007) although legislation such as the UK Disability Discrimination Act (1995) has acted as a catalyst to focus attention on the needs of persons with disabilities in general, such legislation has done little to help those persons with disabilities that are further marginalised by low income. Shaw goes on to suggest that a policy of social tourism may be the only way to empower this group.

Social tourism is defined as 'the relationships and phenomena in the field of tourism resulting from participation in travel by economically weak or otherwise disadvantaged elements of society' (Hall 2000: 141). The persons with disabilities are among the main social groups who are most at risk from social exclusion from tourism (McCabe 2009) and would presumably benefit significantly from such a practice. While for many countries there is little knowledge of social tourism, in parts of Europe there is a history of social tourism:

> As early as 1956 Arthur Haulot (a former prisoner of Dachau), initiated a movement that subsequently led to the *Bureau Internationale du Tourisme Sociale*, and which has, in 2000, a large number of organisations scattered around the world. The Bureau seeks to establish a right to a paid vacation, and to provide those on low income with subsidised travel.
>
> (Ryan 2002: 18)

Within the UK, there have been past initiatives to aid single parents and disabled groups (Ryan 2002), and the 'Tourism for All' charity works to create equality of access to tourism opportunities, focusing mostly on older people and PWD (McCabe 2009) (see *Tourism for All* <http://www.tourismforall.org.uk>). Families with either adults or children with disabilities were included in McCabe's (2009) study of the demand for subsidised social tourism experiences in the UK. His study found that holiday participation impacts positively on people's sense of wellbeing, their life experiences and horizons. McCabe raises the question of the role of holidays 'as an enabler to help [disadvantaged] people contribute positively to wider society through work, attitudinal and behavioral change, and normalised consumption practices' (2009: 684). However, he does note that social tourism initiatives to combat social exclusion will 'require a particular ethical orientation at either the level of government or society' (McCabe 2009: 670).

8.5 SOCIAL MODEL OF DISABILITY

Despite access being more broadly conceptualised, the tourism industry continues to pay a 'disproportionate amount of attention to issues of physical access' (Shelton and Tucker 2005: 211). With respect to nature-based recreation, most of the effort has gone into improving physical access for the disabled (Burns et al. 2009). A contributing factor to this is that in general disability is commonly equated only with physical impairment (i.e. wheelchair users) and that the broader needs of people with other disabilities are often overlooked (Burns et al. 2009).

The continued focus on physical access is also considered to be due to an uncritical acceptance of the medical or person-centred model of disability (Shelton and Tucker 2005). Instead, the tourism industry would better be directed to consider the social model of disability in which disability is not viewed simply as a medical problem, but rather as a product of the disabling tourism environment (Shelton and Tucker 2005; Darcy and Pegg 2011). The social model of disability views disability as 'a product of the disabling environmental, social and attitudinal barriers that compound a person's impairment and prevent their [full] participation in society' (Darcy and Pegg 2011: 470). In this model, the need for societal change is emphasised, rather than individuals adapting to the disabling environment: 'It is not the person's impairment that is disabling but the social exclusion that they are subjected to by environmental design or service attitude' (Darcy and Pegg 2011: 470). To illustrate, a person with a given mobility impairment is not disabled in an environment where he or she can use accessible public transport and gain full access to buildings and their respective facilities in the same manner that a person without an impairment might do (Barnes et al. 2010 in Darcy and Pegg 2011). Separating out 'impairment' from 'disability' is the cornerstone of the social model of disability (Morris 2001). Conversely, the medical model of disability reinforces the idea that impairments need always equate with disability, and with this comes a perpetuation of the tourism industry's focus on a narrow version of access, rather than on providing 'opportunities to participate'(Shelton and Tucker 2005).

It must be noted that the social model is not without its critics, who argue that it is seriously flawed, because of the claim that once the social dimensions of disability have been resolved no seriously disabling features remain (Harris 2001). On their own, neither model is adequate, although both are partially valid. The World Health Organization's position is that disability is always an interaction between features of the person and features of the overall context in which the person lives (WHO 2002: 9). Thus, both medical and social responses are appropriate to the problems associated with disability. They advocate a model of disability that synthesises the medical and social models into what might be called the *biopsychosocial model* (WHO 2002). (See Smith 2009 for a fuller discussion of the social and medical models of disability.)

Figure 8.2 shows the competing views of disability and disablement and the social responsibilities that attach to each formulation (Rioux and Valentine 2006: 49). The authors identify four social and scientific formulations of disability that are reflected in the treatment of PWD in law, policy, social programmes and human rights instruments (Rioux and Valentine 2006: 49).

8.6 TOURISM INDUSTRY AND THE DISABLING ENVIRONMENT

It appears that the tourism industry is facing some challenges in addressing the disabling environment and the associated range of constraints faced by persons with disabilities. For example, in a study of accommodation managers in Australia, Darcy and Pegg (2011: 475) found that 'far from embracing disability, there were a series of omissions that maintained a disabling accommodation environment'. These included no proactive approach to developing disability as a market segment; low levels of disability awareness/training; a lack of understanding of what constitutes suitable accessible accommodation; and an omission to document, market and promote this information to PWD (see also Daruwalla and Darcy 2005; Eichhorn et al. 2008). In sum, there are a number of commonalities in terms of the specific requirements of the disability 'market' (Buhalis and Michopoulou 2011: 159):

- Accessibility of physical/built environment
- Information regarding accessibility
- Accessible information online.

However, as has been pointed out 'the accessibility market is not homogenous, but it entails different sub-segments with distinct needs and requirements' (Buhalis and

INDIVIDUAL PATHOLOGY	
Biomedical approach (consequency of biological characteristics)	**Functional approach** (consequency of functional abilities and capacities)
• **Treatment:** through medicine and biotechnology • **Prevention:** through biological or genetic intervention or screening • **Social responsibility:** to eliminate or cure	• **Treatment:** through rehabilitation services • **Prevention:** through early diagnosis and treatment • **Social responsibility:** to ameliorate and provide comfort
SOCIAL PATHOLOGY	
Environmental approach (consequency of environmental factors and service arrangements)	**Human rights approach** (consequency of social organization and relationship of individual to society)
• **Treatment:** through increased individual control of services and supports • **Prevention:** through elimination of social, economic, and physical barriers • **Social responsibility:** to eliminate systemic barriers	• **Treatment:** through reformulation of economic, social, and political policy • **Prevention:** through recognition of conditions of disability as inherent in society • **Social responsibility:** to provide political and social entitlements

Figure 8.2 *Social and scientific formulations of disability.*
Source: Rioux and Valentine (2006).

Michopoulou 2011: 145). These authors depict a pyramid of demand types, based upon a continuum of abilities, noting that each individual, with their unique abilities and disabilities, has a unique set of requirements. They then identify seven disability sub-segments, and outline the importance of information required by each segment prior to travel: 'Different types of disability place importance on different criteria while the degree of ability/disability determines the significance of those criteria for individual travellers' (2011: 160). Shaw (2007) also identifies a continuum of impacts of impairment, but

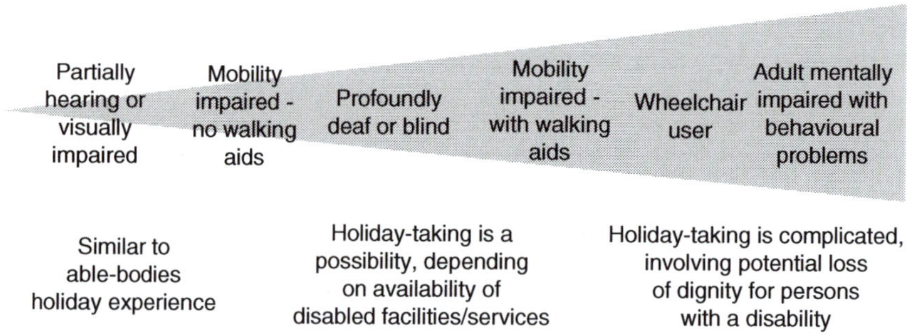

Figure 8.3 *A continuum of impacts of disability on holidaymaking.*
Source: Shaw (2007).

differing from that above, in the way that it highlights that certain types of impairment may lead to greater impacts on holidaymaking (Figure 8.3).

The complexity and diversity of disabilities is certainly challenging, and the range of potential disabilities so enormous, that the question is 'how does one begin to talk about a group characteristic such as disability without slipping into communalistic claims that reproduce claims of inclusion and exclusion' (Devlin and Pothier 2006: 14). There is also the compounding issue of 'intersectionality' where considerations of disability may be too generic because they do not give significant emphasis to other aspects of a disabled person's identity, including gender, ethnicity, sexual orientation or class (Devlin and Pothier 2006: 14).

Despite these complexities, however, it is suggested that segmenting the disabled by type and level of impairment may be a useful approach to understanding and meeting the needs of those with disabilities (Buhalis and Michopoulou 2011; Burnett and Bender Baker 2001).

While the report card for the industry is far from perfect, there is some evidence, however, that some destinations (e.g. South Africa, Finland, the State of Victoria in Australia) are starting to take a more proactive approach at the destination level to issues around disability (Darcy and Pegg 2011).

Making your tourism business accessible

To successfully cater for human rights issues and a growing market, tourism businesses should be aware of some of the main barriers experienced by travellers with a disability. These include:

- Physical barriers such as inaccessible buildings and facilities
- Inaccessible information, for example text that is too small to read
- A lack of disability awareness and negative staff attitudes
- Poor promotion of existing accessible services and facilities.

Useful sources

Tourism Victoria: Accessible Tourism <http://www.tourism.vic.gov.au/industry-resources/industry-resources/accessible-tourism/>
Tourism Victoria's Accessible Tourism Plan 2010–2013 <http://www.tourism.vic.gov.au/images/stories/Documents/StrategiesandPlans/final-accessible-tourism-plan-2010-2013.pdf>
Be Accessible (New Zealand) <http://www.beaccessible.org.nz/>

8.7 MORAL IMPERATIVE FOR ADDRESSING NEEDS OF THE DISABLED

Notwithstanding the legal and human rights requirements to address the needs of persons with disabilities, and the market-based economic imperative to do so, is there a *moral imperative* for society to provide for their needs? And, furthermore, specifically for the tourism industry to provide for their touristic needs? One problem in developing an ethical argument for the touristic care of PWD is that people with impairments, in the view of some ethical theories and theories of social justice, are 'marginal human beings'. The tenets of Western moral philosophy suggest that people with impairments are 'morally less human then others' (Vehmas 2004: 218). This suggests that conventional ethics may be imperfect in terms of addressing the touristic needs of the disabled.

Such problems are aptly illustrated by the view of Aristotle (384–322 BC), a founding father of virtue theory. Aristotle did not, however, have a particularly enlightened view of disability, explicitly endorsing in the *Politics,* the Greek practice of leaving 'deformed' babies to die of exposure. However, such a view can perhaps be forgiven in that it was very much shaped by common understandings of the human body in Ancient Greece (Merriam 2010).

Utilitarianism and disability

That similar sentiments emerge in contemporary bioethics, however, is a little more challenging. We refer here in particular to the work of bioethicist Peter Singer. Singer (2000) promotes an extreme version of Jeremy Bentham's utilitarian philosophy, which defines any act that increases the total amount of pleasure or decreases the total amount of suffering in the world as moral. The concept of human rights is not really important to utilitarians, although some utilitarians may see the application of human rights as a means to the end of increasing happiness and reducing suffering (McPherson and Sobsey 2003). As discussed in Chapter 10, in relation to animal rights, self-awareness is intrinsic to 'moral considerability', and in Singer's view people with severe cognitive disabilities have no such status. Thus they should not be considered in our moral reasoning. Singer suggests excluding from personhood everyone who has severe disabilities. He argues that a person's potential for happiness is limited by their disability, and that allowing them to live is morally wrong because we are prolonging their suffering and using resources that might increase the happiness of others with a greater quality of life potential (Singer 2000; McPherson and Sobsey 2003). Critics argue that PWD rate their quality of life just as highly as people without disabilities, and compare Singer's approach with that of the Nazis, who exterminated the disabled and minorities on the grounds that these actions decreased suffering and increased happiness in the world (McPherson and Sobsey 2003).

However, utilitarianism has been defended as providing an argument for positive social response to disability. Tannsjo (2010) applies classical hedonistic utilitarianism to the issue of disability. (Because Bentham's concept of *utility* comprised happiness and suffering, ethicists refer to him as a hedonistic utilitarian – *hedonism* is the view that the best life is one that maximises pleasure. See Chapter 2.) Tannsjo argues that because utilitarianism requires us to act to maximise the sum total of wellbeing (happiness) in the world, we need to understand the 'hedonistic status' of disabled people – to what extent their impairments and resulting disabilities make them unhappy. This, in a way, parallels tourism research into the different levels and types of impairment and how they impact differently upon the touristic experience (see Buhalis and Michopoulou 2011; Shaw 2007). Tannsjo identifies a range of disabilities including 'mere' disabilities which result in no loss of happiness; 'simple' disabilities, which do not seem to make people less happy than those who do not have them, although this happiness may rely upon society taking measures to facilitate the disabled person's life; 'problematic' disabilities include those which impact the hedonic status of the person with the disability; and the final category comprises those with 'tragic' disabilities that are so severe 'they rob the disabled person of a life worth living' (Tannsjo 2010: 96). Tannsjo argues that utilitarianism may suggest different solutions to issues arising for people whose disability lies in each of these categories.

Importantly, given utilitarianism, Tannsjo argues that PWD have a strong claim on scarce resources. While Tannsjo's focus is upon medical resources, we can extend the utilitarian argument to scarce tourism resources – for example transport, accommodation and activities. 'Classical hedonistic utilitarianism seems to give the "right" answer to how society should react to disability' (Tannsjo 2010), and can thus inform us as to how touristic resources may be allocated between those with and without disability.

It should be noted that there is a range of alternative ethical approaches to the question of disability, but that space in this book precludes our coverage of all. However, readers should be aware of egalitarianism (the view that we should try to level out happiness between people – even at some cost – and considered from the point of view of the sum-total of happiness (Tannsjo 2010: 100)) and prioritarianism (a version of utilitarianism), an approach that recognises 'a diminishing marginal moral importance of happiness' (2010: 100). The latter advocates a focus on increasing the happiness of those who are least happy, rather than increasing the happiness of those who already possess high levels of happiness. Arneson (2000) points out that prioritarianism may require us to aid only those people with impairments, who are disadvantaged, compared to those with the same impairments who are not disadvantaged. Prioritarianism thus gels with the social model of disability in recognising that social factors are paramount in defining a disability and by extension defining access to and assistance required in tourism experiences. Yet Tannsjo (2010) rejects both egalitarianism and prioritarianism, believing them to not support the case for social assistance for persons with disabilities, as strongly as does utilitarianism.

Despite the extreme views espoused by Aristotle and the 'Singerites' noted above, there are those who *do* argue that 'No disability, however slight, nor however severe, implies lesser moral, political or ethical status, worth or value' (Harris 2001: 383). As such, an ethic of care is advocated for persons with disabilities. And with regard specifically to the provision of services, Takeda and Card (2002) refer to a legal *and* moral obligation of providing tourism services to everyone. However, there is an issue around the cost of provision of such services, which is seen as a disincentive to investing in disability-related interventions and raises the issue of who should bear the cost for such interventions – the public, the government, the industry, the provider or the disabled user. Richter and Richter (1999) play the devil's advocate in questioning whether individuals with disabilities should be subsidised in order to equalise their opportunities. The utilitarian approach that they offer, could see disabled tourists paying the extra travel costs required for the provision of services such as sign language, Braille information, wheelchair access and personal attendants. They note, however, that such issues raise ethical questions of fairness and distributive justice.

Distributive justice

Distributive justice refers to the extent to which society's institutions ensure that benefits and burdens are distributed among society's members in ways that are fair and just. According to Stein (2006), theories of distributive justice are most severely tested in the area of disability. Stein uses disability as a testing ground for utilitarian and egalitarian theories of distributive justice. He argues that disability tends to reduce welfare, and as utilitarianism seeks to maximise welfare, it will endorse measures to ameliorate disability. However, utilitarianism, as a theory of distributive justice, 'tells us to help those who can most benefit, those who can gain the greatest increase in welfare' (Stein 2006: 5). Egalitarian theories of distributive justice tell us to help those who are in some way worse off. Stein advocates utilitarianism, believing it to address distributive issues involving disability better than egalitarian theories. He critiques egalitarian theory from a utilitarian perspective, addressing the work of egalitarian theorists such as John Rawls.

However, Malhotra (2006) describes how Rawls's theory of justice may be used to the advantage of persons with disability. Rawls's theory of distributive justice, influenced by Kantian theory, sets out to create a society in which equality is important. Parties reach a set of principles in what Rawls describes as the 'original position'. In the original position, 'mutually disinterested contracting parties make their decisions out of enlightened self-interest as approximate equals behind a veil of ignorance about their own socio-economic characteristics. They are also unaware of their own race, gender and disability status' (Malhotra 2006: 74). The Rawlsian agenda is to 'focus on the redistribution of social primary goods to members of the least advantaged class so that they can fulfill their life plans and achieve their goals' (2006: 76). Social primary goods include liberties, opportunities and income. With respect to disability, this is where the Rawlsian approach falls down, as Rawls requires that all persons in his model have 'physical needs and psychological capacities within the normal range' and that the consideration of people with significant physical or mental disabilities, as 'objects of pity' may distract our ability to make accurate moral judgements (Malhotra 2006: 76). Because of this and other shortcomings some have criticised the capacity of Rawls's framework to address the needs of those with disabilities (e.g. Brighouse 2001 in Malhotra 2006). Malhotra, while acknowledging some weaknesses in the Rawlsian approach, 'tinkers' with it by engaging with critical theory and the social model of disability, to make it more applicable to the disability issue. He argues that with such reconfiguration, a duty to accommodate PWD in the workplace (and by extension in other spheres of life such as the leisure–touristic space) fits well with Rawls's model.

Rights movements

As noted above, other ethical approaches can be used to help us understand how the tourism industry can engage with PWD. Notably, the disability rights movement (as do other rights-based movements) appeals to Kantian universal values of equal rights (Smith 2005). Universalism, as expressed in Kantian ethics, holds that there are general moral principles applicable to all persons. Human rights declarations – such as the UN *Convention on the Rights of Persons with Disabilities* (2006) addressed at the beginning of this chapter – 'are typically universal as they delineate general moral principles for all people in all circumstances and under all social and cultural conditions' (Smith 2005: 559). Thus some commentators justify the state meeting individuals' needs (including individuals with disabilities) using Kantian arguments.

However, there are problems with the traditional ethical theories discussed above, regarding their assumptions and norms about what makes us distinctively human – and thus how

Figure 8.4 *New developments in access now allow wheelchair users to experience heritage sites, such as the Colosseum, Rome. Photo: Simon Darcy.*

this may impact upon expectations for how society treats PWD (Vehmas 2004). Vehmas proposes a new ethical theory of disability that would have to take into account, at least, virtue-based, duty-based and outcome-based ethics. Such an approach also 'requires understanding of different impairments and how they affect people's well being in different cultures' (2004: 219). Virtue ethics, with its focus on the importance of having a good character, may be such an approach, as it emphasises the cultural nature of morality, and fits nicely with the social model of disability, in which disability is seen as 'socially constructed, culturally shaped and produced' (Vehmas 2004: 220).

8.8 HERITAGE TOURISM SITES, ACCOMMODATION AND DISABILITY

While meta-ethicists struggle with different ethical approaches to the question of disability, the fact remains that on a day-to-day basis persons with disabilities live in a largely disabling environment. Policy and legislation tries to redress this situation through seeking accommodation for needs of the disabled. The UN *Convention on the Rights of Persons with Disabilities* (2006) requires that States Parties shall take all appropriate steps to ensure that reasonable accommodation is provided: 'Reasonable accommodation' meaning necessary and appropriate modification and adjustments not imposing a disproportionate or undue burden (on others). In individual destinations, such as New Zealand, for example, there is an obligation to accommodate PWD to the extent that it is 'unreasonable' to expect a provider to do so (New Zealand Human Rights Commission 2011; and see Air New Zealand example above). But there is a level of ambiguity or subjectivity that leaves the law open to interpretation, in terms of what is reasonable and what is unreasonable.

The question of reasonable accommodation is particularly vexing when it comes to modifying special environments – natural or cultural heritage sites – for the needs of disabled visitors. While the principles of universal design (also known as inclusive design, design-for-all, or lifespan design (Green 2011)) and a built environment friendly to all users regardless of impairment are very important, historic sites date from periods when access for the disabled was not considered, and it can be a challenge for heritage providers to make the necessary access improvements whilst maintaining the historic integrity of a site. Goodall et al. (2004) provide a good discussion of disability in relation to heritage property in the UK, where conservation and access are to be negotiated in a complex legal environment. The interests of the disabled are catered for by the UK 1995 Disability Discrimination Act which requires the service provider 'to remove, alter or avoid any physical feature that makes it impossible or unreasonably difficult for a disabled person to access that provider's service' (2004: 347). However, for listed (protected) buildings, improving access for disabled visitors could conflict with conservation aims, since listing often protects both the interior and exterior of a building. And planning legislation that protects the historic integrity of buildings may take precedence over disability discrimination legislation.

Interestingly, the UK Disability Discrimination Act does allow for a reasonable alternative method of making the service available. Goodall et al. (2004) note that where conservation values are paramount and/or the costs of adaptation to the needs of the disabled far exceed the benefits, that alternative methods involving 'intellectual access' may be acceptable solutions. They cite the example of Shakespeare's birthplace (in Stratford-upon-Avon, England), a Grade I listed building, in which a photo-real virtual reality replica of the upper floor allows disabled visitors to negotiate around rooms, open chests and examine fabrics via a touch-screen. Of course the value and meaning of a virtual tour compared to a physical tour is open to debate.

CASE STUDY: HOSPITALITY AND ACCESS

A disabled man has won £3,000 damages in a landmark legal case against a Scottish hotel for failing to provide adequate disabled access.

In the first case to go to court under the Disability Discrimination Act 1995, Isaac Curran took Redstones hotel in Uddingston, Lanarkshire, to court for not taking adequate measures to ensure reasonable changes had been made to facilitate disabled access.

Curran was originally offered a £50 voucher by the hotel owner but has now been awarded £3,000 in compensation and his £2,000 legal expenses paid, after taking the case to court.

Yesterday Curran told *The Herald* newspaper: 'Disabled access is not something I take for granted but this is a big company which can afford to make the changes needed. They could have done it for a couple of thousand pounds. Now it has cost them a lot more.'

During his visit to the hotel, for a relative's birthday lunch, Curran had to be carried into the property as there was no ramp, the dining room was located up five flights of stairs and the only disabled toilet was in the ladies.

The hotel has now applied for planning permission to improve its disabled access.

Source

Manson, E. (2006) *Disabled man wins landmark case against Scottish hotel.* Available at <http://www.caterersearch.com/> (Accessed 30 October 2011).

Discussion questions

1 From an ethical perspective, discuss the breach in ethics experienced by the disabled person in the example above.
2 From an ethical perspective, do compensation payments actually compensate for the injustice experienced by a disabled person?

8.9 DISABILITY AND ACCESS TO NATURE AND WILDERNESS

Natural heritage sites, too, pose special challenges, and their unmodified nature, or 'wilderness' is strongly defended by wilderness advocates. In the USA, within the US National Parks context access for those with disabilities is governed by the 'reasonable modification' requirement, but must not fundamentally alter the nature of the programme or services required. This is a vexing issue, especially when it has been said that the realities and limitations of being disabled may make contact with nature 'just that much more precious' for PWD (McAvoy 1996 in Jaquette 2005: 9). Studies have also demonstrated additional benefits to PWD from their visits to wilderness settings, in that they transfer the outcomes they gain in wilderness into their daily lives (McAvoy et al. 2006).

Yet people with disability are under-represented in terms of access to natural sites and are more likely to identify constraints to participation in outdoor recreation than those without disabilities due to inadequate facilities (among other constraints) (Williams et al. 2004). Does this place an onus upon natural area managers to provide reasonable accommodation to natural sites and to wilderness for PWD? The view of PWD themselves on this issue would seem to be important. In one of the few studies undertaken, PWD were split on the need to enhance access to wilderness. Lovelock's (2010) New Zealand study, a survey comparing disabled and able-bodied respondents, found that the group with mobility disabilities expressed a significantly stronger desire for enhanced access to remote natural environments than did the able-bodied group. Also, they viewed the potential impacts of such development as being more benign and less harmful than did those without disabilities. However, less than half of the mobility-disabled sample approved of further motorised access. There was no support for large-scale (e.g. gondola, monorail) type of transport developments in remote natural environments.

Figure 8.5 *Large-scale motorised access to wilderness, such as this gondola, allow access for persons with disabilities – but is this the best use of wilderness? Photo: Brent Lovelock.*

Despite such evidence, commercial developers and their advocates continue to use the disability discrimination argument to support tourism development plans for wilderness settings. As such, they have been accused of co-opting disability concerns in order to push their own agendas for development within such settings. In New Zealand, proposers of a motorised 'skytrail' through a conservation park stated it 'would allow those aged and less physically mobile visitors to experience ... wilderness landscapes en route to Milford Sound [World Heritage Area]' (Skytrail 2001 in Lovelock 2010: 357). This has been called a 'phoney issue, supported and perpetuated mainly by those having little or no interest in the welfare of the handicapped' (Bricker 1995: 12).

DISCUSSION POINT: WILDERNESS, ACCESS AND DISABILITY

Adirondack Park is a 25,000 sq. km park in New York State, and is an extremely popular area for ATVs (All-Terrain Vehicles). However, conservationists have argued for the restriction of ATV use in the park, because of their environmental and social impacts, identified by the park managers, the New York State Department of Environmental Conservation (DEC). But a lawsuit filed in 1998 on behalf of a group of PWD, charged that the state's laws regarding ATV access constituted discrimination in public services, which is prohibited under the Americans with Disabilities Act (ADA). This case held the potential to significantly affect ATV access issues nationwide, with the possibility that Americans with disabilities might be granted motorised access to trails, even in wilderness areas (Karasin 2003). The initial finding of the court was that the disabled plaintiffs' rights were violated when they were not allowed to use all-terrain vehicles in an area of the park closed to motorised vehicles. The court judged that 'meaningful access' must be provided, and that the 'remaining pristine portions of the environment should not be available only to the able-bodied' (Skidmore n.d.). However, ultimately, access to trails was not expanded, but disabled individuals with permits were given ATV access to 65 specified roads in wild forests.

Below are posts on a park user website from a disabled person who uses an ATV in the park, and a response from an able-bodied person to the posting (Williams 2011):

> *'Bob'*: I am disabled with FSH dystrophy. i can barely walk and if i fall i can't get up. i drive [an ATV]. i respect the land and drive safely. what gives a healthy man/woman the right over me to hike back into a 10 mile trail when i can't. u call it it illegal, i call it being selfish.

> Reply: *'Jim'*: I'm sorry for your disability and would stand beside you to fight with you to make sure public buildings had access to everyone with any type of disability. Sadly we can't make every place accessible to everyone. Do we need to have paved trails to every remote pond in the park? I can get there does that mean we have to provide access to someone in a wheel chair? Should we put a chair lift to all the high peaks? Following your argument you have the right so we need to make it accessible.

Discussion question

From different ethical perspectives (including utilitarianism and the theory of distributive justice) who has the greatest claim above – the disabled ATV driver or the wilderness advocate?

References

Karasin, L.N. (2003) *All-terrain vehicles in the Adirondacks: Issues and options*, Wildlife Conservation Society Working Paper No. 21.

Skidmore, M. (n.d.) *Disabled rights to the wilderness: Whose waterfall is it anyway?* Available at <http://law.fordham.edu/publications/articles/700flspub226.pdf> (Accessed 13 June 2009).

Williams, S. (2011) *ATVs still running amuck*. Available at <http://www.adirondackexplorer.org/stories/2011/08/22/atvs-still-running-amuck/> (Accessed 22 August 2011).

CHAPTER REVIEW

This chapter has introduced the problems faced by persons with disabilities in engaging with the tourism industry. Despite an increasingly inclusive policy and legal environment, many tourism providers appear to be failing in their duty to reasonably accommodate the needs of the travelling PWD. We discussed the problems around defining 'reasonable' accommodation. We identify that most work in this field has focused on issues of physical access, but suggest that, more importantly, the problems of offering persons with disabilities the same touristic opportunities as the able-bodied lie around the social and economic disadvantages that they face. The potential role of and argument for social tourism as a means of redressing this imbalance was discussed.

While there is a legal imperative in many destinations to meet the tourism needs of the disabled community, and a clear economic incentive to do so, in terms of the size of the market, the moral imperative is open to debate. Ethically a range of different approaches can be applied to the provision of services for persons with disabilities. Utilitarianism is a contested approach to the issue; at one extreme, problems arise around the concept of moral considerability and its application to persons with disabilities. Other conceptualisations of utilitarianism, in particular hedonism, however, provide an argument for providing special services for persons with disabilities. We also visited distributive justice as an approach to consider how the disabled could be treated within society and by the tourism industry. Finally, we pointed out the problems associated with addressing multiple demands upon some 'special' tourism resources – in particular, built and natural heritage – and raise the difficult question of how we can provide worthwhile experiences in such settings as wilderness, or historic sites, without impacting negatively on the site itself and on the experiences of other visitors.

SUMMARY OF KEY TERMS

Disability Any restriction or lack (resulting from impairment) of ability to perform an activity in the manner or within the range considered normal for a human being (United Nations 2006).

Impairment Problems in body function or structure such as a significant deviation or loss (WHO 2002).

Reasonableness requirement Reasonable accommodation means a provider of a service is required to take reasonable steps to accommodate a person's disability unless it would cause the provider undue hardship or would be considered unreasonable to do so.

Social model of disability views disability as a social problem: 'a product of the disabling environmental, social and attitudinal barriers that compound a person's impairment and prevent their [full] participation in society' (Darcy and Pegg 2011: 470).

Medical model of disability is presented as viewing disability as a problem of the person, directly caused by disease, trauma or other health condition. The medical model of disability reinforces the idea that impairments equate with disability.

Accessible tourism is intended as the set of services and facilities capable of allowing persons with specific needs to enjoy a holiday and their leisure time with no particular barriers or problems.

Social tourism Participation in travel by economically weak or otherwise disadvantaged elements of society.

Moral considerability A morally considerable being is a being who can be wronged in a morally relevant sense. For some ethicists, people with severe cognitive impairments are not accorded full status, and are denied moral considerability.

Prioritarianism A modern variation of utilitarianism and is the view that a benefit has greater moral value the worse the situation of the individual to whom it accrues is. Therefore argues that we ought to give priority to those who are worse off.

Hedonism Proposes that pleasure is the only value, and is therefore the measure and standard of ethics, morality, right and wrong. Thus our fundamental moral obligation is to maximise pleasure or happiness. Is associated with the Ancient Greek philosopher Epicurus (342–270 BC).

Distributive justice Principles of distributive justice are normative principles designed to guide the allocation of the benefits and burdens of economic activity. The first principle of distributive justice, egalitarianism, advocates the allocation of equal material goods to all members of society. John Rawls's alternative distributive principle, the Difference Principle, allows allocation that does not conform to strict equality so long as the inequality has the effect that the least advantaged in society are materially better off than they would be under strict equality.

QUESTIONS FOR REFLECTION

Do you think that the social tourism model is one that could be applied to persons with disabilities?

1 Who do you think should pay for these holidays? The government? Charities?
2 Develop an ethical argument for social tourism for PWD.
3 Should tourism attractions and activities be available at a subsidised price for persons with disabilities?

EXERCISES

1 Consider some tourism attractions from your town, and compile a typology (a list of categories) of the 'accessibility' of these to persons with disabilities.
2 If you consider the multiple interpretations of accessibility, how does this affect your typology?

3 If you consider the range of different disabilities (hearing disability, sight disability, physical disability and intelligence deficiency), how does this affect your typology of accessibility?

4 Within your typology, are there some attractions that are more essential that access is provided for persons with disabilities? If so, why?

FURTHER READING

Buhalis, D. and Darcy, S. (2011) *Accessible Tourism: Concepts and Issues*, Bristol: Channel View.

Buhalis, D., Darcy, S. and Ambrose, I. (2012) *Best Practice in Accessible Tourism: Inclusion, Disability, Ageing Population and Tourism*, Bristol: Channel View.

NOTES

a Helen Keller (1880–1968), American author and educator who was blind and deaf.

b Albert Schweitzer (1875–1965), German theologian, philosopher and medical missionary. Available at <http://en.wikiquote.org/wiki/Talk:Albert_Schweitzer> (Accessed 12 September 2012).

c Hubert H. Humphrey (1911–78), US Vice President (1965–69). From his speech at the dedication of the Hubert H. Humphrey building in Washington, DC, on 4 November 1977.

REFERENCES

Arneson, R.J. (2000) 'Disability, discrimination and priority', in Francis, L.P. and Silvers, A. (eds) *Americans with Disabilities: Exploring Implications of the Law for Individuals and Institutions*, New York: Routledge, pp. 18–33.

Blichfeldt, B.S. and Nicolaisen, J. (2010) 'Disabled travel: not easy, but doable', *Current Issues in Tourism*, 14(1): 79–102.

Bricker, J. (1995) 'Wheelchair accessibility in wilderness areas: the nexus between the ADA and the Wilderness Act', *Environmental Law*, 25(4): 1243–70.

Buhalis, D. and Michopoulou, E. (2011) 'Information-enabled tourism destination marketing: addressing the accessibility market', *Current Issues in Tourism*, 14(2): 145–68.

Burnett, J. and Bender Baker, H. (2001) 'Assessing the travel-related behaviors of the mobility-disabled consumer', *Journal of Travel Research*, 40(1): 4–11.

Burns, N., Paterson, K. and Watson, N. (2009) 'An inclusive outdoors? Disabled people's experiences of countryside leisure services', *Leisure Studies*, 28(4): 403–17.

Christofle, S. and Massiera, B. (2009) 'Tourist facilities for disabled people on the French Riviera: a strategic model of the controversial plans to develop the seafront areas', *Journal of Coastal Conservation*, 13(2): 97–107.

Daniels, M.J., Drogin Rodgers, E.B. and Wiggins, B.P. (2005) '"Travel Tales": an interpretive analysis of constraints and negotiations to pleasure travel as experienced by persons with physical disabilities', *Tourism Management*, 26(6): 919–30.

Darcy, S. and Dickson, T. (2009) 'A whole-of-life approach to tourism: the case for accessible tourism experiences', *Journal of Hospitality and Tourism Management*, 16(1): 32–44.

Darcy, S. and Pegg, S. (2011) 'Towards strategic intent: perceptions of disability service provision amongst hotel accommodation managers', *International Journal of Hospitality Management*, 30(2): 468–76.

Darcy, S., Cameron, B. and Pegg, S. (2010) 'Accessible tourism and sustainability: a discussion and case study', *Journal of Sustainable Tourism*, 18(4): 515–37.

Daruwalla, P. and Darcy, S. (2005) 'Personal and societal attitudes to disability', *Annals of Tourism Research*, 32(3): 549–70.

Devlin, R. and Pothier, D. (2006) 'Introduction: toward a critical theory of dis-citizenship', in Pothier, D. and Devlin, R. (eds) *Critical Disability Theory: Essays in Philosophy, Politics, Policy and Law,* Vancouver: UBC Press, pp. 1–24.

Eichhorn, V., Miller, G., Michopoulou, E. and Buhalis, D. (2008) 'Enabling access to tourism through information schemes?', *Annals of Tourism Research*, 35(1): 189–210.

Etravelblackboard.com (2010) *Australia misses the plane on accessible tourism*, 12 October. Available at <http://www.etravelblackboard.com/article/109845/australia-misses-the-plane-on-accessible-tourism> (Accessed 12 November 2011).

Freeman, I. and Selmi, N. (2010) 'French versus Canadian tourism: response to the disabled', *Journal of Travel Research*, 49(4): 471–85.

Goodall, B., Pottinger, G., Dixon, T. and Russell, H. (2004) 'Heritage property, tourism and the UK Disability Discrimination Act', *Property Management*, 22(5): 345–57.

Green, R.J. (2011) 'An introductory theoretical and methodological framework for a Universal Mobility Index (UMI) to quantify, compare, and longitudinally track equity of access across the built environment', *Journal of Disability Policy Studies*, 21(4): 219–29.

Hall, C.M. (2000) *Tourism Planning: Policies, Processes and Relationships*, Harlow: Prentice Hall.

Harris, J. (2001) 'One principle and three fallacies of disability studies', *Journal of Medical Ethics*, 27: 383–7.

Hetherington, K. (2000) 'Museums and the visually impaired: the spatial politics of access', *Sociological Review*, 48(3): 444–63.

Hillis, C. (2005) 'Talking images: museums, galleries and heritage sites', *International Congress Series*, 1282: 855–9.

Israeli, A. (2002) 'A preliminary investigation of the importance of site accessibility factors for disabled tourists', *Journal of Travel Research*, 41: 101–4.

Jaquette, S. (2005) 'Maimed away from the earth: disability and wilderness', *Ecotone*, Spring, 8–11.

Lovelock, B. (2010) 'Planes, trains and wheelchairs in the bush: attitudes of people with mobility-disabilities to enhanced motorised access in remote natural settings', *Tourism Management*, 31(3): 357–66.

McAvoy, L., Holman, T., Goldenberg, M. and Klenosky, D. (2006) 'Wilderness and persons with disabilities: transferring the benefits to everyday life', *International Journal of Wilderness*, 12(2): 23–31.

McCabe, S. (2009) 'Who needs a holiday? Evaluating social tourism', *Annals of Tourism Research*, 36(4): 667–88.

McPherson, G.W. and Sobsey, D. (2003) 'Rehabilitation: disability ethics versus Peter Singer', *Archives of Physical Medicine and Rehabilitation*, 84: 1246–8.

Malhotra, R. (2006) 'Justice as fairness in accommodating workers with disabilities and critical theory: the limitations of a Rawlsian framework for empowering PWD in Canada', in Pothier, D. and Devlin, R. (eds) *Critical Disability Theory: Essays in Philosophy, Politics, Policy and Law,* Vancouver: UBC Press, pp. 70–86.

Merriam, G. (2010) 'Rehabilitating Aristotle: a virtue ethics approach to disability and human flourishing', in Ralston, D.C. and Ho, J. (eds) *Philosophical Reflections on Disability,* New York: Springer, pp. 133–54.

Miller, G.A. and Kirk, E. (2002) 'The Disability Discrimination Act: time for the stick?', *Journal of Sustainable Tourism*, 10(1): 82–8.

Morris, J. (2001) 'Impairment and disability: constructing an ethics of care that promotes human rights', *Hypatia*, 16(4): 1–16.

New Zealand Human Rights Commission (2011) *What does the Human Rights Act mean by disability?* Available at <http://www.hrc.co.nz/enquiries-and-complaints-guide/what-can-i-complain-about/disability> (Accessed 2 September 2011).

Packer, T.L., McKercher, B. and Yau, M.K. (2002) 'Understanding the complex interplay between tourism, disability and environmental contexts', *Disability and Rehabilitation,* 29(4): 281–92.

Packer, T., Small, J. and Darcy, S. (2008) *Tourist experiences of individuals with vision impairment,* Gold Coast, Australia: Sustainable Tourism Cooperative Research Centre.

Poria, Y., Reichel, A. and Brandt, Y. (2009) 'People with disabilities visit art museums: an exploratory study of obstacles and difficulties', *Journal of Heritage Tourism,* 4(2): 117–29.

Poria, Y., Reichel, A. and Brandt, Y. (2010) 'The flight experiences of people with disabilities: an exploratory study', *Journal of Travel Research,* 49(2): 216–27.

Pühretmair, F. and Buhalis, D. (2008) 'Accessible tourism introduction to the special thematic session', in Miesenberger, K., Klaus, J., Zagler, W. and Karshmer, A. (eds) *Computers Helping People with Special Needs: 11th International Conference ICCHP 2008 Proceedings,* Berlin: Springer-Verlag, pp. 969–72.

Richards, V., Pritchard, A. and Morgan, N. (2010) '(Re)Envisioning tourism and visual impairment', *Annals of Tourism Research,* 37(4): 1097–116.

Richter, L.K. and Richter, W.L. (1999) 'Ethics challenges: health, safety and accessibility in international travel and tourism', *Public Personnel Management,* 28(4): 595.

Rioux, M.H. and Valentine, F. (2006) 'Does theory matter? Exploring the nexus between disability, human rights and public policy', in Pothier, D. and Devlin, R. (eds) *Critical Disability Theory: Essays in Philosophy, Politics, Policy and Law,* Vancouver: UBC Press, pp. 47–69.

Ryan, C. (2002) 'Equity, management, power sharing and sustainability: issues of the "new tourism"', *Tourism Management,* 23: 17–26.

Shaw, G. (2007) 'Disability legislation and the empowerment of tourists with disabilities in the United Kingdom', in Church, A. and Coles, T. (eds) *Tourism, Power, and Space,* London: Routledge, pp. 83–100.

Shaw, G. and Coles, T. (2004) 'Disability, holiday making and the tourism industry in the UK: a preliminary survey', *Tourism Management,* 25(3): 397–403.

Shelton, E. and Tucker, H. (2005) 'Tourism and disability: issues beyond access', *Tourism Review International,* 8(3): 211–19.

Singer, P. (2000) *Writings on an Ethical Life,* New York: Harper Collins.

Small, J., Darcy, S. and Packer, T. (2011) 'The embodied tourist experiences of people with vision impairment: Management implications beyond the visual gaze', *Tourism Management,* 33(4): 941–50.

Smith, S.R. (2005) 'Equality, identity and the disability rights movement: From policy to practice and from Kant to Nietzsche in more than one uneasy move', *Critical Social Policy,* 25: 554–76.

— (2009) 'Social justice and disability: competing interpretations of the medical and social models', in Kristiansen, K., Vehmas, S. and Shakespeare, T. (eds) *Arguing About Disability,* Abingdon: Routledge, pp. 15–29.

Stein, M.S. (2006) *Distributive Justice and Disability: Utilitarianism against Egalitarianism,* New Haven, CT: Yale University Press.

Takeda, K. and Card, J. A. (2002) 'U.S. tour operators and travel agencies: barriers encountered when providing package tours to people who have difficulty walking', *Journal of Travel & Tourism Marketing,* 12(1): 47.

Tannsjo, T. (2010) 'Utilitarianism, disability and society', in Ralston, D.C. and Ho, J. (eds) *Philosophical Reflections on Disability,* New York: Springer, pp. 91–108.

United Kingdom Office of Public Sector Information (1995) *Disability Discrimination Act 1995*, National Archives.

United Nations (1948) *Universal Declaration of Human Rights*. Available at <http://www.un.org/en/documents/udhr/index.shtml> (Accessed 27 July 2011).

— (2006) *Convention on the Rights of Persons with Disabilities*. Available at <http://www.un.org/disabilities/default.asp?navid=12&pid=150> (Accessed 22 November 2007).

United Nations Economic and Social Commission for Asia and the Pacific (UNESCAP) (2007) *Promoting Tourism for People with Disabilities* (Press release 22 November). Available at <www.scoop.co.nz/stories/wo0711/s00956.htm> (Accessed 27 November 2007).

United Nations World Tourism Organization (UNWTO) (2011) *Ethics and Social Dimensions of Tourism* Available at <http://ethics.unwto.org/en/content/accessible-tourism> (Accessed 4 October 2011).

Var, T., Yesiltas, M., Yayli, A. and Öztürk, Y. (2011) 'A study on the travel patterns of physically disabled people', *Asia Pacific Journal of Tourism Research*, 16(6): 599–618.

Vehmas, S. (2004) 'Ethical analysis of the concept of disability', *Mental Retardation*, 42(3): 209–22.

Williams, R., Vogelsong, H., Green, G. and Cordell, K. (2004) 'Outdoor recreation participation of people with mobility disabilities: selected results of the national survey of recreation and the environment', *Journal of Park & Recreation Administration*, 22(2): 85–101.

World Health Organization (WHO) (1980) *International Classification of Impairments, Disabilities and Handicaps*, Geneva: WHO.

— (2002) *Towards a Common Language for Functioning, Disability and Health: International Classification of Functioning, Disability and Health*, Geneva: WHO.

Yau, M.K., McKercher, B. and Packer, T.L. (2004) 'Traveling with a disability: more than an access issue', *Annals of Tourism Research,* 31(4): 946–60.

9 Nature-based tourism

'In all things of nature there is something of the marvellous.'

Aristotle[a]

'Look deep into nature, and then you will understand everything better.'

Albert Einstein[b]

'The last word in ignorance is the man who says of an animal or plant: "What good is it?"'

Aldo Leopold[c]

'We do not inherit the earth from our ancestors, we borrow it from our children.'

Navajo proverb[d]

LEARNING OBJECTIVES

After reading this chapter you will be able to:

- Identify and discuss the different conceptualisations of the human–non-human nature relationship.
- Define the terms anthropocentrism and ecocentrism and discuss their role in how the tourism industry interrelates to the natural world.
- Discuss the use of common pool resources by tourism interests.
- Consider cultural relativism and how it may influence the development of tourism attractions and activities within different destinations.
- Understand, from an environmental ethics position, the ethical problems relating to the concept of sustainable tourism.

9.1 INTRODUCTION

The Millenium Ecosystem Assessment, a comprehensive analysis involving over 1,000 scientists and conducted over a four-year period, concluded in the report *Living Beyond our Means*, that 'human activity is putting such strain on the natural functions of the Earth that the ability of the planet's ecosystems to sustain future generations can no longer be taken for granted' (MAWEB 2005: 5). The bare facts that up to one-half of the Earth's land surface has been transformed by human action, that CO_2 in the atmosphere has increased by 30 per cent since the industrial revolution, that over half of all accessible surface fresh water is appropriated by humanity, and that one-quarter of the world's bird species have been driven to extinction (Vitousek et al. 1997) are all clear messages that humans need to renegotiate their relationship with nature and that we are in need of a new environmental ethic to guide us in this renegotiation.

Nature is a critical component within the tourism industry – as an attraction, as a setting for tourism and as a provider of ecological services (fresh air, fresh water) that are essential resources for the industry. Writing about the relationship between tourism and nature over three decades ago, Gerardo Budowski, then director general of the International Union for the Conservation of Nature and Natural Resources (IUCN), identified three possible types of relationship that can exist between the promoters of tourism and conservationists: conflict, coexistence and symbiosis; and for the majority of cases the relationship between tourism and conservation is usually one of coexistence moving towards conflict. He noted that:

> The net result has been a widespread degradation or reduction in the assets of nature, and, with it, of tourism…Many of the places visited by tourists support fragile ecosystems that cannot endure heavy disturbance…After 'saturation point' is reached or when a critical threshold is passed, rapid degradation seems inevitable.
>
> (Budowski 1976: 27)

Arguably, since the scale of tourism as an industry since that time has grown considerably (from 220 million international arrivals in 1976 to 980 million in 2011) the impacts of tourism upon nature and natural systems have also grown accordingly – prompting further questions over whether tourism and the environment is in accord or discord (Romeril 1989). One underlying problem has been the lack of recognition that tourism is an industry. And like many industries, it requires the development of infrastructure, it consumes resources and it generates waste. But *unlike* other industries, tourism does this in some of the most ecologically fragile locations on the planet (Williams and Ponsford 2009). In recognition of this environmental paradox – whereby tourism requires the protection of the ecological integrity of natural resources for its ongoing growth and competitiveness – the tourism industry has responded with what are purported to be more sensitive approaches. These include, among others, green tourism, ecotourism and sustainable tourism.

This chapter explores the ethics of our relationship with nature, and more specifically of nature-based tourism. It asks questions about alternative forms of tourism, such as ecotourism, and investigates ways and means of putting tourism's relationship with nature back on a more ethical footing.

9.2 NATURE-BASED TOURISM – SCOPE, SCALE, IMPACTS

Nature-based tourism is any form of tourism that relies primarily on the natural environment for its attractions or settings (TIES 2012). This form of tourism is having 'explosive growth' (Newsome et al. 2002), with visitation to natural areas having risen from only

2 per cent of all tourism in the late 1980s to about 20 per cent of all leisure travel by the turn of the twenty-first century (Weaver and Oppermann 2000).

With an annual growth rate of 10–30 per cent, nature-based tourism seems to be the fastest-growing tourism sector. Its share in the world travel market is currently about 20 per cent (Kuenzi and McNeely 2008). The United Nations Environmental Programme (UNEP) and Conservation International report that most of the tourism industry's expansion is occurring in and around the world's remaining natural areas (TIES 2006).

However, despite recognition of the impacts of tourism in such sensitive environments, the economic imperative for tourism to persist and grow in these areas is strong. Nature-based tourism is a very important component of the overall tourism market – for example, contributing US$122.3 billion to the USA's tourism market in 2006 (UNWTO 2010). In Europe, nature-based tourism comprises 42 per cent of Europe's international tourism, while in Australia this figure is as high as 75 per cent (UNWTO 2010).

Impacts of nature-based tourism

The impacts of nature-based tourism are broad and varied, and beyond the scope of this book to describe in detail. Readers would best be advised to read a specialist text on the subject such as Newsome et al. (2002, see Chapter 3 in particular), Mason (2008, see Chapter 6), Wall and Mathieson (2006, see Chapter 5), Holden (2008, Chapter 3) or Hill and Gale (2009). Suffice to say that tourism impacts have been recorded in a variety of ecosystems, ranging from high alpine environments to marine coral reefs, and from deserts to tropical rainforest. One disturbing trend is for the impacts of tourism to be seen to be emerging in more isolated, previously inaccessible regions and habitats. Polar regions, for example, are parts of the world that have traditionally only been accessible to explorers and scientists. This is changing with improved accessibility and visitor safety provision, along with greater demand for this type of experience, fuelled by media coverage and increasing disposable incomes. As Holden (2008) points out, with technological advances it would seem that no environment is too remote or inaccessible for tourism. (For a good coverage of the impacts of tourism in polar regions see Hall and Saarinen 2010.)

Overall, a number of factors have been identified that influence the level and type of impact that tourism has upon natural systems – these include the obvious, such as the level of visitation (numbers of visitors), the spatial or temporal concentration of visitors, the activities of visitors, and the extent of modification of habitats required (e.g. for roads, buildings and other infrastructure). However, the behaviours of visitors have also been linked to the level of impacts within natural settings and, of course, behaviours are linked to attitudes, which in turn are influenced by individuals' (and groups') ideas of nature and of the way that humans should behave in and towards non-human nature.

9.3 ENVIRONMENTAL ETHICS

Environmental ethics addresses the relationship between humans and non-human nature. It should be noted here that some authors in this field (e.g. Curry 2006) prefer to use the term 'ecological ethics' rather than environmental ethics, as they feel that the latter is harmful in that it makes two assumptions: first, that only humans matter; second, that the value of everything else only need concern humans to the extent that it 'enables us to get on with our own show' (Curry 2006: 4). For the purposes of this chapter, we use the more common term 'environmental ethics'; however, implicit in our usage is a more ecocentric, holistic interpretation of this term.

Christianity and nature

Many discussions of environmental ethics (at least in the Western context) and, indeed, of the origins of environmental problems in the world today, begin with reference to the Bible. White (1967) believes Christianity to be the primary historical cause of the contemporary ecological crisis. White refers to what is known as the Dominion thesis, sourced from the Bible's Book of Genesis (1: 26, 28 English standard version) in which it is stated that humans shall 'have dominion over the fish of the sea, and over the fowl of the air, and over every living thing that moveth upon the earth'. It is argued that Christianity removed the sacred focus away from the Earth and its creatures to humankind, with negative consequences for non-human nature. Such a thesis is open to criticism, however. For example, there is evidence of *pre*-Christian ecological destructiveness; and the eco-crisis did not occur until the nineteenth century – nearly two thousand years after the founding of Christianity (Curry 2006). Non-Christian people also exhibit ecological destructiveness. And while other religions (e.g. Hinduism, Buddhism, Taoism) may not be as overtly anthropocentric as Christianity, cultures following these religions still despoil the environment (Holden 2003).

Defenders of the Christian position would point out that there are other interpretations of nature within the Bible. The Stewardship thesis (Genesis 1: 24; 2: 15 English standard version), for example, states that 'the Lord took the man, and put him into the Garden of Eden, to dress it and to keep it'. Of course the stewardship thesis is not only restricted to Christianity, but has relevance to many cultures and societies that have other faith systems. The indigenous Māori in New Zealand, for example, have a concept of stewardship or 'kaitiangitanga', which has been articulated in legislation and, notably, in tourism policy. Kaitiangitanga refers to the 'guardianship and sustainable management of natural, built, and cultural resources for the collective benefit of current and future generations' (Ministry of Tourism et al. 2007: 77). As appealing as the concept of stewardship sounds, however, environmental ethicists question its underlying rationale, in particular, its link to sustainability (discussed below), and the centrality of humankind within this ethic.

Deontology, utilitarianism and nature

Such challenges did not begin to arise in Western society until the emergence of a secular ethic in the mid-seventeenth century. The emergence of Humanism placed an emphasis on humankind, and challenged the role of divinity as the central focus of life (Curry 2006). Of the three main schools of ethical thought that emerged from this time – virtue ethics, deontology and utilitarianism – a number of limitations have been pointed out in terms of their application to environmental problems. Deontology, or 'rights' based ethics, in particular has been described as 'decidedly anthropocentric' (Curry 2006: 35). Proponents of deontology, such as Kant, considered both rights and duties to be limited to human beings. The basis of Kantian philosophy is to treat nature as non-divine, thus assigning the right to humanity to dominate over it (Holden 2008). (Note that American philosopher John Rawls (1921–2002) went so far as to say that 'the status of the natural world and our proper relation to it is not a constitutional essential or a basic question of justice' (in Curry 2006: 35)). Rather, deontology has typically been focused upon human rights, and has limitations with respect to environmental ethics: first, its tendency to dissociate rights from corresponding duties; and, second, its focus upon individualism leaves questions (important questions!) about the common good 'dangerously unattended' (Curry 2006: 35).

These inherent problems have not precluded some environmental ethicists from extending deontology to non-human animals, however. Most notably, this has been the approach of Regan (1984), with his case for animal rights. Others have tried to extend deontology to non-human components of nature – for example, to individual plants (e.g. Taylor 1986). But overall, as Curry observes, 'it is difficult to see how a fully ecological ethics could be developed while still remaining within the deontological fold' (2006: 36).

Utilitarianism as an environmental ethic also has some drawbacks, the most notable of which derives from its position that 'actions are right or wrong, good or bad, according to how they affect the experiences of beings capable of experience' (Wenz 2001: 85). This limitation, to sentient beings, is problematic when seeking to apply utilitarianism to non-sentient beings, species, ecosystems or places (Curry 2006). However, utilitarianism has, most famously, been extended to animals by philosopher Peter Singer (see Chapter 10).

9.4 ANTHROPOCENTRISM AND ECOCENTRISM

It is considered by some environmental philosophers that environmentally, all established ethics are inadequate (Sylvan and Bennett 1994). The root cause of this inadequacy is anthropocentrism – the human-centred approach of most of our established system of ethics. The premise of anthropocentrism is that all value, for humans, is anthropogenic – generated by human experience; anthropocentrism is thus the 'unjustified privileging of human beings…at the expense of other forms of life' (Curry 2006: 43). Alternative ethical positions have been mooted, most notably, biocentrism, described as an intermediate position, and ecocentrism, described as a more inclusive concept and value. The latter position, unsurprisingly, has been criticised as simply being an inverse of anthropocentrism, of being misanthropic, and for preserving the human/nature dualism inherited from Platonism, Christianity and Cartesianism (Curry 2006).

Curry (2006) identifies a range, or spectrum, of ethical positions in relation to the environment, from light green or shallow (anthropocentric) to mid-green or intermediate ethics, to dark green or deep (ecocentric) ethics. In relation to the first position, consideration for the non-human is only indirect, with the main focus being on the wellbeing of humans. Critics tend to lump sustainable development into this camp (see discussion below), which of course is an important point for tourism scholars to consider, as much of tourism policy and management is increasingly centred around concepts of sustainability. While not an ideal approach, under such an ethic, for tourism to be ecologically sound would require (Curry 2006: 48):

- A very strong precautionary principle (acting cautiously, assuming that our knowledge of the effects of our actions is limited)
- A definition of sustainability that rules out all practices except those that are *indefinitely* sustainable
- A conviction that as much rather than as little as possible of nature should be preserved.

An important concession of the mid-green ethic is its denial of the 'Sole Value Assumption' – that humans alone have any intrinsic value. Rather, this ethic subscribes to the 'Greater Value Assumption', that natural items have some intrinsic value, but wherever this conflicts with human interests, the latter must take precedence. For example, wilderness preservation may be defended under a mid-green ethic, but if the provision of other 'vital' needs, such as oil or minerals is affected, the wilderness values must give way (Curry 2006). Of course this brings into question what are 'vital' human interests – and in a tourism scenario, many would argue (from an ecocentric perspective) that the interests of most tourism businesses would not fall into this category.

Figure 9.1 *Often the negative impacts of tourism on nature are unintentional. Here, the tourists don't realise that they are threatening the sea lion by coming too close and getting between it and the sea. Photo: Brent Lovelock.*

CASE STUDY: ISSUES OF ENVIRONMENTAL ETHICS AND TOURISM'S USE OF WILDERNESS AND NATURE – *ANDREW HOLDEN*

The growth in international mass and niche market tourism from the mid-twentieth century onwards has meant that nature has increasingly been turned into a 'resource' and lent an economic value through tourism. This increased interaction between nature and tourism raises ethical issues over the judgement of what is 'right' or 'wrong'. In the view of Nash (1989), the idea that the human–nature relationship should be treated as a moral issue represents one of the most extraordinary developments in recent intellectual history, having potential future implications for thought and behaviour comparable to that of the ideal of human rights at the time of democratic revolution in the eighteenth century. This case study evaluates how we can use environmental ethics to construct judgements on the tourism and nature interaction, related to the extent of recognition of the intrinsic rights of nature to an independent existence.

It seems that sometimes we could expect a level of near universal agreement on what is 'right' and 'wrong' in our interaction with nature. For example, in the case of tour operators advertising 'ecotourism' tours to the rainforest of Ecuador, it is likely that the majority view would be it is wrong for an ecotourism experience to involve throwing a stick of dynamite into a river to witness dead fish come floating to the top. This would dictate against the conservation ethic that now underwrites much of human philosophy and policy about how we should be interacting with nature, emphasised in the loosely defined term of sustainability. This action would likely be judged to be causing harm to the fish, violating their rights to existence, and posing a threat to the ecosystem.

Nevertheless, the judgement of whether an interaction between tourism and wildlife is acceptable using environmental ethics may be more difficult than it may at first appear. For example, these dramatic headlines refer to the interaction of tourists with seal pups in the Arctic Circle.

> *'Tourists rush for kill a seal pup holiday'* and *'It's the new sport for tourists: killing baby seals'*

These two emotive headlines are based upon the decisions by governments in Canada and Norway to allow tourists to participate in the killing of baby seals as part of annual culling programmes. The justification for this action is that there are too many seals resulting in a decline in fish stocks. Following the government ruling, tour operators decided to promote holidays based on seal pup culling. The Canadian decision was taken in the early 1990s, with package holidays being marketed for US$3,000 in America, to buy the 'right' to club seal pups to death on the Newfoundland ice in the annual culling programme. The packages were popular, as Mike Kehoe, the executive director of the Canadian Sealers Association, commented: 'People want to come out and kill and it's a good market for us' (Evans 1993).

In Norway, the involvement of tourists in seal culling was set to begin in January 2005, with one company NorSafari advertising culling trips on the Internet. Jowit and Soldal (2004: 3) comment: 'The company's website shows photos of hunters posing with their kill and offers trips that not only include accommodation and food but help with cutting up and preserving seal carcasses.' Although professional seal hunters have traditionally used clubs, tourists would kill the seals by shooting, a presumably more humane but expensive way of execution.

Utilising a framework of environmental ethics to judge the participation of tourists in seal culling, from an 'instrumental' perspective, i.e. an ethic for the 'use of the environment' as humans deem appropriate, the action would be understood as deriving human benefit from the pleasure of killing a sentient being. The evidence of this ethic in action in tourism has a long history. It was associated with shooting on safari in the early twentieth century in the then British East Africa. For example, in an expedition led by Theodore Roosevelt and his son, 5,000 animals of 70 different species were killed, including one of East Africa's rare white rhinos (Monbiot 1995).

Yet, if we judge tourist participation in seal culling utilising the environment ethic of 'eco-holism', our judgement of 'right' and 'wrong' may be more problematic. The emphasis within eco-holism rests upon the conservation of the ecosystem and its right to existence, rather than the right to existence of the individual animal. The 'right' or 'wrong' of an action is judged upon its outcome for the 'greater good', the interests of the majority and not the individual. In this sense, eco-holism can be understood as having a synonymous relationship with John Stuart Mill's influential ethical principle of 'utilitarianism', which advocates that the basic principle of moral action should be the maximisation of happiness for the greatest number, the difference in this case being the emphasis on the wellbeing of non-human species.

The issues of the rights of nature to an independent existence is epitomised in the seminal work of Stone (1972) who drew attention to the rights and legal status of sentient and non-sentient beings in his seminal *Should Trees Have Standing?* He comments:

> It is not inevitable, nor is it wise, that natural objects should have no rights to seek redress on their own behalf. It is no answer to say that streams and forests cannot have standing because streams and forests cannot speak.
>
> (Stone 1972: 450)

The application of this latter ethic as the rationale for environmental law could have dramatic implications for tourism development, challenging an established legal system that is centred upon human rights. The concept of 'Wild law' or 'Earth jurisprudence' recognises the rights of an 'Earth community', in which humans as part of that community cannot ignore the rights of the rest of it (Thornton 2007). Under this law, for example, a hotel owner could be sued on behalf of the diversity of species belonging to a coral reef, whose habitat was being damage by sewage emissions from the hotel, on the basis of their right to exist.

In summary, the interaction of tourism with wildlife and nature poses challenging problems, and environmental ethics has a role in helping to distinguish and define the 'right' and 'wrong' of stakeholder actions.

References

Evans, G. (1993) 'Tourists rush for kill a seal pup holiday', *Evening Standard*, London, 5 July, p. 10.

Jowit, J. and Soldal, H. (2004) 'It's the new sport for tourists: killing baby seals', *The Observer*, London, 3 October, p. 3.

Monbiot, G. (1995) 'No man's land', *Tourism in Focus*, 15: 10–11, London: Tourism Concern.

Nash, R.F. (1989) *The Rights of Nature: A History of Environmental Ethics*, Madison: University of Wisconsin Press.

Stone, D.C. (1972) 'Should trees have standing? Towards legal rights for natural objects', *Southern California Law Review*, 25: 450–501.

Thornton, J. (2007) 'Can lawyers save the world?', *The Ecologist*, June, pp. 38–46.

9.5 MORAL EXTENSIONISM

The moral extensionism referred to in the case study above, or extending moral considerability to non-human subjects, is a matter of great debate. But to many, the idea of the abiotic community being morally considerable, or 'rocks having rights', seems, as Jamieson describes it, as 'somewhere between unacceptable and mad' (2008: 153).

Defenders of a human-centred ethic argue that moral considerability should rest upon 'being a moral agent' (moral agents are aware of their moral obligations to others). This has attracted criticism, as under such an argument, we would have to exclude from considerability, babies, children, sentient animals, non-sentient animals, plants, inanimate objects, species, ecosystems, landscapes and places, and the biosphere (Midgely 1992).

Arguably, the most extreme form of moral extensionism would be Lovelock's Gaia Theory (1979), in which the Earth is seen as more like a living super-organism, comprised of highly complex interacting ecosystems. While not an ethical theory per se, under this eco-holist approach, inanimate components by necessity have moral considerability.

This is the point of difference of dark green or deep (ecocentric) ethics in which entities as well as individuals can be objects of ethical concern, and these entities may be non-living or living. This ethic rejects the Sole and the Greater Value assumptions, and 'the ecological community forms the ethical community' (Sylvan and Bennett 1994: 91).

Included within a dark green ethic, and arguably a foundation for this ethic, is the Land Ethic of Aldo Leopold. Leopold (1887–1948) was an American forester, wildlife biologist and conservationist, whose writings about nature are best known from *A Sand County Almanac*, in which he proposed that:

> The Land Ethic simply enlarges the boundaries of the community to include soils, waters, plants, and animals, or collectively, the land … a land ethic changes the role of Homo sapiens from conqueror of the land community to plain member and citizen of it.
>
> (Leopold 1949: 239, 240)

For Leopold, human action within nature is right when it acts to 'preserve the integrity, stability and beauty of the biotic community' (1949: 262). Importantly, the Land Ethic marks a paradigm shift from individualism to holism (Keller 2010). As reasonable as it sounds, however, the Land Ethic is not without its critics, notably animal rights advocate Tom Regan describes it as 'environmental fascism' (1984: 362), as he believes it subordinates the rights of individual beings to those of the collective whole.

The Deep Ecology of Norwegian philosopher Arne Naess (1989) has also been influential. Naess offers eight 'Platform Principles' that recognise the intrinsic value of nature, and presents the changes in human thought and action required to maintain the 'flourishing of human and non-human life'. The call for individual and institutional change is also evident in Deep Green Theory (Sylvan and Bennett 1994), the premise of which is that all established or traditional ethics are, ecologically speaking, inadequate (Curry 2006). Under this ethic, what is required 'is that reasons be given *for* interfering with the environment, rather than reasons for not doing so' (Sylvan and Bennett 1994: 147). The authors call for ' "thinking like a mountain" instead of thinking like a cash register' (Sylvan and Bennett 1994: 182).

In summary, environmental ethics is premised on the notion that human beings, as moral agents, have obligations to entities other than humans (Keller 2010). And depending on the particular 'brand' of ethical theory, these entities may be sentient animals, living things, or entire ecosystems. Environmental ethics would seek that human beings live their lives as best we can, recognising that we are embedded in 'webworks of ecological relationships' (Keller 2010: 19).

Keller (2010) pictures the development of environmental ethics as a series of widening concentric spheres of inclusion of membership in the moral community, radiating out from a core of orthodox anthropocentrism (Figure 9.2).

Importantly, most environmental policy relevant to tourism (and indeed for most industries that exploit nature), originates from a light to mid-green ethic, where the environment has an instrumental value, in which it is not seen as an end in itself, but as a means of gaining pleasure and/or profit (Holden 2000).

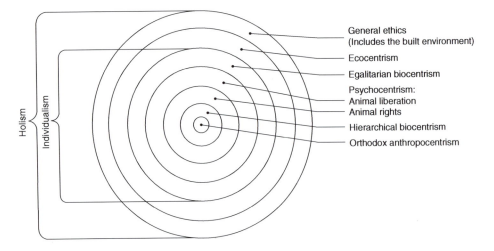

Figure 9.2 *Spheres of moral considerability.*
Source: Keller (2010).

DISCUSSION POINT: GALAPAGOS ISLANDS

'If there's one place in the world where we should draw a line in the sand, it's the Galapagos.'

(US Scientist Michael Lemonick in *Time* magazine
1995 cited in Honey 2008)

Earlier in this chapter we referred to the work of Budowski (1976), who wrote of the potential for 'symbiosis' between conservation and tourism interests. He noted at the time that the Galapagos Islands were a good case of where this had been achieved. The Galapagos Islands comprise a chain of volcanic islands, located in the Pacific Ocean about 1,000 km west of Ecuador. They became famous as the site of Darwin's study of evolution in the 1830s, Darwin referring to them as a 'Garden of Eden'. More recently they have become well known as a nature-based tourism destination, famous for their endemic wildlife, including tortoises, iguana, and a wide variety of birdlife and marine mammals. The islands are a UNESCO World Heritage Site and Biosphere Reserve, and have been considered a model for tourism management worldwide (Hohl and McLaren 2003). But surprisingly, only a few years after Budowski's praise, de Groot (1983) noted that 'unless decisive action is taken soon, Galapagos will become another example of man's dangerous habit of preferring short-term economic gains over long-term ecological and economic interests' (1983: 291), referring to it as a 'lost paradise'.

The source of this concern has been a parallel increase in both visitor numbers and residents of the islands – drawn to migrate there by the opportunities arising from the growth in nature-based tourism. Large-scale tourism development began in the late 1960s, following the establishment of the Galapagos National Park in 1959. The growth of both land-based and cruise ship visitors has increased substantially since that time. In 1972 there was only one cruise ship visit, while in 1997, there were 84; over that period, visitor numbers grew from 5,000 to 60,000 (Hohl and McLaren 2003), and now exceed 170,000 per annum (Gardener and Grenier 2011). The number of residents on the islands has also grown from an original (pre-tourism) population of less than 1,000 to over 20,000. The lack of will to implement limits on tourism is in part linked to the value of tourism to the local economy and to the Ecuadorian economy as a whole: tourism is the country's third largest foreign exchange earner, and the Galapagos provide about one-third of that income (Honey 2008). As Fennell (2008: 205) points out, 'The lure of tourists and associated tourist spending is too powerful'.

Consequently, environmental problems arising from the increase in tourism have become apparent. Grenier (1996 in Gardener and Grenier 2011) noted that 'The ecological damage is being done at a terrific speed; more people, tourists, boats, concrete, introduced plants and animals.' In 2007 UNESCO added the islands to its 'World Heritage in Danger' list, noting specifically the negative effects of 'unbridled tourism'. However, in 2010 the islands were removed from that list in response to the Ecuadorian Ministry of Tourism's measures, including their pledge to consider limiting tourist numbers, activities and new tourism permits.

The refusal to place limits on visitor numbers speaks of an anthropocentric approach to tourism on the islands, and is representative of many so-called 'protected areas' around the world that are exploited for tourism. The fact that tourism on the Galapagos is essential for the livelihoods of thousands of locals raises some interesting questions about the social and economic roles of nature-based tourism, and the extent to which government and private (business) sectors are prepared to prioritise their own interests above the interests of individual non-human beings, non-human species and ecosystems.

The situation in the Galapagos also raises questions about the ethics of touristic use of common pool resources. Common pool resources are those for which exploitation by one user reduces the amount available for others (subtractability), but for which exclusion of additional users is difficult or impossible (nonexcludability). (Note: common pool resources are also discussed in Chapter 11 in relation to global environmental change.) The issue of common pool resources was popularised by Hardin's (1968) essay on the 'Tragedy of the Commons', a model of unsustainable resource use based upon the pursuit of self-interest (Holden 2005). As Briassoulis (2002) notes, common pool resources play a central role in tourism – and management of such resources is thus an important part of sustainable tourism development. In the Galapagos there are both terrestrial and marine common pool resources, comprising the landscapes, ecosystems and wildlife within these environs.

Typically, common pool resources, such as tourism landscapes, are faced with the problem of exploitation, free-riding and overuse (Healey 1994).

Elinor Ostrom, winner of the 2009 Nobel Prize in Economics, identifies the common pool resource problem as a collective example of a 'social trap'. The trap is that an individual will continue to work to his/her own advantage, even though collectively the resource is damaged to the extent that he/she (and others) can no longer benefit from it (Platt 1973 in Fennell 2008). Fennell believes the Galapagos to be a good example of the social trap phenomenon 'whereby the decisions by policy makers to increase visitation yearly undermine initial attempts to control the impacts of tourism in this sensitive region' (2008: 205). Similarly, referring to the cruise industry, Fennell (2008) notes that as no one owns the oceans, and therefore cannot regulate activities that take place on the oceans, 'cruise companies are free to pollute their waters' (2008: 205).

Solutions to common pool issues have been identified and include privatisation, management by government or collective/cooperative management. In the Galapagos, to an extent, management by government *is* practised; however, this behoves the government to recognise the intrinsic value of the resource, and to prioritise this over a purely extrinsic value (i.e. economic returns) – something that has been lacking to date. While acknowledging the role of such resource management regimes, Holden (2005), however, advocates an alternative approach to addressing the problems of common pool resources. Drawing on what he describes as an overlooked part of Hardin's (1968) 'Tragedy of the Commons' essay, Holden supports Hardin's view that only 'a shift in morality will ultimately provide a more balanced model of existence between human needs and CPRs [common pool resources]' (2005: 340). He advocates the application of a strong environmental ethic to address common pool resource issues in tourism.

Discussion questions

1 Would privatising protected areas such as the Galapagos National Park help overcome problems associated with CPRs?
2 How may the 'shift in morality' advocated by Holden, as outlined in the section above, be achieved in practice?

Useful sources

Epler, B. (2007) *Tourism, the Economy, Population Growth, and Conservation in Galapagos*, Ayora, Galapagos Islands: Charles Darwin Foundation. Available at <http://www.eastue.org/media/100519_Galapagos/news/Epler_Tourism_Report-en_5–08.pdf>

Honey, M. (2008) *Ecotourism and Sustainable Development: Who Owns Paradise?* Washington: Island Press. Chapter 4, 'The Galapagos Islands: Test site for Theories of Evolution and Ecotourism', pp. 121–59.

9.6 CULTURAL RELATIVISM AND THE ENVIRONMENT

The discussion to this point has been quite Western-centric in terms of how the relationship between human and non-human nature can be conceptualised. We have hitherto ignored the extent to which ethnicity may influence this relationship, and the implications for environmental ethics, and nature-based tourism development in non-Western destinations. While it is beyond the scope of this chapter to fully explore the broad literature in this area, researchers are aware of the possibility that different cultural groups may be more concerned about different aspects of the environment. To generalise, traditional Eastern (Asian, African) and Native American groups are purported to believe that humans exist in a harmonious relationship with nature (Altman and Chemers 1980 in Johnson et al. 2004). There are problems around homogenising 'the East', and in drawing boundaries around the environmental values of different ethnic groups. Despite this, however, a Western visitor to a national park in the East – China, for example – may be struck by the extent of commercial tourist development within the park; developments that protected area managers and advocates in the West are at pains to keep outside of the park boundaries.

This raises the question of cultural relativism, and its connection to environmental ethics. Relativism has been defined as the thesis that 'cognitive, moral, or aesthetic claims involving such values as truth, meaningfulness, rightness, reasonableness, appropriateness, aptness, or the like are relative to the context in which they appear' (Krausz 1989: 1). In other words, cultural relativism maintains that morality is grounded in the approval of one's society (see Chapter 2). The opposing view, moral absolutism, assumes that all moral issues can be measured by one universal standard without regard for cultural differences. A cultural relativist approach would therefore defend the right of Chinese park managers, park visitors and tourism entrepreneurs to establish tourism businesses within a protected natural area, despite the fragility of the environment, or the endangered status of plant and animal species living there. A problem arises, however, with natural attractions that are *international* in significance.

DISCUSSION POINT: WULINGYUAN WORLD HERITAGE AREA, CHINA

In 2002, the world's tallest outdoor elevator opened in the scenic area of Zhangjiajie, China. Bailong Elevator is built onto the side of a huge cliff in Zhangjiajie and at 1,070 feet high has three Guinness World Records, i.e. world's tallest full-exposure outdoor elevator, world's tallest double-deck sightseeing elevator and world's fastest passenger traffic elevator with biggest carrying capacity.

There is concern, however, about the impact of the elevator on the surrounding landscape, especially considering that it is located within the Wulingyuan UNESCO World Heritage Area, designated for its outstanding scenic beauty.

Figure 9.3 Bailong Elevator, Wulingyuan World Heritage Area, China. Photo: Pin Ng.

The elevator has been subject to mounting disputes and criticism since its construction began. Critics argue that digging tunnels and shafts and building steel structures at the heritage site obviously go against the principles of World Heritage. Furthermore, others argue that the number of tourists should be reduced to help preserve the site, as the scenic spot already suffers from excessive tourism (five million tourists visited in 2000 alone) (Beijing Review 2010).

Some critics point out that it is hard to imagine such a development occurring within Western World Heritage Sites, and question the environmental ethics or commitment of the Chinese.

The question is: Is it ethical for Chinese authorities to allow such developments within World Heritage Areas (ostensibly created for the protection of global heritage, for a global population and for global visitation)? Han (2008) notes that the traditional Chinese view of nature, with its origins in Confucianism and Taoism, maintains a philosophical, humanist and holistic attitude to the human–nature relationship, which is distinguished from the traditional Western human detachment from nature. From the Chinese point of view, nature has never excluded human activities. Historically, wild nature has not been the focus of Chinese appreciation, rather, the Chinese seek 'humanised' nature, as it is more beautiful than pristine nature. To Chinese people, the idea of 'repair[ing] to nature in order to experience solitude, taking only pictures and leaving only footprints, as Westerners wish to do, is foreign' (Han 2008: 256).Chinese tourists seek three things from their visits to a scenic spot (Han 2008: 256; Lovelock et al 2011).

- Beautiful scenery
- Cultural refinement of the scenery
- Convenient access and tourist facilities (e.g. hotels, shops, restaurants) that enhance the comfort and enjoyment of the visit.

Sadly, these demands have resulted in 'huge environmental impacts in these areas' (Han 2008: 256). So when Chinese protected area managers come to apply the principles of World Heritage protection, based as they are upon contemporary Western environmental philosophies (including sustainability), they suffer from 'cross-cultural confusion' (Han 2008). The controversy over developments such as the Bailong Elevator (arguably an example of humanised nature), are in effect 'battles between international universal values and traditional Chinese values' (Han 2008: 258). In that case, the idea that culture can be guided by but should not be suppressed in the process of preserving nature, has won out. Thus such developments are generally acceptable to most Chinese visitors.

> *Wang Zhe* (Tourist): 'The natural environment can't be preserved exactly as it is, just as we cannot live in the past. The questions are, how much should we alter it, and what methods should be used….So we must be open-minded toward some alterations to nature.
> *Sun Delong* (Bailong Elevator manager): 'I do not agree with the experts. They say building elevators will harm the mountain. But as we all know, the mountain is lifeless. The successful operation of the elevator offers a model for other scenic spots.'
>
> (Beijing Review 2010)

Discussion questions

1 Should such developments as the Bailong Elevator be permitted within World Heritage Areas?

2 Would your answer to the above question be different if the area did not have World Heritage status?

3 What are the implications for protected natural areas in other parts of the world, with increasing numbers of outbound tourists from countries such as China, who may have different conceptions of the human–nature relationship?

Sources

Beijing Review (2010) 'Construction in scenic spots: protection or destruction?' *Beijing Review*, 6 September. Available at <http://www.bjreview.com/Cover_Story_Series_2010/2010–09/06/content_296545.htm> (Accessed 9 October 2011).

Han, Feng (2008) 'Cross cultural confusion: the application of World Heritage concepts in scenic and historic interest areas in China', in Nelson, M.P. and Baird Callicott, J. (eds) *The Wilderness Debate Rages On: Continuing the Great New Wilderness Debate*, Athens: University of Georgia Press, pp. 252–63.

Lovelock, Kirsten, Lovelock, Brent, Jellum, Carla and Anna Thompson (2011) 'In search of belonging: immigrant experience of outdoor nature based settings in New Zealand', *Leisure Studies* 30 (4): 513–529.

9.7 SUSTAINABLE TOURISM

Sustainable tourism development is espoused as a means of addressing the needs of the tourism industry, visitors and communities while protecting the resources upon which it depends. It is espoused as a useful framework for guiding nature-based tourism, with its often fragile resource-base. Critics of the concept, though, argue that, at best, sustainable tourism development is a potentially damaging compromise between interests of conservation and development (see Chapter 1). While much debate has gone into trying to define and refine the concept, few commentators have questioned the relationship between sustainable tourism and ethical tourism (Pawlowski 2008).

Sustainable development

Broadly speaking, there are two approaches to sustainable development – weak or strong – that may be thought of as relating to different ethical concepts: the 'domination of nature' and the 'intrinsic right of nature' (Jabareen 2008). Weak sustainability adopts an anthropocentric approach to the relationship between humans and nature: humans are separate from nature; nature is a 'resource' to be used for the benefit of humans; and humans have the right to dominate nature – and as such it does not question the core values concerning dominant attitudes towards nature (Williams and Millington 2004). It is also characterised by 'technocentrism', or a belief in technical solutions to environmental problems. In a 'stronger' version of sustainability, a different view of the relationship between human and non-human nature is adopted, in which nature has biotic rights, and anthropocentrism is replaced by biocentric egalitarianism (Williams and Millington 2004). Such an approach questions the underlying principle of economic growth, and redefines 'wealth' as 'wellbeing'.

The connection between sustainable development and environmental ethics is further investigated by Jabareen (2008) who teases out the conceptual underpinnings of sustainable development. He believes that sustainable development may be interpreted as a 'discourse of ethics', in which human conduct with regard to good or evil is articulated. Indeed, *Our Common Future* concludes that 'human survival and well being could depend on success in elevating sustainable development to a global ethics' (WCED 1987: 308). However, the ethics behind sustainable development have been questioned, for example by Kothari who argues that the concept is ecologically destructive because it is 'ethically vacuous – not impelled by basic values, and not anchored in concepts or rights and responsibilities' (1990: 28). Norton (2007) notes that the ethical debate over sustainable development is essentially one of instrumental versus intrinsic values, where economists and environmental ethicists are essentially speaking different languages. Because of their rejection of economic (anthropocentric) frameworks of analysis for environmental problems, the latter group are at odds with current formulations of sustainable development.

Some argue that there are more than the three typically described dimensions of sustainable development (economic, ecological, socio-cultural). Pawlowski (2008) identifies no less than seven dimensions, one of which is a moral (ethical) dimension. He draws a link between German philosopher Hans Jonas's (1984) 'Ethic (or Imperative) of Responsibility' and the principle of sustainable development, pointing out that the 'old ethics' with limited temporal and spatial application are no longer applicable, because of the tremendous technological power that humankind has to destroy the global environment.

Ethics of sustainable tourism

Before progressing to a discussion of the ethics of sustainable tourism, we first need to question whether or not we can simply apply the concept of sustainable development to tourism. For most, such an extension is automatic – however, some question the logic of doing so. Sharpley believes that there are significant differences between the concepts of sustainable tourism and sustainable development – suggesting that the principles and objectives of sustainable development cannot be transposed onto the specific context of tourism. He warns that '"true" sustainable tourism development is unachievable' (2000: 23), and that the concept is a 'red herring', drawing attention away from the realities of tourism development – much of which stand in stark opposition to the principles of sustainable tourism. Holden (2000) is also critical of the concept, differentiating 'sustainable tourism' which emphasises the customer and the industry, from tourism used as a means to achieve sustainable development, with wider social and environmental goals in mind. He too points out that the goals of so-called sustainable tourism may not necessarily equate with those of sustainable development.

But discussion of the ethics of sustainable tourism and the moral appropriateness of sustainable tourism has been limited (Butler 1991). Macbeth believes that 'without a clearly articulated and utilized ethical stance, it [sustainable tourism development] will simply serve the interests of short term development and profit takers' (2005: 980). The dominant approach to sustainable tourism has been technical, rational and scientific – and this has eclipsed the emergence of an ethical response (Hughes 1995). Hughes proposes a brand of sustainable tourism 'fashioned out of an ethical interest in the development of people, as tourists, and destination populations, as communities' (1995: 49).

Tourists as practitioners of sustainable tourism

This interest in individuals (tourists, developers, locals) as proponents of sustainable tourism also underlies Jamal's (2004) exploration of the underlying purpose, or 'telos' of sustainable tourism. Delving into Aristotelian virtue ethics, in which the goodness of a thing is measured by the extent to which it achieves its purpose, Jamal questions the connection between sustainable tourism, 'good tourism' and leading a good life. She notes that sustainable tourism generally focuses upon macro-level outcomes – for example at the societal or ecosystem level. Questions of how sustainable tourism can promote good tourism and good actions on a micro (personal) scale are not really addressed under current conceptualisations: 'the telos of sustainable tourism is especially unclear with respect to the development of individual character and habits that contribute to the "good life"' (Jamal 2004: 535). She notes that sustainable tourism is mainly influenced by contemporary moral philosophy's focus on rightness, obligation and duty (e.g. inter and intra generational equity). Jamal argues the benefits of a neo-Aristotelian approach that focuses 'more upon the type of person we ought to be rather than the things we do' (2004: 543). By combining this virtues approach with the 'right action' approach, both macro and micro issues may be more readily addressed within a sustainable tourism framework.

In order to better understand and operationalise sustainable tourism development, there appears a need for researchers, planners and developers to gain a better understanding of environmental ethics – and to position themselves on the anthropocentric–ecocentric continuum (Macbeth 2005). They will then be in a better position to relate to the varied interpretations of sustainable tourism development. Macbeth calls for the adoption of a non-anthropocentric ethic and suggests that we be prepared to argue, on ethical grounds, for '…no tourism!' (2005: 980).

DISCUSSION POINT: ECOWARRIORS AND TOURISM

On the evening of 19 October 1998, Earth Liberation Front (ELF) eco-activists firebombed a lodge, ski patrol headquarters and four ski lifts at a ski resort in Vail, Colorado, causing US$12 million worth of damage. The stated goal of ELF is 'economic sabotage and guerrilla warfare to stop the exploitation and destruction of the environment'. In a statement, they said that:

> Vail, Inc. is already the largest ski operation in North America and now wants to expand even further. The 12 miles of roads and 885 acres of clearcuts will ruin the last, best lynx habitat in the state. Putting profits ahead of Colorado's wildlife will not be tolerated.

> (Earth First! 2011)

This and other actions earned them the label of 'eco-terrorists', and the FBI named them as one of the top domestic terror threats in the United States. ELF, Earth First! and other similar movements carry out acts of ecological sabotage, or 'eco-tage'. Dave Foreman, co-founder of Earth First! in describing the philosophy behind the movement (see *Confessions of an Eco-Warrior* (1991)) notes: 'An individual human life has no more intrinsic value than does an individual Grizzly Bear life....Ours is an ecological perspective that views Earth as a community.'

The tactics of ecotage are supposedly inspired by the writings of Edward Abbey, author of the novel *The Monkeywrench Gang* (1975), in which 'monkey-wrenching' or sabotage of environmentally unfriendly industrial projects is featured (Abbey discusses the impacts of 'industrial tourism' on nature in his book *Desert Solitaire* (1968)). Earth First! has even published a book entitled *Ecodefense: A Field Guide to Monkeywrenching* (Foreman and Haywood 1985).

The ethics of ecological sabotage are complex – but captured to some extent in an exchange between the Editor of the journal *Environmental Ethics*, Eugene Hargrove, Edward Abbey and Dave Foreman in 1975 (in Keller 2010). Hargrove is critical of ecotage, describing activists as 'criminally and morally reprehensible by normal and moral standards' (Keller 2010: 336). Abbey defends the actions of the characters in his novel, noting that they engage in sabotage (Keller 2010: 335):

> only when it appears in certain cases and places all other means of defense of land and life have failed and that force – the final resort – becomes morally justified. Not only justified but a moral obligation, as in the defense of one's own life, one's own family, one's own home, one's own *nature*, against a violent assault.

The ethical issue boils down to a question of whether the means are justified by the ends. Can we judge the ethics by the ends pursued, or by other moral standards, or both? In his article *The Morality of Ecosabotage*, Young considers arguments against destroying property as a means of defending the environment, and concludes that there can be a consequentialist justification of particular acts of ecosabotage. In particular a 'constrained utilitarianism' can, at least in principle, justify some acts of strategic ecosabotage in a democratic society (Young 2001) (also see Martin 1990; and Welchman 2001, who address ecosabotage from a civil disobedience perspective).

Discussion questions

1 Is eco-sabotage ethically justified to prevent tourism development from impacting upon natural values?
2 Is your answer to the above question different if there is an endangered species of animal that would be wiped out as a result of the tourism development?

3 Is your answer to the above question impacted if the eco-sabotage may physically harm humans? (e.g. in 1987 activists in Goa greeted tourists at the airport with a shower of cowdung.)

4 How can an action be considered ethical if it is illegal?

References

Abbey, E. (1968) *Desert Solitaire*, New York: McGraw-Hill.

—— (1975) *The Monkey Wrench Gang*, Philadelphia, PA: Lippincott. (The *Monkey Wrench Gang*. Facebook http://www.facebook.com/...Monkey-Wrench-Gang/108463352514329)

Foreman, D. (1991) *Confessions of an Eco-Warrior*, New York: Crown Publishing.

Foreman, D. and Haywood, B. (eds) (1985) *Ecodefense: A Field Guide to Monkey wrenching*, http://theanarchistlibrary.org/HTML/Various_Authors_−_Ecodefense_−_A_Field_Guide_to_Monkeywrenching.html

Martin, M. (1990) 'Ecotage and civil disobedience', *Environmental Ethics*, 12(4): 291–310.

Welchman, J. (2001) 'Is ecotage civil disobedience?', *Philosophy and Geography*, 4(1): 97–107.

Young, T. (2001) 'The morality of ecosabotage', *Environmental Values*, 10: 385–93.

9.8 ECOTOURISM

Ecotourism, like sustainable tourism, has been put forward as a solution to the negative impacts of tourism in sensitive natural environments. Ecotourism is defined as 'Responsible travel to natural areas that conserves the environment and improves the well-being of local people' (The International Ecotourism Society (TIES) 1992). Honey (2008: 29–31) expands on the TIES definition by describing seven characteristics of ecotourism:

- Involves travel to natural destinations
- Minimises impact
- Builds environmental awareness
- Provides direct financial benefits for conservation
- Provides financial benefits and empowerment for local people
- Respects local culture
- Supports human rights and democratic movements.

Some, however, question the veracity of ecotourism, saying that it is just another example of 'greenwash', and is simply a 'buzzword' used as a marketing ploy to attract undiscerning tourists (e.g. Wheeler 1995). The array of ecotourism products certainly seems to be expanding and now includes activities that are patently antithetical to the principles of ecotourism, such as 'eco-jetboating' on rivers in New Zealand. As McLaren notes, 'the term is being used for almost any travel as long as something green is seen along the way' (2003: 91). Referring to an 'Ecotourism Lite', Honey (2008) is also critical of the concept, believing it to bring only marginal financial benefits, but often with serious environmental and social consequences. Fennell, in his book on ecotourism, concurs, believing that it can be just as unsustainable as other more intrusive forms of tourism. He argues for a stronger philosophical grounding of ecotourism that would allow the consideration of 'the bigger picture beyond concerns for our own immediate self-interest' (2008: 226). Despite positive examples of ecotourism products (e.g. Higham and Carr 2003), it would appear that ecotourism does require a more ethical approach, if it is to avoid being what Butler (1992) would describe as just another 'snake oil panacea' for the ills of tourism development.

DISCUSSION QUESTIONS

1 How does sustainable tourism compare with ecotourism as an ethical tourism activity?
2 How does ecotourism relate to environmental ethics – where does it fit into the anthropocentric–biocentric continuum?
3 Ethically, how can the dilemma of ecotourism's requirement to meet both social and natural goals be resolved?

Exercise

Conduct an Internet search to identify what you consider to be a true ecotourism product – what are the features of that product that make it truly ecotourism?

Useful sources

Fennell, D. (2008) *Ecotourism* (3rd edn), Routledge: London.
Higham, J. (ed.) (2007) *Critical Issues in Ecotourism: Understanding a Complex Tourism Phenomenon*, Oxford: Elsevier.
Honey, M. (2008) Ecotourism and Sustainable Development: Who Owns Paradise? Washington: Island Press.

CHAPTER REVIEW

This chapter has outlined the importance of the natural world to tourism and noted some of the negative impacts of human interaction with non-human nature. This has largely been attributed to an anthropocentric approach to non-human nature. These, in the Western world, have been attributed to Christian origins, where the ethical conceptualisation of the human–nature relationship, is influenced by the Dominion thesis. We introduce some more contemporary conceptualisations of the relationship that are more ecocentric in their approach.

In a discussion of the application of the mainstream ethical frameworks of deontology and utilitarianism to the nature problem, the shortcomings of both are outlined. Moral extensionism is noted as a necessary advance in order to address the environmental problems associated with tourism and associated development. This led to an introduction to some more 'radical' ethical approaches, including holism and deep-green ethics, including the Gaia hypothesis. The problem of tourism's reliance often on common pool resources was noted, and the ethics of this examined and illustrated by a case study of tourism development in the World Heritage site of the Galapagos Islands.

And while sustainable development and sustainable tourism have been promoted as approaches to address such complexities, from a more ecocentric environmental ethics position, the concept of sustainable development is problematic. Similarly, ecotourism is challenged as a remedy for tourism's ills. The need to challenge tourism development in natural areas – for a zero-tourism policy – is raised, and the issue of ecological sabotage as an ethical action to defend nature debated.

While the discussion in the chapter was limited mainly to Western environmental ethics, it is noted that different cultures may conceptualise nature differently. This can lead to different understandings of what is 'right' in the way of tourism developments and activities in different destinations. Such cultural relativism is problematic with attractions that may be considered 'global property'.

SUMMARY OF KEY TERMS

Anthropocentrism A human-centred ethic or world view. The ethical position that humans are the most important entity in the universe, and that only humans have moral considerability (or at least moral primacy).

Common pool resource A resource that benefits a group of people, but which provides diminished benefits to everyone if each individual pursues his or her own self-interest. The value of a common pool resource can be reduced through overuse because the supply of the resource is not unlimited, and using more than can be replenished can result in scarcity. Overuse of a common pool resource can lead to the 'Tragedy of the Commons' problem.

Cultural relativism Cultural (or moral) relativism argues that good and bad, or 'ethical truth', is relative to culture. Thus moral principles are not objective, but rather, must be based on the norms of our society (cf. moral universalism).

Ecocentrism A nature-centred ethic or world view. An ethical position that places an emphasis on ecological wholes rather than individual plants or animals. A holistic rather than individualistic ethic.

Ecotourism Responsible travel to natural areas that conserves the environment and improves the wellbeing of local people (The International Ecotourism Society).

Land ethic From Aldo Leopold (1949). Recognises that communities include not just people but all elements of the natural world, including soils, waters, plants and animals; or, collectively, 'the land'. For an extract from Leopold's *A Sand County Almanac,* see http://www.waterculture.org/uploads/Leopold_TheLandEthic.pdf

Moral extensionism Moral (or ethical) extensionism widens the moral community, arguing that moral standing ought to be extended to non-human things (e.g. animals, plants, species or the Earth as a whole).

Sustainable development From the United Nations Commission for the Environment and Development (WCED 1987) (the 'Brundtland Report'): development that meets the needs of the present generation without compromising the needs of future generations to meet their own needs.

Sustainable tourism Tourism that takes full account of its current and future economic, social and environmental impacts, addressing the needs of visitors, the industry, the environment and host communities (UNWTO).

Tragedy of the Commons From Hardin (1968). If a resource is held in common for use by all (a common pool resource), then ultimately that resource will be destroyed by individuals trying to maximise their personal utility from the resource. The concept can be traced back to Aristotle who noted that 'what is common to the greatest number has the least care bestowed upon it'.

QUESTIONS FOR REFLECTION

1 Does sustainable development and sustainable tourism provide a new ethical framework for considering how tourism should interact with nature?
2 As a tourist, when visiting a different culture and observing what are in your view abuses of nature by tourism, is it ethical for you to criticise your host society?
3 Nature-based tourism tends to rely heavily upon common pool resources – will the ethical problems around the use (and abuse) of these resources be addressed by privatising them?

EXERCISES

1 Conduct an Internet search for ecotourism attractions/activities. Find the most radically ecocentric one and try to analyse what the underlying environmental ethic is behind it. Position the attraction/activity on the blue–green environmental ethic spectrum.
2 Identify a range of actions that could be taken by you as an individual to help prevent inappropriate tourism development within a natural area. Outline the ethical problems and 'acceptability' of each action.

3 Consider the human–non-human relationships espoused within the faiths of Islam, Buddhism, Hinduism and Taoism. How do they compare with that of Christianity? And to what extent are these different relationships manifested within the tourism industries of destinations that practise these different faiths?

NOTES

a Aristotle (384–322 BC), Greek philosopher and scientist. From *Parts of Animals* I.645a16.

b Albert Einstein (1879–1955), theoretical physicist.

c Aldo Leopold (1887–1948), author, ecologist, environmentalist. From *A Sand County Almanac,* New York: Oxford University Press, 1949.

d Ancient Native American quote. See <http://www.ilhawaii.net/ stony/quotes.html>

REFERENCES

Briassoulis, H. (2002) 'Sustainable tourism and the questions of the Commons', *Annals of Tourism Research*, 29(4): 1065–85.

Budowski, G. (1976) 'Tourism and environmental conservation: conflict, coexistence, or symbiosis?', *Environmental Conservation,* 3(1): 27–31.

Butler, R.W. (1991) 'Tourism, environment, and sustainable development', *Environmental Conservation,* 18(3): 201–9.

—— (1992) 'Alternative tourism: the thin edge of the wedge', in Smith, V.L. and Eadington, W.R. (eds) *Tourism Alternatives: Potentials and Problems in the Development of Tourism*, Philadelphia: University of Pennsylvania Press, pp. 31–46.

Curry, P. (2006) *Ecological Ethics: An Introduction*, Cambridge: Polity Press.

de Groot, R.S. (1983) 'Tourism and conservation in the Galapagos Islands', *Biological Conservation,* 26: 291–300.

Earth First! (2011) 'Earth First! accused of burning down Colorado ski resort', in '98 https://earthfirstnews.wordpress.com/2011/06/08/earth-first-accused-of-burning-down-colorado-ski-resort-in-98/

Gardener, M.R. and Grenier, C. (2011) 'Linking livelihoods and conservation: challenges facing the Galapagos Islands', in Baldacchino, G. and Niles, D. (eds) *Island Futures and Development Across the Asia-Pacific Region*, Tokyo: Springer, pp. 73–85.

Hall, C.M. and Saarinen, J. (eds) (2010) *Tourism and Change in Polar Regions: Climate, Environments and Experience,* Abingdon: Routledge.

Hardin, G. (1968) 'The Tragedy of the Commons', *Science*, New Series, 162(3859): 1243–8.

Healey, R. (1994) 'The "common pool" problem in tourism landscapes', *Annals of Tourism Research*, 21: 596–611.

Higham, J. and Carr, A. (2003) 'Defining ecotourism in New Zealand: differentiating between the defining parameters within a national/regional context', *Journal of Ecotourism,* 2(1): 17–32.

Hill, J. and Gale, T. (eds) (2009) *Ecotourism and Environmental Sustainability: Principles and Practice,* Burlington, VT: Ashgate.

Hohl, N. and McLaren, D. (2003) 'The Galapagos Islands: tourism in (the lack of) a social setting', in McLaren, D., *Rethinking Tourism and Ecotravel,* Bloomfield, CT: Kumarian Press, pp. 12–124.

Holden, A. (2000) *Environment and Tourism* (1st edn), London: Routledge.

—— (2003) 'In need of new environmental ethics for tourism?', *Annals of Tourism Research*, 30(1): 94–108.

—— (2005) 'Tourism, CPRs and environmental ethics', *Annals of Tourism Research*, 32(3): 805–7.

—— (2008) *Environment and Tourism* (2nd edn), Abingdon: Routledge.

Honey, M. (2008) *Ecotourism and Sustainable Development: Who Owns Paradise?* Washington: Island Press.

Hughes, G. (1995) 'The cultural construction of sustainable tourism', *Tourism Management*, 16(1): 49–59.

Jabareen, Y. (2008) 'A new conceptual framework for sustainable development', *Environment, Development and Sustainability,* 10(2): 179–92.

Jamal, T.B. (2004) 'Virtue ethics and sustainable tourism pedagogy: phronesis, principles and practice', *Journal of Sustainable Tourism,* 12(6): 530–45.

Jamieson, D. (2008) *Ethics and the Environment: An Introduction*, New York: Cambridge University Press.

Johnson, C., Bowker, J. and Cordell, H.K. (2004) 'Ethnic variation in environmental belief and behavior: an examination of the New Ecological Paradigm in a social psychological context', *Environment and Behavior*, 36: 157–86.

Jonas, H. (1984) *The Imperative of Responsibility. In Search of an Ethics for the Technological Age,* Chicago, IL: University of Chicago Press.

Keller, D.R. (2010) 'Introduction: What is environmental ethics?', in Keller, D.R. (ed.) *Environmental Ethics: The Big Questions*, Chichester: Blackwell, pp. 1–24.

Kothari, R. (1990) 'Environment, technology and ethics', in Engel, J.R. and Engel, J.G. (eds) *Ethics of Environment and Development: Global Challenges, International Response,* Tucson: University of Arizona Press, pp. 27–35.

Krausz, M. (ed.) (1989) *Relativism: Interpretation and Confrontation*, Notre Dame, IN: University of Notre Dame Press.

Kuenzi, C. and McNeely, J. (2008) 'Nature-based tourism', in Renn, O. and Walker, K.D. (eds) *Global Risk Governance: Concept and Practice Using the IRGC Framework*, International Risk Governance Council Bookseries, Dordrecht: Springer, pp. 155–78.

Leopold, A. (1949) *A Sand County Almanac,* New York: Oxford University Press.

Lovelock, J. (1979) *Gaia: A New Look at Life on Earth,* Oxford: Oxford University Press.

Macbeth, J. (2005) 'Towards an ethics platform for tourism', *Annals of Tourism Research,* 32(4): 962–84.

McLaren, D. (2003) *Rethinking Tourism and Ecotravel,* Bloomfield, CT: Kumarian Press.

Mason, P. (2008) *Tourism Impacts: Planning and Management*, Oxford: Elsevier.

MAWEB (2005) *Living Beyond Our Means: Natural Assets and Human Well-being: Millenium Ecosystem Assessment.* Available at <http://www.maweb.org/documents/document.429.aspx. pdf> (accessed 4 September 2011).

Midgely, M. (1992) *Science as Salvation: A Modern Myth and its Meaning,* London: Routledge.

Ministry of Tourism, Tourism New Zealand and Tourism Industry Association (2007) *New Zealand Tourism Strategy 2015,* Wellington, NZ: Ministry of Tourism.

Naess, A. (1989) *Ecology, Community and Lifestyle*, Cambridge: Cambridge University Press.

Newsome, D., Moore, S. and Dowling, R. (2002) *Natural Area Tourism: Ecology, Impacts, and Management*, Clevedon: Multilingual Matters.

Norton, B. (2007) 'Ethics and sustainable development: an adaptive approach to environmental choice', in Atkinson, G., Dietz, S. and Neumayer, E. (eds) *Handbook of Sustainable Development*, Cheltenham: Edward Elgar, pp. 27–44.

Pawłowski, A. (2008) 'How many dimensions does sustainable development have?', *Sustainable Development,* 16: 81–90.

Regan, T. (1984) *The Case for Animal Rights*, Berkeley: University of California Press.

Romeril, M. (1989) 'Tourism and the environment – accord or discord?', *Tourism Management*, 10(3): 204–8.

Sharpley, R. (2000) 'Tourism and sustainable development: exploring the theoretical divide', *Journal of Sustainable Tourism*, 8(1): 1–19.

Sylvan, R. and Bennett, D. (1994) *The Greening of Ethics: From Anthropocentrism to Deep Green Theory,* Tucson: University of Arizona Press.

Taylor, P. (1986) *Respect for Nature,* Princeton, NJ: Princeton University Press.

The International Ecotourism Society (TIES) (1992) *Uniting Conservation and Travel Worldwide,* North Bennington, VT: The Ecotourism Society.

—— (2012) *What is Ecotourism? The International Ecotourism Society.* Available at <http://www.ecotourism.org/what-is-ecotourism> (Accessed 23 February 2012).

United Nations World Tourism Organisation (UNWTO) (2010) *2010 Statistics and TSA Programme,* Madrid: World Tourism Organisation.

—— (2010) *Tourism and Biodiversity: Achieving Common Goals Towards Sustainability*, Madrid: World Tourism Organisation.

Vitousek, P.M., Mooney, H.A., Lubchenco, J. and Melillo, J.M. (1997) 'Human domination of Earth's ecosystems', *Science,* 277(5325): 494–9.

Wall, G. and Mathieson, A. (2006) *Tourism Change Impacts and Opportunities,* London: Prentice Hall.

Weaver, D. and Oppermann, M. (2000) *Tourism Management*, Brisbane: Wiley.

Wenz, P. (2001) *Environmental Ethics Today*, Oxford: Oxford University Press.

Wheeler, M. (1995) 'Tourism marketing ethics: an introduction', *International Marketing Review,* 12(4): 38–49.

White, L. (1967) 'Historical roots of our ecological crisis', *Science*, 155: 1203–7.

Williams, C.C. and Millington, A.C. (2004) 'The diverse and contested meanings of sustainable development', *Geographical Journal,* 170(2): 99–104.

Williams, P.W. and Ponsford,I.F. (2009) 'Confronting tourism's environmental paradox: transitioning for sustainable tourism', *Futures*, 41: 396–404.

World Commission on Environment and Development WCED (1987) *Our Common Future*, Oxford: Oxford University Press.

10 Animals and tourism

'The greatness of a nation and its moral progress can be judged by the way its animals are treated.'

Mohandas Gandhi[a]

'I am in favor of animal rights as well as human rights. That is the way of a whole human being.'

Abraham Lincoln[b]

'The question is not, Can they *reason*? nor Can they *talk*? but, Can they *suffer?*'

Jeremy Bentham[c]

LEARNING OBJECTIVES

After reading this chapter you will be able to:

- Discuss relevant ethical theories and how they relate to animals and tourism.
- Identify and discuss the different conceptualisations of the human–animal relationship.
- Define the terms 'animal rights' and 'animal welfare' and explain the key ethical approaches associated with these concepts.
- Identify and explain the difference between intrinsic and instrumental value in relation to animals.

10.1 INTRODUCTION

Throughout history, people have had a close relationship with animals, and the demand for this interaction has been argued to be fundamentally important to humans (Orams 2002). In the contemporary world, animals have become an integral part of the tourism product and, some would argue, are also important as consumers of tourist experiences themselves (Carr 2009). The importance and growth of nature-based tourism and wildlife tourism in particular necessitates a focus upon animals and how they are treated by the tourism industry.

Much effort in recent years has gone into ascertaining the impact of tourism upon animals, in particular upon animals in natural ecosystems – wild animals. However, recently, captive animals have also been the focus of some research, as zoos, animal parks and related attractions continue to be important attractions for domestic and international visitors alike (see e.g. Frost (2011) *Zoos and Tourism*, and the special issue in the journal *Current Issues in Tourism*: 'Animals in the Leisure and Tourism Experience', Volume 12 (2009), Issues 5–6). Of course animals are used in a wide variety of roles within the tourism industry, from passive objects of the tourist gaze, to active sources of labour (e.g. beasts of burden, elephant rides). Some animals make the 'ultimate sacrifice' and appear on the menus of tourist restaurants and then on the plates of tourists.

Issues of human carnivorism aside, the main ethical areas of concern continue to be around wildlife viewing, and its associated impacts upon the viewed species, along with 'consumptive wildlife tourism'. The latter category includes hunting and fishing – which, although a relatively small niche international tourism activity in most destinations, is a very important regional or local tourism/recreation activity. And for some less developed African nations, it is a substantial economic activity. But hunting in particular continues to be highly controversial, especially in regions with well-developed animal rights movements (e.g. Europe, North America).

While the ethics of human–animal interactions has been addressed in general, there has been relatively little attention paid to this within the tourism context. In a recent work, however, Fennell (2012) in an attempt to address what he describes as a critical lack of

Figure 10.1 *Animals, both wild and in captivity, are a popular visitor attraction.*
Photo: Brent Lovelock.

involvement in the area of tourism and animal ethics provides a very good coverage of ethical issues in relation to animals in captivity, in tourism service, in competition and combat, for sport and subsistence and wildlife viewing.

This chapter begins by outlining the main ethical arguments for and against incorporating animals into the tourism product, and introduces the concepts of animal rights and animal welfare. The discussion then moves to tourism and wild animals, addressing the impacts and benefits of exposing wild populations of animals to tourists. Tourism and captive animals is addressed, before the chapter moves on to focus on the ethical issues associated with consumptive wildlife tourism.

10.2 ANIMALS AND TOURISM

Wildlife tourism can be broadly defined as trips to destinations where the main purpose of the visit is to observe or interact with the local fauna. Newsome et al. (2005) note that this may take place in a variety of settings including captive, semi-captive and wild, and can encompass a variety of interactions from passive observation to feeding or touching the wildlife. However, we include consumptive interactions in this discussion, along the lines of Reynolds and Braithwaite (2001) who depict wildlife-based tourism (WBT) as comprising consumptive (e.g. hunting and fishing) and non-consumptive (ecotourism uses) (see Figure 10.2). Freese (1998) defines consumptive wildlife tourism (CWT) as a practice that involves animals being deliberately killed or removed, or having any of their body parts utilised. The consumptive/non-consumptive dichotomy has been challenged however (e.g. Tremblay 2001; Lemelin 2006) in that it erroneously suggests that some tourism activities that do not harvest or remove specimens from their habitats have no impacts. Tremblay maintains that non-consumptive tourism and ecotourism is also potentially

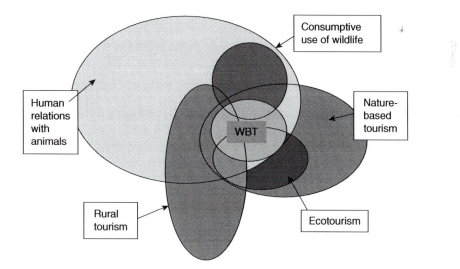

Figure 10.2 *Wildlife-based tourism.*
Source: Reynolds and Braithwaite (2001).

Types of interaction							
a. Groups fishing for sport	b. Fishing in the service of the tourism industry	c. Individuals fishing for sport	d. Individuals fishing for sport	e. Fishing in the service of the tourism industry	f. Fishing for subsistence	g. Fishing for subsistence	h. Viewing fish
Competition	Trophy or pleasure	Trophy	Pleasure	To feed clients	Taking more to meet one's long-term needs	Meeting one's own immediate needs	Learning/ appreciation
Mainly catch-and-release	Intentional kill or catch-and-release	Intentional kill	Catch-and-release	Intentional kill	Intentional kill	Intentional kill	No direct physical handling

Consumptive/non-essential ←——————————————→

Other nature-based tourism ←——————————————————————→

Increasingly anthropocentric ←——————————————————→	Increasingly biocentric
Human ethics	Universal ethics
Sanctity of human life	Sanctity of all life
Human interests first	Interests of nature first
Harm to life for human benefit	No intentional harm to life

Figure 10.3 *Human priorities and actions in recreational interactions with fish*
Source: Fennell (2012).

liable for large-scale damage to ecosystems and habitats and, in the longer run, to animals themselves (2001: 85).

As illustrated by Fennell (2012) (Figure 10.3) using the example of fish, there is a broad range of wildlife tourism activities, with a range of motivations and, accordingly, different styles of interaction with the animals concerned.

The global market for wildlife tourism today is an estimated 12 million trips annually, and is growing at 10 per cent per annum (Mintel 2008). Africa accounts for around one-half of all these trips, with South Africa, Kenya, Tanzania and Botswana being the top destinations. This is not to forget, however, that many countries have huge domestic wildlife tourism markets. For example, according to a US Fish and Wildlife Service study, birdwatchers contributed US$36 billion to the US economy in 2006, with one-fifth (20 per cent) of Americans self-identifying as birdwatchers. Birdwatching is reported as being the fastest growing outdoor activity in America with 51.3 million Americans claiming to watch birds (US Department of the Interior 2006). In the UK, the Royal Society for the Protection of Birds (RSPB) has a membership of over 1 million people.

The figures for hunting and fishing tourism are less clear, although it is likely in terms of international travel that, at least for most destinations, this is a niche market. Domestically, however, hunting and fishing are large markets: in the USA for example, US$18 billion was spent on trip-related expenses for both hunting and fishing in 2006 (US Department of the Interior 2006). Wildlife tourism clearly generates significant economic benefits, with some developing world destinations relying heavily on wildlife tourism receipts. For example, wildlife tourism contributes roughly $500 million to the Kenyan economy, or 14 per cent of GDP. Destinations such as the Galapagos Islands rely almost exclusively on wildlife tourists, with wildlife tourism contributing over $100 million to the local economy each year (One Caribbean 2011). In the UK, angling is the most popular sport, with £2.75B spent on the activity, and 20,000 people employed in angling-related jobs. Wildlife tourism also brings non-monetary benefits in the way of conservation and educational benefits to visitors by providing first-hand experiences of viewing wildlife in natural surroundings. The indirect conservation benefits of marine wildlife tours, for example, have been cited in terms of the enhanced educational and conservation outcomes (both on-site and off-site) (e.g. Zeppel and Muloin 2008). Some studies suggest that wildlife tourism has a positive effect on visitors' contributions to environmental organisations, helps strengthen pro-conservation attitudes towards the protection of species and encourages tourists to take positive actions to help conserve endangered species. For example, a survey of tourists visiting Mon Repos Conservation Park in Queensland showed that seeing sea turtles in a natural setting was effective in increasing the willingness of tourists to pay for the conservation of sea turtles (Tisdell and Wilson 2002). The study also suggested this would not have been the case if the setting had been a non-natural habitat such as a zoo.

However, the sustainability of wildlife tourism has been challenged. Higham and Bejder (2008) note that there are few examples in the world of tourism of a genuine symbiosis between tourism and conservation, and that this is particularly the case for wildlife tourism. What is more concerning is that there are a number of emerging wildlife destinations, e.g. Antarctica (whales, penguins and seals) that pose challenges to the sustainability of this form of tourism, because of the fragility of their environments (see Chapter 9).

A number of researchers have contributed frameworks for wildlife tourism, often depicting the impacts of tourism upon animals, species, habitats and ecosystems. The wide range of impacts upon wild animals is illustrated by Reynolds and Braithwaite (2001) (Figure 10.4)

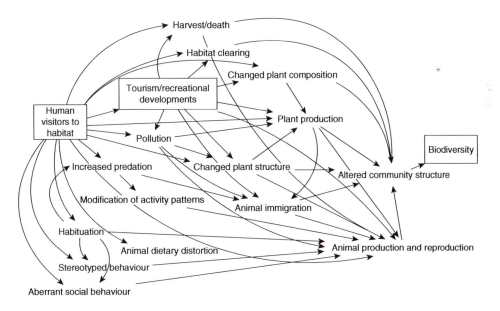

Figure 10.4 *Impacts of tourism on wildlife.*
Source: Reynolds and Braithwaite (2001).

and is shown to vary from modification of habitats, distortion of animal diets, and aberrant social behaviour to harvest and death. Ultimately many tourism interactions with wildlife impact negatively upon animal production and reproduction.

A number of tourism researchers have provided models that categorise tourist–wildlife interactions. Orams's (1996) model uses a scale with 'captive', 'semi-captive' and 'wild' settings. While not addressed in that model, each setting (e.g. zoo, wildlife park, natural habitat) and activity (e.g. passive observation, feeding, hunting/harvest) may pose a different and unique ethical problem for the tourism industry and the tourist. However, tourism researchers are yet to collate and systematise the ethical challenges associated with this broad range of wildlife tourism interactions. Table 10.1 presents a range of tourist–animal interactions and outlines the ethical issues associated with each activity, together with the potential benefits of that interaction.

Table 10.1 *Ethical issues and benefits of tourist–animal interactions*

Tourist activity	Ethical issues	Benefits?
Viewing animals in wild locations	Range of individual animal (production and reproduction), species, and ecosystem impacts	Pleasure to tourist, conservation knowledge and benefits, benefits to species and ecosystem
Feeding animals in the wild	Habituation, behavioural changes, health impacts on individual animals, group dynamics	Pleasure to tourist, intense human–animal interaction, conservation knowledge and benefits, benefits to species and ecosystem
Viewing and feeding animals in captive environments	Rights of individual animals, loss of benefits, impact on production and reproduction	Contributes to conservation programmes (captive breeding of endangered species), pleasure for viewers, education for conservation purposes, generates funds for conservation
Performing animals, captive environments	Harm in training, loss of individual benefits	Support for wild populations, revenue generation for conservation programmes
Hunting and fishing – harvesting wild animals	Death of animal, loss of future preferences, individual rights breached	Pleasure to hunter/fisher, game meat/fish, social bonding, intense animal–hunter experience

Continued

Table 10.1 Continued

Tourist activity	Ethical issues	Benefits?
Hunting and fishing – as part of conservation programme	Death of animal, loss of future preferences, individual rights breached	Benefits to species or ecosystem, pleasure to hunter/fisher, game meat/fish, social bonding, intense animal–hunter experience
Catch-and-release fishing, 'green hunting'	Pain and stress caused to individual animal (note debate over sentience of fish, however)	Pleasure to hunter/fisher, intense animal–hunter experience, conservation benefits (e.g. if part of a tagging programme)
Observing subsistence hunting as part of cultural tourism product	Death of animal, loss of future preferences, pain to animal, stress	Game meat to local people, income for tourism, cultural knowledge transfer, intense natural and cultural experience
Eating wild animals on tourist menu	Death of animal, loss of future preferences, pain to animal, stress, impact on species and ecosystem if over-harvesting	Pleasure for tourist, income to local people

Tourism experiences have traditionally been designed to cater for the desires of the human population, utilising animals as products rather than 'sentient creatures with individual "rights" and "needs" in the process' (Carr 2009: 409). For centuries it was theological and philosophical dogma that animals have no psychological lives at all – that they are mindless organic automata (Jamieson 2008). In the seventh century French philosopher Malebranche wrote 'they eat without pleasure, they cry without sorrow, they desire nothing, they fear nothing, they know nothing' (in Jamieson 2008: 189). In contrast, English philosopher Jeremy Bentham (1748–1832), one of the first proponents of animal rights, believed 'the question is not, Can they *reason*? Nor, can they *talk*? But, Can they *suffer*?' (in Fennell 2006: 184).

Mainly in response to the perceived abuse of animals in other industries and activities (e.g. agriculture) a number of ethical arguments have been developed to enhance the interests and wellbeing of animals. Such arguments can be readily applied to tourism. The main two ethical arguments that are used against hunting (and farming/slaughter of animals), and by extension can be employed in the analysis of touristic use of animals, are animal welfare and animal rights. While differing in their approaches, both are similar in the way that they extend to animals a moral value that usually would only apply to humans. This is in keeping with Plato, who thought it was no more feasible to divide living creatures into humans and non-humans than cranes and non-cranes (Plato, in *The Statesman*). Indeed, to not recognise the moral worth of all or some non-humans is described as 'speciesism' – the discrimination of others based upon species membership (Noske 1999 in Lemelin 2009). The implication of an animal rights or an animal welfare approach to tourism is that any touristic activity that harms animals requires a moral justification in terms of countervailing human rights or interests (Cahoone 2009).

Animal welfare

The animal welfare argument has been championed by the work of Peter Singer (notably in his book *Animal Liberation* (2001)), drawing on the utilitarian approach of Bentham. Utilitarianism (see Chapter 2) is an ethical approach that considers the right action to be one that maximises good consequences. The basic tenet of Singer's work is that of 'having an interest'. Creatures that have interests fall within the bounds of moral considerability. The capacity to feel pleasure or pain (often referred to as sentience) is a necessary and sufficient condition of having interests. If a creature cannot feel pleasure or pain then it has no interests, whereas if it is sentient, then it has, at the very least, an interest in avoiding pain (Dickson 2009). All and only sentient creatures count – ethically – thus Singer expands the moral circle beyond humans to include (some) animals.

As noted above, utilitarians are interested in maximising the satisfaction of interests, with an equivalent interest counting equally, whoever's (or whatever's) interest it is. Thus the pain of an animal should count equally as the pain of a human. However, Singer distinguishes between creatures that are 'persons' and those that are not. This is not the same as a human/non-human distinction. A person is defined as a rational and self-conscious being. Some non-human animals are persons and some (although they may be sentient) are not. Most mammals are persons, birds are not. In this respect, some ethicists are at odds with the allocation of sentience, and believe there is a need to broaden the current human–animal leisure and tourism narrative away from the privileged warm-blooded animals more to the cold-blooded species (Lemelin 2009).

That debate aside, killing a person would typically be worse than killing a non-person, because a person will typically have many future-oriented preferences that will remain unsatisfied if it is killed. A non-person does not see itself as an entity with a future and will have fewer such preferences. But killing a sentient creature is also wrong as its life may be pleasant, and death will lead to loss of pleasant experiences.

In Singer's approach, entities such as species and ecosystems do not count, morally, for they are not sentient and so do not have interests. However, it is suggested that we may still have to conserve species and ecosystems because that will often be essential to avoid harming individual members of those species and ecosystems that do have interests.

Animal rights

Rights theorists, Kantians and utilitarians have all argued that many non-human animals have rights. The animal rights approach (Regan 2004) posits that some types of animals are 'subjects of a life' – if they can perceive and remember, if they have desires and preferences, and if they are able to act intentionally and have some sense of the future. Such animals are said to have a unified psychological presence (e.g. mammals). Regan claims that subjects of life have equal inherent value, and anything with equal inherent value has an equal right to treatment respectful of that value. Foremost among those rights is the right not to be killed. Hunting, for example, violates this right and would therefore be wrong. Regan also argues that we should treat other animals as if they were also rights-holders – and thus hunting of those animals (e.g. birds, fish) should also be prohibited.

The main difference between the animal welfare and animal rights approaches is that the former does take into account the sum of consequences in a weighing-up process. For example, if we consider safari hunting, an animal welfare approach would consider the exercise benefits to hunters, the value of individual hunters communing with nature, the contribution of hunting to conservation of the species and habitat, and the economic and social benefits to poor communities, etc. The animal rights approach rejects such a weighing-up, saying that this cannot justify violating the rights of individuals. Individuals cannot be sacrificed to advance the greater good (of a species, ecosystem or human community). Deep ecology is a philosophical position widely advocated by animal rights advocates. Such a position is a 'clear effort to diverge from the anthropocentric view of nature and its common utilitarian and often consequentialist ethical perspective' (Reis 2009: 576). Deep ecology espouses the principle that life forms have value in their own right – and that humans have no right to reduce this richness of life and diversity 'except to satisfy *vital needs*' (Devall and Sessions 1985: 70 in Reis 2009: 576).

Virtue ethics

While animal rights and animal welfare are the two main approaches to the animal question, virtue ethics has also been employed in this area. Virtue ethics (from Aristotle – see Chapter 2) is person- (or agent-) rather than action-based. It considers the moral character of the person carrying out an action, evaluating moral actions based on what a virtuous person should do, disregarding the consequences of the actions or the duty to carry them out. Under such an approach, most touristic hunting would be wrong, because it is done for fun, and the people who participate in it are behaving selfishly and not as a virtuous person would. Since their behaviour is not virtuous, their behaviour is morally wrong. However, this is questioned by some. If we consider fox-hunting, previously a substantial 'domestic' tourism activity but made illegal in England in 2004, there are arguments using a virtue ethics approach for the continuation of this activity. Scruton (1996) notes that the pleasure derived from fox-hunting is not specifically from the suffering or death of the fox, but rather from the associated activities. He believes that fox-hunting displays the virtues of traditional social solidarity, respect for the hunted animal and concern for the countryside – and is thus a morally acceptable activity.

10.4 INSTRUMENTAL AND INTRINSIC VALUE

Central to the debate over the use of animals in tourism and leisure is the intrinsic versus the instrumental value of animals. In contrast to both the animal welfare and animal rights arguments, in an environmentalist approach, Callicott (1980) argues that only the biotic community as a whole has intrinsic value – individual animals only have value in so far as they contribute to that whole. This approach can be used to defend touristic activities that will impact upon individual members of a species (e.g. hunting, feeding wild animals, placing animals in zoos), but may benefit the entire population (e.g. through raising conservation awareness, or generating funds for conservation programmes).

In sum, it appears that none of the approaches on their own provides the perfect ethical framework for considering the 'animal question' in tourism. As Anderson (2004) suggests, each of the three main approaches (animal rights, animal welfare and environmentalism) raises relevant moral considerations, but none on its own recognises all of the relevant sources of value concerning the human–animal interaction. However, the debate has moved forward, and today, as Fennell (2006) notes, it is acceptable to view animals as having rights, despite the fact that they cannot claim those rights (Regan 1983 in Fennell 2006).

DISCUSSION POINT: CAN HUNTING BE ECOTOURISM?

A standard definition of ecotourism is 'Responsible travel to natural areas that conserves the environment and improves the well-being of local people' (TIES 2012). About 10 years ago there was a debate in the literature between tourism and wildlife academics about whether or not fishing could be seen as ecotourism. Holland et al. (1998, 2000) suggested that 'catch and release' of bill-fish (e.g. marlin, swordfish) is an ethical treatment of fish, and could be considered a form of ecotourism. Fennell (2000) responded that no form of fishing could really be classed as ecotourism, because of the consumptive nature of the activity. He argued that catch-and-release fishing was only slightly more non-consumptive than consumptive, and that it did not show evidence of the respect for plants and animals that ecotourism should be based on. As Lovelock (2008) points out, this practice does result in stress to the target species (and death to some) when they are removed (consumed) from their natural environment, albeit temporarily, by fishers. See Figure 10.3 in which Fennell depicts the various ethical aspects of touristic interaction with fish.

Hunting, despite animal rights advocates considering it to be the least acceptable form of wildlife use (Cohn 1999), is another activity that under some circumstances could be considered an ecotourism activity. Some researchers believe that ecotourism can embrace forms of consumptive wildlife tourism that are beneficial to the economy, the environment, and to local communities (Novelli et al. 2006). In destinations such as New Zealand, which is a popular hunting tourism destination, where all game species are introduced (and are even legally classified as pests, hunting could be considered as a restorative form of ecosystem management (Lovelock 2007), and by extension a form of ecotourism. Indeed, Callicott (1980) argues that 'to hunt or kill a white-tailed deer in certain districts may not only be ethically permissible, it might actually be a moral requirement, necessary to protect the local environment' (1980 in Dickson 2009: 68).

Buckley (2009), while acknowledging this, notes that hunting is not generally considered a form of ecotourism. Other writers go to the extent of removing hunting (and fishing) from their definitions of wildlife tourism. For example, Newsome et al. (2005: 20) in their book on wildlife tourism state that '[we] have deliberately delimited our definition of wildlife tourism to exclude any activity which results in the killing of wildlife as it does not sit comfortably with the ecocentric worldview that engenders respect for all living creatures'.

Knight (2005) argues that focusing on the population rather than the individual animals presents hunters with arguments that try to neutralise the moral objections raised by animal welfarists over recreational hunting. However, it is argued by Reis (2009) that hunting practice is a cultural ritual that at some part is intended to reunite the human animal with the environment in which it belongs – a laudable and acknowledged aim of ecotourism. Other writers go further to argue that the embodied experience of hunting (or fishing) is the ultimate form of engagement with the natural world (e.g. Franklin 2001; Marvin 2005).

Even animal welfare advocates, whose arguments for animal welfare centre upon animal suffering, raise possibilities about the ethical value of hunting – in comparison to other acts against animals. Singer, for example, asks 'why, for instance is the hunter who shoots a deer for venison subject to more criticism than the person who buys a ham at the supermarket? Overall it is probably the intensively reared pig who has suffered more' (1995 in Dickson 2009: 62). Should the touristic hunting of animals for trophy heads or for 'fun' be considered differently?

While this debate continues to rage, hunting as a form of tourism will continue to be vigorously attacked by animal rights groups, and equally as vigorously defended by hunters and hunting operators. The pressure is starting to tell, as countries such as Namibia and Botswana face pressure to ban hunting. Botswana has banned lion hunting since 2000 and is considering reductions in the hunting of some species. The Botswana government wishes to encourage photographic tourism and gradually limit but not ban wildlife hunting.

Codes of practice (see Chapter 14) will also play an important role, both in animal welfare and in maintaining the quality of the wildlife tourism experience.

Discussion question

Are some forms of hunting (or fishing) more ethical than others?

Exercise

Develop a list of different consumptive wildlife tourism activities and a set of criteria for ranking them from 'least ethical' to 'most ethical'.

Figure 10.5 *Inuit man preparing skin from a polar bear shot by a tourist. Photo: Martha Dowsley.*

CASE STUDY: INUIT PERSPECTIVES ON THE ETHICS OF POLAR BEAR CONSERVATION HUNTING IN NUNAVUT TERRITORY, CANADA – *MARTHA DOWSLEY*

Conservation hunting, which uses sport hunting as a means to promote both short- and long-term management of the target species through financial support for conservation programmes and local economies, is an important mechanism for maintaining viable populations of game species in poor, rural and often indigenous areas around the world. Despite the success of conservation hunting in maintaining wildlife populations, there is debate about the ethics of trophy hunting as a form of tourism, due to its consumptive nature. Trophy, or sport, hunting is often seen as killing an animal for recreation, and such an idea does not fit with the ethical standards of many cultures.

In the Canadian arctic territory of Nunavut, aboriginal Inuit communities are permitted to outfit and guide polar bear conservation hunts for non-aboriginal tourists under a strict quota system that ensures the long-term health of the bear populations. Each biologically defined polar bear population is assigned a sustainable quota each year. The communities that are located in a particular polar bear population receive a share of the quota, and may divide the quota between sport hunts and traditional subsistence hunting. The ethical issues around conservation hunting for Inuit are complex and expand beyond the concern regarding the motivation of the sport hunter to include concerns about human–polar bear relationships, the use of a quota system, and the appropriate sharing of financial and employment opportunities in such a way as to support today's hunters while ensuring hunting can be continued into the future.

In Inuit cultural tradition, animals are seen as non-human people who are sentient and have their own way of life. Polar bears are ascribed a particularly powerful consciousness that includes the ability to choose to have interactions with people based on evaluations of an individual's motivations, thoughts and past actions. A polar bear may make itself available to a hunter who respects it through various actions and thoughts. For example, such a hunter does not think or say negative things about bears, he or she intends to share the meat or other by-products of the hunt (including money), and has shared meat in the past. The relationship between bears and people also extends beyond the relationship between an individual hunter and individual polar bear to include the communities to which each belongs. Humans, as a group, are expected to share meat from animals, who share themselves with hunters. Polar bears are thought to know how humans treated other bears and whether humans participated in the sharing cycle amongst themselves. Based on that information, polar bears may perpetuate the sharing relationship by making themselves available to hunters or they may withdraw from the relationship by leaving the area, or attacking humans or human objects.

Given this cultural tradition, the involvement of tourist sport hunters in the human–polar bear relationship is of importance to their host communities because it could potentially damage the relationship and reduce community hunting success in the future. The traditional conceptualisation of the human–bear relationship, however, is able to accommodate the visiting hunters in two ways. First, since polar bears are often viewed as sentient, the success of a sport hunter is viewed, in part, to be due to the decision by the bear to make itself available to the hunter. It is not respectful to question a bear's decision, so Inuit do not overly concern themselves with the motivation of the hunter. That evaluation is left to the bear. Second, the meat from sport hunted polar bears is not generally of great interest to the sport hunter, who is more interested in the hide and skull for taxidermy. Thus, the Inuit hunting guides are able to distribute the meat through community social networks, which perpetuates the human obligation of sharing. Therefore, the relationship between humans and bears can be continued on good terms in a sport hunting situation.

Of greater ethical concern to many Inuit communities, is the use of a quota system. The system was implemented in order to control harvest levels and allow for a conservation hunt, but some Inuit have expressed anxiety about its effects on the human–bear relationship. First, setting a harvest quota suggests that humans are so arrogant as to think they are the sole decision makers in how many polar bears they will catch in a given year. Once the quota is filled, humans will also refuse to hunt bears that may make themselves available. These problems, along with the common practice of assigning hunting tags to individual hunters, reduce the role of polar bears in the harvest decision-making process. Quotas assume animals are merely resources and do not have the consciousness that Inuit tradition assigns them. Some Inuit communities have arrived at systems that allow successful compromise between the principles of conservation hunting and the principles of the traditional Inuit world view.

The economic return from outfitting and guiding polar bear conservation hunts is another ethical issue. In using their quota, communities must decide how to compensate Inuit hunters (either individually or as a group) for the loss of hunting tags to the sport hunt and who to hire for sport hunt outfitting and guiding. These discussions are often held against the backdrop of moral concerns about offending polar bears by not sharing.

Conservation hunting of polar bears provides support for Inuit cultural traditions and economic opportunities in Nunavut, but also creates some ethical dilemmas for Inuit communities that are not expected given our social discourse around sport hunting. The traditional Inuit world view values sharing and recognises polar bears are sentient beings, capable of making decisions regarding their interactions with humans. For Inuit, the ethics of conservation hunting are less about the motivations of individual sport hunters, and more about how to fit conservation hunting into a cultural world view where animals and humans are both considered people who respect each other by sharing.

Discussion questions

1 How does conservation hunting, despite the death of an animal, fit the definition of ecotourism?
2 Discuss the Inuit perspective on polar bear–human relationships.
3 What ethical conflicts do Inuit see in polar bear sport hunting?
4 What ethical issues do Inuit have with the conservation hunting paradigm?

5 In which two ways do Inuit attempt to ensure polar bear hunting will occur in the future?

References

Dowsley, M. (2009) 'Inuit organized polar bear sport hunting in Nunavut Territory, Canada', *Journal of Ecotourism*, 8(2): 161–75.

—— (2010) 'The value of a polar bear: Evaluating the role of a multiple use resource in the Nunavut mixed economy', *Arctic Anthropology*, 47(1): 39–56.

Freeman, M.M.R. and Wenzel, G.W. (2006) 'The nature and significance of polar bear conservation hunting in the Canadian Arctic', *Arctic*, 59(1): 21–30.

Freeman, M.M.R. and Foote, L. (eds) (2009) *Inuit, Polar Bears, and Sustainable Use: Local, National and International Perspectives*, Edmonton: CCI Press.

Sandell, H. and Sandell, B. (1996) 'Polar bear hunting and hunters in Ittoqqortoormiit/ Scoresbysund, NE Greenland', *Arctic Anthropology*, 33(2): 77–93.

Schmidt, J.J. and Dowsley, M. (2010) 'Hunting with polar bears: problems with the passive properties of the commons', *Human Ecology*, 38: 377–87.

Wenzel, G.W. (1983) 'Inuit and polar bears: cultural observations from a hunt near Resolute Bay, N.W.T.', *Arctic*, 36(1): 90–4.

10.5 WILD ANIMALS AND TOURISM

Wildlife tourism continues to grow and will make the 'animal question' increasingly relevant as pressures for more intense interactions with animals grow. It is useful therefore to have an understanding of how we 'view' wildlife in a tourism context. Bentrupperbaumer (2005) outlines four universal values that she believes to be important in understanding our view of wildlife: control (dominionistic); use (utilitarian); rights and responsibilities (moralistic); and conservation (protectionistic). The way in which we view wildlife has implications for how the interaction is promoted and managed, the impact upon animals, and the nature and quality of the experience for visitors.

Orams (2002) notes that the underlying philosophical position of the wildlife tourism industry (indeed in most Western cultures) is that animals are subordinate to humans and, as a consequence, humans have the right to utilise animals for human benefit. This dominionistic view (Kellert 1996), based on Judeo-Christian belief, is predominant in most Western cultures today. Such a view is most obvious in activities such as hunting and fishing, but is also apparent in zoos and wildlife parks where animals are confined in highly artificial environments, and subject to a constant tourist gaze. Where animals have to behave or perform in a circus-like way, this demonstrates the mastery, control and dominance humans have over animals (Bentrupperbaumer 2005: 94; Kellert 1996).

The utilitarian view (not to be confused with the utilitarianism ethics discussed above) reflects a benefit to humans. This may refer to the economic value of wildlife tourism activities, to operators and/or communities, or the psychophysiological benefits to individual tourists (there is evidence that animal contact has significant health benefits and that it positively influences transient psychological states, morale and feelings of self-worth (Rowan and Beck (1994)). Bentrupperbaumer (2005) notes that while many tourism activities involving animals comprise a combination of these views, the utilitarian view is nevertheless common to all. She does note, however, that the nature of the psychophysi-ologial benefits is highly variable.

Animals are manipulated for the enjoyment of tourists and for the economic benefits to tourism providers – they have instrumental value rather than intrinsic value in the tourism industry (Hughes 2001). The moralistic view noted above would argue to address this shortcoming, or what Bentrupperbaumer (2005: 95) describes as an 'absence of moral considerations at an industry level, that is the considerations for animal welfare, animal rights and the responsibilities of the tourist and tourism provider'. Indications are that change is happening within parts of the wildlife tourism sector, and some tourism opera-tors recognise animal rights. For example, the development of codes of conduct and codes of practice in wildlife tourism can be seen as a step forward – although shortcomings have been identified in this area (Malloy and Fennell 1998; see also Chapter 14). While these developments may be a sign of a move towards granting animals moral standing in tour-ism, that is not necessarily the case: the key to judging this will be whether animals are granted individual moral worth (Hughes 2001). There is, however, some evidence to sug-gest that there have been structural shifts in the ways that wildlife are being presented within the tourism product. This especially applies to captive settings, e.g. zoos, aquaria (see Frost 2011; Hughes 2001; Beardsworth and Bryman 2001).

DISCUSSION POINT: DOLPHINS AND AQUARIA

In 2001, Hughes described how there were no dolphinaria remaining in the UK, with tourist–dolphin encounters now only possible in the wild. This was in part due to the public action and lobbying campaigns of animal rights NGOs such as ZooCheck and the Whale and Dolphin Conservation Society. The 'zoological gaze' is changing because of shifts in attitude to the displayed captivity of animals (Franklin 1999). Many consider zoos and aquaria to be an anachronism in a time when we are increasingly aware of the negative impacts on captive animals.

However, in contrast to the UK experience, Cater (2010) describes aquaria, globally, as one of the fastest growing sectors in the industry. For example, in 2006 US SeaWorld facilities attracted 22 million visitors, making a profit of US$233 million (Anheuser-Bush 2006 in Cater 2010). Visitors from the UK simply visit dolphinaria in other countries where animal rights and welfare movements have yet to restrict industry practices (Hughes 2001).

And while researchers warn of the need to manage visitors' desire for close interaction with marine wildlife (e.g. Higham and Lück 2008; Zeppel and Muloin 2008), visitors continue to flock to aquaria to 'get up close and personal' (Cater 2010) with wildlife – an action which is seemingly at odds with many visitors' expressed concern for animal welfare. Furthermore, the recent quest for 'authentic' 'embodied' touristic interaction encourages zoos and aquaria to offer increasingly intimate experiences (Cater 2010). Such experiences may come at a cost for wildlife, however, and there are, for example, a number of arguments against captive dolphin attractions:

- Dolphins are captured and removed from the wild
- They are forced to perform unnatural tricks for food
- Their lifespan is reduced considerably
- They can suffer stress-related disorders.

Their performances fuel an anthropocentric and distorted understanding of dolphin behaviour (Curtin and Wilkes 2007: 133). In response, aquaria have begun to reposition their activities from entertainment to education, conservation and breeding programmes. But 'The moral issues of keeping such wide-ranging marine animals in a cramped space performing for their food under the guise of education and research is now being questioned' (Curtin and Wilkes 2007: 133). On a wider scale, there is little evidence to support the contribution of such research and conservation programmes in aquaria to the survival of dolphins and other marine mammals (Wearing and Jobberns 2011). Of the hundreds of millions of dollars profit made by SeaWorld, for example, only US$4 million is contributed to conservation or stranding rescue programmes.

From an ethical perspective, it is questionable whether the above repositioning within the tourism industry is reflective of a truly moralistic view or whether it is motivated by more anthropocentric (i.e. economic) concerns (Bentrupperbaumer 2005), with aquaria and dolphinaria simply adapting to survive. The same basic ethical questions and concern for individual animal welfare and rights thus still remain unaddressed (Hughes 2001).

On the positive side, it is argued that tourists' interaction with captive, trained animals may take some of the pressure off wild animals (Deng et al. 2002) – the impact of tourism on which is well documented (e.g. Constantine 1999; Lusseau et al. 2006). In the UK, a consequence of the closure of aquaria and dolphinaria has been that the number of dolphin boat operators, onshore dolphin visitor centres and interpretation sites at coastal viewing points has increased (Hughes 2001). However, in reality, non-captive 'wild' marine mammal tourism will likely continue to grow despite the existence of captive attractions.

Figure 10.6 *Tourists riding elephants, Nepal. Photo: Andrea Farminer.*

Useful source

World Society for the Protection of Animals <http://www.wspa-international.org/
    helping/animalfriendlyliving/captivedolphins.aspx>

The protectionistic view towards wildlife is expressed by those providers and consumers (tourists) who consider the primacy of conservation and preservation of species within the tourism activity (Bentrupperbaumer 2005). Tourism activities with such a view may occur in captive or wild settings – for example zoos and wildlife parks may have captive breeding programmes that are supported by the entrance fees of visitors. In wild settings, through park fees, or participation in guided concession activities, visitors may contribute to in-situ conservation breeding or habitat enhancement programmes. The protectionistic view is based on an eco- or biocentric value orientation, which acknowledges the intrinsic value of wildlife, independent of human value systems (Bentrupperbaumer 2005).

Wearing and Jobberns (2011) are critical of claims that wildlife tourism, even ecotourism, are adopting the principles espoused by animal rights (or welfare) advocates such as Singer. They write that for ecotourism to 'philosophically align itself to environmental ethics and to present itself as an alternative form of tourism, it must incorporate some intention to include in its agenda the rights of animals' (2011: 57). They believe that any claim on the part of the ecotourism sector to have included such an ethic, appears to be a long way off.

DISCUSSION POINT: ELEPHANTS AND TOURISM

Elephants are one the most loved of the 'charismatic megafauna'. They live a long time, form strong family groups, protect their young and display many of the 'human' characteristics that tourists admire. It is logical therefore, that the tourism industry has incorporated elephants into a variety of products, ranging from observing and photographing elephants in the wild, to feeding elephants in zoos. Elephant riding, however, is a controversial use of elephants – although most tourists arguably would not be aware that this is the case. Indeed, the use of elephants for elephant-back tourism is 'fraught with a series of ethical issues centred around animal rights and animal welfare' (Duffy and Moore 2010: 759). Indeed, the International Fund for Animal Welfare, and the Humane Society of the United States, are both strongly opposed to any form of elephant training for the tourism industry, on the grounds of cruelty.

Recent research (e.g. Kontogeorgopolous 2009; Duffy and Moore 2010) highlights the contradictory use of elephants in the industry. Although elephant-back riding is practiced in various destinations across Africa and Asia, Thailand is the most popular destination for this activity. Kontogeorgopoulos (2009) notes that elephants form a crucial component of the tourism industry, and that nearly every domesticated elephant in Thailand is employed in the tourism industry. Most elephants work in semi-captive 'elephant camps', and while they may lead better lives than elephants working on logging camps or those performing in circuses, there are still issues around the welfare of these animals. Notably, problems exist around the training or 'breaking in' of elephants to make them take tourists for rides, a process that involves physical force or pain; often elephants are said to be forced to take too many rides, or for too long a period of time; elephants are chained; foodstuffs and nutrition are sometimes inadequate; and there are problems with the artificial herd situation, leading to aggressive interactions with other elephants. Up to 70 per cent of baby elephants used in tourism in Asia are believed to have been poached from the wild where they are classified as highly endangered (Thai World View 2012).

An irony is that elephants in circuses and elephant riding have been banned in many Western countries or are being actively campaigned against by organisations such as People for the Ethical Treatment of Animals (PETA), but it is mainly Western tourists who are fuelling the ongoing demand for elephant-back tourism in destinations such as Thailand and Botswana.

However, the problem is not as easily solved as banning the activity and just letting the elephants go to the wild. Apart from the strong history and culture of elephant husbandry in Thailand, and the economic dependence of thousands of mahouts (and their families) upon working elephants, there are problems with reintroducing elephants to the wild – the expense of doing so and lack of suitable habitat.

Jane Crouch is the Responsible Travel Manager for Intrepid Travel (www. intrepidtravel.com), which runs trips that include elephant treks:

> At Intrepid Travel we are endeavouring to find a balance between elephant welfare, client education and demand. There are dozens of places offering elephants, and they range from very bad – with terrible husbandry conditions or where animals are trained (using cruel methods) to perform unnatural acts – through to very good where the animals are free to roam in a natural environment.

Discussion questions

1 Based upon the ethical approaches outlined in this chapter, is it ethical to visit an elephant camp?
2 Similarly, is it ethical to ride an elephant?

Useful sources

Wemmer, C. and Christen, C.A. (eds) (2008) *Elephants and Ethics: Toward a Morality of Coexistence*, Baltimore, MD: Johns Hopkins University Press.
Duffy, R. and Moore, L. (2011) 'Global regulations and local practices: the politics and governance of animal welfare in elephant tourism', *Journal of Sustainable Tourism*, 9(4–5): 589–604.

Websites

Wanderlust <http://www.wanderlust.co.uk/magazine/blogs/would-you-/is-it-ethical-to-go-elephant-trekking> Presents different perspectives on elephant trekking.
Elephant Nature Foundation <http://www.elephantnaturefoundation.org> Is a non-profit organisation which advocates and acts on behalf of the rights of Asian elephants in Thailand.
Animals Asia <http://www.animalsasia.org/> Has information on a variety of animal uses for tourism.

10.6 CAPTIVE ANIMALS AND TOURISM

In a recent collection on zoos, Frost (2011a) acknowledges the problematic nature of zoos – and the periodic and widespread calls for their abolition. Zoos are important attractions for tourism and, although much of this is local and domestic, they still attract significant numbers of international travellers. In Australia, for example, 3 million of the annual 8 million visitors to zoos are from overseas (Tribe 2004). Over half (53 per cent) of Australia's international visitors visit a zoo, wildlife park or aquarium (Frost 2011a).

The impacts of captivity on animals have been observed – especially on the large roaming nomadic predators such as tigers and polar bears. Many exhibit atypical, stress-related behaviours, illustrated by Gus the polar bear at Central Park Zoo in New York, who, suffering from depression, became the first animal in captivity to be treated with the antidepressant Prozac (Newkirk 1999 in Wearing and Jobberns 2011). The stress of captivity has been noted by other researchers, including aberrant behaviours such as pacing, and the condition of 'zoochosis' – or zoo-induced psychosis – in animals (Clubb and Mason 2003).

However, keeping animals in zoos might be seen as a valid infringement of animal welfare 'if the purpose of confinement was to protect and ultimately reintroduce a species into the wild, or if there was some educational element to captive display, such that the species as a whole were better respected by people' (Hughes 2001: 324). But some environmental ethicists would reject this, arguing that captive animals are 'meaningless' outside their natural habitat – for example a condor ceases to be a condor in a zoo, because it cannot do what a condor in the wild could do (Hughes 2001). From an animal rights perspective, putting animals in captivity may be rejected outright. However, a grey area is that of sanctuaries that provide ostensible natural (or reconstructed natural) habitats for species, and are often located in accessible areas for visitors with the idea of educating visitors about the value of species and habitat protection. Such sanctuaries often attract substantial visitor numbers because of their urban-proximate locations. In such cases it may be ethical to relocate endangered species to such sanctuaries (e.g. relocating endangered

Figure 10.7 *Bear in a zoo, Norway – education or entertainment? Photo: Brent Lovelock.*

kiwi to the Zealandia sanctuary in Wellington city, New Zealand – see <http://www.visitzealandia.com>).

While the arguments for retaining zoos are largely based upon their educational and conservation value (and there are examples of success, e.g. Catibog-Sinha 2011), they do have rather a poor record of conserving species (Frost 2011b). Only five species have been saved from extinction by zoos (Hancocks 2001 in Frost 2011c). And, even worse, some endangered species have suffered or died in zoos – the last Tasmanian Tiger perished in a Hobart Zoo after its keeper forgot to return it to its enclosure on a cold winter's night (Frost 2011b). Looking at the bigger picture, of the 10,000 zoos worldwide, only 12 per cent are registered for captive breeding and conservation (Shackley 1996). Rather, there is strong evidence that zoos are primarily for entertainment (Tribe 2004; Frost 2011; Linke and Winter 2011). Casamitjana (2004 in Frost 2011) in a study of UK aquaria found that few facilities actually offer educational talks or events, or educational packs. And even where interpretation was provided, few visitors actually read the interpretative signage. More worryingly, some staff employed in these facilities provided incorrect information to visitors about their animals. He concluded that the public would be better educated through watching documentaries.

DISCUSSION POINT: BULLFIGHTING

Bullfighting is one tourism attraction that tends to polarise opinion, and provides a good example of where cultural 'rites' clash head-on with animal rights and welfare interests. Still practised in nine countries in the world, the activity is mainly espoused now as a cultural tourism attraction. Many countries have legal bans on bullfighting, and the most recent area to ban bullfighting is the Spanish region of Catalonia. In a highly controversial debate (which attracted over 180,000 signatures on the 'Enough' campaign's petition), bullfighting was banned in 2010. Opponents of the ban argued for its protection as a cultural landmark – even seeking World Heritage Status for the activity (Keeley 2007). They also argued that the ban would have adverse economic effects, including job losses (Chu 2010).

Discussion questions

1 What countries practise bullfighting?
2 What is the status of the bullfighting industry – visitor numbers, profile, impacts?
3 What support is there from the travelling public for bullfighting?
4 What is behind the claims of animal rights and welfare advocates that bullfighting is a cruel industry?
5 To what extent is bullfighting a cultural tourism attraction, and does this justify its retention?

6 Are there alternative forms of bullfighting that are ethical?
7 What other animal combative activities are employed as tourist attractions, and where?

Useful sources

Yates, R. (2009) 'Rituals of dominionism in human–nonhuman relations: Bullfighting to hunting, circuses to petting', *Journal for Critical Animal Studies*, 7(1): 132–71.
CAS International (Comité Anti Stierenvechten) <http://www.cas-international.org/en/news/>
Stop Our Shame <http://www.stopourshame.com/en/home.htm>
For a bullfighting free Europe <http://www.bullfightingfreeeurope.org/>
World Society for the Protection of Animals <http://www.wspa-international.org/helping/animalfriendlyliving/travel.aspx>
League Against Cruel Sports <http://www.league.org.uk/>
The Humane Society <http://www.humanesociety.org/>

CHAPTER REVIEW

This chapter has outlined some of the issues associated with the involvement of non-human animals in the tourism product/experience. Animals are identified as an important component of the tourism product yet a raft of negative impacts on animals are recognised. The chapter discussed the main approaches currently used to address the 'animal question' in tourism: animal rights and animal welfare. The concept of sentience was introduced. Virtue ethics was presented as a complementary approach and the issue of instrumental versus intrinsic value addressed. The human 'view' of wildlife was discussed, and the four universal values that determine this view described. Following sections focused on the problems around consumptive wildlife tourism (hunting and fishing) and captive animals in tourism (zoos, aquaria).

SUMMARY OF KEY TERMS

Animal rights The animal rights viewpoint holds that humans do not have the right to use animals for their own gain, whether as a source of labour, in entertainment (e.g. zoos, performances) or in the wild. This applies whether or not the animals are treated humanely. It would violate the 'moral inviolability' of an animal to consider it as a resource for use by people.

Animal welfare The animal welfare viewpoint advocates the humane use of animals which involves maintaining animal wellbeing and prohibiting cruelty. Animals can contribute to human wellbeing (e.g. by providing entertainment) but humans have moral obligations to protect their welfare and provide for their wellbeing. Animal welfare advocates do not believe that animals should have rights equal to those of people.

Instrumental value Value as a means to another end or value. Includes the value of objects, both physical objects and abstract objects, not as ends-in-themselves but a means of achieving something else (e.g. animals as attractions in zoos, to generate income). Money has instrumental value, but no or little intrinsic value. Sometimes called extrinsic value.

Intrinsic value is the value something has 'in itself', 'for its own sake' or 'in its own right', e.g. the intrinsic value of animals can be defined as a value placed on the inherent qualities of a species, independent of any financial, instrumental or practical value attributed by humans. Intrinsic value is central to animal ethics as a basis to grant animals specific rights based upon the idea of sentience and/or interests.

Sentience is the ability to feel, perceive or be conscious, or to have subjective experiences; roughly defined as the capacity for emotion, pleasure and pain. In the philosophy of animal rights, sentience is commonly seen as the ability to experience suffering. It is a necessary and sufficient condition of having interests, and thus moral considerability.

QUESTIONS FOR REFLECTION

At the beginning of this chapter, the economic significance of animals to the tourism industry was outlined. Can you picture how a tourism industry would appear without animals? Would it be a better tourism industry?

1 Are there actions that we can take in other spheres of our personal lives that will make it ethically acceptable for us to participate in animal tourism? e.g. does adopting a stray dog from the local pound, or becoming a vegetarian give you the right to participate in a whale watching tour?

2 Do you agree with the concept of sentience – do you think that 'higher order' animals (e.g. mammals) should have greater moral standing than others (e.g. reptiles, insects)?

EXERCISES

This chapter describes the main ethical approaches to animals, i.e. animal rights and animal welfare. Investigate what other ethical theories have been used to effectively address the human–animal relationship, and which could be useful in tourism.

1 Conduct an informal web-based 'survey' of animal-related tourism attractions/activities in your town/region. See what evidence you can find that they are operating ethically.

2 Imagine that you are a tourism operator, conducting wildlife tours. If you were to adopt an animal rights perspective, what policies and practices might you have to put in place across your wildlife tourism operation to operate ethically?

FURTHER READING

Fennell, D.A. (2012) *Tourism and Animal Ethics*, London and New York: Routledge.

Frost, W. (2011) *Zoos and Tourism: Conservation, Education, Entertainment?* Clevedon: Channel View.

Newsome, D., Dowling, R. and Moore, S. (2005) *Wildlife Tourism*, Bristol: Channel View.

Regan, T. (2004) *The Case for Animal Rights*, Berkeley: University of California Press.

Singer, P. (2001) *Animal Liberation*, New York: Harper Collins.

NOTES

a Mohandas Gandhi (1869–1948), leader of Indian nationalism.

b Abraham Lincoln (1809–65), 16th President of the USA.

c Jeremy Bentham (1748–1832), English philosopher and social reformer. Source: *An Introduction to the Principles of Morals and Legislation* (1823), Ch. 17: 'Of the Limits of the Penal Branch of Jurisprudence'.

REFERENCES

Anderson, E. (2004) 'Animal rights and the values of nonhuman life', in Sunstein, C. and Nussbaum, M. (eds) *Animal Rights: Current Debates and New Directions*, Oxford: Oxford University Press, pp. 277–98.

Beardsworth, A. and Bryman, A. (2001) 'The wild animal in late modernity: the case of the Disneyization of zoos', *Tourist Studies*, 1(1): 83.

Bentrupperbaumer, J.M. (2005) 'Human dimension of wildlife interactions', in Newsome, D., Dowling, R. and Moore, S. (eds) *Wildlife Tourism: Ecology, Impacts, and Management*, Clevedon: Channel View, pp. 82–112.

Buckley, R.C. (2009) *Ecotourism: Principles and Practices*, Wallingford: CABI.

Cahoone, L. (2009) 'Hunting as a moral good', *Environmental Values*, 18(1): 67–89.

Callicott, J. Baird. (1980) 'Animal liberation: a triangular affair', *Environmental Ethics*, 2: 311–38.

Carr, N. (2009) 'Animals in the tourism and leisure experience', *Current Issues in Tourism*, 12(5&6): 409–11.

Cater, C. (2010) 'Any closer and you'd be lunch! Interspecies interactions as nature tourism at marine aquaria', *Journal of Ecotourism*, 9(2): 133–48.

Catibog-Sinha, C. (2011) 'Zoo tourism and the conservation of threatened species: A collaborative programme in the Philippines' in Frost, W. (ed.) *Zoos and Tourism: Conservation, Education, Entertainment?* Bristol: Channel View, pp. 13–32.

Chu, H. (2010) 'Catalonia is first region in mainland Spain to ban bullfighting', *Los Angeles Times*, 29 July. Available at <http://articles.latimes.com/2010/jul/29/world/la-fg-spain-bullfight-ban-20100729> (Accessed 9 September 2011).

Clubb, R. and Mason, G. (2003) *Captivity effects on wide-ranging carnivores.* Retrieved from ZooCheck Canada. Available at <http://www.zoocheck.com/articlepdfs/Carnivore%20Mason.pdf> (Accessed 17 August 2011).

Cohn, P. (ed.) (1999) *Ethics and Wildlife*, Lewiston, NY: Edwin Mellen Press.

Constantine, R. (1999) *Effects of Tourism on Marine Mammals in New Zealand*, Wellington: Dept. of Conservation.

Curtin, S. and Wilkes, K. (2007) 'Swimming with captive dolphins: current debates and post-experience dissonance', *International Journal of Tourism Research,* 9(2): 131–46.

Deng, J., King, B. and Bauer, T. (2002) 'Evaluating natural attractions for tourism', *Annals of Tourism Research,* 29: 422–38.

Dickson, B. (2009) 'The ethics of recreational hunting', in Dickson, B., Hutton, J. and Adams, W.M. (eds) *Recreational Hunting, Conservation and Rural Livelihoods,* Chichester: Blackwell, pp. 59–72.

Duffy, R. and Moore, L. (2010) 'Neoliberalising nature? Elephant-back tourism in Thailand and Botswana', *Antipode,* 42(3): 742–66.

Fennell, D.A. (2000) 'Comment: ecotourism on trial – the case of billfish angling as ecotourism', *Journal of Sustainable Tourism,* 8(4): 341–5.

—— (2006) *Tourism Ethics*, Clevedon: Channel View.

—— (2012) *Tourism and Animal Ethics*, London: Routledge.

Franklin, A.S. (1999). *Animals and Modern Culture: A Sociology of Human–Animal Relations in Modernity*, London: Sage.

—— (2001) 'Neo-Darwinian leisures, the body and nature: hunting and angling in modernity', *Body & Society*, 57–76.

Freese, C. (1998) *Wild Species as Commodities: Managing Markets and Ecosystems for Sustainability,* Washington, DC: Island Press.

Frost, W. (ed.) (2011a) *Zoos and Tourism: Conservation, Education, Entertainment?* Bristol: Channel View.

—— (2011b) 'Rethinking zoos and tourism' in Frost, W. (ed.) *Zoos and Tourism: Conservation, Education, Entertainment?* Bristol: Channel View, pp. 1–8.

—— (2011c) 'Zoos and tourism in a changing world', in Frost, W. (ed.) *Zoos and Tourism: Conservation, Education, Entertainment?* Bristol: Channel View, pp. 227–35.

Higham, J. and Lück, M. (eds) (2008). *Marine Wildlife and Tourism Management: Insights from the Natural and Social Sciences*, Wallingford: CABI.

Higham, J.E.S. and Bejder, L. (2008) 'Commentary: managing wildlife-based tourism: edging slowly towards sustainability?', *Current Issues in Tourism,* 11(1): 75–83.

Holland, S.M., Ditton, R.B. and Graefe, A.R. (1998) 'An ecotourism perspective on billfish fisheries', *Journal of Sustainable Tourism,* 6(2): 97–116.

Holland, S.M., Ditton, R.B. and Graefe, A.R. (2000) 'A response to "ecotourism on trial – the case of billfish angling as ecotourism"', *Journal of Sustainable Tourism,* 8(4): 346–51.

Hughes, P. (2001) 'Animals, values and tourism-structural shifts in UK dolphin tourism provision', *Tourism Management,* 22(4): 321–9.

Jamieson, D. (2008) 'The rights of animals and the demands of nature', *Environmental Values,* 17: 181–99.

Keeley, G. (2007) 'Bullfighting fans in plea for World Heritage Status', *The Independent,* 27 April. Available at <http://www.highbeam.com/doc/1P2–5880895.html> (Accessed 14 December 2011).

Kellert, S.R. (1996) *The Value of Life: Biological Diversity and Human Society,* Washington, DC: Island Books.

Knight, J. (ed.) (2005) 'Introduction', in Knight, J. (ed.) *Animals in Person: Cultural Perspectives on Human–Animal Intimacies,* Oxford: Berg, pp. 1–13.

Kontogeorgopoulos, N. (2009) 'Wildlife tourism in semi-captive settings: a case study of elephant camps in northern Thailand', *Current Issues in Tourism,* 12(5 & 6): 429–49.

Lemelin, R.H. (2006) 'The gawk, the glance, and the gaze: ocular consumption and polar bear tourism in Churchill, Manitoba, Canada', *Current Issues in Tourism,* 9(6): 516–34.

—— (2009) 'Goodwill hunting? Dragon hunters, dragonflies and leisure', *Current Issues in Tourism,* 12(5): 553–71.

Linke, S. and Winter, C. (2011) 'Conservation, education or entertainment: What really matters to zoo visitors?', in Frost, W. (ed.) *Zoos and Tourism: Conservation, Education, Entertainment?* Bristol: Channel View, pp. 69–82.

Lovelock, B.A. (2007) '"If that's a moose, I'd hate to see a rat!": Visitors' perspectives on naturalness and the consequences for ecological integrity in peripheral natural areas of New Zealand', in Muller, D.K. and Jannson, B. (eds) *Tourism in Peripheries: Perspectives from the North and South,* Wallingford: CABI, pp. 124–40.

—— (ed.) (2008) *Tourism and the Consumption of Wildlife: Hunting, Shooting and Sportfishing,* London: Routledge.

Lusseau, D., Slooten, L. and Currey, R.J.C. (2006) 'Unsustainable dolphin-watching tourism in Fiordland, New Zealand', *Tourism in Marine Environments,* 3(2): 173–8.

Malloy, D.C. and Fennell, D.A. (1998) 'Codes of ethics and tourism: an exploratory content analysis', *Tourism Management,* 19(5): 453–61.

Marvin, G. (2005) 'Sensing nature: encountering the world in hunting', *Etnofoor,* 18(1): 15–26.

Mintel (2008) *Wildlife tourism – International,* June.

Newsome, D., Dowling, R. and Moore, S. (2005) *Wildlife Tourism: Ecology, Impacts, and Management,* Clevedon: Channel View.

Novelli, M., Barnes, J.I. and Humavindu, M. (2006) 'The other side of the ecotourism coin: consumptive tourism in Southern Africa', *Journal of Ecotourism,* 5(1/2): 62–79.

One Caribbean (2011) *Wildlife Tourism.* Available at <http://www.onecaribbean.org> (Accessed 12 July 2011).

Orams, M.B. (1996) 'A conceptual model of tourist–wildlife interaction: the case for education as a management strategy', *Australian Geographer,* 27(1): 39–51.

—— (2002) 'Feeding wildlife as a tourism attraction: a review of issues and impacts', *Tourism Management,* 23(3): 281–93.

Plato (1992) *The Statesman,* translated by J.B. Kemp, edited and with an introduction by M. Oswald, Indianapolis, IN: Hackett.

Regan, T. (2004) *The Case for Animal Rights,* Berkeley: University of California Press.

Reis, A.C. (2009) 'More than the kill: hunters' relationships with landscape and prey', *Current Issues in Tourism,* 12(5/6): 573–87.

Reynolds, P.C. and Braithwaite, D. (2001) 'Towards a conceptual framework for wildlife tourism', *Tourism Management,* 22(1): 31–42.

Rowan, A.N. and Beck, A.M. (1994) 'The health benefits of human–animal interaction', *Anthrozoos,* 7(2): 85–9.

Scruton, R. (1996) *Animal Rights and Wrongs,* London: Demos.

Shackley, M. (1996) *Wildlife Tourism,* London: International Thomson Business Press.

Singer, P. (2001) *Animal Liberation,* New York: Harper Collins.

Singer, P. (ed.) (2006) *In Defense of Animals,* Malden, MA: Blackwell.

Thai World View (2012) *Elephants.* Available at <http://www.thaiworldview.com/animal/animal2.htm> (Accessed 8 July 2012).

The International Ecotourism Society (TIES) (2012) *What is Ecotourism?* Available at <http://www. ecotourism.org/what-is-ecotourism> (Accessed 10 October 2011).

Tisdell, C. and Wilson, C. (2002) 'Ecotourism for the survival of sea turtles and other wildlife', *Biodiversity and Conservation,* 11: 1521–38.

Tremblay, P. (2001) 'Wildlife tourism consumption: consumptive or non-consumptive?', *International Journal of Tourism Research,* 3: 81–6.

Tribe, A. (2004) 'Zoo tourism' in Higginbottom, K. (ed.) *Wildlife Tourism: Impacts, Management and Planning*, Victoria, Australia: Common Ground, pp. 35–56.

US Department of the Interior, Fish and Wildlife Service, and US Department of Commerce, Census Bureau (2006) *National Survey of Fishing, Hunting, and Wildlife-Associated Recreation*, Washington, DC: USDOI.

Wearing, S. and Jobberns, C. (2011) 'Ecotourism and the commodification of wildlife: animal welfare and the ethics of zoos' in Frost, W. (ed.) *Zoos and Tourism: Conservation, Education, Entertainment?* Bristol: Channel View, pp. 47–58.

Zeppel, H. and Muloin, S. (2008) 'Conservation benefits of interpretation on marine wildlife tours', *Human Dimensions of Wildlife,* 13(4): 280–94.

11 Climate change

'If your sister-in-law is getting married in Buenos Aires, it is both immoral to travel there, because of climate change, and immoral not to, because of the offence it causes.'

George Monbiot[a]

'I think we're going to find, with climate change and everything else...that things are going to become very complicated.'

Prince Charles[b]

'We simply must do everything we can in our power to slow down global warming before it is too late. The science is clear. The global warming debate is over.'

Arnold Schwarzenegger[c]

LEARNING OBJECTIVES

After reading this chapter you will be able to:

- Conceptualise climate change as an ethical problem.
- Discuss issues of responsibility and harm in relation to tourists, aviation and climate change.
- Use the 'Prisoner's Dilemma' and 'Tragedy of the Commons' to help explain the ethical problems of flying in relation to climate change.
- Describe the ethical issues pertaining to each of the solutions posed for reducing carbon omission from tourist flights.
- Critically discuss the tensions between the environmental, social and economic impacts of touristic aviation.

11.1 INTRODUCTION

As academics, a part of our job is to present our work at international conferences. Often these are held in Europe, and thus require a long journey by air from home in New Zealand. Usually this involves a 10-hour flight from New Zealand through an Asian hub, such as Hong Kong or Singapore, followed by a longer flight of around 12 hours to a European hub, such as Frankfurt, then a shorter flight in the vicinity of 2–3 hours, to the conference venue. A conference presentation, although it is usually based upon several months of research planning, data collection and analysis, will only take about 20 minutes. We will stay for the duration of the conference (usually 2–3 days) and sometimes partake in a short post-conference fieldtrip (perhaps a day), then return home. Presenting our research to peers is an important aspect of the job. But every time we phone our travel agent to make the flight arrangements there is that nagging feeling that perhaps 44 hours of flying may be producing a little too much carbon than is warranted for a 20-minute presentation.

The flights involved above, according to climatecare.org, are a total of 24,000 miles (38,000 km) and produce about 6.52 tonnes of carbon dioxide (CO_2). In a world already suffering from a serious glut of CO_2 this amount is already well over what climate change researchers argue should be our annual personal CO_2 allowance. We could assuage our conscience and purchase 'carbon offsets' thus 'neutralising' the carbon produced by the travel, and reducing our net emission to zero. This would cost us (as our university will not pay for carbon offsetting the travel of their staff) US$12.69/tonne of CO_2 or about US$82 (ClimateCare 2012). (Note that this doesn't include the CO_2 emissions associated with any local travel when we get to the conference venue, or emissions associated with the conference or the accommodation.)

Should we stay or should we go? This is turning out to be the big ethical question of twenty-first-century tourism. This chapter sets out to explore the ethics of air travel in relation to global environmental change. We employ ethical principles to try to weigh up the pros and cons of air travel in a complex environment with a high level of uncertainty – uncertainty in the minds of travellers concerning the impacts of their individual travel upon climate change, and uncertainty whether or not the positive benefits of their flying (especially to developing world destinations) may outweigh the negative environmental consequences. The basic ethical juxtaposition is the individual freedom to travel against the wider harm to the environment and society as a whole. Sager (2006 in Graham and Shaw 2008) refers to mobility as a 'right', but notes that these rights may be problematic in that they have to be balanced against the rights of others in society (and those of non-human actors).

11.2 GLOBAL ENVIRONMENTAL CHANGE

It is beyond the scope of this chapter to detail the impacts of anthropogenic induced climate change on the world. Instead, we take as a given that there is substantial and incontrovertible evidence of this, and would refer readers to the reports of the Intergovernmental Panel on Climate Change (IPCC) (http://www.ipcc.ch/). Briefly, the IPCC reports from 1990 to the current day are consistent in showing that increases in global average surface temperatures over the twentieth century are likely to have been the largest of any century in the last 1,000 years. The present atmospheric CO_2 concentration is the highest it has been in 420,000 years, and possibly up to 20 million years (IPCC 2001: 155). Ongoing increases in atmospheric CO_2 will likely exacerbate the trend of global warming, and will result in a decrease in snow and ice cover, with associated sea-level rise, among a range of other bio-geo-climatic changes.

It is also beyond the scope of this chapter to consider the complex physical, social and economic relationship between tourism and global environmental change. Rather, the focus of this chapter is specifically on the contribution of touristic air travel to global environmental change. Suffice to say that destinations, host communities, the tourism industry and tourists' experiences will be impacted in a myriad of ways, both positively and negatively, by human-induced global environmental change. Estimates are that by 'the year 2065, on current trends, damage from climate change will exceed global GDP' (Dlugolecki 2004: n.p). The impact upon low-lying nations such as Bangladesh, Tuvalu and many others will be profound, to the extent that global warming has been described as 'climatic genocide' (Timmons Roberts and Parks 2007). We recommend a number of specialist books that address this topic:

Becken, S. and Hay, J.E. (2007) *Tourism and Climate Change: Risks and Opportunities*, Clevedon: Channel View.
Gössling, S. and Hall, C.M. (eds) (2006) *Tourism and Global Environmental Change: Ecological, Social, Economic and Political Interrelationships*, Abingdon: Routledge.
Hall, C.M. and Higham, J.E.S. (eds) (2005) *Tourism, Recreation, and Climate Change*, Clevedon: Channel View.
United Nations World Tourism Organisation and United Nations Environment Programme (2008) *Climate Change and Tourism: Responding to Global Challenges*, Madrid: UNWTO and UNEP.

11.3 GLOBAL ENVIRONMENTAL CHANGE AS AN ETHICAL ISSUE

Most of us would conceptualise anthropogenic global environmental change (or simply 'climate change' from hereon) as a scientific problem, and are aware of the substantial political debate around the issue. But, increasingly, writers and researchers in this field are beginning to describe climate change as an ethical problem. In the movie *An Inconvenient Truth*, Nobel Prize winner Al Gore describes climate change as 'not a political issue so much as a moral issue' (2006). Similarly ex-prime minister of the United Kingdom, Gordon Brown, refers to the 'moral duty' of the developed world to tackle climate change (in Gardiner 2010).

While an economist would refer to the climate change problem as one of costs (of abatement), a moral philosopher would see it as more about *values*. According to environmental philosopher Dale Jamieson our present value system evolved relatively recently, and in low population density and low technology societies. In the latter half of the twentieth century, with the growth of the human population, wealth, industry and technology, our capacity to change the environmental circumstances of the planet is unprecedented in history – to the extent that, as Jamieson puts it, our species now 'dances with the devil' (2010: 82). Unfortunately our dominant value system is 'inadequate and inappropriate for guiding our thinking about global environmental problems' arising from this 'success' of the human race (Jamieson 2010: 83).

A feature of our current value system is its underlying concept of responsibility. For this concept to work hinges upon harms and their causes being individual, being readily identified, and local in space and time. Jamieson provides an example of Jones breaking into Smith's house and stealing Smith's television set. Jones's intent is clear: she wants

Smith's TV set. Smith suffers a clear harm: he is made worse off by having lost his TV. Jones is responsible for Smith's loss, as she was the cause of harm and no one else was involved. In this example, we can clearly identify harms and assign responsibility. We can respond to the breach of our norms by punishing Jones and/or requiring compensation from Jones to redress the harm caused to Smith (Jamieson 2010: 83).

This paradigm collapses when we apply it to global environmental problems such as climate change when apparently innocent acts (e.g. riding in a plane) can have devastating consequences; cause and harms may be diffuse; and causes and harms may be remote in time and space (Jamieson 2010: 83). Thus moral (and political) confusion arises about the issue of climate change, as despite clearly identifiable harms (to the environment, and to human life) conventional morality has trouble finding someone to blame. No one intended the bad outcome, or brought it about, or was even able to foresee it (Jamieson 2010). Jamieson believes, however, that despite these complexities, climate change is an ethical problem for all of us to address – as political actors and as individual everyday moral actors.

Prisoner's dilemma

But everyday moral actions are not as easy to perform as they may seem. Gardiner (2010) in discussing moral agents' decisions over whether or not to engage in a polluting activity (e.g. to take a holiday flight) employs the Prisoner's Dilemma.[1] The Prisoner's Dilemma is a short parable about two prisoners, arrested for a crime, who are individually offered a chance to rat on each other for which the 'ratter' would receive a lighter sentence and the 'rattee' would receive a harsher sentence. The 'dilemma' faced by the prisoners here is that, whatever the other does, each is better off confessing than remaining silent. But the outcome obtained when both confess is worse for each than the outcome they would have obtained had both remained silent. The dilemma illustrates a conflict between individual and group rationality. A group whose members pursue rational self-interest may all end up worse off than a group whose members act contrary to rational self-interest. More generally, if the payoffs are not assumed to represent self-interest, a group whose members rationally pursue any goals may all meet less success than if they had not rationally pursued their goals individually (Stanford Encyclopedia of Philosophy 2012).

The Prisoner's Dilemma is thus a case in which actions determined by self-interest are not in the group's interest. Schenk (2011) notes that the Prisoner's Dilemma would have pleased English philosopher Thomas Hobbes (1588–1679) who proposed the individual as the starting point of social analysis, asserting that people are motivated by self-interest (i.e. the first principle of human behaviour is egoism). Hobbes believed that the unrestrained pursuit of self-interest would result in chaos and that government, with its power to coerce people, was necessary to bring order out of chaos.

In relation to polluting actions and climate change, Gardiner (2010) notes that while it is *collectively rational* to cooperate and restrict overall pollution, is it *individually rational* not to restrict one's own pollution. In Chapter 9 we evoked the Tragedy of the Commons (Hardin 1968) to discuss the impact of tourism activities on nature; Gardiner points out that a Tragedy of the Commons is essentially a Prisoner's Dilemma involving a common resource (e.g. the atmosphere).

Gardiner also points out that in fact the climate change problem is a bit more complex than the Prisoner's Dilemma scenario above suggests, because it also involves *intergenerational ethics*. Human-induced climate change is a severely lagged phenomenon. A CO_2 molecule will stay in the atmosphere from 5–200 years, but a significant amount will last thousands or even tens of thousands of years (Gardiner 2010). The mean lifetime of fossil fuel CO_2 is 30,000 to 35,000 years (Archer 2005). Thus the actions we take today will impact upon humans many generations into the future. Such an intergenerational problem is more difficult to resolve, as the standard solutions to the Prisoner's Dilemma are not available – we cannot appeal to the mutually beneficial interaction, or to the usual notions of reciprocity: 'This is a large moral problem...the intergenerational problem dominates the Tragedy of the Commons aspect in climate change' (Gardiner 2010: 92). Gardiner refers to the climate change issue being subject to 'morally relevant multiplier effects' – i.e. the current generation does not simply pass the problem on to future people, rather,

Figure 11.1 *Air travel brings benefits to developing world destinations. Photo: Brent Lovelock.*

it adds to it, making the problem worse (2010: 92, 93). The issue of temporal impartiality versus temporal distance is therefore important to this problem. Some philosophers believe that we should care more about the people who live close to us in time than those who will live in the more distant future. Others, however, abide by the principle of temporal impartiality – that the date on which a harm occurs makes no difference to its value (Broome 2008). There can be little doubt, however, about the impact of our current carbon emissions on future human life, to the extent that Urry (2008) describes the whole twentieth century as a 'free lunch' to be enjoyed at the expense of following centuries.

Responsibility

To date much of the filibustering surrounding climate change has to do with who is causing it and who will take responsibility for it. Peter Singer (of animal ethics fame – see Chapter 10) provides a good analogy to help understand the problem:

> One advantage of being married to someone whose hair is a different colour or length from your own is that when a clump of hair blocks the bath outlet, it's easy to tell whose hair it is. 'Get your hair out of the tub' is a fair and equitable household rule.
>
> (Singer 2010: 189)

He notes that the USA, which comprises 5 per cent of the world's population, from 1950 to 1986 was calculated to contribute to 30 per cent of the world's carbon emissions (Hayes and Smith 1993 in Singer 2010).

> It's as if, in a village of twenty people, all using the same bathtub, one person had shed 30% of the hair blocking the drain hole...who pays the bill for the plumber to clear out the drain?
>
> (Singer 2010: 189)

CASE STUDY: CLIMATE CHANGE AND TOURISM DEVELOPMENT – *STEFAN GÖSSLING*

Organisations such as the United Nations World Tourism Organization (UNWTO) (2006), World Travel and Tourism Council (WTTC) (2004), World Economic Forum (WEF) (2008), as well as many government agencies concerned with development aid have emphasised the importance of tourism as a means of poverty alleviation. Based on indicators such as the contribution made by tourism to gross domestic product (GDP), it is argued that this economic sector should be further developed: 'Tourism development, if properly developed and supported, can indeed be a "quick-win" in overcoming the economic and social conditions that prevail in LDCs [least developed countries] and in accelerating their integration into the world economy' (UNWTO 2005: 3; for a more comprehensive review of arguments in favour of tourism development in LDCs see UNWTO 2006; for more balanced views see e.g. Hall and Lew 2009; Telfer and Sharpley 2008).

Although the vast majority of international tourism currently occurs in developed countries, international tourism in emerging and developing markets has grown more rapidly in recent years than in industrialised countries, with for instance tourist arrival growth rates averaging 9 per cent per year in least developed countries in the period 1996–2006 (UNWTO 2008). In particular in tropical island states, visitor spending now accounts for a significant share of GDP (in some cases more than 50 per cent of GDP), highlighting the economic importance of this sector for these countries (Hall et al. 2009). As there is currently no country in the world that seeks to limit or stabilise tourist arrivals, further growth in all of the world's tourism economies can be expected.

Though still being small on an overall basis, with an estimated share of 5.2–12.5 per cent of the global warming caused by human activities in 2005 (measured as radiative forcing), tourism is an increasingly significant contributor to global warming (Scott et al. 2010). This is because technology can be expected to make a contribution to the reduction of specific energy use – estimated at 1.5–2.0 per cent per year – but efficiency gains are outpaced by growth in tourist numbers in the order of about 4 per cent per year (Airbus 2011; Boeing 2011). Emissions from global tourism are consequently expected to grow by more than 130 per cent over 2005 by 2035 (UNWTO-UNEP-WMO 2008).

Transport and associated emissions of greenhouse gases are thus one of the main sustainability issues to be solved in global tourism; and one which is particularly important for remote islands dependent on long-haul air travel to attract high value tourism markets (Hall et al. 2009). Emissions associated with air transport to/from these countries, often also including energy-intense cruise tourism, are often equal to or even larger than the emissions caused by the rest of the economy. In the case of the Maldives, for instance, emissions associated with the air travel of 650,000 international tourists are equal in size to the emissions from 310,000 inhabitants and the stay of the tourists (BeCitizen 2010). Results also indicate that the tourism system of many less wealthy countries generates emissions that exceed, if calculated on a per capita basis, those that are found in developed countries.

A wide range of reports has warned of the consequences of continued emissions of greenhouse gases for humanity (e.g. Stern 2006; see also Stern 2009). The Global Humanitarian Forum (GHF 2009: 1) emphasises, for instance, that climate change already seriously affects the livelihoods of 325 million people, causing 300,000 deaths per year and economic losses of US$125 billion. Four billion people are regarded as vulnerable to climate change, and 500 million people are at extreme risk with an estimated half a million lives expected to be lost because of climate change by the 2030s. The tourism sector may be seen as responsible for a contribution to climate-change related deaths and economic losses proportional to the sector's emissions. Paradoxically, as tourism is most energy-intense where it is largely based on long-haul flights, tourism may thus contribute to destabilising the living conditions of the poor in many countries that are particularly dependent on the economic contribution of tourism.

From these observations the paradoxical conclusion may be drawn that while tourism lifts a share of humanity out of poverty, it simultaneously jeopardises the living conditions of another share of humanity through its contribution to climate change. The situation is further complicated by the fact that the Kyoto Protocol, which regulates emission reductions on a global basis, does not consider bunker fuels, i.e. omitting in many countries a considerable share of emissions arising from the activities of their citizens.

Discussion questions

1 Who should be responsible for greenhouse gas emissions from tourism – the originating countries, those receiving the tourists, or both?
2 Is there an individual responsibility for greenhouse gas emissions? And can it be justified that some individuals – usually highly mobile travellers – emit greenhouse gases several orders of magnitude larger than others?
3 Is it feasible to alleviate poverty through particularly energy-intense economic sectors, such as tourism?
4 In light of the absence of technology solutions for aviation and cruise ships, is it justified to wait for such solutions to (perhaps) emerge in the future, or should a precautionary principle apply, ultimately restricting aviation and cruise tourism?

References

Airbus (2011) *Airbus Global Market Forecast 2010–2029*. Available at <http://www.airbus.com/company/market/gmf2010/> (Accessed 3 April 2011).

BeCitizen (2010) *The Maldives' 2009 Carbon Audit*, Paris: BeCitizen.

Boeing (2011) *Current Market Outlook 2010–2029*. Available at <http://www.boeing.com/commercial/cmo/> (Accessed 3 April 2011).

Global Humanitarian Forum (GHF) (2009) *The Anatomy of a Silent Crisis*, London: GHF.

Hall, C.M. and Lew, A. (2009) *Understanding and Managing Tourism Impacts: An Integrated Approach*, London: Routledge.

Hall, C.M., Scott, D. and Gössling, S. (2009) 'Tourism, development and climate change', in: D'Mello, C., Minninger, S. and McKeown, J. (eds) *Disaster Prevention in Tourism – Climate Justice and Tourism*, Chiang Mai: Ecumenical Coalition on Tourism and German Church Development Service (EED), pp. 136–61.

Scott, D., Peeters, P. and Gössling, S. (2010). 'Can tourism deliver its "aspirational" emission reduction targets?', *Journal of Sustainable Tourism*, 18(3): 393–408.

Stern, N. (2006) *The Economics of Climate Change: The Stern Review*, Cambridge: Cambridge University Press.

—— (2009) *The Global Deal: Climate Change and the Creation of a New Era of Progress and Prosperity*, New York: Public Affairs.

Telfer, D. and Sharpley, R. (2008) *Tourism and Development in the Developing World*, London: Routledge.

United Nations World Tourism Organisation (UNWTO) (2005) *Tourism Market Trends. World Overview and Tourism Topics, 2004*, Madrid: UNWTO.

—— (2006) *Tourism and Least Developed Countries: A Sustainable Opportunity to Reduce Poverty*. Available at <http://www.unwto.org/sustainable/doc/tourism-and-ldc.pdf> (Accessed 3 April 2011).

—— (2008) *Emerging Tourism Markets – The Coming Economic Boom*, Press Release, UNWTO Madrid, 24 June.

United Nations World Tourism Organization (UNWTO), United Nations Environment Programme (UNEP) and World Meteorological Organization (WMO) (2008) *Climate Change and Tourism: Responding to Global Challenges*. Madrid: UNWTO, UNEP and WMO.

World Economic Forum (WEF) (2008) *The Travel and Tourism Competitiveness Report 2008: Balancing Economic Development and Environmental Sustainability*, Geneva: WEF.

World Travel and Tourism Council (WTTC) (2004) *The Caribbean. The Impact of Travel and Tourism on Jobs and the Economy*, London: WTTC. Available at <http://www.caribbeanhotels.org/WTTC_Caribbean_Report.pdf > (Accessed 11 February 2008).

11.4 TOURISM AND GLOBAL ENVIRONMENTAL CHANGE

The aviation sector is one of the culprits, as it were, of blocking the drain and not taking its turn to clear out the plug. Air travel, at least up until now, has remained off the radar as far as culpability for greenhouse gas emissions. Transport makes up between 75 and 90 per cent of greenhouse gas emissions caused by tourism, and within the transport component (even though most tourism transport is car-based), aviation contributes 75 per cent of all tourism-related transport emissions, and is the most environmentally damaging form of transport per passenger kilometre (Graham and Shaw 2008). And this is projected to increase to 80–90 per cent by 2020 (Peeters et al. 2006). Since the 1960s global air passenger traffic has increased by nearly 9 per cent per year (Barnett 2009), with 42 per cent of all international arrivals being by air (Gössling et al. 2007). Today, the global airline industry consists of over 1,600 airlines operating more than 27,000 aircraft, providing service to over 3,700 airports. In 2010, the world's airlines flew almost 30 million scheduled flight departures and carried over 2 billion passengers (IATA 2011). It has (at least for a significant proportion of the world's population) never been easier or cheaper to fly. Indeed, airfares are around 42 per cent cheaper today than they were 10 years ago, in real terms (Barnett 2009).

Air travel contributes around 700 million tonnes of CO_2 into the atmosphere each year, and this emission is growing by 5 per cent each year. Collectively, this comprises around 3 per cent of total global emissions (Barnett 2009). The global air industry tends to highlight this low figure; however, the issue is slightly complicated by the fact that green-house gases emitted at high altitudes by long-haul international flights have an enhanced greenhouse effect – indeed, aircraft emissions are reported to be at least twice as damaging as ground-level emissions (Adam 2007).

Despite its current low(ish) contribution to greenhouse gases, some climatologists are worried that aviation is the fastest growing cause of climate change (Holden 2008). With increased demand for flying, CO_2 from aircraft will reach 1.2–1.4 billion tonnes by the year 2025 (Adam 2007). Scenarios run in the UK show that all other industry sectors would need to reduce their carbon emissions substantially to allow the aviation sector to grow (Bows et al. 2006). With current high-growth emission trends in tourism, the sector could become a major source of greenhouse gases in the future if other sectors achieve significant emission reductions; to reduce emissions substantially in tourism hinges largely upon 'major policy and practice changes in air travel' (Scott et al. 2010: 393).

Basically there are ethical concerns around aviation on two levels: at the industry level, and at the individual level. At an industry level there has been a lack of serious action to address current and predicted emissions. NGO Tourism Concern is critical of the tourism industry, believing that it 'lags behind many others in recognising its responsibilities in relation to climate change and the environment' (Barnett 2009: 47). The aviation sector in particular has been picked out as one that enjoys the benefits of unfair fuel tax advantages but is not included in any emission trading schemes (Peeters et al. 2006).

Despite advances in addressing the issue of greenhouse gas emission, and identifying culpability (at least in liberal and advanced states) aviation continues to remain outside of the Kyoto Protocol. The Kyoto Protocol, which was adopted by the Conference of the Parties to the UN *Framework Convention on Climate Change* in December 1997, entered into force on 16 February 2005, and calls for developed countries (Annex I parties) to pursue limitation or reduction of greenhouses gases from 'aviation bunker fuels' work-ing through the International Civil Aviation Organisation (ICAO) (Article 2.2 of the Protocol).

The International Air Transport Association (IATA), the international trade body representing 230 airlines, comprising 93 per cent of scheduled international air traffic, explains how a 'global sectoral approach' is needed to address the carbon emissions of the sector.

> For a typical flight, CO_2 will be emitted over several different countries, over international waters and even different continents…While it is simple for governments to account for emissions from fixed sources within their borders, it is difficult to do this with mobile sources such as aircraft used in international aviation'.
>
> (IATA 2009)

Thus national carbon reduction targets often exclude international aviation emissions (Anderson et al. 2008 in Smith and Rodger 2009). But there are a number of ways in which the carbon emissions from flying may be addressed: reductions (e.g. through air-craft/engine/fuel technology, demand, efficient routing), carbon offsetting and carbon trading.

Figure 11.2 *Is this a view we should feel guilty about? Photo: Brent Lovelock.*

DISCUSSION POINT: INDUSTRY DISCOURSES ON FLYING

The flyer's dilemma is exacerbated by positively biased social representation of air travel (Becken 2007). The public discourse around the efficiencies and benefits of air travel legitimise tourists' desire to participate in global travel (Gössling and Peeters 2007). There are four major industry discourses (2007: 402):

- Air travel is energy efficient and accounts for only marginal emissions of CO_2
- Air travel is economically and socially too important to be restricted
- Fuel use is consistently minimised and new technology will solve the problem
- Air travel is treated unfairly in comparison to other modes of transport.

Exercise

Conduct a search of a sample of airline websites and see if/how they present the issue of carbon emissions.

DISCUSSION POINT: LOW-COST CARRIERS

The continued liberalisation of air transport and expansion of low-cost carriers (LCC) have been implicated in fostering 'excessive' holiday flying (Graham and Shaw 2008; Cohen et al. 2011). Graham and Shaw point out the 'Incompatibility of environmental sustainability with a business as usual model that promotes rapid growth in air travel without meeting its external costs, but simultaneously claims to be socially and geographically inclusive' (2008: 1439). The 'ubiquitous and commodified leisure mobility brought about by cheap (and even "free") air flights' is at odds with efforts to address greenhouse gas emissions (Burns and Bibbings 2009: 31).

LCCs originated in North America and are now found in most regions, including Europe, Asia and Australasia. In Europe LCCs, comprise about 20 per cent of all air traffic, and 50 per cent of the UK–continental Europe market (in 2005) (Graham and Shaw 2008). Their low-cost structures have led to behavioural changes in leisure and business travel patterns. LCCs have been instrumental in the development of weekend, city or short-break tourism, and in expanding the list of available destinations (Graham and Shaw 2008). Such short-haul flights make a disproportionately large contribution to the aviation sector's greenhouse gas emissions (Royal Commission on Environmental Pollution 2002). They have also attracted passengers away from more sustainable forms of surface transport (Graham and Shaw 2008).

Ryanair, the archetypal LCC, is now the biggest airline in the world, and together with rival easyJet provides 30 million return seats per year. LCCs such as Ryanair claim to make flying accessible to poorer groups. This is somewhat supported by research, for example Hares et al.'s (2010) interviews with tourists about LCCs:

> They give accessibility to people to travel at an affordable cost. I think back years ago when I was a kid, we never thought of going abroad because our family could never afford that, and suddenly, everyone can *get on a plane and go somewhere*.
> (Interviewee in Hares et al. 2010: 466)

The new social inclusiveness of LCCs, however, is disputed (CAA 2006; Randles and Mander 2009). The Civial Aviation Authority (CAA) study in the UK found that rather than the working class entering the market in significant numbers, it is the middle and higher income socio-economic groups who are flying more often than in the past, and often on shorter trips (CAA 2006: 5). Flying has changed from something that a generation ago was an extraordinary activity for those of moderate socio-economic status, to an 'everyday' and 'locked-in' social institution. In defence of LCCs, they do play a positive role in the economic development of more remote and economically disadvantaged destinations, and have facilitated the movement of migrant labour (Graham and Shaw 2008).

Sadly, LCCs continue to attract negative attention to themselves, through comments such as those made by Michael O'Leary, the owner of Ryanair, who when asked about global warming said:

> I believe it's all a load of bullshit...I mean, it is absolutely bizarre that the people who can't tell us what the fucking weather is next Tuesday can predict with absolute precision what the fucking global temperatures will *be in 100 years' time. It's horseshit.*

(in Hickman 2010)

Ryanair has been accused by a junior environment minister in the UK Parliament of being 'the irresponsible face of capitalism' for its record on greenhouse gases. In defence, O'Leary said that Ryanair was Europe's greenest airline because it operated modern aircraft and fitted as many passengers as possible on each flight. He went on to comment that 'There is no link between aviation and climate change' and that 'I am far too busy doubling Ryanair to be joining any carbon emissions trading scheme' (Webster 2007).

Discussion questions

1 Are LCCs unethical or simply aggressive business operations?
2 How do we balance the social and economic gains against the environmental losses that LCCs allegedly contribute to?
3 Do civil aviation authorities in countries or regions have an ethical duty to address the practices of LCCs?

Useful sources

Graham, B. and Shaw, J. (2008) 'Low-cost airlines in Europe: Reconciling liberalization and sustainability', *Geoforum*, 39(3): 1439–51.

Ryanair (2008) Europe's Greenest Airline <http://www.ryanair.com/doc/about/ryanair_greenairline_2008.pdf>

11.5 TECHNOLOGY AS A SOLUTION?

Peeters et al. (2006) in addressing the question of whether or not technology may help to reduce carbon emissions from aviation, note that innovation in tourism as a whole is low. They characterise tourism as a sector that aims primarily to satisfy consumer needs, increase market share and competitiveness rather than addressing environmental impacts. Furthermore, aviation is described as a 'mature' field in which most of the innovations and breakthroughs have already been made (Kroo 2004 in Peeters et al. 2006). Increasing fuel efficiency, therefore, is likely to only be incremental. The IPCC in their report on aviation in 2007 do acknowledge that medium-term mitigation for CO_2 emissions from the aviation sector can potentially come from improved fuel efficiency, but that such improvements are expected to only partially offset the growth of CO_2 aviation emissions (ICAO 2011).

Other options for saving fuel include high density seating (note that low-cost carriers score well on this), more efficient air traffic management and passenger routing.

Biofuels, however, have been identified as having promise for reducing aviation carbon emissions. Biofuels are sourced from crops, and are mixed with conventional jet fuel in blends. In 2009, Air New Zealand, an airline committed to becoming 'the world's most environmentally sustainable airline' ran a Boeing 747–400 on a 12-hour (5,800 nautical miles) test flight using a 50/50 blend of second generation jatropha[2] sustainable biofuel and traditional Jet A1. Using this biofuel blend, the fuel burn improved by 1.2 per cent, saving 1.43 tonnes of fuel (Air New Zealand 2009).

Air New Zealand say that they are committed to a goal of having 10 per cent of their fuel needs by 2013 met by sustainable alternative biofuels – but for them and for other airlines considering this option, just how feasible is it as a means of reducing emissions, how sustainable is it, and how ethical? (see Discussion Point that follows). Peeters et al. (2006) believe that marketing flights fuelled by biofuels as 'green air travel' is problematic because it requires land currently devoted to agricultural production becoming dedicated to meeting the energy needs of air travel. The economic and social implications of this are immense. Furthermore, the land area requirements to meet the biofuel needs of aviation are immense. One Boeing 747–400 flight of 10,000 kilometres would consume 112 tonnes of biofuel, the equivalent production of 52 hectares of jatropha plantations. In 2005, global consumption of jet fuel was 232 Mt, which would require an area of around one million square kilometres (an area equivalent to Germany, France, the Netherlands and Belgium combined). This area would grow by a factor of two in the next 15 years (Scott et al. 2010).

Figure 11.3 *Are there more ethical modes of travel, such as this TGV in Switzerland? Photo: Brent Lovelock.*

DISCUSSION POINT: THE ETHICS OF BIOFUELS

One of the 'technical' solutions to the emissions of aviation is substituting a portion of traditional aviation fuel (kerosene) with biofuels. However, in addition to the technical problems around the viability of this, a number of ethical issues have been raised. These revolve mainly around the conversion of productive agricultural lands from food production to biofuel production, with concomitant impacts upon communities who had relied upon that food production. Similarly there are concerns that 'The rapid expansion of biofuels production in the developing world has also led to problems such as deforestation and the displacement of indigenous people' (Professor Joyce Tait, Nuffield Council on Bioethics Working Party on Biofuels). Some of these problems are illustrated by the case study of Malaysia, summarised below:

> Malaysia is the second largest producer of palm oil in the world (after Indonesia)...In 2008, Malaysia produced approximately 1.3 million litres of biofuel, and production is expected to increase steeply. The rapid expansion of Malaysian palm oil biodiesel has led to worries over the conversion of forests to oil palm plantations that might have detrimental impacts on South-East Asia's biodiversity. The potential impacts of lost forestland and biodiversity in this region are particularly significant given that, by some estimates, South-East Asia contains 11 per cent of the world's remaining tropical forests which are home to many rare species, and reports have warned of the extinction of, for example, the orang-utan of Borneo. Moreover, the conversion of lowland tropical rainforest would result in significant GHG emissions. Malaysia also faces issues of illegal logging, which at current scales poses significant threats to the environment and local communities. There have also been accusations of so-called 'land-grabs' by palm oil producers. Companies have been accused of clearing large areas of land and displacing indigenous tribes who, despite often not having official title to the land, may exercise Native Customary Rights because they have lived there for generations and depend on the land for their livelihood.
>
> (Nuffield Council on Bioethics 2011: Biofuels: Ethical Issues (Summary and Recommendations), pp. xxi–xxii, xxv)

The Nuffield Council on Bioethics is concerned that rushing to meet aggressive biofuel targets could harm the environment and violate human rights. They urge that a 'comprehensive ethical standard' be adopted worldwide to guide the ethical production of biofuels. This standard would address six ethical principles surrounding production of biofuels:

Six ethical principles

> The first five Principles specify the conditions that should be met for biofuels development to be permissible. These are as follows:
>
> i. Biofuels development should not be at the expense of people's essential rights (including access to sufficient food and water, health rights, work rights and land entitlements).
> ii. Biofuels should be environmentally sustainable.

iii. Biofuels should contribute to a net reduction of total greenhouse gas emissions and not exacerbate global climate change.

iv. Biofuels should develop in accordance with trade principles that are fair and recognise the rights of people to just reward (including labour rights and intellectual property rights).

v. Costs and benefits of biofuels should be distributed in an equitable way.

We then consider whether in some cases there may be a duty to develop biofuels. To address this we propose a sixth Principle:

vi. If the first five Principles are respected and if biofuels can play a crucial role in mitigating dangerous climate change then, dependency on additional key considerations, there is a duty to develop such biofuels.

> (Nuffield Council on Bioethics 2011: Biofuels: Ethical Issues
> (Summary and Recommendations), pp. xxi–xxii, xxv)

Similarly energy reformer, Sharon Astyk (2006) proposes a set of 12 ethical principles around the production and use of biofuels. These include:

> *Ethical Principle 1* – Biofuels cannot and must not be a strategy for maintaining the present situation.
> *Ethical Principle 3* – We must not allow people to starve to fuel our [planes].
> *Ethical Principle 5* – Either we must address the more basic injustices that lead to hunger or we must acknowledge that large-scale use of biofuels will increase hunger and inequity.

Discussion questions

1 What are the Nuffield Council on Bioethics referring to when they write about the 'essential rights' of people (ethical principle i.)? How do we define what is an essential right? Could people's rights to fly be considered an essential right?

2 How do we ensure that the ethical principles espoused above are implemented? What are some processes through which this may happen?

3 There are many investment opportunities available for biofuel production, including from jatropha. Is it ethical to invest in jatropha production?

4 How do airlines determine whether or not it is ethical to use biofuel substitutes? What factors need to be taken into consideration in their ethical decision making?

Useful sources: for information on the debate of food security versus energy:

Achten, W.M.J., Maes, W.H., Aerts,R., Verchot, L., Trabucco, A., Mathijs, E., et al. (2010) 'Jatropha: from global hype to local opportunity', *Journal of Arid Environments*, 74: 164–5.

Escobar, J.C., Lora, E.S., Venturini, O.J., Yanez, E.E., Castillo, E.F. and Almazan, O. (2009) 'Biofuels: Environment, technology and food security', *Renewable and Sustainable Energy Reviews*, 13(6–7): 1275–87.

Naylor, R.L. Liska, A.J., Burke, M.B., Falcon, W.P., Gaskell, J.C., Rozelle, S.D. and Cassman, K.G. (2007) 'The ripple effect: Biofuels, food security, and the environment', *Environment*, 49(9): 30–43.

Websites

Nuffield Council on Bioethics (2011) Biofuels: Ethical Issues <http://www.nuffieldbio-ethics.org/biofuels-0>

Astyk, S. (2006) Ethics of biofuels <http://www.energybulletin.net/node/24169>

11.6 CARBON OFFSETTING

Carbon offsets are another approach to addressing the emissions of flying. Carbon offsets are a system in which the traveller pays for an emissions-reducing project elsewhere, that negates the amount of carbon that would be emitted from their travel. Many airlines offer carbon offsets, and they can include a range of carbon-reducing activities. Carbon offsets are advocated by travel guides *Lonely Planet* and the *Rough Guide*. However, there are substantial differences between offsetting organisations with respect to emission calculation processes, prices charged and verification processes – all having 'consequences for the efficiency and credibility of voluntary offsetting schemes' (Gössling et al. 2007: 241). Taylor (2009) cites examples of offsetting for a flight for two people London to Sydney return: ClimateCare 11.23 tonnes CO_2 (£98); Carbon Clear 2.82 tonnes CO_2 (£21); Offset Carbon 8 tonnes CO_2 (£76); the Carbon Neutral Company 6.1 tonnes CO_2 (£52). Examples of offsetting schemes include tree planting in China, eco-fuelled boilers in India and solar panels in Thailand (Barkham 2006).

Trading in such emissions credits is big business, worth US$705 million in 2008. Some offset schemes have been criticised, however, for being unsustainable. Wambi (2009) writes of a scheme established by a Dutch organisation involved in the voluntary carbon market, that has resulted in the displacement of indigenous Benet people in the Mount Elgon region of Uganda, to clear the way for a tree-planting project. The Dutch company, Green Seat, had a number of airline companies as clients.

Based on current uptake of carbon offsetting, it is unlikely that voluntary carbon offsets could make a significant contribution to making tourism more sustainable, as uptake would have to increase by a factor of 400 to achieve just a 10 per cent reduction in the greenhouse gas emissions from aviation (Gössling et al. 2007: 241). But, more importantly, some researchers in the field perceive carbon offsets to be negative, in that they encourage people to believe that they don't need to change their behaviour (Gössling et al. 2007). The authors describe such schemes as an 'ambiguous solution to aviation's environmental impacts' and call for more attention to the ethical dimensions of compensation schemes, noting that they ignore intra and inter generational equity (Gössling et al. 2007: 242). Wambi (2009) describes participating in such schemes as buying the right to keep on polluting.

NGO Tourism Concern's *Ethical Travel Guide* questions whether carbon offsetting does anything more than 'making owners of offsetting companies wealthy and appeasing our own guilt', pointing out that offsetting does not prevent our flights from contributing to climate change, and allows travellers to think that they don't need to reduce their emissions at source (Barnett 2009: 44). Offsets have been said to allow airlines to 'greenwash' their activities, while lulling consumers into believing that their flights are 'neutralised' with no impact on climate (Equations 2008 in Barnett 2009: 44)

In response to such concerns, Responsibletravel.com, one of the United Kingdom's leading ethical travel operators has recently stopped offering offsets to its customers. Justin Francis, the company's founder, sees offsets as a 'medieval pardon that allows people to continue polluting' and that 'Carbon offsetting is an ingenious way to avoid genuinely reducing your carbon emissions. ...It's a very attractive idea – that you can go on living exactly as you did before when there's a magic pill or medieval pardon out there that allows people to continue polluting' (Taylor 2009). Instead, Responsible Travel will now attach 'carbon warnings' to their holiday packages.

11.7 REDUCING VOLUME AND DEMAND

Given the limitations around technical emission reduction, and the fundamental flaws around offsetting, meeting emission reduction targets seems unlikely without 'volumetric changes' (Scott et al. 2010). However, currently there is little evidence that tourists are willing to voluntarily change their travel behaviour, in order to reduce emissions. Researchers have recently begun to focus on the decision-making behaviours of tourists with respect to carbon emissions. These studies, ostensibly of ethical decision making of tourists, reveal a reluctance to relinquish any 'rights to fly'. Becken concluded from her study of international tourists in New Zealand that people are less concerned about the environment when on holiday, and that 'the value of freedom of travel is firmly established in the minds of [the study's participants]' (2007: 364).

Part of the problem lies around addressing the travel behaviours of what have been termed the 'hypermobile' (Peeters et al. 2006). Only 2–3 per cent of the world's population travel annually by air and a portion of these exhibit 'hypermobility'. In one study, the most frequent travellers came from three countries – South Africa, Australia and New Zealand (Gössling et al. 2006). In that study, compared to the average distance flown in two years by study participants (34,000 km), the hypermobile travellers flew 180,000 km each, visiting up to 24 countries. Addressing emissions from aviation will involve changing the lifestyles of such hypermobile travellers – encouraging more benign travel patterns (Peeters et al. 2006). This also raises questions about the ethics of airlines' 'frequent flyer' programmes.

Evidence suggests that persuading people away from flying will not be an easy task. Research into the psycho-social responses of air-passengers to their carbon emissions (the so-called 'flyer's dilemma' (Adams 2000 in Becken 2007)) reveals strategies of guilt suppression and denial used to span a cognitive dissonance between the short-term personal benefits of tourism and the long-term consequences (of their flying) for climate change (Cohen et al. 2011). Becken's interviews with travellers show that they are aware that the privilege of flying conflicts with the socially desirable behaviour of being a 'good citizen'. However, this discrepancy or dissonance (gap between attitude and behaviour), and the discomfort associated with it, is 'insufficiently strong to induce behavioural change when it comes to air travel' (2007: 364). Becken notes that travellers seek to dissolve this dissonance by denial, and by seeking scapegoats (e.g. airlines, business travellers (the hypermobile)) thus deferring personal ethical responsibility (see also Hares et al. 2010; McKercher et al. 2010; Cohen et al. 2011). More positively, there is some evidence to suggest that among *some* travellers there is a 'growing negative discourse towards frequent short haul tourist air travel' (Cohen et al. 2011). For example, more eco-friendly attitudes have been found in Norwegian tourists, who demonstrate what Cohen and Higham (2011) refer to as 'air travel with a conscience'.

11.8 CARBON TAXES

Carbon taxes, environmental taxes or green taxes are one mechanism that could be used to temper demand, and thus the volume of people flying. Ethically, though, there are problems, with green taxes having been compared to 'indulgences' in the Catholic faith (Goodin 2010). In Catholic theology, indulgences were granted by Church officials to those who had sinned, in order to remit time that would have to be served by the sinner in purgatory. Goodin compares selling God's grace with selling nature's benefice, arguing that we are essentially selling something that cannot be sold. He questions the morality of paying (a tax) for something that you know is wrong and that you are going to do now or in the future.

Taxes would of course be passed on to the customer and would increase the cost of airfares. Holden (2008) questions though, whether increased costs (assuming that they *do* reflect the full environmental costs of flying) will actually result in a decrease in demand – given the high elasticity of the recreational tourism market. Taxes, while internalising the climate-change cost of aviation, would not prevent demand from growing overall – and will not provide an incentive for airlines to reduce their emissions (Peeters et al. 2006).

11.9 ETHICAL DECISION MAKING AND TRANSPORT CHOICE

Back to the question we posed at the start of this chapter – should we stay or should we go? To fly or not to fly? Holden believes that this is an ethical question hinging upon the willingness of individuals 'to forgo the personal pleasures gained from flying for the greater good of the natural environment and future generations' (2008: 219). There is an elementary moral principle that could be useful in addressing this question – 'that you should not do something for your own benefit if it harms another person' (Broome 2008: 97). We have a moral obligation not to perform an act that causes harm to others (Sinnott-Armstrong 2010). However, when considering our flight, we could argue that global warming will still occur even if we don't fly, and that our individual act is neither necessary nor sufficient for global warming. In response to such an evasion, Sinnott-Armstrong asks us to picture a scenario:

> Imagine it takes three people to push a car off a cliff with a passenger locked inside, and five people are already pushing. If I join them, my act of pushing is neither necessary nor sufficient to make the car go off the cliff. Nonetheless, my act of pushing is a cause (or part of the cause) of the harm to the passenger.
>
> (Sinnott-Armstrong 2010: 334)

Sinnott-Armstrong then extends this Harm Principle to the Indirect Harm Principle 'We have a moral obligation not to perform an act that causes harm to others indirectly [or] by causing someone to carry out acts that cause harm to others' (2010: 336). Further to this, he identifies the Contribution Principle, whereby 'We have a moral obligation not to make problems worse'; a Risk Principle: 'We have a moral obligation not to increase the risk of harms to other people'; and even a Gas Principle where 'We have a moral obligation not to expel greenhouse gases into the atmosphere' (2010: 337).

Utilitarians would argue for us to 'do what is best' – to calculate the greatest good from flying, taking into account the complex equations involving social and economic well-being, and environmental harm. But some environmental philosophers argue that utilitarianism cannot account for the value of biodiversity or ecosystems as it is too anthropocentric, and is a theory that has brought us to the edge of environmental catastrophe (Jamieson 2010). Defending utilitarianism, however, Jamieson believes that from such a perspective, 'agents should minimize their own contributions to global environmental change and act in such a way as to cause others to minimize their contributions as well' (2010: 318). He identifies three aspects of utilitarianism: non-contingency – that our actions should not be contingent upon our beliefs about the behaviour of others; non-complacency – that our ways of life and patterns of action should be dynamically responsive to changing circumstances; and progressive consequentialism – that requires us to produce a progressively better world rather than the best world (2010: 318). In discussing the value of utilitarianism to the issue of climate change, Jamieson concludes that 'when it comes to global environmental change, utilitarians should generally be inflexible, virtuous greens' rather than flexible 'calculators' of net wellbeing. Also, he notes that ethically, our behaviour in producing and consuming is important not only for its immediate environmental impacts but also for the 'example-setting and role-modelling of that behavior' (2010: 322, 324).

11.9 THE SOLUTION – ETHICAL FLYING?

So, as individuals, how do we address the carbon emissions from our flying? NGO Tourism Concern does not advocate simply stopping flying, as this would have profound effects on the livelihoods of those who depend on tourism for their income (Barnett 2009). Rather, they suggest taking longer less frequent trips rather than lots of short-break trips: one big trip per year, if flying – or every other year if long-haul flying is involved. And they advise being energy/carbon aware when we get to our destination. This latter point is important when we consider that many tourism destinations are inefficient users of energy and are substantial carbon emitters – air conditioning to keep us cool in the tropics, heating to keep us warm in snow resorts. One study in an Alpine tourist region of Switzerland has shown that per capita carbon emissions are 25 per cent higher than the national average (Walz et al. 2008). 'Slow tourism' is recommended as a solution (Peeters et al. 2006), as are 'staycations' (Cohen et al. 2011). Becken refers to the need to distinguish between 'legitimate holiday' versus 'dispensable' air trips (2007 in Cohen et al. 2011). Responsible Travel recommend to their clients to 'fly less and when you do fly, make it count' (Taylor 2009).

At the other end of the spectrum, tongue in cheek, Urry (2008) envisages a 'digital panopticon' that will be able to track and trace each person's carbon allowance. Under such an authoritarian approach, in the future when flying is even more of an 'elitist and privileged activity' (Holden 2008) perceivably, those wishing to indulge in international air travel would have to make sacrifices elsewhere in their lives to fit within their carbon allocation – live in unheated (or uncooled) houses, forgo car ownership, grow and eat their own (raw) food, etc.

Climate change is fundamentally an ethical issue because to successfully address climate change will require a fundamental paradigm shift in our ethics (Gardiner 2010) and in how we view travel. It was once written that 'When most people see a large automobile and think first of the air pollution it causes rather than the social status it conveys, environmental ethics will have arrived' (Durning 1992 in Jamieson 2010: 325). In a similar vein, perhaps when most people envisage a flight on a large aeroplane and think first of the carbon emissions of their journey, will an environmental travel ethic have arrived?

CHAPTER REVIEW

This chapter has outlined the ethical issues around air travel, pointing to air travel's link with global environmental change, and related environmental, social and economic impacts. Climate change is positioned as an ethical issue, and one that will require action on the part of different stakeholders: the consumer, airlines, destinations, governments and international bodies.

We discuss the concept of harm and identifying and assigning responsibility for actions such as flying where harm is indirect, not readily observable, the victims not easily identifiable, and responsibility not easily assigned. We invoke the Prisoner's Dilemma and Tragedy of the Commons scenarios to illustrate the ethical outcomes of individual actions upon collective wellbeing.

Mechanisms to address the impacts of carbon emissions from flying are outlined, including technology, fuel substitution (biofuels), carbon offsetting and carbon taxes. There are ethical problems with each of these, and it is concluded that a key change must come from consumers – and in particular addressing the travel behaviours of the hypermobile, but ultimately of all of us.

SUMMARY OF KEY TERMS

Hypermobility Refers to a minority of highly mobile individuals, who account for a large share of the overall kilometres travelled, especially by air. These travellers are 'hypermobile' in terms of participation in frequent trips, often over large distances (Gössling et al. 2006).

Intergenerational ethics A system of ethics that address intergenerational issues, and how to balance the interests of those people alive now and those who will be in the future.

The ethical principle of equity, particularly intergenerational equity, is central to the concept of sustainable development. Some claim that our obligations to future generations deserve to be the central topic of moral philosophy.

Low-cost carrier or a low-cost airline (also referred to as a no-frills, discount or budget carrier or airline) is an airline characterised by lower fares and fewer comforts. Originally developed in the USA, it is now a model widely applied around the world.

Prisoner's Dilemma A paradox in decision analysis in which two individuals acting in their own best interest pursue a course of action that does not result in the ideal outcome. The dilemma illustrates a conflict between individual and group rationality. A group whose members pursue rational self-interest may all end up worse off than a group whose members act contrary to rational self-interest.

Responsibility Originally a concept developed by Aristotle. Put simply, people are morally responsible for what they do. People who have moral responsibility for an action are referred to as *moral agents*. Moral agency, and thus moral responsibility, necessitates free will. There is debate over whether individuals do have free will or if their actions are causally determined. The latter position would question whether people are ever morally responsible for their actions.

QUESTIONS FOR REFLECTION

1 Think about the last flight you took – to what extent was it necessary, and how did you (or how *could* you) ethically justify the flight?
2 Does your ethical defence of your flight differ when you take into consideration future generations?
3 Are business travellers who are required to fly as a part of their job (who may also travel *business class*) more morally responsible than holiday travellers? Do their employers have any moral responsibility?
4 How ethical are airlines' frequent flyer programmes?

EXERCISES

1 List some of the strategies that could be put in place at destinations in order for the carbon emissions of flying there to be 'neutralised'. Who are the tourism stakeholders that would need to make these changes?
2 Are there further ethical implications associated with reducing in-destination carbon consumption?
3 Consider alternative transport modes, such as rail or car, and discuss whether there are similar or different ethical issues around these transport choices.

FURTHER READING

Gardiner, S.M. (2010) *Climate Ethics: Essential Readings,* Oxford: Oxford University Press.

Gössling, S. (2011) *Carbon Management in Tourism: Mitigating the Impacts on Climate Change,* Abingdon: Routledge.

Gössling, S. and Upham, P. (2009) *Climate Change and Aviation: Issues, Challenges and Solutions,* London: Earthscan.

IPCC (2001) *Aviation and the Global Atmosphere* <http://www.grida.no/publications/other/ipcc_sr/?src = /climate/ipcc/aviation/index.htm>

Mulgan, T. (2006) *Future People: A Moderate Consequentialist Account of Our Obligations to Future Generations*, Oxford: Clarendon Press.

NOTES

a George Monbiot (1963–), environmental and political writer. From 'On the Flightpath to Global Meltdown', *The Guardian*, 21 September 2006. Available at <http://www.guardian.co.uk/environment/2006/sep/21/travelsenvironmentalimpact.ethicalliving> (Accessed 13 June 2011).

b Prince Charles (1948–) Available at <http://www.woopidoo.com/business_quotes/climate-change.htm > (Accessed 1 May 2011).

c Arnold Schwarzenegger (1947–), movie actor, Governor of California 2003–11. In Flam, F. (2008) *Debate Still Heating up on Global Warming.* Available at <http://www.azcentral.com/news/articles/2008/08/17/20080817ClimateChangeDebate0817.html>

1 Puzzles with this structure were devised and discussed by Merrill Flood and Melvin Dresher in 1950, as part of the Rand Corporation's investigations into game theory (which Rand pursued because of possible applications to global nuclear strategy). The title 'prisoner's dilemma' and the version with prison sentences as payoffs are attributable to Albert Tucker (Stanford Encyclopedia of Philosophy 2007).

2 Jatropha oil is vegetable oil produced from the seeds of the *Jatropha curcas* plant.

REFERENCES

Adam, D. (2007) 'Surge in carbon levels raises fears of runaway warming', *The Guardian*, 19 January. Available at <http://environment.guardian.co.uk/climatechange/story/0,01994071,00.html> (Accessed 12 December 2011).

Air New Zealand (2009) *Biofuel Test Flight Report Shows Significant Fuel Saving.* Available at <http://www.airnewzealand.com/press-release-2009-biofuel-test-flight-report-shows-signif-icant-fuel-saving-28may09> (Accessed 10 October 2011).

Archer, D. (2005) 'Fate of fossil-fuel CO_2 in geologic time', *Journal of Geophysical Research Oceans,* 10:C09S05, DOI 10.1029/2004JC002625.

Barkham, P. (2006) 'Oops, we helped ruin the planet', *The Guardian*, 4 March. Available at <http://www.guardian.co.uk/travel/2006/mar/04/travelnews.climatechange.environment> (Accessed 27 July 2011).

Barnett, T. (2009) 'Climate change: To fly or not to fly', in Pattullo, P. and Minelli, O. (for Tourism Concern), *The Ethical Travel Guide,* London: Earthscan.

Becken, S. (2007) 'Tourists' perception of international air travel's impact on the global climate and potential climate change policies', *Journal of Sustainable Tourism,* 15(4): 351–68.

Bows, A., Upham, P. and Anderson, K. (2006) *Contraction and Convergence: UK carbon emissions and the implications for UK air traffic.* Tyndall Centre for Climate Change Research, Technical

Report 40. Available at <http://tyndall2.webapp3.uea.ac.uk/sites/default/files/t3_23_0.pdf> (Accessed 4 January 2012).

Broome, J. (2008) 'The ethics of climate change', *Scientific American.* Available at < Http://www.scientificamerican.com/article.cfm?id¼the-ethics-of-climate-change> (Accessed 6 August 2009).

Burns, P. and Bibbings, L. (2009) 'The end of tourism? Climate change and societal challenges', *21st Century Society*, 4(1): 31–51.

Civil Aviation Authority (CAA) (2006) *No-Frills Carriers: Revolution or Evolution?* CAP 770, London: CAA.

ClimateCare (2012) *Calculate and Offset Your Carbon Footprint.* Available at <http://www.climate-care.org> (Accessed 7 May 2012).

Cohen, S.A. and Higham, J.E.S. (2011) 'Eyes wide shut? UK consumer perceptions on aviation climate impacts and travel decisions to New Zealand', *Current Issues in Tourism,* 14(4): 232–35.

Cohen, S., Higham, J. and Cavaliere, C. (2011) 'Binge flying: Behavioural addiction and climate change', *Annals of Tourism Research*, 38(3): 1070–89.

Dlugolecki, A. (2004) 'Climate change and mounting financial risks: what are the options?' Background Paper for *The Hague Conference on Environment, Security and Sustainable Development,* 9–12 May. Available at <http://www.envirosecurity.org/conference/working/ClimateChangeFinancialRiskOptions.pdf> (Accessed 7 July 2011).

Gardiner, S.M. (2010) 'Ethics and global climate change', in Gardiner, S.M., Caney, S., Jamieson, D. and Shue, H. (eds) *Climate Ethics: Essential Readings*, New York: Oxford University Press, pp. 3–38.

Goodin, R.E. (2010) 'Selling environmental indulgences', in Gardiner, S.M., Caney, S., Jamieson, D. and Shue, H. (eds) *Climate Ethics: Essential Readings*, New York: Oxford University Press, pp. 231–46.

Gössling, S. and Peeters, P. (2007) '"It does not harm the environment!" An analysis of industry discourses on tourism, air travel and the environment', *Journal of Sustainable Tourism,* 15(4): 402–17.

Gössling, S., Bredberg, M., Randow, A., Sandstrom, E. and Svensson, P. (2006) 'Tourist perceptions of climate change: a study of international tourists in Zanzibar', *Current Issues in Tourism,* 9(4/5): 419–35.

Gössling, S., Broderick, J., Upham, P., Ceron, J.-P., Dubois, G., Peeters, P. and Strasdas, W. (2007) 'Voluntary carbon offsetting schemes for aviation: efficiency and credibility', *Journal of Sustainable Tourism,* 15(3): 223–48.

Graham, B. and Shaw, J. (2008) 'Low-cost airlines in Europe: Reconciling liberalization and sustainability', *Geoforum*, 39(3): 1439–51.

Hares, A., Dickinson, J., and Wilkes, K. (2010) 'Climate change and the air travel decisions of UK tourists', *Journal of Transport Geography*, 18(3): 466–73.

Hickman, M. (2010) *Global warming? It doesn't exist, says Ryanair boss O'Leary.* Available at <http://www.independent.co.uk/environment/climate-change/global-warming-it-doesnt-exist-says-ryanair-boss-oleary-2075420.html> (Accessed 4 May 2011).

Hickman, L. (2010) *Michael O'Leary: Global warming is 'horseshit' – and other insights.* Available at <http://www.guardian.co.uk/environment/blog/2010/sep/10/michael-o-leary-ryanair-global-warming> (Accessed 3 October 2011).

Holden, A. (2008) *Environment and Tourism* (2nd edn), Abingdon: Routledge.

Intergovernmental Panel on Climate Change (IPCC) (2001) *Climate Change 2001: Synthesis Report.* Available at <http://www.ipcc.ch/ipccreports/tar/vol4/english/index.htm> (Accessed 11 November 2011).

International Air Transport Association (ATA) (2009) *A global approach to reducing aviation emissions.* Available at <http://www.iata.org/SiteCollectionDocuments/Documents/Global_Approach_Reducing_Emissions_251109web.pdf> (Accessed 3 April 2011).

—— (2011) *Fact Sheet: IATA – International Air Transport Association*. Available at <http://www. iata.org/pressroom/facts_figures/fact_sheets/Pages/iata.aspx> (Accessed 23 October 2011).

International Civil Aviation Organization (ICAO) (2011) 'Climate change', http://www.icao.int/ environmental-protection/Pages/climate-change.aspx

Jamieson, D. (2010) 'Ethics, public policy and global warming', in Gardiner, S.M., Caney, S., Jamieson, D. and Shue, H. (eds) *Climate Ethics: Essential Readings*, New York: Oxford University Press, pp. 77–86.

McKercher, B., Prideaux, B., et al. (2010) 'Achieving voluntary reductions in the carbon footprint of tourism and climate change', *Journal of Sustainable Tourism,* 18(3): 297–317.

Nuffield Council on Bioethics 2011: Biofuels: Ethical Issues (Summary and Recommendations), London: Nuffield Council on Bioethics.

Peeters,P., Gössling, S. and Becken, S. (2006) 'Innovation towards tourism sustainability: climate change and aviation', *International Journal of Innovation and Sustainable Development,* 1(3): 184–200.

Randles, S. and Mander, S. (2009) 'Aviation, consumption and the climate change debate: "Are you going to tell me off for flying?"' *Technology Analysis and Safety Management,* 21(1): 93–113.

Royal Commission on Environmental Pollution (2002) 'Environmental planning, 23rd report', Cm 5459, London: TSO.

Sager, T. (2006) 'Freedom as mobility: implications of the distinction between actual and potential travelling', *Mobilities,* 1: 465–88.

Schenk, R. (2011) *The Prisoner's Dilemma*. Available at <http://ingrimayne.com/econ/ IndividualGroup/PrisDilm.html> (Accessed 6 November 2011).

Scott, D., Peeters, P. and Gössling, S. (2010) 'Can tourism deliver its "aspirational" greenhouse gas emission reduction targets?', *Journal of Sustainable Tourism,* 18(3): 393–408.

Singer, P. (2010) 'One atmosphere', in Gardiner, S.M., Caney, S., Jamieson, D. and Shue, H. (eds) *Climate Ethics: Essential Readings*, New York: Oxford University Press, pp. 181–99.

Sinnott-Armstrong, W. (2010) 'It's not my fault: Global warming and individual moral obligations', in Gardiner, S.M., Caney, S., Jamieson, D. and Shue, H. (eds) *Climate Ethics: Essential Readings*, New York: Oxford University Press, pp. 332–46.

Smith, I.J. and Rodger, C.J. (2009) 'Carbon emission offsets for aviation-generated emissions due to international travel to and from New Zealand', *Energy Policy*, 37(9): 3438–47.

Stanford Encyclopedia of Philosophy (2007) *Prisoner's Dilemma*. Available at <http://plato.stanford.edu/entries/prisoner–dilemma/> (Accessed 19 February 2012).

Taylor, J. (2009) 'Ethical travel company drops carbon offsetting', *The Independent*. Available at <http://www.independent.co.uk/environment/green-living/ethical-travel-company-drops-carbon-offsetting-1816554.html> (Accessed 2 June 2011).

Timmons Roberts, J. and Parks, B. (2007) *A Climate of Injustice*, Cambridge, MA: MIT Press.

Urry, J. (2008) 'Climate change, travel and complex futures', *British Journal of Sociology,* 59(2): 261–79.

Walz, A., Calonderb, G.P., Hagedornc, F., Lardellia, C., Lundströma, C. and Stöcklia, V. (2008) 'Regional CO_2 budget, countermeasures and reduction aims for the Alpine tourist region of Davos, Switzerland', *Energy Policy,* 36(2): 811–20.

Wambi, M. (2009) Uganda: Carbon Trading Scheme Pushing People off their Land. Available at <http://business.highbeam.com/409433/article-1G1–206960002/uganda-carbon-trading-scheme-pushing-people-off-their-land> (Accessed 30 September 2011).

Webster, B. (2007) *Ryanair chief flies into a rage over green taunts*, 29 November. Available at <http://www.timesplus.co.uk/welcome/index.htm> (Accessed 29 September 2009).

Hospitality and
12 marketing ethics

'The market has no morality.'

Michael Heseltine[a]

'Being good is good business.'

Anita Roddick[b]

'Advertising is the rattling of a stick inside a swill bucket.'

George Orwell[c]

'Don't tell my mother I work in an advertising agency; she thinks I play piano in a whorehouse.'

Jacques Seguela[d]

LEARNING OBJECTIVES

After reading this chapter you will be able to:

- Present an overview of the range of ethical issues facing the hospitality industry and marketers of hospitality and tourism products.
- Apply key ethical frameworks to issues of tourism and hospitality marketing.
- Apply virtue ethics and social contract theories to marketing issues.
- Discuss ethical approaches to achieving truth in representation.

12.1 INTRODUCTION

Many readers will be familiar with Academy Award winning movie *Slumdog Millionaire* (2008) directed by Danny Boyle. Set in Mumbai, India, in the movie there is a scene in which careful observers will witness one of the main characters, Salim, a 'restaurant boy' filling a mineral water bottle with tap water and then resealing the cap with glue. The apparently clean and safe bottled water is then served to customers. This fascinating and potentially harmful practice is said to be widespread in railway stations and lower-end restaurants across India, and some travel advisers recommend checking the seal of your water bottle carefully. We refer to this as a great micro-example of unethical practice within the hospitality industry. The act itself may result in harm to the consumer (illness through drinking contaminated water), and benefits the restaurateur (at least in the short term) by reducing their production costs.

One response to ethical issues around products and services is *caveat emptor,* or let the buyer beware. If someone is foolish enough to not check their water bottle for tampering, then surely they almost deserve to get sick? However, is such a response an ethical response? Is there a role for the hospitality industry in providing checks and balances, and encouraging ethical (and safe) practices that may preclude such behaviour?

This chapter considers such questions, ranging from the micro issues such as the water-bottle scam above, to wider and more pervasive ethical infringements, particularly around the representation (or misrepresentation) of products and services. We illustrate a range of unethical practices from across the hospitality sector, and from associated marketing activities, and discuss why practitioners should behave more ethically. We include within this discussion the links between ethical practice and quality management. The chapter considers how managers within the sector currently approach ethical decision making, and examines alternative frameworks for a more ethical industry.

12.2 THE CASE FOR A MORE ETHICAL HOSPITALITY INDUSTRY?

Two decades ago, the comment was made that ethics is the central element in most of the critical issues of the hospitality industry (Whitney 1990). Commentators at the time called for the development of a more ethical approach within the industry (e.g. Krohn and Ahmed 1992). In their 1999 article entitled 'Ethics in tourism: reality or hallucination?' Fleckenstein and Huebsch assert that international tourism and hospitality operate within a paradigm of 'profit-driven megabusiness' (1999: 137) and that this results in many ethical problems for the industry. Such problems range from quality control and maintaining truth in the representation of products and services to wider macro-scale issues that pervade the industry – such as 'greenwashing' or unethical marketing practices that misrepresent the environmental aspects of products and services (e.g. Wight 1993; Lansing and De Vries 2007). Hudson and Miller (2005), for example, describe as 'exploitive' the marketing behaviour of mountain resorts that communicate a strong environmental message within their promotional material but have little or no environmentally responsible action.

The accommodation sector faces its own set of ethical problems; Haywood (1987) writes of serious ethical issues facing hoteliers, including the taking of kickbacks and gifts from suppliers within the sector, the hiding of income from tax authorities, the lack of investment in installing and maintaining safety and security systems, and the raiding of competitors' staff (Haywood 1987 in Whitney 1990). Whitney (1990) adds to the list – overbooking, a standard practice in the accommodation sector (asking if it is not a lie to 'guarantee' a non-existent room for a guest?) and liability for customer safety/behaviour around the use of liquor (Wheeler and Cooper 1994).

Upchurch (1998) provides the following list of ethical issues confronting hospitality management (see also Lynn (2012) for a review of recent hospitality ethics research):

- Guest rights
- Empowerment of employees
- Sexual harassment
- Equal opportunity
- Departmental relations
- Vendor relationships
- Yield management
- Community and public relations
- Balancing personal and organisational values.

Perhaps the most commonly reported problems, however, are around the issue of truth in advertising (Dunfee and Black 1996). Many of us have experienced something like that of the individual described below by Fleckenstein and Huebsch, who sees a brochure promotion for a 'luxury' hotel...

> The tourist is intrigued and calls for reservations at the 'five star' hotel and plans a fun-filled vacation for the family no matter what it costs...Upon arrival, one finds a 'one star' hotel with a pond in the back stocked with minnows; a nine-hole overgrown par-three golf course; a wading pool that hasn't been cleaned in years, and includes a 'hunt' for the maid with the towels and clean sheets. There is plenty of quiet, since there is nothing to do.
>
> (Fleckenstein and Huebsch 1999: 138)

The questions is, was the brochure accurate or ethical in its presentation or was it only (harmlessly) exaggerating a bit? (Fleckenstein and Huebsch 1999: 138). They believe that little attention has been paid to the ethical marketing of the tourism/hospitality product, and that, overall, quality is not a concern, rather, just the bottom line. In fact, ethical representation has been such an issue within the industry that in 1989, an NGO, the International Institute for Quality and Service in Ethics and Tourism, was founded with the express purpose of promoting ethical practices within the tourism industry.

But truth in advertising, fair pricing and ethical business practice have been concerns since ancient times. Over two thousand years ago philosophers such as Aristotle and Cicero were analysing marketing ethics problems not too different from what we face today (Nill and Schibrowsky 2007). Aristotle gave lectures on the vices and virtues of merchants and tradesmen, while both the New and Old Testaments of the Bible referenced proper ways to do business (Fennell 2006). And while we might think that shrinking steaks and smaller burgers are a problem of the twenty-first century, as long ago as 1923, the US National Restaurant Association was addressing concerns over how restaurateurs were representing their fare. The association actually published standards that included accuracy in menus – yet there are still ongoing problems regarding truth-in-menu standards (Whitney 1990). Whitney asks 'do consumers have a right to full and accurate disclosure regarding menu items'? (1990: 60).

From an ethical perspective the *caveat emptor* argument is not ideal, and it certainly does little to enhance the reputation of the industry. Such an approach assumes that the consumer appropriates all liability at the time of purchase, and arguably while such an approach may be defensible for *some* products, in the tourism and hospitality industry where an often distant product is pre-purchased, sight-unseen and untested, *caveat emptor* is even less justifiable. Importantly, *caveat emptor* is not unconditional, and if the seller uses deceit to promote the virtues of a product or service, and that product or service is 'faulty' then there are grounds for redress (Gibson 2007). But neither is the opposite scenario of strict liability the ethical solution, where the provider is responsible for *all* the consequences from a product or service. Obviously, an ethical path lies in between these extremes.

Note that conspicuous in its absence from lists of ethical issues in the hospitality industry is the issue of guest health and safety. This is perhaps attributable to health and safety being conceived of as *legal* rather than *ethical* responsibilities – both by industry and researchers in the field. Although this chapter does not specifically address tourism health and safety, the frameworks that we discuss below can be applied to ethical responsibilities in this respect. We also recommend these additional sources:

Mansfeld, Y. and Pizam, A. (2006) *Tourism, Safety, and Security: From Theory to Practice*, Oxford: Elsevier Butterworth-Heinemann.
Hall, C.M.,Timothy, D.J. and Duval, D.T. (eds) (2003) *Safety and Security in Tourism: Relationships, Management and Marketing*, Binghamton, NY: Haworth Hospitality Press.
Hall, D. and Brown, F. (2006) *Tourism and Welfare: Ethics, Responsibility and Sustained Wellbeing*, Wallingford: CABI (Chapter 3).

12.3 MANAGERS' APPROACHES TO ETHICS

The poor ethical practices observed within the hospitality sector have been explained away by the argument that 'hotel managers do not tend to be philosophers' (Whitney 1990: 61). The counter-argument to this is that we don't need to be a police officer to obey the law. Specialised knowledge of moral philosophy is not a precursor to (nor a guarantee of) ethical behaviour. Nevertheless, Whitney does make the useful distinction between 'operational' and 'ideological' components of ethics. He notes that managers tend to approach ethical problems in technical terms (e.g. using financial data, product specifications, marketing strategies and occupancy rates in their decision making). Any ethical aspect of a problem is thus only partly addressed, and then only in operational, technical and/or behavioural terms. The point that Whitney is making is that managers are generally poorly prepared to deal with problems 'holistically', since such an approach would include the philosophical aspect. Holistic, in-depth solutions are difficult to find due to (Whitney 1990: 61):

1 The complex philosophical nature of ethics
2 A lack of descriptive categories which managers can find practical and applicable
3 The absence of a dynamic code of ethics which would guide managers in decision making.

In a study of the ethical orientations of over one hundred hotel managers, it was found that managers commonly based their behaviour on 'tried and true' principles developed in their formative years (Whitney 1990). This, however, becomes problematic when the demands of business are not harmonious with such traditional values, because in a 'business is business' scenario, the manager's strong traditional values may 'get shoved aside' (1990: 66). Whitney (1990: 67) goes on to define what makes a good manager:

> The marks of excellence in managers is that they be technically skilled in their craft, experienced, educated, mature, and have the ability to hold high ethical ground under fire. More than any attribute, the latter characterises the true professional.

In another study that sought to determine the ethical principles used by managers in hotels and motels, Upchurch and Ruhland (1996) identified the three main ethical precepts of:

- Egoism (self-interest)
- Benevolence (care and concern for others)
- Principle (adhering to internalised or external rules and regulations).

In applying these ethical precepts, the managers drew upon three main referent sources: individual values; values emanating from the immediate work setting; and values exerted from society at large. Most decisions, however, were based upon benevolence with managers employing values from the immediate work setting. While Upchurch and Ruhland describe this as maximising the best interest for organisational members within the prescribed boundaries of the organisation, it does pose problems for organisations that do not have well-established ethical norms, or for those organisations whose norms are substantially at odds with those of greater society.

12.4 MARKETING ETHICS

Marketing is the functional area within business most often cited with ethical abuse (Dunfee et al. 1999; Murphy and Laczniak 1981 in Wheeler 1995). This is attributed to the link between marketing and the process of exchange (Chonko and Hunt 1985; Dubinsky and Loken 1989; both in Wheeler 1995). The marketing professional has relationships with other parties in the exchange process: 'Each party is owed duties and has responsibilities to the extent that the fulfilment of these leads to conflicts and marketing ethical problems' (Wheeler 1995: 38). Exacerbating matters, the global integration of markets and marketing assisted by rapid improvements in electronic communication have helped to compound ethical problems for marketers (Nill and Schibrowsky 2007).

Evidence from the Gallup Polls, that report on the perceived ethics of different professions, show that marketers rank near the bottom in terms of honesty and ethical standards (Advertising Age 2002 in Nill and Schibrowsky 2007). Ethical issues around marketing include (2007: 257):

- Product liability
- Personal selling techniques
- False or misleading advertising
- Product dumping

- Price gouging
- Marketing to low-income earners ('disadvantaged consumers')
- Foreign child labour.

Subsequently, Nill and Schibrowsky (2007) pose a range of questions for marketers, some of which are presented below:

- How should firms define their ethical responsibility?
- How should firms make ethical decisions in marketing?
- What should be the marketers' responsibility towards vulnerable consumers?
- What ethical decisions should marketers take when operating in foreign cultures with different value systems?
- What should marketers' ethical responsibility be towards society?
- What should be the role of consumer sovereignty?
- What is the relationship between ethics and profits?

With such a range of 'sticky' issues, it is unsurprising that commentators have called for a greater focus on marketing ethics, which has been defined as 'an inquiry into the nature and grounds of moral judgements, standards and rules of conduct relating to marketing decisions and marketing situations' (Vitell 1986 cited in Yaman and Gurel 2006: 470).

While there is a broad range of ethical issues facing the marketing sector, a particularly common theme is that of 'truth', and specifically the distinction between consumer and scientific truth in product claims (Davis 1992 in Wheeler 1995). Truth is especially important in the marketing of services, as they cannot readily be examined and tested before purchase. For tourism and hospitality, the service can be conceived of as a 'performance' rather than a physical good, leading to problems of standardisation and control. Similarly, the tourism 'product' is an amalgam of several products (e.g. transport, accommodation, attractions) often from different suppliers. As tourism is an experience based upon expectation, it is the marketer's role to present this image (of a service or destination) and create awareness. But Wheeler (1995) notes that the role of the marketer is also to ensure that the image they present is consistent with reality and introduces no product violations (of truth). However, it could be argued that this is not the *sole* responsibility of just the marketer, and is, rather, a shared responsibility of all stakeholders on the supply side – particularly those who take profit from such marketing activities.

In a similar manner to that described above for hospitality managers, marketing professionals are also 'torn' between the conflicting demands of the different stakeholders within the marketing exchange. This includes their own individual ethics (beliefs and values), their professional ethics (those dictated by the marketing profession) and the organisation's ethics (those dictated by the particular firm or body for which they work) (Wheeler 1995). However, it is argued that marketers must first perceive that ethics is important or beneficial to their organisation before their behaviours will become more ethical (Yaman and Gurel 2006).

So how can marketers behave more ethically? From a review of the prescriptive literature (i.e. literature that tells us how we *ought* to behave) on marketing ethics, Gaski (1999) concluded that marketers would be acting ethically as long as they heeded the law and acted in their own self-interest. Such a stance has been rejected, however, by writers such as Smith (2001) who point out that obeying the law, while being necessary, is not sufficient requirement for good conduct: 'There are many situations where the law and self interest are too inconsistent to provide any guidance for marketers' (2001: 8).

To help guide us in this respect, Laczniak and Murphy (1993: 49–51 in Dunfee et al. 1999: 16) propose a list of questions that could be used to evaluate the ethics of marketing practices:

1 Does the contemplated action violate the law? (*legal test*)
2 Is this action contrary to widely accepted moral obligations? (*duties test*)
3 Does the proposed action violate any other special obligations that stem from the type of marketing organisation at focus? (*special obligations test*)
4 Is the intent of the contemplated action harmful? (*motives test*)
5 Is it likely that any major damages to people or organisations will result from the contemplated action? (*consequences test*)
6 Is there a satisfactory alternative action that produces equal or greater benefits to the parties affected than the proposed action? (*utilitarian test*)
7 Does the contemplated action infringe on property rights, privacy rights, or the inalienable rights of the consumer? (*rights test*)
8 Does the proposed action leave another person or group less well off? Is this person or group already a member of a relatively underprivileged class? (*justice test*)

A 'yes' to any of the questions indicates that the marketer's decision is probably unethical and should be reconsidered. However, there are pragmatic problems with this approach: 'If every type of ethical theory must be satisfied, few marketing decisions would be likely to pass muster' (Dunfee et al. 1999: 16). Furthermore, it is also noted that a 'yes' to some questions may be a 'no' in other contexts. For example, 'a duty of justice that contemplates some reasonably equivalent distribution of benefits may consistently conflict with shareholder property rights' (1999: 16).

DISCUSSION POINT: ETHICAL DESTINATION MARKETING

The 'sun sand and sea' mass tourism market is very important for destinations. Some destinations, it would seem, are prepared to go to extremes to sell the quality of their offerings, as revealed in the following three news items.

> The images of beautiful beaches accompanied by humorous slogans were meant to tempt British tourists over to France during the London Olympics. But yesterday the joke was on the French after it emerged that posters designed to advertise the delights of Northern France and the Mediterranean actually show a beach in South Africa. Tourism bosses in France spent more than £500,000 on the campaign, which involved newspaper adverts and 23 posters plastered all over the London Underground for three weeks this month.

Figure 12.1 *A beautiful beach ... but where is it?*

Unfortunately for them, however, the advertising agency inadvertently used an image of a beach in Cape Town – some 5,500 miles away from France – in two of the posters. The offending poster features a family running along the sand and the words 'Sprint finish on the Northern France Coast' – one of what the French tourist board describes as 'humorous' Olympics-related slogans...the South African Llandudno is one of Cape Town's most exclusive suburbs and is famed locally for its spectacular beach and impressive surf...Having been alerted to the error, French tourism bosses replaced the 'Northern France' image on their website.

Source: Newling, D. (2012) 'France's shifting sands: Tourist chiefs tempt Brits...with a picture of Cape Town' <http://www.dailymail.co.uk/news/ article-2121120/Frances-shifting-sands-Tourist-chiefs-tempt-Brits – picture-Cape-Town.html#ixzz22Sa5HrFp>

Talk about false advertising...a tourism board in Spain has admitted to using images of the Caribbean in their travel campaign, as their own beaches didn't cut the mustard. The picture, taken by Getty Images in the Bahamas, was used in posters produced by the Costa Brava tourism board in Spain...Tourism board director Dolors Batallé was unrepentant when called out on the scam. She said she was unable to find images 'of sufficient quality' of the real Costa Brava.

Source: Whitley, D. (2010) 'Worst ever travel promos' <http://travel. ninesn.com.au/world/920875/worst-ever-tourism-promotions>

Tourism Australia chiefs have been left red-faced over a misleading scene in a $250 million advertising campaign. The campaign, aimed at 18 key markets, was launched in Shanghai....However, in Australia some media organisations were yesterday sent an inaccurate promotional package, with a screenshot of Seal Bay on Kangaroo Island off South Australia wrongly labelled as the Freycinet

Peninsula in Tasmania. Compounding the confusion, the scene shows a couple walking unaccompanied along the beach at Seal Bay, with a bottle of wine and two glasses in hand. Access to the beach is in fact by guided tour only in the presence of a ranger. Visitors also have to stay in a group, and they can only observe the rare sea lions there from a distance. Alcohol is not allowed...'There was a bit of creative licence used in the end.' A Tourism Australia spokeswoman said a ranger was present at all times during the filming.

Source: Owen, M. (2012) 'Fur flies over romantic ad's false promise' <http://www.theaustralian.com.au/national-affairs/fur-flies-over-romantic-ads-false-promise/story-fn59niix-1226383952182>

Discussion questions

1 In the first two cases above, if the beaches used in the promotional images are similar to the beaches that they are meant to portray, then is this really an ethical issue?
2 Is it ethical for destination marketers to use digitally manipulated images to enhance the attractiveness of their destinations?
3 In the third case, is 'creative licence' an excuse for unethical marketing practices?
4 If destinations and communities benefit from increased tourism spending resulting from the use of such images in marketing campaigns, does this outweigh any ethical problems associated with their use?

Exercise

Apply Laczniak and Murphy's (1993) set of questions (as listed in the previous section) to each of these cases.

12.6 ETHICAL BEHAVIOURS IN MARKETING AND HOSPITALITY

To understand different management approaches towards ethical issues in the tourism and hospitality industry, it is important to draw upon normative theories which attempt to explain ethical decision making (Yaman and Gurel 2006). One such theory is 'Ethics Position Theory' (EPT) developed by Forsyth (1980). EPT maintains that individuals' personal moral philosophies influence their judgements, actions and emotions in ethically intense situations. The theory is grounded in the work of psychologists Kohlberg (1976) and Piaget (1932) (both in Forsyth and O'Boyle 2011). This theory assumes that moral actions and evaluations are the outward expression of a person's 'integrated conceptual system of personal ethics, or ethics position' (Forsyth and O'Boyle 2011: 354). Forsyth's framework identifies two basic dimensions of personal moral philosophy – idealism and relativism. Relativism refers to the extent to which the individual 'rejects universal moral rules' (Forsyth 1980: 175). Idealistic individuals, on the other hand, 'tend to make use of moral absolutes when making judgements and believe the morally "right" behaviour always leads to positive and desirable consequences' (Forsyth 1980: 175). Forsyth uses this dichotomy to develop a taxonomy supporting four distinct moral philosophies (Figure 12.2).

	Low Relativism	High Relativism
High Idealism	**Absolutists:** Principled idealists who believe people should act in ways that are consistent with moral rules, for doing so will in most cases yield the best outcomes for all concerned	**Situationists:** Idealistic contextualists who favor securing the best possible consequences for all concerned even if doing so will violate traditional rules that define what is right and what is wrong
Low Idealism	**Exceptionists:** Principled pragmatists who endorse moral rules as guides for action, but admit that following rules will not necessarily generate the best consequences for all concerned	**Subjectivists:** Pragmatic relativists who base their ethical choices on personal considerations, such as individualized values, moral emotions, or an idiosyncratic moral philosophy

Figure 12.2 *Ethical position matrix.*
Source: Forsyth (2012) Available at <http://donforsyth.wordpress.com/ethics/the-epq/>

The four positions relate to specific moral philosophies, for example the absolutist position is consistent with deontology, while the exceptionist position is consistent with teleology, and utilitarianism. Forsyth (1980) developed the Ethics Position Questionnaire (EPQ) to assess personal moral philosophy. It asks individuals to indicate their acceptance of items that vary in terms of relativism and idealism.

> The relativism scale includes items such as 'Different types of moralities cannot be compared as to "rightness"' and 'What is ethical varies from one situation to another.' The idealism scale, measures one's perspective on positive and negative consequences with such items as 'A person should make certain that their actions never intentionally harm another even to a small degree' and 'If an action could harm an innocent other then it should not be done.'
>
> (Forsyth, 1980: 178 in Forsyth and O'Boyle 2011: 354)

Studies undertaken in the USA have shown that the situational position is the common preference of marketing managers there (Pratt 1994). However, such situational ethics has been criticised as being a 'non-ethics' or an 'anti-ethics'. Merrill (1975) argues that when a matter of ethics is watered down to subjectivism, to situations or contexts, it loses all its meaning as ethics:

> if there are no absolutes in ethics, then we should scrap the whole subject of moral philosophy and simply be satisfied that each person can run his life by his whims or 'consideration' that may change from situation to situation.
>
> (Merrill 1975: 16 in Pratt 1994: 73)

Yaman and Gurel (2006) have undertaken one of the few empirical studies of the ethical ideologies of tourism marketers, applying EPT in their study. They were interested in identifying the antecedents for ethical decision making, e.g. some research indicates that gender, culture, education and size of organisation are influential factors. The study compared tourism marketers in Australia and Turkey, revealing some cultural differences, in that Turkish marketers were more idealistic *and* more relativistic than their Australian counterparts. Another significant finding relates to organisational size: the larger the organisation, the less likely were marketing managers to consider that ethics is important for the organisation (2006: 483).

CASE STUDY: CULTURE AND ETHICS IN THE SUPPLY CHAIN

Outbound tourism from China has grown substantially in recent years, and destinations such as Australia have faced issues over maintaining the quality of the visitor experience for this relatively new inbound market. Unethical practices in the tourism supply chain from China to Australia are described as one of the biggest issues for tourism practitioners and authorities in Australia (Keating 2008). The problem is associated with package tours, heavily discounted, for which the costs for the operators are heavily subsidised by commission-based shopping. Such tours are referred to as 'zero-fare' tours, and are problematic not only because of the impact upon the travel experiences of individuals, but also because of the shear dominance of package tours within the industry (Chen and Mak 2011; March 2008).

The problems experienced by Chinese tourists participating in such tours include (Chen and Mak 2011; Keating 2008):

- Misrepresentation of the product
- Default on contracted services
- Changing travel itinerary without consultation or approval
- Inducing tourists to spend money on what they do not need
- Low service quality
- Inadequately skilled guides
- Limited choice in shopping
- Requesting tips from tourists
- Deceitful dealings at the destination.

Table 12.1 elaborates on such unethical practices in Australia. The China National Tourism Authority has reported complaints from Chinese nationals visiting Australia and experiencing the problems listed above, for example being asked to pay more for their tours because they did not spend enough in gift shops (DRET 2008 in Keating 2008). The main problem in this issue appears to be unethical practices within the supply chain, especially in terms of the financial relationships between outbound tourism operators in China and inbound tourism operators in Australia.

In Figure 12.3 March (2008) presents the antecedents, impacts and outcomes of unethical practices in the supply chain. Importantly, March identifies that different ethical norms apply in the tourism industries of the destination and

Table 12.1 *Categories of unethical practice in the Chinese inbound market*

Category	Practices
Business-to-business (B2B) practices	• *Gifts/Favours/Entertainment*: lavish gifts, gifts after completion of transaction, funding of personal expenses through provision of (limitless) credit card • *Pricing*: includes unfair differential pricing, questionable invoicing (where the buyer requests a written invoice showing a price other than the actual price paid), and providing some component services at below cost (e.g. hotel accommodation) • *Excessive Commissions to Channel Members*: unreasonably large commissions or fees paid to channel members, such as overseas wholesalers, inbound tour operators, and guide companies • *Unfair market entry barriers*: duty-free stores and other retailers offer coaches and tour guides free of charge to overseas wholesalers, thereby erecting barriers to market entry.
Consumer practices	• *Overcharging*: (1) fees applied under guise of local council fees (e.g. for permission to enter a national park) when no fees apply; (2) charging separately for a departure tax, even though the said tax is already included in the price of the air ticket; (3) prices are quoted in US$ instead of A$ and the difference is pocketed; and (4) forcing customers into retail outlets that charge exorbitant prices • *Degrading the tourism experience*: (1) the location of major retail shopping precincts is withheld from tourists to ensure intermediaries control where and when tourists shop; (2) tour commentaries focus on selling products and not on educating tourists about Australian history or culture; (3) charging inflated prices for goods due to large commissions paid to intermediaries by retail outlets; and (4) incorrectly representing a product as made in Australia, or that the shop is a licensed duty-free store.

Source: March (2008).

source market: 'practices viewed as unethical in Australia are regarded simply as "how business is done around here" in certain overseas countries' (2008: 295). While acknowledging these cultural differences in business practice, Keating (2008) defines unethical business practice to be (universally) 'those specific actions by a travel intermediary that impact negatively on the tourists'

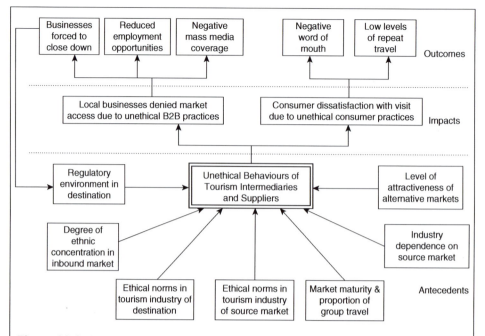

Figure 12.3 *Antecedents, impacts and outcomes of unethical practices.*
Source: March (2008: 293).

satisfaction with the travel experience and their perception of the destination'
(2008: 404). He proposes a 'best practice model' for managing ethics in the
tourism supply chain (2008: 407) which includes (among others) 'Creat[ing]
a strong business case for managing ethics in the tourism supply chain and
us[ing] this to generate stakeholder support'.

Discussion questions

1 In previous chapters we have discussed cultural and ethical relativism.
   Does cultural relativism apply here?
   a Can a business practice that is acceptable (ethical) in China be
      unacceptable (unethical) in Australia?
   b How do we resolve the two sets of business norms?
2 What actions do you think could be included in a best practice model for
   ethics in the tourism supply chain?
3 Who has ethical responsibility for ensuring that such actions are taken?
4 The Australian Tourism Export Council (the 'peak body' for inbound
   tourism) 'encourages' rather than 'requires' its members to engage in
   appropriate behaviour (March 2008).
   a Are there problems with this approach?
   b Is the Council behaving ethically?
   c If not, why not?

References

Chen, Y. and Mak, B. (2011) 'Testing for moral hazard at the tourist destination', *International Journal of Tourism Sciences*, 11(2): 1–37.

Keating, B. (2008) 'Managing ethics in the tourism supply chain: The case of Chinese travel to Australia', *International Journal of Tourism Research*, 11(4): 403–8.

March, R. (2008) 'Towards a conceptualization of unethical marketing practices in tourism: a Case-study of Australia's inbound Chinese travel market', *Journal of Travel & Tourism Marketing*, 24(4): 285–96.

Useful sources: best practice in non-western cultures

It is beyond the scope of this book to consider the range of business practices in non-Western cultures, however, the sources below may be useful:

Alshersan, B.A. (2011) *The Principles of Islamic Marketing,* Farnham: Gower.

Christie, P., Kwon, I. and Stoeberl, P. (2003) 'A cross-cultural comparison of ethical attitudes of business managers: India, Korea and the United States', *Journal of Business Ethics,* 46: 263–87.

Commers, M.S.R., Vandekerckhove, W. and Verlinden, A. (2008) *Ethics in an Era of Globalization,* Aldershot: Ashgate.

Enderle, G. (ed.) (1999) *International Business Ethics: Challenges and Approaches*, Notre Dame, IN: University of Notre Dame Press.

Fennell, D. (2006) *Tourism Ethics*, Clevedon: Channel View (see Chapter 10: Theerapappisit's model of Buddhist ethics).

Gosh, B. (2006) *Ethics in Management and Indian Ethos*, New Delhi: Vaikos Publishers.

Jayamami, C.V. (2008) *Hindu Business Values.* Available at <http://manomohanam-manomohanam.blogspot.co.nz>

LeFebvre, R. (2011) 'Cross-cultural comparison of business ethics in the U.S. and India: A study of business codes of conduct', *Journal of Emerging Knowledge on Emerging Markets.* Available at <http://digitalcommons.kennesaw.edu/cgi/viewcontent.cgi?article=1055&context=jekem>

Lu, X. and Enderle, G. (eds) (2006) *Developing Business Ethics in China*, New York: Palgrave.

12.7 A GENERAL THEORY OF MARKETING ETHICS

A number of ethical frameworks have been applied to marketing. However, broadly, deontology and teleology have been favoured (Williams and Murphy 1990) (see Chapter 2 for a description of these ethical theories). Hunt and Vitell (1986) posit that 'any positive theory of ethics must account for both the deontological and teleological aspects of the evaluation process' (1986: 7). Similarly, Ferrell et al. (1989) propose a 'synthesis' model of ethical decision making.

Hunt and Vitell's (1986, 2006) general theory of marketing ethics (Figure 12.4) has dominated ethical debate within the field. The theory is based on deontological and teleological traditions in moral philosophy. To remind readers about these positions, for deontologists, 'certain features of the act itself, other than the value it brings into existence' make an action or rule right (Frankena 1963: 14 in Hunt and Vitell 2006: 144); while

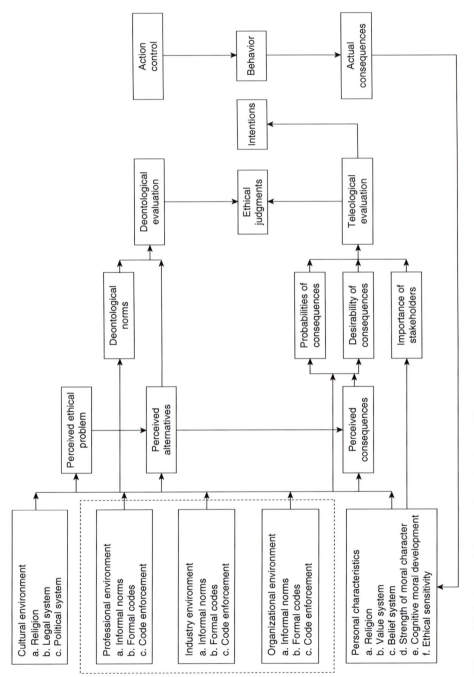

Figure 12.4 *General theory of marketing ethics.*
Source: Hunt and Vitell (2006).

teleologists believe 'that there is only one basic or ultimate right-making characteristic, namely the comparative value (non moral) of what is, probably will be, or is intended to be brought into being' (Frankena 1963: 14 in Hunt and Vitell 2006: 144).

However, the general theory of marketing ethics also incorporates other concepts:

- Integrative social contracts (see below in this chapter)
- Moral intensity (also see Chapter 4)
- Opportunity
- Religiosity
- Organisational commitment
- Machiavellianism
- Strength of moral character
- Cognitive moral development
- Ethical sensitivity.

The theory, although developed originally for the marketing context, has wider application. It addresses situations where an individual encounters problems perceived to have an ethical content. This perception triggers the process depicted in Figure 12.4, producing an evoked set of alternative actions (note the evoked set will be smaller than the complete set of possible alternatives, simply because the individual will not be aware of all alternatives) which are evaluated using deontological or teleological frameworks (Hunt and Vitell 2006). In a deontological evaluation the individual evaluates the inherent rightness or wrongness of the behaviours implied by each alternative:

> the process involves comparing each alternative's behaviours with a set of predetermined deontological norms. These norms represent personal values or rules of moral behaviour. They range from (1) General beliefs about things such as honesty, stealing, cheating and treating people fairly to (2) Issue specific belief about things such as deceptive advertising, product safety, sales 'kickbacks' etc.
>
> (Hunt and Vitell 2006: 145)

Deontological norms may represent 'hypernorms' or universal principles, and local norms. The teleological evaluation process focuses on four constructs (Hunt and Vitell 2006: 145):

1 The perceived consequences of each alternative for various stakeholder groups
2 The probability that each consequence will occur to each stakeholder group
3 The desirability or undesirability of each consequence
4 The importance of each stakeholder group.

The core of the model is ethical judgement – or the belief that a particular alternative is the most ethical alternative, and is a function of the individual's deontological and teleological evaluation. These evaluations exist in various mixes of importance: some individuals in some situations may be strict deontologists and may completely ignore the consequences of alternative actions; in other situations, some may be strict teleologists (Hunt and Vitell 2006: 145).

The model recognises several personal characteristics that might influence the ethical decision-making process such as age, gender and religiosity (strength of religious convictions), along with the role of the cultural, industry, professional and organisational environments (Hunt and Vitell 2006: 146). One important factor is 'action control' or the extent to which the individual 'exerts control in the enactment of an intention in a particular situation' (2006: 146). For example, in some scenarios, an employee may not be able to enact what they consider the most ethical action because they are precluded from doing so by a directive from their supervisor, or board of directors.

Hunt and Vitell (2006) note that there have been 'scores' of empirical studies that, overall, provide strong support for their theory. They are confident that the general theory of marketing ethics can provide a framework that assists business practitioners in 'navigating the moral mazes of contemporary business practice' (2006: 151).

12.8 VIRTUE ETHICS FOR TOURISM MARKETERS?

Apart from deontology and teleology, other ethical frameworks have seldom been explored for marketing. Considering the multitude of ethical frameworks, a focus on these two is perhaps short-sighted (Nill and Schibrowsky 2007). The acknowledged shortcomings of deontological and teleological approaches have led to other ethical frameworks being advocated. As noted in Chapter 2, utilitarianism faces problems around forecasting unknowable futures and with comparing different types of utilities. Duty-based (deontological) approaches also face problems in that for some situations there may be no obvious duties that can be invoked, or such duties may be in conflict: 'In many business related contexts, duty-based theories produce conflicting obligations without any clear-cut method for resolving the conflicts' (Dunfee et al. 1999: 16). The shortcomings of the above approaches have led some researchers in the area to comment that these 'grand narratives' of moral philosophy seem inadequate for the complex context of marketing (Robin and Reidenbach 1993 in Dunfee et al. 1999: 16).

In light of these shortcomings, virtue ethics is one alternative ethical framework that has been promoted as having promise for guiding the behaviour of marketers (Williams and Murphy 1990; Ross 2003). Virtue ethics was the main form of ethical theory in ancient and medieval times, but has experienced a revival in recent years and is now the third 'big' ethical theory beside deontology and teleology (Kuusela 2011). This re-emergence is largely due to dissatisfaction with Kantian ethics (deontology) and utilitarianism (teleology) both of which 'largely ignore issues of moral education, moral character and issues of emotion in relation to morality' (Kuusela 2011: 109).

Based on Aristotle's (384–322 BC) ethics of virtue, this approach argues that ethics are acquired, that acting virtuously is its own reward, and that virtuous decision makers act primarily to be true to themselves: 'An ethics of virtue assumes that being human entails living in a community and developing certain virtues or skills required for a human life with others' (Williams and Murphy 1990: 23). Such virtues include honesty, truthfulness, compassion, loyalty and justice – virtues relating to and developed from the classical virtues espoused by Plato, Aristotle and Cicero (prudence, justice, courage and temperance). It is argued that only a person who has developed these moral virtues will perceive the right moral dilemmas and make correct judgements. According to Aristotle, virtues entail 'affectivity', a learned behaviour that influences a person's ability to 'see' the moral dimensions of a situation.

Virtues are not entirely ignored in Kantian ethics or in utilitarian approaches; however, they are seen as means to an end, rather than as ends themselves. For virtue ethics, it is the virtues that form the foundation of morality: 'The morally good or right is not determined in terms of some overarching moral principle, but good or right is whatever is virtuous or whatever the virtuous person would choose' (Kuusela 2011: 110). This theory is thus agent-centred rather than rule- or consequence-centred.

To come back to the issue of tourism marketing, the theory of virtue has a bearing on the type of marketing mix decisions a company or manager makes, and has implications for product, pricing, channel and promotional decisions (Williams and Murphy 1990). For example, for product decisions, the theory of virtue would emphasise the product's effect on consumers' lives. For pricing, a virtue approach would require marketers to place price in a perspective understandable to the potential market, e.g. 'confusing airline fares may not meet the moral requirements of pricing products. Yet complex fares may be viewed as more ethical (that is, virtuous) than a simple monopoly price charged to consumers' (1990: 27). Williams and Murphy note that 'the theory of virtue would emphasise the price–value trade-off about which consumers are concerned when entering into the exchange process for products' (1990: 27).

In discussing the relationship between virtue ethics and promotions, Williams and Murphy note that the literature is divided among those who believe that persuasive advertising is either: moral as long as it promotes a useful or essential product; never good; or good as long as it does not affect individual autonomy. They believe that the theory of virtue would demand that marketers 'think about how advertising influences recipients' (1990: 27). Overall, it is the focus of virtue ethics on the character of the person that can bring value to the analysis of marketers' and entrepreneurs' activities within the tourism industry (Ross 2003).

Further reading on virtue ethics

Gardiner, S.M. (ed.) (2005) *Virtue Ethics, Old and New,* Ithaca, NY: Cornell University Press.
Winter, M. (2012) *Rethinking Virtue Ethics*, New York: Springer.

12.9 INTEGRATED SOCIAL CONTRACT THEORY

Social contract theory is a further ethical alternative that has been advocated for guiding marketing practices. Social contract theory (see also Chapter 8) has its origins in the social upheavals of the seventeenth and eighteenth centuries. The decline of feudalism and rejection of the divine right of kings as a basis for obedience to the state gave rise to a search for a philosophy that legitimised state authority (Dunfee et al. 1999). John Locke (1632–1704), building on the work of Thomas Hobbes (1588–1679), proposed that a 'social contract' justified the existence of the state, and identified the obligations of citizens and the state (Dunfee et al. 1999) (e.g. Locke's ideas informed the American Revolution, the US Declaration of Independence and the US Constitution).

Three elements are common to most social contract theories:

1 The consent of the individual
2 Agreement among moral agents
3 A device or method by which an agreement is obtained.

Note that an 'agreement' may be actual or hypothetical. However, critics of the theory deny the existence of actual contracts, and argue that hypothetical contracts cannot provide for meaningful consent and agreement (Dunfee et al. 1999). These criticisms aside, social contract theory is relevant to tourism and business settings, as it goes beyond defining the roles of the state and its citizens, and extends to business entities. Indeed, Donaldson (1982 in Dunfee et al. 1999) uses social contract theory to establish the moral foundation of the corporation, his argument based on the ethical advantages of a productive organisation versus a 'state of individual production'. According to Donaldson, the firm offers advantages to society (and its customers and employees) in exchange for the right to exist and prosper.

The relevance of social contract theory for marketing ethics (and ultimately to tourism and hospitality) lies in its shared focus on exchange. As noted earlier, the exchange relationship is central to marketing. Social contract theory, which is an exchange-based model of ethics, sheds light on a domain that is dominated by economic exchange (Dunfee et al. 1999). Dunfee et al. (1999) propose an 'Integrative' Social Contract Theory (ISCT) that incorporates the two different types of contract described above: hypothetical macrosocial contracts and actual microsocial contracts.

Central to the ISCT decision process (Figure 12.5) are norms of behaviour. These include norms based upon the 'millions' of community-based microsocial contracts that are

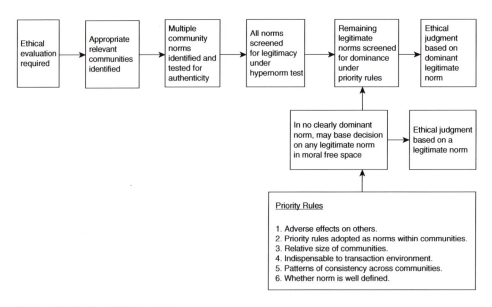

Figure 12.5 The ISCT decision process.
Source: Dunfee et al. (1999).

generated every day, but also the 'hypernorms' – principles that are fundamental to human existence (Dunfee et al. 1999). Dunfee et al. explain that some of the more challenging issues of marketing ethics involve conflicting legitimate norms. For example, in a tourism context, destination marketers may believe that some 'soft' deception in destination promotional material is acceptable in order to meet their clients' objectives and to contribute to the general economic welfare of the destination. The broader social community (including tourists) may have an opposite norm and believe that more accurate representation of the destination is required.

The ISCT addresses these problems by introducing three concepts: 'authentic norms' which clarify culturally specific norms, 'priority rules' which determine the rules of engagement when authentic norms clash, and 'hypernorms' which measure the value of authentic norms against a set of universally upheld values (Douglas 2000). In the above destination example, both norms are recognised as authentic, and both may be considered legitimate because neither violates a hypernorm. The ISCT outlines a process for resolving conflict between norms by specifying a set of six priority rules 'derived from the basic assumptions and terms of the macrosocial contract and influenced by concepts that underlie principles of international conflicts of law and dispute resolution' (Dunfee et al. 1999: 20). These rules include:

1 Transactions solely within a single community, which do not have significant adverse effects on other humans or communities, should be governed by the host community's norms;
2 Community norms for resolving priority should be applied, as long as they do not have significant adverse effects on other humans or communities;
3 The more extensive the community that is the source of the norm, the greater the priority that should be given to the norm;
4 Norms essential to the maintenance of the economic environment in which the transaction occurs should have priority over norms potentially damaging to that environment;
5 When multiple conflicting norms are involved, patterns of consistency among the alternative norms provide a basis for prioritisation;
6 Well-defined norms ordinarily should have priority over more general, less precise norms.

ISCT has advantages over other ethical approaches to business in that it specifies a core set of principles (hypernorms) 'that may be used to specify the line of the moral minimum that no marketing practitioner should ever cross' (Dunfee et al. 1999: 30). It also recognises that different communities (or interests) have different norms and it has a process for resolving potential conflict arising from these differences.

Despite some criticism around the identification and justification of hypernorms for actual decision making in companies, the ISCT has been described as 'arguably the most sophisticated and promising concept of business ethics to date' (Gilbert and Behnam 2009: 215). However, it is yet to be applied to issues within the tourism and hospitality industry. Considering the global nature of tourism and hospitality, coupled with the inherent ethical problems faced by the sector in terms of representing the tourism product, along with the range of stakeholder values or norms associated with many tourism issues, ISCT would seem to offer a useful framework.

Useful source

Donaldson, T. and Dunfee, T.W. (1999) *Ties That Bind: A Social Contracts Approach to Business Ethics*, Boston, MA: Harvard University Press.

DISCUSSION POINT: WEB 2.0 AND ETHICS IN HOSPITALITY

The term Web 2.0 is defined as a 'perceived second generation of Web-based services – such as social networking sites, wikis, communication tools…that emphasise online collaboration and sharing among users' (Wikipedia in O'Connor 2010). As an empowering tool for consumers, Web 2.0 relies on user-generated content, harnessing the power of 'prosumers' – users who simultaneously produce and consume online content (Tapscott and Williams 2006). Such user-generated content is becoming increasingly important in the decision making of consumers, including tourists. Basically, the data posted on Web 2.0 about products and services are web-based 'word-of-mouth' recommendations – but with a quantum increase in reach and power. As such, this content has a high level of credibility in the eyes of the consumer as being unbiased and relevant (O'Connor 2010). Prosumption empowers consumers whose choices have until now been constrained by a top-down corporate culture and marketing industry (Bruns 2008). It is now more difficult for marketers to craft sales messages and position them in front of an uninformed and uncritical consumer (Kuehn 2011; O'Connor 2010).

Web 2.0 offers a mechanism, for example, through which the hospitality industry can become more ethical in its practices. TripAdvisor.com, is the world's largest online network of travel consumers. It claims to have over 32 million members and features over 75 million user-generated reviews and opinions on nearly half a million hotels and attractions worldwide. Their websites attract nearly 56 million monthly visitors (TripAdvisor 2012). By way of comparison, travel publisher Frommer's sells about 2.5 million paper guidebooks each year (O'Connor 2010). TripAdvisor displays 'detailed, rich and relevant' data for use by consumers in their travel planning (O'Connor 2010). The two reviews below (both at www.tripadvisor.com) are typical of negative feedback from users of accommodation (bear in mind that positive reviews, however, abound.)

'False advertising'

[We] Booked the room primarily because according to the web site they had hot tub rooms. We booked one and received confirmation. When we checked in we were told 'oh no – we don't have hot tub rooms.' They took a whopping $4.25 off our bill to compensate us. That will be the last time we stay at any Ramada Inn.

'Bed bugs and false advertising'

The staff was not very concerned or surprised when I awoke with bug bites on my body, head, hands and legs, and then reported this to them. No compensation has been tendered and I have been told that I would have to go to a physician to get the bites diagnosed at my expense, of course. The ad in the 'Travel Buddy' is misleading, there is only a waffle, no hot breakfast, and no restaurant on the premises.

Critics argue that sites such as TripAdvisor can be abused by hospitality providers, providing false reviews to enhance a hotel's reputation or to tarnish that of competitors. But O'Connor's (2010) analysis of 100 London hotels, suggests that fears that the system is compromised by false reviews posted are unfounded.

Discussion questions

1 Should critics be able to place anonymous reviews of a hotel or restaurant?
2 Is it ethical for hoteliers to post false 'positive' reviews of their premises, even if they are providing a high quality, faultless service?
3 Is it ethical for a service provider who has received a bad review, to then respond by posting a likewise 'bad review' of the guest?
4 Some critics view consumer-generated content as a form of free labour and prosumption as an exploitative practice (e.g. Cohen 2008). Discuss.
5 How does Web 2.0, and the Internet generally, challenge current models of ethical decision making and practice within the tourism and hospitality industry?

12.10 ETHICS AND QUALITY IN HOSPITALITY – A CONNECTION?

Some authors in the field have drawn a connection between ethical behaviour and quality in service provision (e.g. Lynch 1992 in Wong 1998; Wong 1998; Holjevac 2008). In the service industry, and in the hotel industry in particular, the ethical standards and behaviours of the direct service providers (i.e. the staff members) are described as critical components of the host–guest transaction:

> Consumers are not satisfied with just the 'hardware' or tangible elements of the hotel experience – their satisfaction depends much more on how they perceive they are treated by the hotel's staff.
>
> (Wong 1998: 107)

How they are treated includes how they are *ethically* treated. Total Quality Management (TQM) is a management approach that originated in the USA in the 1980s and which was adopted widely in Japan and elsewhere. It has long been used in hotel chains such as Ritz-Carlton and Marriott. TQM is a commitment to long-term success through customer satisfaction, and involves all members of an organisation participating in improving processes, products, services and the culture in which they work. TQM does not explicitly incorporate ethical behaviour, but some authors (e.g. Holjevac 2008) emphasise the importance of ethics as a dimension of TQM. It is proposed that the principles of quality together with ethics can transform TQM into 'total care management' (Lynch 1992 in Wong 1998).

In practice, this may be achieved through controlling the 'moments of truth', i.e. every interface between clients and staff members (Wong 1998). Wong believes that in order to ensure a consistently high quality service based on high ethical standards, it is important for managers to understand and influence the ethical values and job-related behaviours of employees. Sadly, however, a recent study of hotel general managers tells us that while managers realise that business ethics is an essential part of business success, 'most hotel companies have not incorporated or implemented ethics education into their training programmes' (Yeh 2012: 72).

Hotels pose an interesting challenge for ensuring ethical behaviour of their staff. Often they employ a young, lowly paid, diverse staff with rapid turnover (including staff in management positions). And to complicate matters, sometimes, as Wong (1998) points out, hotel guests themselves will attempt to induce employees to behave in an unethical manner (e.g. they may request a room upgrade, or may bribe an employee to ignore theft of hotel property). Wong (1998) undertook a survey of 299 employees from Hong Kong hotels, to investigate their job-related ethical beliefs. Three major service environments were chosen: housekeeping, front office and food and beverage departments. He found that workers' ethical behaviours could be grouped into four categories, examples of which are provided below (Wong 1998: 110):

1 No Harm
   • Making a telephone call in a guest room
   • Using the toilet in a guest room
   • Listening to the radio in a guest room
   • Watching TV or a hotel movie in a guest room
   • Drinking or eating company food at the back of the house.

2 Unethical behaviours
   • Consuming soft drinks in the bar before the bar is in operation
   • Not issuing a captain's order to the cashier while still getting food from kitchen to serve friends in the restaurant
   • Offering free coffee or tea to friends in the restaurant without issuing a captain's order
   • Consuming minibar beverages and charging them to a guest's account.

3 Actively benefitting
   • Breaking a glass or plate but blaming it on a guest's carelessness
   • Collecting leftover fruit from guests for self-consumption.

4 Passively benefitting
   • Accepting tips to arrange a room change for a guest
   • Eating leftover food items from the buffet at the back of the house.

Happily, the study found that most employees had higher than expected ethical standards. However, the study did indicate that problems could arise when employees needed to choose between satisfying a guest and following company policy. The study was set in Hong Kong, and the issue of competing norms was perhaps more of an issue in this location, because, as Wong points out, within the Chinese culture, reciprocity is highly recognised and practised. Thus employees tended to be more tolerant of unethical behaviour when a guest 'treats them well'. Thus it is OK to 'pay back the favour' to a guest even when the activity is unethical, e.g. accepting tips to arrange a room change for a guest.

CHAPTER REVIEW

This chapter has outlined the ethical issues facing the hospitality industry. A range of challenges exist within the sector, and currently there is little in the way of formal education or training in how to deal with ethical issues. The core issue in many ethical situations is the competing sets of norms that ethical decision makers must choose between or incorporate within their decision-making processes: personal, professional, organisational and wider societal norms of behaviour. The marketing practices of tourism and hospitality providers have been singled out as facing the greatest challenges of all. In particular, issues of truth in representation haunt the activities of marketers.

Ethics Position Theory (Forsyth 1980) provides a framework for considering the ethical behaviours of managers and employees within the sector. Currently, the ethical decision making of most managers within the sector is informed by personal experience and organisational norms. It would seem that there is potential to expand the ethical horizons of decision makers and, to this end, the chapter offers some frameworks including the General Theory of Marketing Ethics (Hunt and Vitell 1986, 2006) that can also be applied in a broad range of business-related settings, as tools to assist managers and employees to work through and resolve ethical problems. While this framework is largely informed by deontological and teleological evaluations of the problem, some authors suggest that alternative ethical theories may be of value within the sector. In particular, virtue ethics, and contract theory have been put forward, with the Integrated Social Contract Theory (Dunfee et al. 1999) offering value for ethical decision making.

While marketing faces challenges around misrepresentation of tourism products and services, we point to developments in the form of Web 2.0, where user-generated content can empower consumers through the availability of unbiased and credible online reviews of tourism and hospitality offerings. This phenomenon seriously challenges the ways that destinations and tourism providers have marketed their products, altering the balance of power in the marketing relationship.

Finally, the role of ethics has been hypothetically linked to quality management within the hospitality sector – to potentially produce a 'total care management' (Lynch 1993 in Wong 1998). However, ethical behaviour is yet to be substantively incorporated into such approaches.

SUMMARY OF KEY TERMS

Caveat emptor Latin for 'let the buyer beware'. With respect to commercial transactions, is the principle that the buyer purchases at their own risk.

Ethics Position Theory (EPT) Developed by Forsyth (1980), it maintains that individuals' personal moral philosophies influence their judgements, actions and emotions when faced with ethical problems. Assumes that moral evaluations and actions are the outward expression of a person's system of personal ethics, or ethics position. EPT employs two basic dimensions of personal moral philosophy – idealism and relativism – to develop a taxonomy of four distinct moral philosophies: absolutists; exceptionists; situationists; and subjectivists.

Hypernorm Hypernorms are broad, foundational norms that encompass all actors everywhere. They are principles so fundamental to human existence that they serve to evaluate lower-order norms.

Idealism refers to the tendency to make use of moral absolutes when making judgements and believe the morally 'right' behaviour always leads to positive outcomes. One of the dimensions of Ethics Position Theory.

Integrated Social Contracts Theory An application of social contract theory to business ethics developed by Donaldson and Dunfee (1994). Provides a framework by which managerial and business decisions can be made with respect to their impact on relevant communities, ethical norms and possible universal moral standards (hypernorms).

Norm A standard or pattern of social behaviour that is typical or expected of a group or social unit. Norms tend to reflect the values of the group and specify those actions that are proper or improper.

Relativism refers to the extent to which the individual rejects universal moral rules. One of the two dimensions in Ethics Position Theory.

Social contract An agreement among the members of an organised society and the governing body that defines and limits the rights and duties of each. Originated from work of philosophers John Rawls and Thomas Locke. In business refers to the agreement between business and society.

Total Quality Management (TQM) is a management approach to long-term success through customer satisfaction, involving all members of the production team.

Virtue ethics is an approach that de-emphasises rules (deontology) and consequences (teleology) and places the focus on the character of a moral agent as a driving force for ethical behaviour. Virtue ethics is person- rather than action-based. The origins of virtue ethics are traced back to Aristotle.

EXERCISE

Scenarios

1 Employees at a hotel sometimes receive gifts from suppliers, e.g. one year the food and beverage manager was given a case of wine to 'thank her' for purchasing the hotel wine from a certain supplier. The hotel has a policy

that all gifts are to be reported and jointly shared, on the basis that the gifts are given to the hotel and not to an individual employee. A bartender at the hotel received tickets to a football game from a guest. He reported the gift to his manager, but then asked if he could keep the tickets, since they were intended for him personally. At first the manager hesitated, but then told him he could keep the tickets.

2 A man from Russia arrived for a two week stay in a luxury hotel in France. With him was an entourage of ten other people who would be staying in seven additional rooms. Before his arrival he informed the manager that he did not want to be served by any people of Jewish, Asian or African descent. This was to include bartenders, waiting staff, housekeeping and any other area of service involving personal contact. The hotel manager, not wanting to lose this amount of business, agreed to his demands.

3 The maître-d' at a popular, exclusive and heavily booked restaurant sometimes gets offered bribes by people desperate to make a booking at the last minute. On this night, he was offered $100 to make a specific table available for a regular diner, but who had no booking. The table in question had been booked by a couple one month in advance, who were to celebrate their 20th wedding anniversary at the restaurant with a romantic dinner. The maître-d' accepted the bribe of $100 and told the romantic couple that there had been a mistake with their booking and that there was no table available for them.

For each of the scenarios above, use one of the ethical frameworks outlined in this chapter to consider whether the staff members were behaving ethically.

Source: 1 and 2 adapted from Stevens (2001: 240–1).

Stevens, B. (2001) 'Hospitality ethics: Responses from human resource directors and students to seven ethical scenarios', *Journal of Business Ethics* 30: 233–42.

NOTES

a Michael, Lord Heseltine (1933–), British politician. Source: Interview on *Panorama*, BBC (June 1988). Available at <http://www.qfinance.com/home> (Accessed 21 September 2012).

b Annita Roddick (1942–2007, British businesswoman, human rights activist and environmental campaigner, founder of The Body Shop. Source: Phillips, M. (2003) 'The Body Shop founder says being good is good for business', *Business Review,* 10 March. Available at <http://www.bizjour-nals.com/albany/stories/2003/03/10/story8.html?page=all> (Accessed 21 September 2012).

c George Orwell (1903–1950), British novelist and journalist. Source: *Keep the Aspidistra Flying* (1936), p. 55.

d Jacques Seguela (1934–), French advertising guru.

REFERENCES

Bruns, A. (2008) *Blogs, Wikipedia, Second Life, and Beyond: From Production to Produsage*, New York: Peter Lang.

Chonko, L.B. and Hunt, S.D. (1985) 'Ethics and marketing management: an empirical examination', *Journal of Business Research*, 13: 339–59.

Cohen, N.S. (2008) 'The valorization of surveillance: Towards political economy of Facebook', *Democratic Communiqué*, 22: 5–22.

Donaldson, T. and Dunfee, T.W. (1994), Towards a unified conception of business ethics: Integrative Social Contracts Theory, *Academy of Management Review*, 19: 252–84.

Douglas, M. (2000) 'Integrative Social Contracts Theory: Hype over hypernorms', *Journal of Business Ethics*, 26: 101–10.

Dubinsky, A.J. and Loken, B. (1989) 'Analysing ethical decision making in marketing', *Journal of Business Research*, 19: 83–107.

Dunfee, T.W. and Black, B.M. (1996) 'Ethical issues confronting travel agents', *Journal of Business Ethics,* 15: 207–17.

Dunfee, T.W., Craig Smith, N. and Ross, W.T. (1999) 'Social contracts and marketing ethics', *Journal of Marketing*, 63(3): 14–32.

Fennell, D. (2006) *Tourism Ethics*, Clevedon: Channel View.

Ferrell, O.C., Gresham, L.G. and Fraedrich, J. (1989) 'A synthesis of ethical decision models for marketing', *Journal of Macromarketing*, 9: 55–64.

Fleckenstein, M.P. and Huebsch, P. (1999) 'Ethics in tourism: reality or hallucination', *Journal of Business Ethics*, 19: 137–42.

Forsyth, D.R. (1980) 'A taxonomy of ethical ideologies', *Journal of Personality and Social Psychology*, 39(1): 175–84.

Forsyth, D.R. and O'Boyle, E.H. (2011) 'Rules, standards, and ethics: Relativism predicts cross-national differences in the codification of moral standards', *International Business Review*, 20: 353–61.

Gaski, J. (1999) 'Does marketing ethics really have anything to say? A critical inventory of the literature', *Journal of Business Ethics*, 18(3): 315–34.

Gibson, K. (2007) *Ethics and Business: An Introduction*, Cambridge: Cambridge University Press.

Gilbert, D.U. and Behnam, M. (2009) 'Advancing Integrative Social Contracts Theory: A Habermasian perspective', *Journal of Business Ethics*, 89: 215–34.

Haywood, K.M. (1987) 'Ethics, value systems and the professionalization of hoteliers', *FIU Hospitality Review*, 25.

Holcomb, J.L., Upchurch, R.S. and Okumus, F. (2007) 'International corporate social responsibility: what are top hotel companies reporting?', *Journal of Contemporary Hospitality Management*, 19(6): 461–75.

Holjevac, I.A. (2008) 'Business ethics in tourism – As a dimension of TQM', *Total Quality Management*, 19(10): 1029–41.

Hudson, S. and Miller, G.A. (2005) 'The responsible marketing of tourism: the case of Canadian Mountain Holidays', *Tourism Management*, 26: 133–42.

Hunt, S.D. and Vitell, S.D. (1986) 'A general theory of marketing', *Journal of Macromarketing*, 6: 5–15.

Hunt, S.D. and Vitell, S.D. (2006) 'The general theory of marketing ethics: a revision and three questions', *Journal of Macromarketing*, 26: 143–53.

Krohn, F.B. and Ahmed, Z.U. (1992) 'The need for developing an ethical code for the marketing of international tourism services', *Journal of Professional Services Marketing*, 8: 189–200.

Kuehn, K.M. (2011) 'Prosumer citizenship and the local: a critical case study of consumer reviewing on Yelp.com'. Unpublished PhD Dissertation in Mass Communications, Pennsylvania State University: Graduate School College of Communications.

Kuusela, O. (2011) *Key Terms in Ethics*, London: Continuum.

Laczniak, G.R. and Murphy, P.E. (1993) *Ethical Marketing Decisions: The Higher Road,* Needham Heights, MA: Allyn and Bacon.

Lansing, P. and De Vries, P. (2007) 'Sustainable tourism: Ethical alternative of marketing ploy?', *Journal of Business Ethics*, 72: 77–85.

Lynn, C. (2012) 'Review of hospitality ethics research in 2009 and 2010', *Journal of Hotel and Business Management*, 1(1): 1–6.

Murphy, P.E. and Laczniak, G.R. (1981) 'Marketing ethics: a review with implications for marketers, educators and researchers', *Review of Marketing*, 251–6.

Nill, A. and Schibrowsky, J.A. (2007) 'Research on marketing ethics: A systematic review of the literature', *Journal of Macromarketing*, 27: 56–273.

O'Connor, P. (2010) 'Managing a hotel's image on TripAdvisor', *Journal of Hospitality Marketing & Management*, 19: 754–72.

Pratt, C.B. (1994) 'Applying classical ethical theories to ethical decision making in public relations: Perrier's product recall', *Management Communication Quarterly*, 8: 70–93.

Ross, G. (2003) 'Ethical beliefs, work problem-solving strategies and learning styles as mediators of tourism marketing entrepreneurialism', *Journal of Vacation Marketing*, (9)2: 119–36.

Smith, C. (2001) 'Ethical guidelines for marketing practice: A reply to Gaski and some observations on the role of normative ethics', *Journal of Business Ethics*, 32(1): 3–18.

Tapscott, D. and Williams, A. D. (2006) *Wikinomics: How Mass Collaboration Changes Everything*, New York: Penguin.

TripAdvisor (2012) About TripAdvisor. Available at:http://www.tripadvisor.com/pages/about_us.html

Upchurch, R.S. (1998) 'Ethics in the hospitality industry: an applied model', *International Journal of Contemporary Hospitality Management*, 10(6): 227–33.

Upchurch, R. and Ruhland, K. (1996) 'The organizational bases of ethical work climates in lodging operations as perceived by general managers', *Journal of Business Ethics*, 9: 1083–93.

Wheeler, M. (1995) 'Tourism marketing ethics: An introduction', *International Marketing Review*, 12(4): 38–49.

Wheeler, M. and Cooper, C.P. (1994) 'The emergence of ethics in tourism and hospitality', in Cooper, C.P. and Lockwood, A. (eds) *Progress in Tourism, Recreation and Hospitality Management*, vol. 6, pp. 46–56, Hoboken, NJ: Wiley.

Whitney, D.L (1990) 'Ethics in the hospitality industry: with a focus on hotel managers', *International Journal of Hospitality Management*, 9(1): 59–68.

Wight, P.A. (1993) 'Ecotourism: Ethics or eco-sell?' *Journal of Travel Research,* 21(3): 3–9.

Williams, O.F. and Murphy, P.E. (1990) 'The ethics of virtue: A moral theory for marketing', *Journal of Macromarketing*, 10: 19–29.

Wong, S.C.K. (1998) 'Staff job-related ethics of hotel employees in Hong Kong', *International Journal of Contemporary Hospitality Management*, 10(3): 107–115.

Yaman, H.R. and Gurel, E. (2006) 'Ethical ideologies of tourism marketers', *Annals of Tourism Research*, 33(2): 470–89.

Yeh, R. (2012) 'Hotel general managers' perceptions of business ethics education: implications for hospitality educators, professionals and students', *Journal of Human Resources in Hospitality and Tourism*, 11(1): 72–86.

13 Labour

'This isn't Paradise – I work here.'

Darcie Vandegrift[a]

LEARNING OBJECTIVES

After reading this chapter you will be able to:

- Discuss the tourism industry and the key features of the labour force.
- Identify and discuss the main ethical issues associated with employment in this industry.
- Describe and explain what is meant by labour mobility and the employment effects of tourism.
- Understand why labour standards are an important ethical issue for the tourism industry.

13.1 INTRODUCTION

It is estimated that the tourism industry provides approximately 3 per cent of global employment which is approximately 192 million jobs (Ladkin 2011: 1135). The International Labour Organization predicts that by 2012 this will rise to 251.6 million, representing one in 11 formal sector jobs (Ferguson 2007 in Ladkin 2011). In this chapter we will consider the nature of the labour market, how it intersects with other labour markets, the nature of work, which encompasses a wide range of service providers, and finally the ethical implications of how the labour force is organised (structured) and how this organisation is shaped by race, class, gender, age and place.

To date there has been considerable attention paid to consumption and the performative aspects of production in the tourism industry (Crang 1997); however, less attention has been paid to productive labour and production, the structural features (how labour is organised) of practice and process and the material and experiential realities for those engaged in producing the tourism product. In late capitalist societies there have been significant changes in the patterns of work and consumption; nowhere is this more evident than in tourism where the new middle classes are embracing consumption as a means of self-fulfilment and advancement (Bianchi 2000) and where tourism offers a wide range of consumptive possibilities. Simultaneously, meeting these new patterns of consumption requires a productive class and in tourism we have seen the emergence of a transnational class responsible for producing the tourist product. However, only a minority of the world consume the tourist product; in contrast, there are a growing number of people involved in its production. While the producers are often local to the destination, there are many temporary and or recently permanent migrants who are meeting the productive needs of the tourism industry. This class of worker is often referred to as the transnational proletariat: not locked into producing in their home locale – but mobile and producing at times in multiple locales for low rates of pay and often working in poor working conditions and with limited legislative protection. When consumption meets production in tourism we see the intersection of travel and class playing out globally. Both are shaped by structured inequities that predate advanced capitalism and globalisation and both raise issues connected to fairness and justice, where the absence of justice threatens the whole social group or in this instance global community.

Tourism labour has primarily been addressed from a management perspective, where practitioners and management academics have addressed practical issues with respect to labour training and supply and employment issues within the industry (Ladkin 2011). There are a range of texts devoted to addressing these practical concerns with most focusing on the hospitality sector (see e.g. Baum 1995; Nickson 2007; Tesone 2008; Ladkin 2011). Here, the subject area is a human resource issue and authors addressing employment issues in the hospitality sector are at the forefront. But this is 'how to' and 'where to' literature rather than theoretically informed critical reflection on the nature of the labour market and employment conditions within this market. More broadly, this literature focuses on issues connected to pay scales, globalisation, shifting global demographics and the implications for employment, skills, skill demand and management style.

Standing alongside the aforementioned literature is a growing body of research embracing a range of social science perspectives and theoretical frameworks. This literature addresses labour relations in tourism and consists primarily of case studies which explore the working conditions of those working in tourism and the hospitality industries (Bianchi 2011). Hospitality, in part, has been the focus of most research because it is easily identifiable and contained with respect to organisational and career structures (Ladkin 2011). Amongst the literature are detailed accounts of the working experiences of those in low-skilled, poorly paid and exploitative workplace relations which have come to characterise employment in this sub-sector (Burns 1993; Lee and Seyoung 1998; Beddoe 2004). Yet despite a substantial body of research that highlights these issues, it is important to note that labour conditions in the tourism industry are more complex and diverse than this, as this labour market also includes skilled and highly paid workers (Bianchi 2011). In addition, there is a body of ethnographic research from anthropologists – for example Hochschild's (2003) study of the working lives of airline workers; and Adler and Adler's (2004) study of the occupational subcultures of resort workers in Hawaii – which provides up-close and in-depth considerations of work experience for these workers.

It, however, remains that there is little research that explores the nature of this international labour market and how employment in this sector is linked to other sectors and a broader political and global economy (Bianchi 2011). One of the reasons is the sheer complexity of examining what is in effect more than one labour market as the industry intersects with a range of other service, transportation and manufacturing industries. Thus, it is probably more accurate to speak of tourism labour markets. Further, there are a range of ethical issues and concerns pertinent to employers and workers and the tourists for whom they labour. We need to understand the structural features of this labour market and how these features are central to the production and reproduction of inequalities in the tourism industry locally and on a global scale. A consideration of the tourism labour market(s) is central to any consideration of ethics in relation to tourism.

In this chapter we will explore the nature of some of the tourism labour markets and emergent ethical issues. No attempt is being made to provide a comprehensive review as the area is broad; rather, the chapter provides some starting points to consider the ethical issues surrounding labour in tourism and what ethical frameworks provide the most utility in this area. We have already touched on aspects of tourism labour in Chapter 6 in relation to sex tourism and in Chapter 3 when addressing mobility. We know that the labour market involves illicit and legitimate movements of people. With respect to the former, trafficking has emerged as a significant ethical issue which is inextricably linked to wealth inequalities and the opportunity that the tourism industry provides for those who desperately seek a means to improve the material realities of their daily lives. This chapter will focus on the legitimate and illegitimate flows of people who work in the industry. We will consider the dominant features of labour in this sector and the ethical issues connected to how various forms of labour reproduce and sustain social inequality. Specifically we will address:

- The tourism labour market(s)
- Gendered work
- Ethnicity, nationality and labour
- Skilled versus unskilled work
- Development and employment
- Demographic shifts in the developed world
- Working holidaymakers.

13.2 THE INDUSTRY AND LABOUR

As Bianchi (2011: 26) observes:

> There can be little argument that the structure and organisation of tourism labour markets are increasingly globalised, cosmopolitan and segmented according to various occupational subcultures defined by ethnicity, nationality and gender.

Age might also be added to this list. Baum (2010) notes that the tourism industry has drawn heavily on young people, but that an ageing workforce in high income countries is going to increasingly impact on the tourism labour market. Tourism is a labour-intensive service sector and has traditionally relied on the employment of young people, who are often mobile. Population decline is predicted to continue for high income countries, while population growth will continue in low and medium income countries, with South Asia dominating (Baum 2010). Thus, in low to middle income countries there will be significant pressure for employment – and for the educated minority there will be a shortage of professional positions. In contrast, in high income countries there will be an ageing work-force and labour shortages and countries will increasingly compete with each other to address these shortages, in particular competing for skilled labour (Castles and Miller 2003). One of the primary means of addressing population decline in the developed world has been through migration and this will, in the next 20 years, continue to be the main means by which developed countries address labour and skills shortages.

Service industries such as tourism foster what are referred to as dual labour markets, where on the one hand there are a large number of jobs that require little skill and on the other a small number of jobs that require high levels of skill, for which the workers receive high incomes (Adler and Adler 2004). Further, the new economies of advanced capitalist societies have moved from a manufacturing economy toward an economy dominated by the service sector. The dual nature of the labour market is further segmented and stratified by race/ethnicity, age, class and gender. Thus, those who are more advantaged can claim the high level skillled and well-remunerated positions and those who are disadvantaged are concentrated in the low skillled and poorly paid occupations. Tourism looks to the second-ary labour market – one that is dominated by unskilled or semi-skilled positions – to fill 'contingent jobs' (Adler and Adler 2004).

Advanced capitalist nations and their industries have been addressing production and labour issues by primarily searching for cheaper labour and cheaper locations for produc-tion. Relocation of production, offshore, where labour is cheaper and where there are fewer regulatory constraints, has been a significant outcome of globalisation. While advanced capitalist countries move production offshore many developing countries have responded by introducing incentives to attract this relocation. For example, the creation of tax havens or special economic zones to encourage investment of foreign capital for indus-trialisation and modernisation has been a strategy adopted in China, South America and South Asia. While this strategy has worked for manufacturing industries, this option is limited for a service industry like tourism. For tourism moving offshore is constrained because of the 'place-specific nature' of much of tourism. Thus, for tourism, rather than moving to the labour pool, labour must be attracted in – domestically and internationally. However, addressing the limitations posed by place-specific tourism has been attempted, for example, through the creation of theme parks located in areas of the world where labour is still cheap, labour laws poor or non-existent and where development is less constrained by environmental or social regulations. In addition, these locations offer access to a large local population of domestic tourists likely to seek this kind of touristic consumption. Disney theme parks in China are one such initiative involving foreign capi-tal investment and offshore non-place specific tourism. In addition, there is the emergence of 'moving a taste of the place' to another destination. For example, within theme parks tourists are offered the opportunity to 'experience' another culture without having to travel to the homelands of that culture. Here foreign nationals are recruited to make the experi-ence as authentic as possible. Yet, despite these developments, it remains that the bulk of

Figure 13.1 *Disneyland. Photo: Brent Lovelock.*

tourism is still place-specific. The movement then that remains dominant is the movement of labour to place-specific tourism ventures (Baum 2010).

13.3 GLOBAL LABOUR MARKET AND FLEXIBILITY

Most discussions of the tourist labour market address globalisation. While globalisation has been variously defined, for the purposes of this chapter we will work with the definition provided by Waters (1995: 3) where globalisation refers to:

> a social process in which the constraints of geography on social and cultural arrangements recede and in which people become increasingly aware that they are receding.

Further to this, these arrangements are played out economically, culturally and politically. Arrangements can be relocated and need not be location-specific: new arrangements can be made that establish networks of connection that have a global dimension. Tourism and the tourism industry provides an apt illustration of the processes of globalisation and how they manifest in the movement of people, tourists, labour and new enterprises involving new networks of connection. As we will see, while much appears new, the inequalities that are being perpetuated are old.

Early attempts to make sense of the labour market and nature of employment in tourism involved focusing on how the labour market was structured and the various functional aspects that occupational niches fulfilled with respect to this market and industry. Thus, Airey and Nightingale (1981) identified a range of occupational classifications in this fashion, which included tourist destination organisations, suppliers of tourist attractions, facilities and services, travel organisations intermediaries, other sectors. All of these classifications remain meaningful, but in an increasingly globalised world, labour markets are no longer so firmly entrenched in localities. For example, arranging travel can potentially involve engaging with workers situated outside of your locality and/or a virtual engagement with functions that are international yet integrated and accessed through one site. We have a highly globalised labour market (Terry 2011) and one where neoliberal capitalism has ensured that employment relations have shifted toward being more malleable and flexible. Flexible labour is not new to tourism and is as much a characteristic of small artisanal enterprises as it is of large hotel chains (Ioannides and Debbage 1998). Migrant labour is also not new to tourism: transient and seasonal workers have always played a role in the industry. However, with the increasing importance of the service sector in late capitalist societies, it is arguably the case that the tourism industry has contributed and in some instances played a key role in exacerbating the emergence and consolidation of flexible labour markets. One of the key characteristics of flexible labour markets is the casualisation of labour; and one of the outcomes of casualised labour is job insecurity, weak negotiating power, poor conditions and low wages for many workers within and outside of the industry (Bianchi 2000).

Overall, the labour market has become more integrated globally; there is increasing diversity in productive arrangements with both producer-driven and consumer-driven commodity chains. Labour arrangements are commonly: flexible, casual, part-time and female dominated. There is a high concentration of transient labourers and immigrant labourers and as with other forms of service work, the work is characteristically labour-intensive (Hudson 1999: 35–40; Bianchi 2000). While the labour force might be characterised as cosmopolitan it is not a flat structure, rather it is hierarchical and structured according to age, ethnicity, gender and country of origin/migratory status. Those who seek employment in the sector do so within and beyond their own national boundaries often in response to the more general nature of labour market conditions in their own society. While the middle class young seek working holidays abroad (Lovelock and Leopold 2011), many others seek employment in the industry to escape poverty. While for the working holiday-maker the engagement with the industry is typically a brief interlude in a career trajectory, for those escaping poverty, flexible labour markets have facilitated the emergence and growth of a transnational working class and reserve army of labour whose movement is governed by economic development, the emergence of new markets, seasonality, customer preference and the labour needs of advanced and emerging capitalist societies. For the poor, it is a trajectory that is precarious but where alternate employment is either non-existent or offers poorer conditions; for these workers a precarious economic existence is normative. Of course this transnational working class is not new. There are many illustrations in history of movements of workers occurring in response to all of the aforementioned processes. We only have to think of the many itinerant labourers who left their countries of origin and laboured in various colonies on plantations, or as servants in the plantation homesteads.

As Mintz (1998: 131) rightly observes:

> The new theories of transnationalism and globalization are not respectful enough of history, especially the history of exploration, conquest, and the global division of labour.

The global division of labour that he speaks of is a division that mirrors and is propelled by the power of economic development, where the under-developed or developing nations of the world continue to provide cheap labour to meet the production and consumption needs of the developed and advanced capitalist nations of the world. Mintz (1998) stresses that we need to ask: What is new? What is new is the contemporary labour mobility and flexible labour market is one that attempts to circumvent or undermine over a century of labour resistance and laws that protect and prevent the exploitation of workers in most high and middle income countries. And, in addition, this new labour mobility and the flexible labour market in practice serves to undermine the development of protective labour legislation for the world's labouring poor. Servicing service production increasingly involves seeking service from those who will most likely engage in servitude and where no protection exists for them. These issues are central to any consideration of ethics in the area of tourism labour. As Terry (2011: 660) notes:

> with the emergence of global labor markets, 'companies are now free to search the world for the most rightless and disempowered workers…in a position of having to accept bargains of desperation' (Bonacich and Wilson 2008: 18). Within this broad purview, 'labor other than as an occasional short term impediment, is no longer a problem for capital' (Cumbers et al. 2008: 371).

DISCUSSION QUESTIONS

1 Who makes up this transnational working class?
2 Who makes up this reserve army of labour?
3 What are the key ethical concerns in relation to this flexible labour force?
4 What divisions of labour have emerged from the conditions of globalisation and neoliberal capitalism?
5 What do these divisions of labour and the associated power asymmetries in specific localities look like?
6 What are the historical antecedents to these asymmetrical power relationships?
7 How are these inequities shaped by relations between specific localities?
8 How is production and consumption organised in the tourism industry and how does this impact on people's everyday lives?

These are just some of a range of questions that we need to ask and explore in order to understand emergent ethical concerns and issues. There is sufficient evidence to observe that there are some exploitative working conditions for workers who also live in impoverished conditions in a range of destinations globally (Belau 2003; Beddoe 2004; Bianchi 2009a). The first thing to note is that consumption in this industry is determined and therefore organised on the basis of unequal wealth and opportunity (Bianchi 2009a). Various flows of goods, capital and people globally intersect with specific markets and different categories of tourists. It has been argued that there has been considerable attention paid to tourism as consumption and those who consume, but less on production and those who labour, yet obviously 'one person's consumption is another person's production' (Perrons in Bianchi 2009b: 494) and in tourism this is often underpinned by significant social inequality.

Tourism is a major avenue of capital accumulation (Britton 1991; Bianchi 2009a). The industry comprises free market forms of enterprise of varying size, from small family firms to large multinational corporations and the industry engages with a range of essential and associated enterprises addressing: modes of travel, accommodation, insurance, tour operators (referred to as commodity chains) (Clancy 1998; Ioannides and Debbage 1998). Further intersections include associations with other industries, including variously: construction, finance, property, hospitality, communications and media. This scope and wide range of interconnections has been referred to as 'hyper-globalising', but Bianchi (2009a) notes it also represents the perfect union of 'freedom of travel' with 'freedom of trade' (O'Byrne 2001: 409). This network, propelled by the seemingly endless tourist product manufactured for consumption in new destinations, is one that is not equally accessed by all. As we have already seen in Chapter 3 on mobility, only a minority of the world's population are mobile and in search of experiential touristic consumption. Further,

> the freedom to consume [tourist products, destinations etc.] often comes at the expense of someone else's welfare, whether through the appropriation/privatisation of public lands for tourism development, the displacement of peasant populations, resource degradation, and the intensified commodification of labour power and/or exploitative working practices.
>
> (Bianchi 2009b: 495)

13.4 DEVELOPMENT AND LABOUR IN TOURISM

Tourism is often presented as a significant force in development for low income societies. The industry invites foreign investment and capital and provides the creation of waged labour for rural migrants and urban dwellers living in transitional economies. The movement from dependency on primary products and their export toward industrialisation and rapid urbanisation is not smooth and high levels of unemployment are normative. Typically in these societies people have low incomes, low education levels, poorer health and higher rates of population growth. Some 80 per cent of the world's population live in developing countries in the Third World. It has been estimated that between 1995 and 2025 the populations of many developing countries will double (Sharpley and Telfer 2002). This growth will determine and exacerbate already high levels of unemployment.

REFLECTION QUESTIONS

1 What will these people do?
2 Where will these people go?
3 What impact will tourism employment have in these societies undergoing such transitions?
4 What are the ethical implications of underpinning assumptions made about what the industry can and cannot do?
5 What are the ethical implications of what the industry currently does?

Most tourism destinations engage with tourism as they perceive economic benefits will result for their communities and specifically there will be improved individual incomes and employment opportunities. What do we know about tourism-related employment experiences in developing countries? Less than we do about experiences of employment in this sector in developed countries. There is some evidence that suggests that the employment experiences for those in developing countries are perceived to be less negative than those in developed countries and that this is in part because tourism employment is assessed in comparison to the other forms of labour available (e.g. rural) (Cleverdon 1979; Blanton 1981; Cukier and Wall 1993). In addition, work in the tourism industry in developing countries does not necessarily suggest that the person occupies a marginal position in the labour market (with all of the disadvantages that marginality conveys), rather research suggests that it can confer high status and invariably pays better than work in the rural sector (Cukier and Wall 1993). Perceptions and experiences are very much shaped by the local context. Thus, in the developed world some roles in the hospitality sector are perceived as menial, and comparatively they are poorly paid. In the developing world, these same occupations are perceived to be comparatively high status and well remunerated, particularly when compared to rural labour. Further, these types of jobs offer entry into the formal labour market – not just for the young, but for women; in the developing world this is considered a positive, whereas in the developed world the lower status jobs held predominantly by women is evident of gendered inequity in employment. However, while assessments of the nature of the employment experience are always going to be relative, we need to explore these claims critically if we are to unpack the overarching ethical issues and moral concerns within localities, between localities and globally. Recall in Chapter 2 the critique of cultural relativism – this critique applies here; further we need to be aware of the implications for all workers globally and over time.

Research on employment in developing countries has been impeded by the large informal sector, where it is common for people to hold multiple jobs and for some of this labour to occur in the informal sector – e.g. hawking goods, selling homemade crafts, selling goods procured on the black market. In terms of identifying the connections to the tourism industry there is considerable variability and it is more difficult to ascertain the levels of engagement in the tourism sector and/or the implications for everyday life for these people. Existing research indicates that tourism does facilitate work in both the informal and formal sectors of the labour market. And while the nature of employment can be precarious, multiple employment and migration are, just as with developed countries, strategies employed to address the associated vulnerability.

While some have challenged ethnocentric readings of what the employment experience and status are in developing societies – namely the transposition of low pay–low status to these settings – it is also important to recognise that while the experience may well be different, the meso and macro material forces of power and inequality generated through liberalised tourism development remain. As Britton (1980, 1982 in Bianchi 2002: 269) has noted: 'Tourism both exacerbates social and economic inequalities between the core and periphery as well as within destinations themselves.' The ethical issue here is one of unequal resource endowments and the need for distributive justice.

DISCUSSION POINT: THE CRUISE INDUSTRY – A LIBERALISED GLOBAL WORK REGIME

Figure 13.2 *Cruise ship – tourists and casualised workers on board. Photo: Brent Lovelock.*

The cruise industry provides an excellent illustration of liberalised global work regimes (Terry 2011). Able to operate within a de-territorialised context that is afforded by ocean-going ships, they can legally recruit anywhere in the world. The cruise industry has aptly been referred to as a 'paradigmatic case of globalization' (Wood 2006). The cruise industry needs to attract workers and seemingly can do this in an unlimited capacity, but they are also constrained by the kind of skill they require to operate and provide services on board a cruise ship. Terry (2011) observes that despite the seemingly limitless pools of labour at their disposal, there are geographical (and cultural) limits to sourcing the workers they require.

> In short, the cruise industry is reliant on global inequalities, skill sets found in local labor markets and cultural alignment with western expectations to produce a very specific type of worker…local geographies that create suitable workers are in constant flux; what was once easy becomes more challenging as typical source countries of the past couple of decades yield fewer skilled workers.
>
> (Terry 2011: 668)

Thus, while global recruitment allows the industry to keep wages and salary costs low while still delivering high levels of customer service, low fares and consumer satisfaction, the industry remains vulnerable to improved labour condition expectations from the pools of labour they have been recruiting from. When labour conditions improve in a recruitment country the cruise companies move on to recruit workers from countries where there is no protection – either minimum wages or other conditions of employment. There is, of course, a limit to the response of moving recruitment to another geographical location; however, it remains the dominant strategy to date. Thus, for example, the Philippines has been a major recruitment destination until reasonably recently. With improved minimum standards for Filipino workers and pay rates now slightly higher for these workers, some cruise lines have sought labour from other countries (Terry 2011: 668).

Cruise tourism, like other forms of tourism, is place-specific, but here the ship is marketed as the destination, not the ports that it docks at (Wood 2000). These ships are essentially floating resorts where viewing the sea can be optional, but where the ship offers sea-based mobility (Wood 2000: 350). The workers on these seaborne resorts are not only recruited from anywhere but are often not protected by labour laws. Flags of convenience (FOC) are a means of manipulating worker protection. These flags allow the cruise liner to identify with any nation/country, rather than their country of origin. Ships which fly flags of convenience are subject to the laws of the country to which they are flagged – and these countries are typically those with poor labour laws or virtually no labour protection laws. Thus, many cruise ships fly Caribbean flags, commonly Panama, Liberia or the Bahamas, despite many of them belonging to US-headquartered lines (Wood 2000: 351).

In addition to these practices, the cruise sector has experienced increased internationalisation with ownership being concentrated in the hands of few. Throughout the late 1990s and early 2000s there were many mergers, acquisitions and bankruptcies (Wood 2000: 352). While relocation serves avoidance of labour laws, ownership in this sector also involves circumventing tax obligations, where ships are registered in places where tax demands are slighter rather than where their headquarters are.

> if economic globalization means the increased mobility of capital and its spatial disembeddedness, cruiseships represent the ultimate globalization: physically mobile; massive chunks of multinational capital; capable of being 'repositioned' anywhere in the world at anytime; crewed with labour migrants from up to 50 countries on a single ship, essentially unfettered by national or international regulations.
>
> (Wood 2000: 353)

The freedom to move and circumvent is not a freedom shared by all. On board, in contrast, the division of labour is rigid, stratified and localised (albeit within the confines of a ship). Those labouring on board ship are engaged in a labour-intensive process of meeting the needs of their guests, and most work seven days a week for six-month periods. The labour force is hierarchical, with officers at the top, followed by staff and then crew with each group accommodated in separate areas, engaging with different passengers and receiving very different pay packages (Wood 2000: 353). The 'hospitality workforce' overlays a parallel organisational hierarchy for the ship which includes the captain, officers, technicians and seamen. For cruise ships in the Caribbean the strata in these hierarchies are also ethnic – where white (Western European and North American) is typically at the top and where Asian, Caribbean and Eastern Europeans are the crew. Wood cites an employment manual intended for North American applicants: 'the most common mistake made [is] applying for a job that is traditionally held by a Filipino or by someone from other "third world" countries' (Landon 1997: 48 in Wood 2000: 353). Yet, some cruise lines also market themselves using the ethnic diversity of their labour force; albeit selectively and often highlighting that the crew have been trained by the cruise operation: the exotic (but civilised) other.

Engaging in this work for migrant workers is not simply an individual choice. Many governments in developing countries encourage this labour migration as it is a means of securing foreign capital. Thus, the Philippines is the largest exporter of labour in the world, with the labour population estimated to be 4.2 million with Filipino contract workers located in over 130 countries and seafaring workers making up a significant proportion of these workers (Ball 1997: 1612). The Philippine state facilitates this labour migration through various agencies and in return demands remittances (percentages of total income) be paid back into the country through Filipino banks, thus securing foreign exchange for their country. China now also represents a large source of cheap labour for seafaring and ultimately is working toward training young workers for cruise lines.

Cruise lines offer the opportunity to consider economic and political deterritorialisation the internationalisation of labour and mobile destinations. Some have noted that there is an increasing trend also toward cruise ships as theme parks – where soon these ships will be akin to artificial islands able to replace real destinations (Wood 2000: 359). The question is will they be islands unto themselves with respect to labour protection and what ports will they be serving? Some cruise companies own private islands – for themed fantasy cruises – and these are preferred ports of call. Further, in the Caribbean where this is on offer, these islands are not inhabited by people of the Caribbean, rather the islanders are employees from all over the world (Sloan 1998; Orenstein 1997) yet, they are marketed 'as if' they were from a Caribbean of the past, a Caribbean that no longer exists. This constructed island paradise is marketed as an authentic experience. And the facilitators of the cruise company vision are transnational workers, who in this instance displace Caribbean workers. Further, these private islands displace the relevance of the local port, which means loss of revenue for locals who provide services and commodities at these port destinations (Wood 2000: 362). The cruise company reaps the rewards and the local ports are bypassed. If, as Wood (2000) observes, 'Globalisation detaches economic life from the constraints of geography – physical, cultural, political', what are the implications for those who are constrained by geography, economically, physically, culturally and politically? Flags of convenience allow bypassing labour legislation and protection for cruise line workers; private islands allow bypassing port consumption – and thereby displacing a market for local production and work for local labourers; private destinations ensure both production and consumption are firmly in the hands of the cruise companies that operate in non-territorial waters. Where development places high hopes on tourism for foreign capital and employment, the locals, on the land, face challenges in attracting mass tourists who seek what the cruise ships can provide and are engaged in production that is increasingly not being consumed – that which is perhaps a little too authentic?

Discussion questions

1 In terms of social responsibility and accountability are these owners and employers exempt because they are a moving target or multiply-located?
2 Is located-ness central to our understandings of social responsibility and ethical conduct?
3 Does dis-location cut these ties? Ironically, locality is more important than ever – where you are from, where you can go and where you are, very much determine the conditions under which you labour and for whom.

Further reading

Cabezas, A.L. (2008) 'Tropical blues: Tourism and social exclusion in the Dominican Republic', *Latin American Perspectives*, 35: 21–36.

13.5 EMPLOYMENT, NEW WORK AND AFFECTIVE LABOUR

In conjunction with the emergence of flexible labour is the notion of new work. New work often involves the blurring of boundaries between work and home, employment that involves combinations of part-time jobs and seasonal work as a means of addressing precarious employment, and increasingly too the role that affective labour plays in the tourism industry (Veijola and Jokinen 2008). Much of tourism work is gendered. The tourism industry employs disproportionately large numbers of women and women are disproportionately represented in the low-skilled, poorly paid and precarious forms of employment in tourism (Ghodsee 2005; Pritchard et al. 2007).

Hospitality, emotional labour and reproductive work

The transformation of unpaid reproductive work into paid reproductive work is one of the outcomes of a wider range of services moving into the labour market. Reproductive work refers to work that aims to sustain workers, that is, labour to feed them, to clean for them and to address personal needs. While once the domain of the home, to which the worker returned, it is now more commonly a domain accessible everywhere; what remains, however, is that it is work done predominantly by women. Paid reproductive work is central to service provision in tourism, evidenced in hotels and other forms of accommodation. Women dominate in paid reproductive work in hotels and other forms of accommodation. For low wages they clean, preen and take care of the residents. Many of these women are also immigrants and members of ethnic minority populations in the country within which they work (Aguiar and Herod 2006). Traditional stereotypes of what the sexual division of labour should look like are mirrored in the division of labour in tourism and in particular the hospitality sector. Many of those who labour to reproduce the creative or 'knowledge class' are central to the economy, yet remain largely invisible while at work, the poorer the pay the more menial the task, the more likely it will be behind the scenes – invisible to the tourist – work. The lower tiers of the employment ladder are dominated by women, immigrants and young people (Zampoukos and Ioannides 2011).

A combination of limited skills (in particular, language), racial prejudice and sexism ensures that the low-end occupations of washing dishes, mopping floors and changing beds are occupations available to many female migrant workers (McDowell 2009; Zampoukos and Ioannides 2011). More generally, it has also been observed that even when non-native

Figure 13.3 *Invisible workers. Service provision in tourism: paid reproductive labourers. Photo: Brent Lovelock.*

immigrant workers are highly educated and have work experience at the high end, this is not a guarantee they will end up in management or in front-line positions (Church and Frost 2004; Devine et al. 2007). Adler and Adler (1999) developed a four-tier typology of hospitality workers, comprising (1) new immigrants, (2) locals, (3) seekers and (4) managers, based on their research focusing on resort workers on the Hawaiian Islands. The locals and the immigrants were reasonably sedentary, but the other two categories were mobile, with the seekers being predominantly white, North American and young. Each type can also be characterised temporally in relation to their connection to this form of employment. New immigrants work hard for the next generation; locals see it as a temporary measure; seekers are doing this work as part of an overall lifestyle strategy with varying commitment (which range from seeking semi-permanent transience to just for the moment) and managers are professionals who are well qualified and enjoy what they are doing. Various observers have noted the flexibility of hospitality positions both with respect to the hours of work and functionality. Overall, some have argued that at the core is the managerial workers who have functional flexibility and on the periphery is a vast army of low- or semi-skilled workers, who respond to various demand categories in the sector.

> the action of freedom in the labour market depends on who you are (identities such as sex, race, class, previous working experience and so on), where you are (geographical setting, sector of economy, firm), and what you aspire to become (dreams for the future, desires)…[in addition] places change.
>
> (Zampoukos and Ioannides 2011: 41)

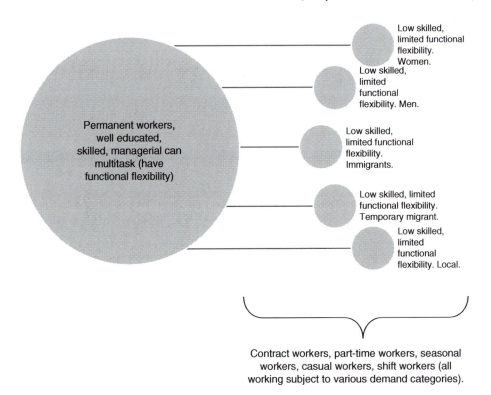

Figure 13.4 Core and periphery in the tourism labour market.

Many workers do not have worker rights protected and many workers on the periphery have their aspirations constrained.

Recommended reading

Beddoe, C. (2004) *Labour Standards, Social Responsibility and Tourism,* A report by Tourism Concern, London; Stapleton House.

CASE STUDY: QUEENSTOWN AND TRANSIENT WORKERS: A MATCH MADE IN HEAVEN? – *TARA DUNCAN*

Queenstown, located in the South Island of New Zealand, is known for its landscapes and adventure activities, initially as a holiday resort for New Zealanders, but from the 1970s it has increasingly attracted international tourists. Queenstown is the home of bungee jumping (the first ever bungee opened in 1988) and jet boating (since 1970) as well as many other adventure activities including skiing, down-hill mountain-biking, parapenting, white water rafting, sky-diving, canyon swings, kayaking and zip-treks. Home to approximately 28,700 residents, Queenstown welcomes over 1.9 million visitors every year (About Queenstown 2012).

With over 160 commercial accommodation providers, Queenstown's tourism and hospitality industries are the largest employer in the town. Whilst the New Zealand government has been promoting the employment of New Zealanders, the industry still tends to rely on an international workforce (Fea 2011) and those on working holiday visas provide much of the labour force in the resort town and on the ski slopes in the area.

Employment in a resort town like Queenstown offers a range of work for transient workers. As Boon's (2006) research highlights many young workers seek combining a job with a lifestyle such as skiing, boarding or mountain-biking. Many young international tourists seek work in the town and area: for example, NZSki, who own the Remarkables and Coronet Peak ski resorts, cap their annual call for 500 workers at 5,000 applicants. The work is seasonal, not highly paid, and in the winter, vulnerable to the amount of snow fall. Employers are also vulnerable to climatic shifts; for example, in 2011, the late arrival of snow caused problems with companies such as NZSki who were unable to pay staff as the ski slopes were not open (McDonald 2012). In addition to seasonal vulnerability, employers of large numbers of international workers are vulnerable to bureaucratic delays with visas (Fea 2011) and balancing how many of their front-line staff are international with the demands of international tourists who seek a 'Kiwi' experience (Hall and Williams 2002).

Yet, whilst those on working holiday visas can have a great experience in Queenstown, and the employers get a steady supply of new labour to choose from, there are a range of impacts on the local community. These impacts include those visiting and working in Queenstown misbehaving (alcohol, drugs, crime) to issues faced by workers on low incomes dealing with a high cost of living. Dramatic seasonal growth of the population places pressure on local health care, housing, education and policing.

So why do the young people keep coming? Morgan et al. (2002: 348) suggest New Zealand's scenery is 'fundamentally...what brings the majority of visitors to the country' and recent research suggests that for many young people this is the case (see Godfrey 2011). Yet it is also the case that Tourism New Zealand, the national tourism promotion organisation, are targeting the younger traveller, having found that young people visiting New Zealand stay longer and spend more (than other tourists). As Godfrey (2011) found, New Zealand tends to be on the backpackers circuit – a must-see place to visit (and work) whilst backpacking or on your gap year.

Therefore, despite the high living costs, unreliable (winter) weather and minimum wages paid for the mostly front-line or entry-level tourism, hospitality and retail positions available, Queenstown still offers something unique to the young people who travel and seek work while taking part in the adventure opportunities. Yet this suggests a certain autonomy to this process that is deceptive. This movement of young temporary workers is part of a larger political economy which is shaped by economic and trade relationships between the various nations who have working holiday agreements. The central ethical issue and concern here is which young people are targeted globally? How do these agreements perpetuate existing global inequities?

Discussion questions

1 What are some of the positive and negative factors for places such as Queenstown which have a large seasonal transient workforce? Why is it important to think about these impacts?
2 Who are the young international workers that provide labour in resort towns such as Queenstown?
3 What are some of the central ethical issues connected to local impact, transient workers and low pay for working holidaymakers?

References

About Queenstown (2012) *Destination Queenstown*. Available at <http://www.queenstownnz.co.nz/information/AboutQueenstown/> (Accessed 15 August 2012).

Boon, B. (2006) 'When leisure and work are allies: the case of skiers and tourist resort hotels', *Career Development International*, 11(7): 594–608.

Fea, S. (2011) 'Plea to cut red tape for work visas', *The Southland Times*. Available at <http://www.stuff.co.nz/southland-times/news/5631728/Plea-to-cut-red-tape-for-work-visas> (Accessed 1 September 2012).

Godfrey, J. (2011) 'The grass is greener on the other side: what motivates backpackers to leave home and why they choose New Zealand as a destination'. Unpublished
Master's thesis, University of Otago, Dunedin, New Zealand. Available at <http://
otago.ourarchive.ac.nz/handle/10523/1736> (Accessed 30 August 2012).

Hall, C.M. and Williams, A.M. (2002) *Tourism and Migration: New Relationships
Between Production and Consumption*, Dordrecht: Kluwer Academic.

McDonald, C. (2012) 'Jobless numbers halved', *Otago Daily Times*, 23 July. Available
at <http://www.odt.co.nz/news/queenstown-lakes/218137/jobless-numbers-
halved> (Accessed 23 July 2012).

Morgan, N., Pritchard, A. and Piggott, R. (2002) 'New Zealand, 100% Pure: The creation of a powerful niche destination brand', *Brand Management*, 9(4–5): 335–54.

Queenstown Lakes Community Housing Trust (2012) *Press Release: Community
Housing Trust Commissions Independent Research into Local Rental Market*.
Available at <http://www.qlcht.org.nz/news-updates/> (Accessed 31 March 2012).

Further reading

Gogia, N. (2006) 'Unpacking corporeal mobilities: the global voyages of labour and
leisure', *Environment and Planning*, 38: 359–75.

Uriely, N. (2001) '"Travelling workers" and "working tourists": variations across the
interaction between work and tourism', *International Journal of Tourism Research*, 3:
1–8.

Working holidaymakers – on behalf of the nation – labour mobility addressing labour futures?

There are a number of assumptions made about the mobile young working tourists internationally. We have addressed a number of issues in Chapter 3 on mobility. The increasing
number of temporary migrants internationally, in the last 30 years, is an outcome of
economic globalisation, the internationalisation of labour markets and transnationalism
(Lovelock and Leopold 2011: 140). Seasonal work, whether in tourist destinations such as
Queenstown, or in other sectors such as agriculture, is a feature of the tourism labour
market. In settler societies such as New Zealand these temporary labour migrants are
granted entry via various policies and bilateral agreements with the tourist's host country.
Underpinning these agreements is a long-term view with respect to permanent settlement.
Attracting skilled migrants in ageing societies such as New Zealand and other settler societies is a priority and working holidaymaker schemes offer a potential future pool of
|permanent settlers who are educated and skilled (Lovelock and Leopold 2011: 142).
These temporary workers in the tourism labour market provide seasonal and casual
labour at rates that support their travel needs, but the rates are low and invariably these
young workers return to their home countries in debt from their trip as their pay has not
covered adequately the cost of living in resort towns (Newlands 2006; Lovelock and
Leopold 2011). Working holidaymakers from developed nations where bilateral agreements
exist are a vastly different class of worker than temporary migrants who fill low pay
occupations and where the view is not to allow permanent settlement. They are rather like
Adler and Adler's (2004) seekers, combining work with leisure pursuits but likely to seek

careers in other sectors once they return home. Working holidaymaker schemes demonstrate that labour migration is not an autonomous process, these schemes and agreements invariably mirror pre-existing trade and migratory flows and/or are often used as a means to establish and strength new trade relationships internationally (Lovelock and Leopold 2011: 149). The ethical questions surrounding this practice hinge on who has the opportunity to become a working holidaymaker and who does not. These schemes exist typically between developed nations and/or are initiated by developed nations seeking trade relations with developing nations. These schemes potentially contribute to the uneven distribution of resources (human capital) and uneven global development.

CHAPTER REVIEW

This chapter has explored the tourism labour market and the ethical implications of the division of labour in various localities and globally. There is a range of research that has addressed consumption and the performative aspects of production in tourism, but less attention has been paid to productive labour and production, the structural features (how labour is organised) of practice and process and the material realities for those engaged in producing the tourism product. Patterns of work and consumption have changed in late capitalist societies and nowhere is this more evident than in tourism with the new middle classes embracing consumption as a means of self-fulfilment and advancement (Bianchi 2000) and an increasingly transnational class, producing the tourist product, for tourist consumption. There are a range of ethical issues connected to the tourism labour market and labour, many of which concern the unequal distribution of resources and how employment practices perpetuate existing structural inequalities. Distributive justice models are particularly useful when considering these ethical issues and concerns in this area.

SUMMARY OF KEY TERMS

Globalisation While globalisation has been variously defined, for the purposes of this chapter we will work with the definition provided by Waters (1995: 3) where globalisation refers to: 'a social process in which the constraints of geography on social and cultural arrangements recede and in which people become increasingly aware that they are receding'. Further to this, these arrangements are played out economically, culturally and politically. Arrangements can be relocated and need not be location-specific; new arrangements can be made that establish networks of connection that have a global dimension. Tourism and the tourism industry provide an apt illustration of the processes of globalisation and how they manifest in the movement of people, tourists, labour and new enterprises involving new networks of connection.

Advanced capitalism refers to those societies where the capitalist economic model has been operating for a prolonged period and where this form of capitalism is distinguished from historic previous forms, including mercantilism and industrial capitalism. According to Habermas (1973), a key feature of advanced capitalism is the privatism (focus on career, leisure and consumption) and commodity fetishism. Advanced capitalism is often used in conjunction with the following descriptors: developed country, post-industrial society, post-Fordist.

Primary and secondary labour markets (dual labour market) The concepts of primary and secondary labour markets (or sectors) have now passed into conventional thought, with the primary labour market commonly understood to mean people with secure jobs and good conditions of work in public-sector employment, the large corporations and highly unionised industries; while the secondary labour market is understood to cover small employers, non-unionised sectors of the economy, and highly fragmented and competitive industries such as retailing, where jobs are less secure and conditions of work and pay generally poorest (Marshall 1998).

Flexible labour Refers to part-time, casual, seasonal work and the job insecurity and underemployment associated with flexible and casualised working arrangements.

Reserve army of labour This term derives from Karl Marx's writing and refers to a disadvantaged section of the proletariat. These workers perform two functions: to regulate wages by the implicit threat posed by available labour; and to supply labour for sudden expansions in production. As the reserve army decreases then wages increase, and vice versa. There has been considerable recent debate about the role of women as reserve labour (Marshall 1998).

QUESTIONS FOR REFLECTION

1 Who comprises the reserve army of labour in the tourism industry?
2 What are the ethical implications of employment practices on the cruise liners?
3 What kind of ethical frameworks are useful when considering the ethical and moral dilemmas produced by the tourism labour market and employment practices?
4 How can individual travellers address these ethical issues and concerns?

EXERCISES

1 Apply the utilitarian model of ethical decision making to labour market conditions for the majority of tourism workers.
2 If you were an employer in the tourism industry how could you apply distributive justice? Find tourist operators who promote themselves in terms of distributive justice on the Internet – what have they changed in their operations?

FURTHER READING

Bianchi, R.V. (2000) 'Migrant tourist-workers: Exploring the "contact zones" of post-industrial tourism', *Current Issues in Tourism,* 3(2): 107–37.

—— (2009b) 'The "critical turn" in tourism studies: A radical critique', *Tourism Geographies,* 11(4): 484–504.

Zampoukos, K. and Ioannides, D. (2011) 'The tourism labour conundrum: Agenda for new research in the geography of hospitality workers', *Hospitality and Society,* 1(1): 25–45.

NOTE

a Vandegrift, Darcie (2008) '"This isn't Paradise – I Work Here": global restructuring, the tourism industry, and women workers in Caribbean Costa Rica', *Gender and Society,* 22: 778–97.

REFERENCES

Adler, P.A. and Adler, P. (1999) 'Resort workers: Adaptation in the leisure-work nexus', *Sociological Perspectives,* 42(3): 369–402.

—— (2004) *Paradise Laborers: Hotel Work in the Global Economy,* Ithaca, NY: Cornell University Press.

Aguiar, L.L.M. and Herod, A. (eds) (2006) *The Dirty Work of Neoliberalism: Cleaners in the Global Economy,* Oxford: Blackwell.

Airey, D., and Nightingale, M. (1981) 'Tourism occupations, career profiles and knowledge', *Annals of Tourism Research,* 8(1): 52–68.

Ball, R. (1997) 'The role of the state in the globalisation of labour markets: The case of the Philippines', *Environment and Planning,* 29: 1603–28.

Baum, T. (1995) *Managing Human Resources in the European Tourism and Hospitality Industry: A Strategic Approach,* London: Chapman and Hall.

—— (2010) 'Demographic change and labour supply in global tourism to 2030: a tentative assessment', in *Contemporary Issues in Irish and Global Tourism and Hospitality,* School of Hospitality Management and Tourism at ARROW@DIT.

Beddoe, C. (2004) *Labour Standards, Social Responsibility and Tourism,* London: Tourism Concern.

Belau, D. (2003) *New Threats to Employment in the Travel and Tourism Industry,* Geneva: International Labour Organisation.

Bianchi, R.V. (2002) 'Towards a new political economy of global tourism', in R. Sharpley and D. Telfer (eds) *Tourism and Development: Concepts and Issues,* pp 265–99, Clevedon: Channel View Publications.

—— (2011) 'Tourism, capitalism and Marxist political economy', in J. Mosedale (ed.) *Political Economy of Tourism: A Critical Perspective,* New York: Routledge, pp. 17–37.

Blanton, D. (1981) 'Tourism training in developing countries: The social and cultural dimensions', *Annals of Tourism Research,* 8(1): 116–33.

Britton, S.G. (1991) 'Tourism, capital and place: towards a critical geography of tourism', *Environment and Planning D: Society and Space,* 9: 451–78.

Burns, P. (1993) 'Sustaining tourism employment', *Journal of Sustainable Tourism,* 1: 81–96.

Castles, S. and Miller, M.J. (2003) *The Age of Migration: International Population Movements in the Modern World,* New York: Guilford Press.

Church, A. and Frost, M. (2004) 'Tourism, the global city and the labour market in London', *Tourism Geographies,* 6(2): 208–28.

Clancy, M. (1998) 'Commodity chains, services and development: Theory and preliminary evidence from the tourism industry', *Review of International Political Economy*, 5(1): 122–48.

Cleverdon, R. (1979) *The Economic and Social Impact of International Tourism on Developing Countries*, London: Economist Intelligence Unit.

Crang, P. (1997) 'Performing the tourist product', in Rojek, C. and Urry, J. (eds) *Touring Cultures: Transformations of Travel and Theory*, New York: Routledge, pp. 137–54.

Cukier, S.J. and Wall, G. (1993) 'Tourism employment: Perspectives from Bali', *Tourism Management*, 14(3): 195–201.

Devine, F., Baum,T., Hearns, N. and Devine, A. (2007) 'Cultural diversity in hospitality work: The Northern Ireland experience', *International Journal of Human Resource Management*, 18(2): 333–49.

Ghodsee, K. (2005) *The Red Riviera: Gender, Tourism and Postsocialism in the Black Sea*, London: Duke University Press.

Habermas, J. (1973) *Legitimation Crisis* (English translation by T. McCarthy), Boston, MA: Beacon.

Hochschild, A. (2003) *The Managed Heart: Commercialization of human feeling* (2nd edn), Berkeley: University of California Press.

Hudson, R. (1999) 'The new economy of the new Europe: Eradicating divisions or creating new forms of uneven development?', in Hudson, R. and Williams, A.M. (eds) *Divided Europe: Society and Territory*, London: Sage, pp. 29–62.

Ioannides, D. and Debbage, K. (1998) 'Neo-Fordism and flexible specializations in the travel industry: Dissecting the polyglot', in Ioannides, D. and Debbage, K. (eds) *The Economic Geography of the Tourist Industry*, London: Routledge, pp. 99–122.

Ladkin, A. (2011) 'Exploring Tourism Labor', *Annals of Tourism Research*, 38(3): 1135–55.

Lee, C-K. and Seyoung, K. (1998) 'Measuring earnings, inequality and median earnings in the tourism industry', *Tourism Management*, 19: 349–58.

Lovelock, K. and Leopold, T. (2011) 'The political economy of temporary migration: seasonal workers, tourists and sustaining New Zealand's labour force', in J. Mosedale (ed.) *Political Economy of Tourism: A Critical Perspective*, New York: Routledge.

McDowell, L. (2009) *Working Bodies: Interactive Service Employment and Workplace Identities*, Oxford: Wiley-Blackwell.

Marshall, G. (1998) *A Dictionary of Sociology. Encyclopedia.com*. (Accessed 16 September 2012).

Mintz, S.W. (1998) 'The localization of anthropological practice: From area studies to transnationalism', *Critique of Anthropology*, 18: 117–33.

Newlands, K.J. (2006) *The modern nomad in New Zealand: A study of the effects of the Working Holiday Schemes on free independent travellers and their host communities*, unpublished thesis, Auckland University, Auckland, New Zealand.

Nickson, D. (2007) *Human Resources Management for the Hospitality and Tourism Industries*, Oxford: Butterworth-Heinemann.

O'Byrne, D.J. (2001) 'On passports and border controls', *Annals of Tourism Research*' 28(2): 399–416.

Orenstein, C. (1997) 'Fantasy island:Royal Caribbean parcels off a piece of Haiti', *The Progressive*, 61(8): 28–31.

Pritchard, A., Morgan, N., Ateljevic, I., and Harris, C. (eds) (2007) *Tourism and Gender. Embodiment, Sensuality and Experience*, Oxford: CABI.

Sharpley, R. and Telfer, D. (eds) (2002) *Tourism and Development: Concepts and Issues*, Clevedon: Channel View Publications.

Sloan, G. (1998) 'When you're young at heart: Disney makes big magic on the high seas', *USA Today*, 16(225): 164–7.

Terry, W.C. (2011) 'Geographic limits to global labor market flexibility: the human resources paradox of the cruise industry', *Geoforum*, 42: 660–70.

Tesone, D. (2008) *Handbook of Hospitality Human Resources Management,* Oxford: Butterworth-Heinemann.

Viejola, S. and Jokinen, E. (2008) 'Towards a hostessing society? Mobile arrangements of gender and labour', *Nordic Journal of Feminist and Gender Research,* 16(3): 166–81.

Waters, M (1995) *Globalization*, London: Routledge.

Wood, R.E. (2000) 'Caribbean cruise tourism: globalization at sea', *Annals of Tourism Research,* 27(2): 345–70.

—— ((2006) 'Cruise tourism: a paradigmatic case of globalization', in Dowling, R. (ed.) *Cruise Ship Tourism,* Cambridge, MA: CABI.

14 Codes of ethics

'Every aspect of Western culture needs a new code of ethics – a rational ethics – as a precondition of rebirth.'

Ayn Rand[a]

'A person who is fundamentally honest doesn't need a code of ethics. The Ten Commandments and the Sermon on the Mount are all the ethical code anybody needs.'

Harry S. Truman[b]

LEARNING OBJECTIVES

After reading this chapter you will be able to:

- Define the terms 'code of ethics' and 'code of conduct'.
- Explain the origins of codes of ethics, their contemporary development, and their connection with corporate social responsibility.
- Explain the ethical basis for codes of ethics, and how this may impact upon their effectiveness.
- Discuss the key criticisms of codes of ethics as an approach to guiding the ethical behaviour of tourism businesses, or tourists.
- Discuss the relative strengths and weaknesses of a moral relativist approach to codes of ethics.
- Outline some key success factors for the development of a code of ethics.

14.1 INTRODUCTION

In an industry that is only lightly regulated in many jurisdictions, and one that is confronted with such a range of ethical challenges, it is not surprising that many codes of ethics have emerged to provide guidance. Fennell and Malloy (2007: 16) refer to there being 'literally thousands of codes of ethics in tourism and outdoor recreation that are geared towards host communities, governments, service providers, individual firms, and tourists throughout the world'.

But given the thousands of codes of ethics that exist across the tourism industry, one would have hoped that the industry would be in a more ethical space than it currently occupies. This begs the question of just how effective codes of ethics are in modifying behaviours of tourism stakeholders, or upholding moral standards. Some commentators criticise tourism codes of ethics as 'little more than a cynical marketing ploy' (Holden 2000: 159), lacking teeth but 'allowing an organisation to claim sensitivity and responsibility' (Honey 1999: 50). Codes have also been labelled an attempt on the part of the tourism industry to stave off government regulation (Mowforth and Munt 2003). Others, however, see codes of ethics as useful tools, that are relatively easy to introduce and effective (e.g. Garrod and Fennell 2004; Roberts and Hall 2001).

The chapter addresses the controversy around codes of ethics. We begin by defining what a code of ethics is, and outlining the philosophical basis for codes of ethics. We then consider their application in tourism and examine the extent to which they have been effective and why.

14.2 TOURISM CODES OF ETHICS – DEFINITIONS AND ISSUES

To clarify what we cover in this chapter under 'codes of ethics', we also include under this umbrella term, codes of conduct and codes of practice. However, Fennell and Malloy (2007) consider that codes of ethics are more philosophical and value-based. Codes of conduct and/or practice in comparison are more technical and specifically tailored to meet the requirements of an organisation or group at a particular time or space. They also argue that of the three functions of codes (to aspire, to educate and to regulate), the aspirational and educational functions are served by codes of ethics, whereas the regulatory function is best served by codes of conduct or practice. While there are subtle differences between these terms, we feel that their common goals of providing guidelines for better moral behaviour provide a basis for treating them under the one heading.

So how can we best define codes of ethics? Genot (1995: 169) refers to a code of ethics as a 'public statement of ethical, rather than legal, commitment to certain values and standards of behaviour'. Building on this Fennell and Malloy (2007: 21) define a code of ethics as:

> a formal, written statement that functions as a *message* to internal and external stakeholders regarding how it wishes to be perceived and it is a *guide* for employees that identifies preferred modes of behaviour. It embodies how an organisation thinks about itself ethically.

In this way, we can see that codes of ethics are related to organisational mission statements, statements of principles and value statements. However, compared to codes of ethics, these other exercises tend to be more aspirational in character (Fennell and Malloy 2007).

While calls for international tourism codes of ethical behaviour are hardly recent (e.g. Krohn and Ahmed 1992), the recent rise in interest in tourism ethics and, consequently, codes of ethics, is linked to other aspirational goals – namely the growth of interest in sustainable tourism and alternative tourism (Fennell and Malloy 2007). With the increased scope, scale and visibility of tourism's impacts, there has been a recognition of the need for tourism to improve its triple bottom-line performance and to contribute to a better world.

A more cynical view may be that the widespread adoption of codes of ethics by the tourism industry, has simply mirrored what was happening in the broader business field, and that codes of ethics (and associated certification programmes) have become linked to competitive advantage (Fennell and Malloy 2007; Harris and Jago 2001).

The power of codes of ethics to the consumer is demonstrated by a survey into consumer attitudes towards ethical and responsible tourism commissioned by Tearfund (a UK-based NGO). The survey revealed strong support among consumers for codes of ethics: 45 per cent of respondents said that they would be more likely to book a holiday with a company 'if they had a written code to guarantee good working conditions, protect the environment and support local charities in the tourist destination' (Tearfund 2000: 8). Tearfund argues that as there is little loyalty shown by tourists to tour operators, there is a positive opportunity for companies to gain competitive advantage by adopting ethical policies.

The controversy around codes of ethics, however, largely rests upon the extent to which they are internalised by the tourism company, and actually become a part of company culture. One of the earlier writers on tourism ethics, Hultsman (1995), believes that there is a need to go beyond simple codes of ethics. He makes the distinction between a 'paradigmatic' ethic and an operational code of ethics. While acknowledging that codes do serve a purpose, he advocates that they need to be grounded in a more paradigmatic footing. He cites Leopold's 'land ethic' developed in his *A Sand County Almanac* (1949) (see Chapter 9 for a discussion of the land ethic) as an example of an ethic that provides an intuitive basis for decision making and action. Hultsman argues for a tourism services ethic that, in a similar way to how the land ethic guides conservationists, could act as a 'foundational and articulated notion of what tourism professionals collectively accept and tacitly understand as being principled behavior' (1995: 556). These sentiments are also reflected in empirical studies of codes of ethics in tourism, in which their shortcomings have been revealed. Malloy and Fennell, for example, call for codes of ethics to be situated within a 'deeper philosophical context' (1998: 460). Thus the extent to which codes are internalised (and then operationalised) depends somewhat on their philosophical origins, and how this has shaped their content and style.

14.3 HISTORY OF CODES OF ETHICS

Fennell and Malloy (2007) provide a very good overview of codes of ethics in tourism, and we direct readers towards their informative volume. They write of codes of ethics being traced back to as early as eighteenth-century BC Babylon. In the fifth century BC, the ancient Greek physician Hippocrates developed an oath 'pledging the medical field to the preservation of life and the wellbeing of mankind' – the well-known Hippocratic Oath (Veatch 2003 in Fennell and Malloy 2007: 19). Many early codes of ethics were related to or developed in association with organised religion. The Ten Commandments, associated with Judeo-Christianity, are a code of ethics for people of this belief system. Similarly, the Smritis, which are held to be an elaboration of the Srutis or Vedas, are the principal codes of social law in Hindu society. They lay down the laws that regulate national, communal, family and individual obligations.

DISCUSSION POINT

Rodrigue Tremblay in his book *The Code for Global Ethics: Ten Humanist Principles* (2010) discusses the possibility of 'morality without religion', and has developed an alternative, secular set of commandments:

1 Proclaim the natural dignity and inherent worth of all human beings.
2 Respect the life and property of others.
3 Practise tolerance and open-mindedness towards the choices and life styles of others.
4 Share with those who are less fortunate and mutually assist those who are in need of help.
5 Use neither lies, nor spiritual doctrine, nor temporal power to dominate and exploit others.
6 Rely on reason, logic and science to understand the Universe and to solve life's problems.
7 Conserve and improve the Earth's natural environment – land, soil, water, air and space – as humankind's common heritage.
8 Resolve differences and conflicts cooperatively without resorting to violence or to wars.
9 Organise public affairs according to individual freedom and responsibility, through political and economic democracy.
10 Develop one's intelligence and talents through education and effort.

Tremblay is just one author to prescribe an alternative set of commandments: others include Richard Dawkins, in his book *The God Delusion* (2006).

Useful sources

Ten Commandment Alternatives <http://en.wikipedia.org/wiki/The_Code_for_Global_Ethics#The_Code_for_Global_Ethics>
Smritis see <http://www.swami-krishnananda.org/hist/hist_8.html>
Dawkins, R. (2006) *The God Delusion*, Boston, MA: Houghton Mifflin.
Tremblay, R. (2010) *The Code for Global Ethics: Ten Humanist Principles*, Amherst, NY: Prometheus Books.

Reflection question and exercise

To what extent are tourism codes of ethics connected to religious codes or scriptures? Conduct a Web search of some tourism codes of ethics and see if you can identify any explicit or implicit links.

Kolk and van Tulder (2002 in Fennell and Malloy 2007) also attribute the growth of codes in some part to the neoliberalisation of government policies adopted widely throughout the West during the 1980s, coupled with globalisation of investment and production, both of which contributed to a regulatory vacuum in many jurisdictions. Societal pressure from various interest groups put pressure on corporates to address this vacuum, which led to an 'explosion of codes in business during the 1990s' (Fennell and Malloy 2007: 21). Also, the concurrent emergence of the concept of Corporate Social Responsibility (CSR) (see Chapter 1) has placed much attention on the concept of responsibility, discussion of which has been dominated by a focus on moral codes of conduct (Loacker and Muhr 2009). Schwartz (2001) reports that over 90 per cent of large corporations in the USA have a code of ethics, Canada 86 per cent and the UK 57 per cent. Indeed, in some countries, listed companies are required (or at least encouraged) to have codes of ethics (e.g. in the USA the Sarbanes–Oxley Act of 2002 has made having a code a necessity; in the UK listed companies are subject to the Combined Code on Corporate Governance (Preuss 2010)). In addition to meeting externally imposed requirements, companies use codes of ethics for a number of reasons, including the provision of normative standards for employees, avoidance of legal consequences and promotion of a public image (Ethics Resource Centre 1990 in Schwartz 2001).

In the well-known Enron case, however, codes of ethics provided no protection for those in the company who perpetrated fraud, nor for innocent employees or the thousands of investors in the company, many of whom lost their life savings. Enron was a US energy, commodities and services company, with revenues of over $100 billion, and employing over 20,000 staff, before collapsing into bankruptcy in 2001 stemming from the exposure of unethical accounting practices. Importantly, Enron had its own comprehensive code of ethics. This comprised a 64-page booklet that refers to the 'moral and honest manner' in which the company's business affairs should be conducted (the booklet is now fetching large sums on the open market due to its curiosity value).

This of course begs the question of whether codes are effective in influencing behaviour. Schwartz (2001), summarising the empirical research addressing code effectiveness in the general area of business, reports that the research findings regarding code efficacy are inconsistent. While some studies suggest that codes lead to 'higher ethical behaviour', or have a 'deterring influence on unethical behaviour', other studies conclude that 'codes by themselves have little impact' (2001: 249). For many studies there was an insignificant relationship between the existence of codes of ethics and enhanced ethical behaviour (e.g. Kaptein and Schwartz 2008). So why is this the case? Researchers have identified the importance not only of the content of codes (level of detail and clarity), but also of monitoring and compliance. In terms of CSR approaches of companies, van Tulder et al. (2009) have synthesised these aspects into a model that classifies companies (from inactive through reactive and active to proactive) based on two dimensions of their codes of ethics: the specificity of the code content and the level of monitoring and compliance.

In addition to company-level codes, codes of ethics may exist at the industry-wide level, at the inter-governmental level, or may be developed by external organisations such as NGOs. But evidence suggests that industry-wide codes are often even less demanding than other codes, due to the need to find common ground among industry members (Kolk and van Tulder 2002). Similarly, codes developed by inter-governmental organisations are often weak in terms of monitoring. NGO codes, on the other hand, can be more demanding in terms of behaviour (Kolk and van Tulder 2002) although the extent to which they are taken seriously by industry members may vary. And finally, a major criticism of all codes of ethics is that they invariably involve self-regulation, and thus they do not have the same degree of 'clout' as government regulation (Sobczak 2006).

14.4 THE BASIS OF CODES

Code approaches to ethics 'try to determine responsible behaviour by way of universally defined rules, instructions and obligations on how to behave and act in a "proper and right way"' (Loacker and Muhr 2009: 266). But many codes have a utilitarian focus that defines responsible conduct from the business perspective: 'from strategic considerations and… organisational interests' (2009: 266). This is reflected in the way that many business ethics approaches advise 'care about the other because the other is useful for us' (Jones et al. 2005: 122), or care about the other because it pays (Francis and Armstrong 2003). Thus code-based approaches to ethics are essentially normative approaches, with a focus on seeking guidance from the 'external invocations and obligations' of others rather than from 'within' (Loacker and Muhr 2009: 266). Critics of this approach argue that the question of responsibility 'cannot be reduced to an abstract, technical and functionalistic codified system' (Loacker and Muhr 2009: 267; see also Weaver 2006).

Some argue for an alternative ethics that is based on practices of the self, as 'ethics is not given *a priori* and cannot be concluded or enclosed' by predetermined codes (Loacker and Muhr 2009). Such an approach draws upon the work of French philosopher Michel Foucault, whose conception of ethics was itself informed by his analysis of the moral prescriptions and behaviour of the ancient Greeks. The Foucauldian concept of ethics, while acknowledging normative codes that define what is morally correct, more importantly requires us to look at context-specific 'practices of the self'. In this way we relate codes to ourselves and try to constitute ourselves as agents of moral conduct (Loacker and Muhr 2009: 268). Individuals constitute themselves as moral subjects through practices such as self-reflection and self-examination (Cummings 2000 in Loacker and Muhr 2009: 268).

Others would argue that codes of ethics serve no good purpose whatsoever. In a similar way to the Foucauldian approach described above, Ladd (1991 in CSEP 2012) argues that ethics should be open-ended and reflective, and that to rely on a code of ethics is to confuse ethics with law. Ladd also questions the need for a separate code of ethics for professionals (e.g. tourism operators), arguing that they should be governed by the same set of ethics that guide ordinary human beings within a moral society. Indeed, ethical codes may not always serve as the highest expressions of moral integrity (Bersoff and Koeppl 1993). They are often 'anachronistic, conservative, protective of [their professional] members, the product of political compromise, restricted in [their] scope, and too often unable to provide clear-cut solutions to ambiguous professional predicaments' (1993: 348).

Likewise, Schwartz argues that codes of ethics are an 'unconscionable regression' to an undesirable earlier time, comparing ethical codes to the methods of control used in feudal times, while noting their elements of 'fascist doctrine' (2000: 173, 174). He believes that business organisations have no business 'prescribing morality' – either to their employees, nor to society. In line with the Foucauldian approach outlined above, Schwartz advocates for businesses to create environments where employees (and clients – tourists – and other stakeholders) 'can be comfortable in choosing to do what they believe is the right thing to do' (2000: 182). While such an approach may be far more difficult than simply developing codes, it will ultimately result in more ethical business operations (Schwartz 2000).

Within the tourism context, Butcher (2003: 71) sees codes of conduct as a part of the 'New Moral Tourism', describing them as 'excess moral baggage' that 'formalise common sense'. However, Butcher's view that tourists do not need help in negotiating their cultural encounter, and that tools such as codes of conduct detract from the tourist experience, has been critiqued by Cole (2007). She points out that host communities have to put up with a 'constant stream of beginners of learners' – tourists who are yet to learn the appropriate 'rules of engagement' for cultures and settings that are unknown to them (2007: 444). It is not enough to simply allow tourists to choose to do what they believe is the right thing to do – especially in destination settings where the cultural norms may be quite different to what they are accustomed to. In these cases, codes of ethics, behaviour or conduct may indeed be useful, if not essential.

What is a good code?

We have discussed a number of criticisms of a code approach to ethics. However, they do appear to have an innate attractiveness to industry, and hence there is a strong likelihood that such an approach *will* persist, so, what are the elements of a good code? They should be clear, comprehensive and phrased to 'emphasise and praise' rather than simply listing a series of prohibitions (Fleckenstein and Huebsch 1999). But, just as importantly, four virtues should be reflected in a code: justice (fairness and good faith in dealings); integrity (honesty, sincerity, respect for self and others); competence (ability, capability and reliability); and utility (efficiency, and providing the greatest good for the greatest number) (Fleckenstein and Huebsch 1999). The assumption that a utilitarian approach should be paramount in developing codes of ethics is, however, open to debate.

DISCUSSION POINT: WHAT MAKES A 'GOOD' CODE OF ETHICS?

It may be useful to look at ethics developments in other industries or professions, as many have considerably longer histories with developing and implementing codes of ethics than the tourism industry. Allan (2011: 438–41) reports on a revision of the codes of ethics in the field of psychology, noting that following a review, a number of principles were settled on to guide the development of a new code, including:

1 *Principled Approach*: It should be based on an ethical theory, principle, or set of principles, e.g. the principles adopted in the United Nations

Universal Declaration of Human Rights (respect for the dignity and rights of people, autonomy, justice, non-maleficence, beneficence, veracity, fidelity and responsibility).

2 *Public Statement*: To provide a clear public statement of the ethical principles of the group or organisation concerned.

3 *Educate, Guide and Support*: To educate and guide new members, to remind experienced members of appropriate behaviour and practice.

4 *Face Value*: Should address issues that are pertinent to the public, stakeholders and members of the group or organisation.

5 *Regulation*: Ensure that the code is enforceable.

Discussion questions

1 To what extent can the tourism industry be informed by ethical codes developed in other fields, such as psychology? What does tourism have in common with other sectors or professions? How does it differ?

2 Tourism has been called a 'partially industrialised' activity – i.e. one that comprises many different industries or sectors, such as hospitality, retail, recreation, education. Does this pose problems in terms of developing good 'tourism' codes of ethics?

Reference

Allan, A. (2011) 'The development of a code for Australian psychologists', *Ethics and Behavior*, 21(6): 435–51.

14.5 PHILOSOPHICAL BASIS FOR CODES OF ETHICS

Deontology and utilitarianism are the two most generally accepted ethical frameworks on which codes of ethics are built (Bersoff and Koeppl 1993; and see Chapter 2). Immanuel Kant (1724–1804), founder of deontology, held that the morality of a behaviour is directly related to its intrinsic or inherent nature, i.e. actions are right or wrong regardless of their consequences. Utilitarianism is often described as the opposite to deontology, in which decision making is guided by maximising happiness (or utility). Alternative approaches to codes of ethics have been proposed that blend aspects of both deontology and utilitarianism. One such approach is that of twentieth-century English philosopher W.D. Ross (1877–1971). Ross argued that maximising the good is only one of seven prima facie duties that outline what a person ought to do in any particular circumstance. These duties include: fidelity; reparation; gratitude; non-maleficence; justice; beneficence; and self-improvement. Such duties may form the basis of codes of ethics. Schfeller (1982 in Getz 1990) similarly advocates an alternative 'hybrid' approach that takes into account respect for rights *and* responsibility for consequences. From this perspective, Getz (1990) analyses codes of conduct for businesses, pointing out that business organisations tend to favour utilitarian reasoning in decision making and policy setting. Thus, Getz argues that an important function of codes of conduct is to provide businesses with a basis for deonto-logical reasoning. In an analysis of international codes of conduct Getz ranks the codes in terms of the number of deontological principles (the more the better) and utilitarian exclu-sions (the fewer the better).

In contrast, when we consider the deontological or teleological (consequentialist) bases of tourism codes of behaviour, some (e.g. Malloy and Fennell 1998; Fennell and Malloy 2007) argue that the teleological basis, because it provides a consequence of non-compli-ance with a rule (rather than just simply a rule to follow), is more appropriate. Deontological codes include ethical perspectives that are rules-based and assess 'rightness' and 'wrong-ness' on the basis of actions and duties, while teleological codes are those that advocate the type of good behaviour 'which produces the best consequences for the greatest number of people' (Garrod and Fennell 2004: 342). Mason (2007) illustrates the differences between deontological and teleological codes: a deontological code might contain an instruction such as 'Please do not feed the wildlife', while a teleological code would contain the statement 'Please do not feed the wildlife, as this may lead to behavioural changes and growing dependency on humans as food providers'. Thus the latter not only provides a prescriptive code, but also indicates the rationale for doing so (Cole 2007).

In a study of 40 tourism operator codes of ethics, however, deontology predominated as the basis for their codes (Malloy and Fennell 1998). This was also the case in an analysis of 58 codes of conduct for whale watching, which were overwhelmingly deontological (Garrod and Fennell 2004). Such codes do not provide the ethical decision maker with any rationale for abiding by the code. Tourists are not given the means to learn through an understanding of the consequences of their actions (Malloy and Fennell 1998).

14.6 MORAL RELATIVISM AND CODES OF ETHICS

As businesses move more into multinational marketing (which is very common in the tourism industry) ethical issues tend to increase (Rallapalli 1999). This raises the question of whether tourism multinationals should develop a code of ethics that is uniform across all their operations in different countries, or instead develop individual codes suited for each country (Laczniak and Murphy 1991). The argument *for* a global code of ethics would be based on the rationale that individual morals that guide ethical decision making tend to be similar in any nation (Rallapalli 1999). Likewise, one might also question whether codes of behaviour for visitors should be tailored to visitors from different source countries, for example should the code for visitors from the USA be different from that for visitors from India?

This leads us to the issue of moral relativism – and its counterpoint, moral universalism (see also Chapters 3 and 9). Moral relativism is the view that moral truth or justification is relative to a culture or society, and that justifications for moral judgements are not univer-sal, but are instead relative to the traditions, beliefs or practices of an individual or a group of people. Moral universalism (or objectivism), on the other hand, holds that some system of ethics, or a universal ethic, applies universally. This would be regardless of culture, ethnicity, religion or any other defining characteristic.

While moral relativism has only emerged relatively recently as a philosophy in its own right, it has ancient roots. Among the ancient Greek philosophers, moral diversity was widely acknowledged but the more common philosophy was that of moral scepticism – the view that there is no moral knowledge (Gowans 2012). With the modern era came an increasing awareness of moral diversity (especially between Western and non-Western cultures), which was an important precursor to the development of moral relativism (Gowans 2012). Gowans points out that there are many examples of moral practices from around the world that may differ radically from those advocated in contemporary Western society: polygamy, arranged marriages, sati (widow suicide in India), stoning for blasphemy or adultery, female genital mutilation and imprisonment for homosexuality. He notes, however, that while there are obvious moral disagreements between cultures, 'it is another matter to say that these disagreements are deep and widespread, and that they are much more significant than whatever agreements there may be' (Gowans 2012: n.p.).

With respect to tourism, Smith and Duffy (2003) argue that it is especially important to know the arguments for and against moral relativism. They present a set of arguments for moral relativism (2003: 34–5).

1   *The fact of moral and cultural diversity*: there are many different cultures in the world, each with its own set of ethical values.
2   *The functional interrelationship between ethics and society*: ethical values are an integral part of each society and cannot be understood outside that context.
3   *The social relativity of evaluation*: what counts as right or wrong depends upon which culture you belong to.
4   *The critique of objectivity*: if all ethical values are socially relative, there cannot be any *objective* ethical values.
5   *The importance of self-reflexivity*: our own ethical values too must be socially relative: they cannot be objective, nor can they provide us with a priviliged perspective of what is right and wrong.
6   *The equality of ethical evaluations*: since there are no objective criteria by which to judge moral values, they must all be treated as equally valid. We should be respectful and tolerant of other people's moral codes, however different they may be from our own.

However, they acknowledge that, apart from the moral objectivist argument, there are other reasons in tourism why one may reject the 'simplistic conclusions' of moral relativism. It is difficult to abandon our own values, and to go along with and respect the values of another social group, especially when they conflict with our core beliefs. Should we respect local views when, for example, we may consider them homophobic, racist or otherwise discriminatory? (Smith and Duffy 2003). Another problem with moral relativism is that it treats societies as easily distinguished, bounded entities – whereas in reality societies do not exist in complete isolation from other societies. In this vein, MacCannell writes that 'otherness is mainly fictional as modernity expands and draws every group, class, nation and nature itself into a single set of relations' (1999: 77 in Smith and Duffy 2003: 35). Thus a society's ethical values are constituted not wholly internally, and there may be shared values across societal boundaries. Also within societies there may be

Figure 14.1 *Tourists feeding dolphins at Tin Can Bay, Queensland, Australia. A wildlife tourism code of ethics might prevent the habituation of wild animals such as this. Photo: Brent Lovelock.*

substantial differences in moral values – meaning that from some sections of society, values may be more aligned with those of other societies (Smith and Duffy 2003).

In terms of developing universal codes of ethics for tourism businesses or a universal code of behaviour for tourists, moral relativism, despite its acknowledged problems, would hold that this may be a difficult task. Developers of such codes would have to consider the fundamental question of whether there is a common core of normative guidelines that all cultures would find agreeable (Rallapalli 1999). The issue of whether or not there *are* universal values is keenly contested in the literature. While some argue that 'the cultural differences in the expression of values precludes the idea of universal values or morals; others argue that there is a high level of agreement about a set of core values, despite differences in other values' (Behnke and Bullock 2010: 308).

What the tourism industry needs to avoid is what Rallapalli calls 'convenient relativism' where tourists or tourism operators can excuse anything (e.g. child labour, sex tourism) in the name of cultural diversity. He proposes that a global code of ethics would comprise two levels: normative guidelines (universally applicable); and specific behaviours (developed with country/culture-specific knowledge) (Rallapalli 1999).

14.7 DO CODES WORK IN THE TOURISM INDUSTRY?

Despite the large number of codes in place across the tourism industry, relatively little research has been undertaken on whether or not they actually work – especially considering that some have been in place since the 1960s (Mason and Mowforth 1996). Mason

(2007: 46), in an article about codes of conduct provocatively titled 'No Better than a Band-Aid for a Bullet Wound', is critical of the piecemeal development of separate codes for individual target audiences (visitors, industry and hosts), advocating for an integrated approach in which codes are incorporated into wider visitor management strategies. He also points to problems around lack of monitoring for effectiveness, reliance on voluntary self-regulation, and potential misuse of codes as marketing tools.

In many parts of the world, but particularly the USA and Canada, tourism codes tend to be sector- or activity-specific or 'single focus' (Wight 2004). One particular sector in which code development has been active is marine mammal tourism, e.g. whale watching and swimming with dolphins. Garrod and Fennell (2004) conducted a study of 58 whale-watching codes from around the world, commenting that the 'results do not appear especially encouraging' considering the variability within codes, the lack of knowledge about impacts on target species and the rapid growth of the industry. One study undertaken in New Zealand on the effectiveness of a voluntary code of conduct in reducing tourist vessel traffic around dolphins concluded that the code was effective in some respects but not others (Duprey et al. 2008). The code was primarily aimed at giving the dolphins a tourist-free rest period; however, while the overall number of visits to the dolphins during the rest period was lower than at other times of the day, visits still occurred. The authors conclude that:

> without increased pressure from either the community or controlling government departments, in the form of public reprimands, media attention, more community support for complying businesses, or the threat of more mandatory regulations, these companies will, most likely, not comply with voluntary codes of conduct.
>
> (Duprey et al. 2008: 635)

They note that voluntary measures such as codes require constant observations, education and encouragement, along with surveillance, to be effective. Similar conclusions were drawn regarding dolphin watching in New South Wales, Australia, where the voluntary code is 'of limited value without revision, education and enforcement' (Allen et al. .2007: 159). In her study of the use of codes in the management of whale watching in Kaikoura, New Zealand, Curtin (2003) concludes that 'spot checks' can help address the problems around self-regulation. She also points to 'consumer power' in the form of complaints potentially assisting with the enforcement of voluntary codes.

The nature of non-compliance with voluntary codes is highly relevant – and raises the question of what it is that makes some tourist operators comply while others do not. Theory on compliance falls into two broad categories: economic and non-economic. The latter is of particular relevance here, and theory would hold that compliance hinges upon individuals' intrinsic (moral) capacities along with extrinsic influences (e.g. incentives or sanctions from their peer group) (Sirakaya 1997). Sirakaya's study of ecotourism operators (from the USA, Ecuador and Canada) highlights the importance of personal morality or ethics in compliance. Out of a broad range of factors, personal ethics was the only factor that explained considerable variation in compliance. Consequently Sirakaya points to the need to include messages in codes or guidelines that 'induce moral obligations' in tourism operators, in order to increase compliance.

Another helpful approach may be to encourage tourism operators to develop their own individual codes of ethics. Fennell and Malloy (1999) investigated the ethical orientations of tourism operators, finding that ecotourism operators are more likely to have a 'more heightened sense of ethical conduct'; they put this down, in part, to the greater use of codes of ethics in the ecotourism operators' own business practices, making them more likely to have a 'heightened awareness of acceptable conduct and a consistent ethical approach throughout their business operation' (1999: 938–9).

14.8 CODES OF CONDUCT FOR TOURISTS

While the above discussion has largely been focused on codes of ethics for tourism businesses, codes of conduct for their clients, the tourists, have also been proposed. A visitor code of conduct is defined as a 'soft' visitor management tool that aims to educate tourists and influence their behaviour, and so reduce the negative impacts of tourism (Cole 2007) (cf. a 'hard' tool that regulates and controls). They have been promoted as a relatively easy tool to introduce to destinations (Garrod and Fennell 2004), and are considered by some to be effective (e.g. Roberts and Hall 2001). However, they are subject to criticism, and there has been limited research into their effectiveness (e.g. Cole 2007; Malloy and Fennell 1998; Mason 2005).

The aims of codes of conduct for tourists are to: raise tourist awareness; educate tourists; increase tourist confidence; prevent conflict between tourists and hosts; improve visitor behaviour; and act as a visitor management tool to reduce negative visitor impacts (Cole 2007: 444). Codes are voluntary and enforced mainly through ethical obligation and peer pressure (Garrod and Fennell 2004). Codes make tourists aware of their potential impact upon host societies and environments, and they provide a set of rules about how to behave in destinations (Roberts and Rognvaldson 2001). However, the very nature of the tourist motivation and tourist experience (escape, hedonistic) poses challenges to the effectiveness of codes of conduct. Cole (2007: 445) notes that if we consider tourists 'to be in "action spaces", released from everyday life and seeking pleasure' that they may be reluctant to adhere to behavioural codes that may 'signify constraints rather than freedom'. To illustrate, Cole points to criticism in the popular press of Venice's 2003 introduction of a code of conduct for visitors to the city. Venice receives 13–15 million visitors each year, and has introduced a 10-point code of conduct, with spot fines (up to 50 Euro) for anyone infringing measures designed to protect monuments and maintain standards of behaviour. One travel writer has described the idea as 'a totally crazy bid…totally daft…Trying to tell them (tourists) how to dress and where to eat is simply ludicrous' (Barrett 2003 in Cole 2007: 445). (For an interesting discussion of the need for tourist codes of conduct see <http://www.tripadvisor.com/ShowTopic-g187870-i57-k2770485-Do_tourists_need_a_Code_of_Conduct-Venice_Veneto.html >.)

Such criticism, however, perhaps points to the need for care in the development, design and dissemination of codes of conduct. Some of the essential characteristics of 'good' codes of conduct include them being negotiated with a wide range of stakeholder input. As Garrod and Fennell (2004) point out, codes are more likely to be actioned by the intended users, if these groups have been involved in the development of the codes.

Figure 14.2 *Tourist codes of conduct may help prevent unwanted intrusions within cultural tourism settings such as this village in Myanmar. Photo: Brent Lovelock.*

They also need to be promoted and the message widely disseminated (Mason and Mowforth 1995 in Cole 2007). Codes should be positively stated and action-oriented, avoiding prohibitive language (WWF 2001 in Cole 2007). They should also be locally relevant, rather than global or general in nature (Cole 2007).

CASE STUDY: CODES OF TOURIST CONDUCT – NGADHA, INDONESIA

Stroma Cole (2007) provides one the few empirical studies of the effectiveness of tourist codes of conduct. She undertook her study in the Ngadha region of Flores, Indonesia, where international tourists are attracted by the traditional culture of the villages. There have, however, been a range of cultural impacts observed, associated with the growth of tourism there. Cole, together with local stakeholders, developed a code of conduct that was distributed to guest houses and included in a marketing leaflet for the region.

The Ngadha code of conduct

In order to be a welcome guest in Ngadha villages the villagers would appreciate it if you observe the following:

1 The villagers appreciate their guests to be appropriately dressed. Please wear long, loose, clean, unrevealing clothing. Avoid wearing short shorts, singlets, tight, transparent or dirty clothes.

2 It is offensive in Ngadha culture to reveal your navel (belly button, ombligo, nombril, nabel). Please ensure your navel is covered.

3 Please do not display affection in public. Avoid handholding, cuddling, hugging and kissing while visiting the villages.

4 Villagers like to talk to tourists. Try to respond to greetings the villagers make and make an effort to communicate with them. Use your guide to facilitate communication.

5 Villagers are generally happy for you to take photographs in the village. However always seek permission before taking photographs of villagers especially if they are in ceremonial costume. Do not offer money for photographs initially refused.

6 Villagers welcome gifts but please do not give to individual children. Gifts should be given to adults so they can distribute them. If children request items from you, try to talk to the children and play games with them. Gift giving, especially sweets, to children may encourage 'begging' behaviour which their parents dislike.

7 Some villages sell tickets to tourists. This is their method of ensuring the amount of money received from tourists is transparent and accountable. The funds are used for village projects. Further donations can be made in donation boxes provided.

8 Some villagers sell handicrafts. It is normal to bargain for such purchases. If you want to be sure of getting the 'best price' bargain first and then consider over-paying (5–10%) as a gesture of goodwill and acknowledgement of your relative wealth.

9 Villagers welcome tourists at rituals and actively invite tourists (often via guides) to participate. If you want to be welcomed, take a contribution, as all local people do, and give it to the hosts of the ritual. For example a kilogram of rice or sugar per tourist would be appropriate.

10 Rituals often take a long time. Be prepared to wait around. It is offensive to attend a ritual and not partake in ritual meals. Always accept ritual food and drink (alcoholic, arak) that is offered to you (it is OK to just taste a little bit).

11 Some rituals involve dancing. If you would like to dance you must be in costume. It is possible to hire a costume (your guide can help you).

12 Ngadha culture is very rich and complex. Tourists are advised to take a guide. You will appreciate your trip a thousand times more with their explanation.

The Ngadha code of conduct was introduced to 'reduce friction and misunderstanding between tourists and villagers, and to ease the job of guides' (Cole 2007: 449). Cole's interviews with tourists revealed that the code of conduct provided tourists with cultural information that they did not know, and that tourists in general responded positively to the code and found the information useful.

For example, during the month of observation, only one tourist fell into the category of 'rudely dressed' and five 'impolitely dressed'. The only person showing their navel was a teenage girl travelling with her parents, who had not seen the code of conduct and was embarrassed when she read the code after her village visit (Cole 2007: 448). However, Cole noted that there were limits to the tourists' compliance, with some tourists admitting that they were not prepared to change or follow some guidelines. For example, there was reluctance over the consumption of (even token amounts of) ritual food and drink (mainly on health grounds). And while tourists did not reject the code's advice about bargaining, the villages noted that the code did not seem to have changed the fierce bargaining behaviour of the tourists – they continued to drive unreasonably hard bargains, the tourists failing to empathise with the villagers' poverty levels (Cole 2007: 449).

Cole concludes that 'in some areas of behaviour the code was effective, while in other areas tourists continued to transgress local cultural norms of behaviour' (2007: 449). She also notes that, despite the suggestions of some (e.g. Garrod and Fennell 2004) that codes of conduct are easy, quick and cheap to introduce, to produce a code that was agreeable to local stakeholders and acceptable to end-users, was a process requiring considerable skill and patience. The language used in the code was also critical in tourists' understanding and compliance. She supports the usage of teleological statements that include reasons for compliance (rather than rule-based deontological guidelines), while acknowledging the complexity of expanding upon the cultural consequences of non-compliance with some guidelines. However, she notes the opportunity for cultural learning provided by attempting to do so.

Reflection questions

1 Consider the items in the Ngadha code of conduct – do you think that many of these may apply to other cultures in other destinations? Would any be applicable in a destination in *your* country? Are any of the items 'universal'?
2 If you were visiting the Ngadha region, how would you feel about adhering to the code of conduct?
3 Are there any items within the code that you may find difficult to adhere to? If so, why?

4 Do any of the items conflict with your own 'personal' code of ethics – or what you inherently understand to be 'good' behaviour?

5 Coles notes that a few tourists still breach the code on occasion. What practices could be put in place to help prevent this?

References

Cole, S. (2007) 'Implementing and evaluating a code of conduct for visitors', *Tourism Management*, 28(2): 443–51.Useful sources

Flores travel guide: <http://wikitravel.org/en/Flores_(Indonesia)>

Kenya Tourist Code of Conduct: <http://www.roveafrica.net/articles/kenya-tourist-code-conduct>

Living Heritage Code of Ethics for Tourists <http://livingheritage.org/tourist-ethics.htm>

Last Frontiers Code of Ethics for Travellers <http://www.lastfrontiers.com/rt_code.php>

WWF International Arctic Programme Code of Conduct for Arctic Tourists <http://wwf.panda.org/what_we_do/where_we_work/arctic/what_we_do/tourism/#tourists>

14.9 THE UNWTO CODE OF ETHICS

It is important to discuss the United Nations World Tourism Organization (UNWTO) Global Code of Ethics for Tourism (GCET) as this code, ideally, serves as the exemplar for other tourism codes of ethics arising at national, regional and local levels and for individual tourism businesses. The UNWTO Code evolved over a number of years, from initially the 1980 World Tourism Organization (WTO) Manila Declaration on World Tourism, the WTO Tourism Bill of Rights and Tourist Code (Sofia, Bulgaria, 1985), and the 1989 WTO The Hague Declaration on Tourism. The UNWTO Global Code of Ethics for Tourism was adopted in 1999.

The GCET is described by the UNWTO as:

> A fundamental frame of reference for responsible and sustainable tourism…a comprehensive set of principles designed to guide key-players in tourism development. Addressed to governments, the travel industry, communities and tourists alike, it aims to help maximize the sector's benefits while minimizing its potentially negative impact on the environment, cultural heritage and societies across the globe.
>
> (UNWTO 2012)

The Code's *10 principles* address the economic, social, cultural and environmental aspects of tourism:

Article 1: Tourism's contribution to mutual understanding and respect between peoples and societies

Article 2: Tourism as a vehicle for individual and collective fulfilment

Article 3: Tourism, a factor of sustainable development

Article 4: Tourism, a user of the cultural heritage of mankind and contributor to its enhancement

Article 5:   Tourism, a beneficial activity for host countries and communities
Article 6:   Obligations of stakeholders in tourism development
Article 7:   Right to tourism
Article 8:   Liberty of tourist movements
Article 9:   Rights of the workers and entrepreneurs in the tourism industry
Article 10: Implementation of the principles of the Global Code of Ethics for Tourism.

(For the full text of the GCET see <http://ethics.unwto.org/en/content/full-text-global-code-ethics-tourism>.)

The UNWTO acknowledges that the GCET is not legally binding. Despite this weakness, it has been described as a good attempt to synthesise most of the ethical concerns raised in the tourism industry (Dubois 2001). However, concerns are raised over inherent contradictions, for example how to reconcile the promotion of transport with the limitation of global warming; and free trade and liberalism with more efficient regulation (Dubois 2001). Dubois also talks of internal contradictions and 'meaningful silences' within the GCET, and believes that the 'attitude' of the GCET is attributable to its internal sector-driven origins. As noted above, such industry-driven codes may have limitations.

Ryan (2002), while acknowledging the aspirations of the WTO in creating the GCET, argues that they will remain 'toothless pieces of paper' unless they are able to be implemented through 'on the ground' actions. He warns, however, that this ground may be 'stony, infertile, and certainly full of those thistles entitled "vested interests"' (2002: 19). Codes of ethics that seek international application may be challenged by local practices, political issues, bribes, government intervention and inappropriate business practices (Fleckenstein and Huebsch 1999). Fennell and Malloy (2007) in their discussion of the GCET are more critical of attempts to produce universal codes of ethics rather than of the GCET per se. They point to the need for agreement on a set of 'hypernorms' or main principles around which such a code may be based. As discussed in Section 14.6 on moral relativism, agreement on such hypernorms may not always be that easy.

Notwithstanding such criticisms, the UNWTO has been active in assessing the effectiveness of the GCET: it conducted three surveys among its member states (in 2000, 2004 and 2008/2009) in order to monitor implementation of the Code. They conclude that the GCET has been 'instrumental in promoting and developing sustainable forms of tourism based upon ethical principles' (UNWTO 2010).

DISCUSSION POINT: *MAKE TRAVEL A GREAT EXPERIENCE: PRACTICAL TIPS FOR THE GLOBAL TRAVELLER* (UNWTO 2010)

To facilitate the understanding of the principles of the GCET by tourists in particular, a more user-friendly version was prepared by the UNWTO. Their *Practical Tips for the Global Traveller* (2010) brochure (below) highlights 'those principles of the GCET directly related to tourists, in order to help guide travellers in making their behaviour ever more responsible' (UNWTO 2012).

Honouring local traditions and customs

- Research your destination to learn all that you can about local customs and traditions. It is a great way to build understanding of the local community and excitement for your adventure ahead.
- Learn to speak a few words in the local language. This can help you connect with the local community and its people in a more meaningful way.
- Experience and respect all that makes an international destination different and unique from its history, architecture and religion to its music, art and cuisine.

Supporting the local economy

- Buy locally made handicrafts and products.
- Respect local vendors and artisans by practising fair trade.
- Do not buy counterfeit products and items that are prohibited by national/ international regulations.

Respecting the environment

- Reduce your environmental impact by being a good steward of natural resources and archaeological treasures.
- Protect wildlife and their natural habitats.
- Purchase products that are not made using endangered plants or animals.
- Take photos instead of protected artefacts as mementos of your trip.
- Leave only your footprint and a good impression behind.

Being an informed and respectful traveller

- Observe national laws and regulations.
- Respect human rights.
- Protect children from exploitation in travel and tourism.
- Take appropriate health precautions.
- Know how to access medical care or contact your embassy in case of an emergency.

Discussion questions

1 Consider the list above – from what ethical theory is it compiled?
2 Is the list effective – can you suggest how it could be improved?

Source

UNWTO (2010) *Make Travel a Great Experience: Practical Tips for the Global Traveller*, <http://ethics.unwto.org/sites/all/files/docpdf/maketravelagreatexperience.pdf>

CHAPTER REVIEW

The increased interest in tourism codes of ethics is in line with a renewed focus on corporate social responsibility, in the light of corporate excesses and abuses of power in recent years. However, as in the corporate world, there are a number of challenges around developing and implementing effective codes of ethics for tourism. While some researchers in the field advocate for a 'tourism services ethic', others are critical of such codes in principle. They advocate for a deeper philosophic approach to an ethical industry, rather than an externally imposed set of rules. Instead, they argue for a focus on 'practices of the self', believing that tourism operators should be guided by basic humanist principles rather than a code of ethics.

We discussed the issue of moral relativism, and how, in the face of an increasingly connected and globalised business environment, many tourism companies operate in multiple cultural environments. This begs the question of whether specific culturally relative codes should be developed, or whether a universal code may apply, irrespective of culture, ethnicity and religion. A blended approach is advocated comprising normative or universal plus locally specific items.

The problems around operationalising codes of ethics were addressed, and were related to the origins of codes, which are predominantly deontological or rules-based. Some workers in the field suggest that a more utilitarian approach, in which the consequences of actions are clearly outlined, may lead to improved observation of codes of ethics. In relation to this we identify the essential steps in developing codes, and useful components and styles within codes. The chapter also discussed the potential for codes of conduct for tourists. We noted, however, that the touristic experience is essentially escapist and hedonistic, posing challenges for tourists' commitment to such codes.

SUMMARY OF KEY TERMS

Code of ethics A set of principles and expectations that are considered binding on any person who is a member of a particular group. The group can consist of tourism businesses or any tourism stakeholder, including the tourists themselves. In relation to business and professions, a code of ethics is a set of guiding principles designed to help professionals conduct business honestly and with integrity.

Code of conduct A set of conventional principles and expectations that are considered binding on any person who is a member of a particular group. In tourism may apply to any tourism stakeholder, including tourists.

Corporate Social Responsibility (CSR) Initiatives or actions by companies to take responsibility for their effects on the environment and impacts on communities. Also referred to as 'corporate citizenship'. Generally conceived as going beyond regulatory requirements and can involve incurring short-term costs that do not provide an immediate financial benefit to the company, but instead promote positive social and environmental change.

Practices of the self From the Foucauldian concept of ethics, and posed as an alternative to normative ethical codes. Requires that we consider context-specific 'practices of the self' in order to constitute ourselves as agents of moral conduct. Individuals constitute themselves as moral subjects through practices such as self-reflection and self-examination.

Responsible tourism Travel conducted in such a manner as to not harm or degrade the cultural or natural environment of the places visited. Responsible tourism adopts a quadruple bottom-line philosophy to contribute to the wellbeing of local communities, cultures, environments and economies and minimise negative impacts

QUESTIONS FOR REFLECTION

1 Throughout this chapter, the problems with enforcing codes of ethics or conduct have been referred to. Think about what would make YOU, as a tourist, abide by a code of conduct?
2 Do you think that there are ways that the tourism industry could use technology to help implement codes of conduct for visitors? How could this be done?

EXERCISES

1 Undertake a Web search for visitor codes of conduct – identify the deontological or teleological aspects of each, along with any other useful approaches employed.
2 Develop a code of conduct for visitors to your own home town, carefully considering the ethical basis of your code.

FURTHER READING

Fennell, D.A. and Malloy, D.C. (2007) *Codes of Ethics in Tourism: Practice, Theory, Synthesis*, Clevedon: Channel View.

NOTES

a Ayn Rand (1905–82), Russian-born American writer and novelist. In Rand, A. (1961) *The Objectivist Ethics*. Available at <http://www.aynrand.org/site/PageServer?pagename = ari_ayn_ rand_the_objectivist_ethics > (Accessed 6 July 2010).
b Harry S. Truman (1884–1972), 33rd President of the United States (1945–53).

REFERENCES

Allen, S., Smith, H., Waples, K. and Harcourt, R. (2007) 'The voluntary code of conduct for dolphin watching in Port Stephens, Australia: Is self-regulation an effective management tool?', *Journal of Cetacean Research and Management*, 9(2): 159–66.

Behnke, S. and Bullock, M. (2010) 'Ethics within, across, and beyond borders: A commentary', *Ethics and Behavior*, 20(3–4): 297–310.

Bersoff, D.N. and Koeppl, P.M. (1993) 'The relation between ethical codes and moral principles', *Ethics and Behaviour*, 3(3&4): 345–57.

Butcher, J. (2003) *The Moralisation of Tourism*, London: Routledge.

Centre for the Study of Ethics in Professions (CSEP) (2012) *The Function and Value of Codes of Ethics*. Available at <http://ethics.iit.edu/research/introduction> (Accessed 4 April 2012).

Cole, S. (2007) 'Implementing and evaluating a code of conduct for visitors', *Tourism Management*, 28(2): 443–51.

Curtin, S. (2003) 'Whale watching in Kaikoura: Sustainable development?', *Journal of Ecotourism*, 3: 173–95.

Dubois, G. (2001) *Codes of conduct, charters of ethics and international declarations for a sustainable development of tourism: Ethical content and implementation of voluntary initiatives in the tourism sector*. TTRA Annual Conference, Fort Myers, Florida, pp. 61–83.

Duprey, N., Weir, J.S. and Wursig, B. (2008) 'Effectiveness of a voluntary code of conduct in reducing vessel traffic around dolphins', *Ocean & Coastal Management*, 51(8–9): 632–7.

Fennell, D.A. and Malloy, D.C. (1999) 'Measuring the ethical nature of tourism operators', *Annals of Tourism Research*, 26(4): 928–43.

Fennell, D. and Malloy, D. (2007) *Codes of Ethics in Tourism: Practice, Theory, Synthesis*, Clevedon: Channel View.

Fleckenstein, M.P. and Huebsch, P. (1999) 'Ethics in tourism – Reality or hallucination?', *Journal of Business Ethics*, 19(1): 137–42.

Francis, R. and Armstrong, A. (2003) 'Ethics as a risk management strategy: The Australian experience', *Journal of Business Ethics*, 45(4): 375–85.

Garrod, B. and Fennell, D.A. (2004) 'An analysis of whalewatching codes of conduct', *Annals of Tourism Research*, 31(2): 334–52.

Genot, H. (1995) 'Voluntary environmental codes of conduct in the tourism sector', *Journal of Sustainable Tourism*, 3(3): 166–72.

Getz, K. (1990) 'International codes of conduct: An analysis of ethical reasoning', *Journal of Business Ethics*, 9: 567–77.

Gowans, C. (2012) 'Moral Relativism', in Zalta, E.N. (ed.), *The Stanford Encyclopedia of Philosophy* (Spring edition). Available at <http://plato.stanford.edu/archives/spr2012/entries/moral-relativism/> (Accessed 10 May 2012).

Harris, R. and Jago, L. (2001) 'Professional accreditation in the Australian tourism industry; an uncertain future', *Tourism Management*, 22: 383–90.

Holden, A. (2000) *Environment and Tourism* (1st edn), London: Routledge.

Honey, M. (1999) *Ecotourism and Sustainable Development: Who Owns Paradise?* (1st edn), Washington: Island Press.

Hultsman, J. (1995) 'Just tourism: An ethical framework', *Annals of Tourism Research*, 22(3): 553–67.

Jones, C., Parker, M. and ten Bos, R. (2005) *For Business Ethics: A Critical Text*, London: Routledge.

Kaptein, M. and Schwartz, M.S. (2008) 'The effectiveness of business codes: A critical examination of existing studies and the development of an integrated research model', *Journal of Business Ethics*, 77: 111–27.

Kolk, A. and van Tulder, R. (2002) 'Child labour and multinational conduct: A comparison of international business and stakeholder codes', *Journal of Business Ethics,* 36: 291–301.

Krohn, F.B. and Ahmed, Z.U. (1992) 'The need for developing an ethical code for the marketing of international tourism services', *Journal of Professional Services Marketing,* 8(1): 189–200.

Laczniak, G.R. and Murphy, P.E. (1991) 'International marketing ethics', *Bridges,* 2: 155–77.

Leopold, A. (1949) *A Sand County Almanac,* New York: Oxford University Press.

Loacker, B. and Muhr, S.L. (2009) 'How can I become a responsible subject? Towards a practice-based ethics of responsiveness', *Journal of Business Ethics,* 90: 265–77.

Malloy, D.C. and Fennell, D.A. (1998) 'Codes of ethics and tourism: An exploratory content analysis', *Tourism Management,* 19(5): 453–61.

Mason, P. (2005) 'Visitor management in protected areas: From "hard" to "soft" approaches?', *Current Issues in Tourism*, 8(2/3): 181–94.

—— (2007) '"No better than a band-aid for a bullet wound!": The effectiveness of tourism codes of conduct', in Black, R. and Crabtree, A. (eds), *Quality Assurance and Certification in Ecotourism,* Cambridge: CABI, pp. 46–64.

Mason, P. and Mowforth, M. (1996) 'Codes of conduct in tourism', *Progress in Tourism and Hospitality Research,* 2(2): 151–67.

Mowforth, M. and Munt, I. (2003) *Tourism and Sustainability: New Tourism in the Third World* (2nd edn), London: Routledge.

Preuss, L. (2010) 'Codes of conduct in organisational context: From cascade to lattice-work of codes', *Journal of Business Ethics,* 94: 471–87.

Rallapalli, K.C. (1999) 'A paradigm for development and promulgation of a global code of marketing ethics', *Journal of Business Ethics,* 18: 125–37.

Roberts, L. and Hall, D. (2001) *Rural Tourism and Recreation: Principles to Practice,* Wallingford: CABI.

Roberts, L. and Rognvaldson, G. (2001) 'The roles of interpretation in facilitating access to and in the countryside', in Roberts, L. and Hall, D. (eds), *Rural Tourism and Recreation: Principles to Practice,* Wallingford: CABI, pp. 92–7.

Ryan, C. (2002) 'Equity, management, power sharing and sustainability – issues of the "new tourism"', *Tourism Management,* 23(1): 17–26.

Schwartz, M. (2000) 'Why ethical codes constitute an unconscionable regression', *Journal of Business Ethics.* 23: 173–84.

—— (2001) 'The nature of the relationship between corporate codes of ethics and behaviour', *Journal of Business Ethics,* 32: 247–62.

Sirakaya, E. (1997) 'Attitudinal compliance with ecotourism guidelines', *Annals of Tourism Research,* 24(4): 919–50.

Smith, R. and Duffy, M. (2003) *The Ethics of Tourism Development,* London: Routledge.

Sobczak, A. (2006) 'Are codes of conduct in global supply chains really voluntary? From soft law regulation of labour relations to consumer law', *Business Ethics Quarterly,* 16: 167–84.

Tearfund (2000) *Tourism an Ethical Issue: Market Research Report.* Available at <http://tilz.tearfund.org/webdocs/Website/Campaigning/Policy%20and%20research/Policy%20-%20 Tourism%20Market%20Research%20Report.pdf> (Accessed 12 May 2011).

United Nations World Tourism Organization (UNWTO) (2010) *Report of the World Tourism Organization on the Implementation of the Global Code of Ethics for Tourism.* Available at <http://ethics.unwto.org/en/content/implementation-reports-global-code-ethics-tourism> (Accessed 10 September 2012).

—— (2012) *Global Code of Ethics for Tourism.* Available at <http://ethics.unwto.org/en/content/global-code-ethics-tourism> (Accessed 16 April 2012).

Van Tulder, R., van Wijk, J. and Kolk, A. (2009) 'From chain liability to chain responsibility: MNE approaches to implement safety and health codes in international supply chains', *Journal of Business Ethics,* 85: 399–412.

Weaver, G.R. (2006) 'Virtue in organizations: Moral identity as a foundation for moral agency', *Organization Studies,* 27(3): 341–68.

Wight, P (2004) 'Practical management tools and approaches for resource protection and assessment', in Diamantis, D. (ed.), *Ecotourism,* London: Thomson, pp. 48–72.

15 Conclusion: ethical futures?

'On the whole human beings want to be good, but not too good, and not quite all the time.'

George Orwell[a]

'Next to doing the right thing, the most important thing is to let people know you are doing the right thing.'

John D. Rockefeller[b]

LEARNING OBJECTIVES

After reading this book you will be able to:

- Discuss the applicability of a range of ethical frameworks in relation to a range of tourism practices.
- Critically explore a range of tourism industry practices and identify the key ethical and moral issues and potential means to address negative outcomes.
- Understand the rationale for an 'ethics' focus on tourism.

15.1 INTRODUCTION

Having read this book the reader will be in no doubt that tourism is not a 'smokeless' industry, that there are a range of impacts – social, cultural, economic and environmental – that require critical scrutiny and an ethics approach if the impacts are to be effectively ameliorated. While there are undoubtedly benefits for communities engaging in tourism, it is also well established that the political and economic benefits of this industry are not equitably distributed and decision making tends to be in the hands of a few, which at times is to the detriment of many. In this book we have attempted to bring ethics to contemporary debates in tourism and explored how a range of ethical frameworks can assist the student, researcher and practitioner of tourism. We have not attempted the impossible task of prescribing what framework should be employed or suggested that there is a single way forward, and the reader will now appreciate why this is not possible. As Smith and Duffy (2003: 3) observe and as noted at the outset of this book:

> a knowledge of ethics is not like a knowledge of mathematics, it will not allow us to 'solve' complex social equations simply, but it might help us interpret and communicate to others what it is that we think is right or wrong about a certain situation and why.

Recall, ethics means 'a habitual mode of conduct' and conduct that ensures that good is being done (Fennell 2009: 213). Morality is beliefs about right and wrong, good and bad and includes judgements about values, rules, principles and theories. The tourism industry cannot avoid ethics – ethics is not outside of social life – it is a fundamental aspect of being human.

15.2 FIVE STEPS AND FOUR KEY ELEMENTS

Central to ethics is critical reasoning. As outlined in Chapter 2, there are five steps to the process of ethical decision making: (1) recognise the problem; (2) analyse the problem and clarify the facts and uncertainties; (3) identify the ethical issues and values central to the decision making; (4) if the values conflict you have an ethical dilemma; (5) prioritise the values in conflict. Here, consider how you can prioritise in terms of what end is sought, what the means to the end is, and authenticity. When these steps are used in conjunction with the four key elements central to ethics – (1) the pre-eminence of reason; (2) the universal perspective; (3) the principle or impartiality; (4) the dominance of moral norms (Vaughn 2008: 7) – you are working toward ethical decision making. We have advocated an eclectic approach to addressing ethical concerns and issues. Schumann's (2001) Moral Principles Framework, which draws from five main ethical theories – (1) utilitarianism; (2) rights; (3) distributive justice; (4) ethics of care; (5) virtue – is a useful tool to employ when considering the diverse range of practices in the tourism industry which provoke ethical concern (see Chapter 2).

In this book we have provided a variety of topical and relevant issues central to contemporary tourism and explored the utility of a range of ethical frameworks. In the first three chapters we commenced with an outline of a range of frameworks and then moved on to critically consider mobility, borders, security and assumptions made about freedom of access and the right to travel. Mobility is not equally shared by people. While some cannot travel others are forced to travel in response to civil unrest, war, famine and human rights abuses. Inequity is the central issue underpinning mobility in the contemporary world and there are significant ethical issues connected to controlling mobility and the surveillance of those who are or attempt to be mobile. With respect to the latter, utilitarian frameworks inform border control and surveillance technologies. Closer inspection of these processes suggests that there would be value in employing a justice framework and closer consideration of the human rights issues that emerge in relation to mobility. We need to question whose interests are being served by those who are legitimately mobile, illegitimately mobile and involuntarily mobile – and an importantly those who will never be able to mobile.

Chapters 4 to 8 consider ethics, host and home communities. There are, as we have seen, a number of challenges for the tourism industry in relation to human rights. Notably, the relativist/universalist dilemma poses ethical questions regarding the enforcement of global human rights. There are a range of human rights issues that emerge in destination communities and all are underpinned by power differentials between stakeholders both within generating regions and destinations. And while the state has been charged with the main responsibility for addressing human rights, increasingly the private sector has also been held to account. We discussed how tourism practitioners face challenges in meeting the human rights needs of those people in distant (host) communities, as ethical decision making within the industry tends to prioritise the client at all costs. Alternative, responsible and justice tourism address human rights issues and suggest various responses that can be adopted by the industry in order to improve industry performance with respect to human rights.

Medical tourism is a growing form of niche tourism that provokes a range of ethical concerns and issues in relation to both destination communities and the communities from which the medical tourist belongs. This range of issues encompasses the resource implications for destination and departure health systems and health care provisions. Especially important is the inequitable access and use of health care resources and the observed emergence of two-tiered health systems in both the developing and developed world which ultimately impact on the provision of public health care for the majority. Distributive justice allows us to consider how unethical practices in this niche might be addressed through closer regulation, involving in particular the redistribution of financing mechanisms (taxes and reinvestment in the public health system), social insurance for those who cannot afford to pay and ensuring that private providers in destination countries, where there are significant public health issues, are obligated to provide free health care for locals. Utilitarian frameworks allow for addressing the needs of the majority and human rights-based frameworks address the fundamental notion that primary health care is a basic human right.

Sex tourism often provokes considerable moral outrage. In Chapter 6 we have explored some of the key issues and in particular focused on the socio-economic factors that underpin the growth and reproduction of sex tourism markets. It is difficult to draw a clear line between tourism and sex tourism and there are definitional problems surrounding whether or not it is 'sex' tourism or 'romance' tourism. However, these conceptual problems do not alter the reality that tourism markets, sex markets, the trafficking of women and children for prostitution and sexual servitude are all interconnected and that poverty is the most significant factor associated with the emergence of the world's largest sex markets. The sex tourism industry is predicated on inequity: women and children are disproportionately represented as the providers of sex for sale in this industry and this is directly linked to their more marginal economic status, the fact that they are more likely to be mobile (and in search of material security) and the hierarchy within this industry, which is structured by class, race and sexuality. Hedonist ethics might provide a legitimation of this search for pleasure, but frameworks that address egalitarian concerns, notions of social responsibility and distributive justice demonstrate that the central ethical issues hinge on significant material inequality – locally and globally. Various measures have been introduced to address trafficking and slavery, with varying success. There are a range of operators and enterprises that are attempting to address the employment of children in this industry, where various codes of conduct have been adopted by employers and educational opportunities provided for those at risk.

There are, as we have seen, a range of ethical issues connected to tourism and indigeneity, including the commodification of culture and fundamental issues surrounding power and control over material and cultural resources that date back to imperial expansion and colonisation of territories. While there have been a range of social movements that have addressed the disenfranchisement of indigenous peoples, with respect to tourism one of the most significant recent developments has been the United Nations *Draft Declaration on the Rights of Indigenous Peoples* (1999), which will arguably have a significant impact on the tourism industry. Central to ethical debate in this area is human rights and the need for distributive justice and or justice approaches, all of which address the need for a fundamental shift in the relationship between tourists and the host community; one that involves a move toward what might be called empathetic respect and the maximisation of local economic, cultural and social benefits (Higgins-Desbiolles 2010: 362).

A range of alternative tourisms have been developed with the aim of focusing on people in poverty. Pro-poor tourism and slum tourism are two examples. The key issues that emerge in relation to both are whether or not they address poverty and what the long-term implications will be for those who live in poverty. Justice and distributive justice frameworks are useful for addressing these issues, as while both of these alternative forms of tourism may well heighten awareness of poverty, what people acknowledge as a reality and how they respond to this reality are two very different things, and the first does not always predicate the latter.

The needs of people with disabilities have generally been inadequately addressed by the tourism industry, and social tourism has been identified as a possible response to the inequities that ensure that those with disabilities do not have the same touristic opportunities as able-bodied tourists. Social tourism focuses on the underlying causes for inequitable access and stresses the need to address economic and social disadvantages that impede access 'for the good of society'. While there is a legal imperative and evidence to suggest that there are economic benefits in engaging more fully with disabled tourists, the moral debate surrounding the provision of services to the disabled is contested. A range of ethical frameworks have been applied, with utilitarianism the most contested. At one end of the continuum Singer (2000) questions whether those with cognitive disabilities have the same ability to be self-aware and thus be subject to moral considerability and at the other end of the continuum is hedonistic utilitarianism – where the view that the best life is one that maximises human pleasure is asserted – and where it is argued that those with disabilities have a strong claim to scarce resources. In addition, egalitarianism, distributive justice and prioritarianism (another form of utilitarianism) are also employed in relation to the disabled. With respect to the latter there is commonality with the social model of disability which stresses that social factors are central to defining disability and how access and assistance are addressed in relation to the disabled tourist. Central to ethical debate on disability is the question of how we can address the multiple demands on resources (built and natural) whilst simultaneously providing worthwhile experiences for persons with disabilities.

Chapters 9 to 11 focus on tourism and the environment. Human interaction with non-human nature provokes a range of ethical issues and concerns, and central to these is the debate that hinges on the dominant anthropocentric approach to non-human nature. While this approach has been attributed various origins, the central question with respect to the tourism industry is how can mainstream ethical frameworks be applied to address the environmental problems which are an outcome of anthropocentrism. The two main approaches to the 'nature problem' have been the frameworks of deontology and utilitarianism. Moral extensionism is also advanced as a useful tool for addressing tourism and development. There are, as we have seen, a range of more 'radical' ethical approaches including: holism and deep-green ethics (including the Gaia hypothesis). Sustainable development has of course been central to debate in this field, but it has also been found to be problematic – as too has ecotourism as a form of tourism that can remedy tourism's ills. We have focused primarily on Western environmental ethics, but acknowledge that this approach is limited as there are differing cultural perspectives, histories of ideas and applications globally – all of which inform understandings about what or which development is 'right' or 'best' and what the ideal outcomes would, could or should be. Yet, here, as with all other illustrations in this book, cultural relativism has limited utility when we are required to address resources from a global perspective, and does not always provide an 'ethical' answer to a social problem.

Animals are considered an important tourism 'product' – the animal question in tourism is typically addressed by focusing on animal rights and welfare. Sentience, that is the ability to feel, perceive or be conscious (or the capacity for emotion, pleasure and pain), ensures moral considerability. With respect to animals, the focus on the ability to experience suffering is usually central to ethical debate. Virtue ethics and the notions of instrumental and intrinsic value allow approaches to the 'animal question', and with respect to the latter emphasise that value in its own right', 'for its own sake' is central to animal rights-based arguments.

Mass tourism has been possible because of air travel and in turn air travel is central to the ethical debate surrounding climate change and the various remedies that have been put forward to address the impact of hypermobility. In this chapter we discussed the concept of harm, and the difficulties in identifying and assigning responsibility for actions such as flying where harm is indirect, not readily observable, the victims not easily identifiable, and responsibility not easily assigned. We invoke the 'Tragedy of the Commons' and 'Prisoner's Dilemma' scenarios to address the ethical problems associated with the touristic use of common pool resources – where individual actions (flying) impact upon collective wellbeing. Addressing climate change requires a fundamental shift in how we view travel and on the kind of trip(s) we choose to take. We note that energy efficiency is not just confined to addressing the resource consumption associated with flying to the destination, but also relies on tourists (and operators) addressing the inefficient use of energy at destinations.

We have considered hospitality, marketing and labour issues. The hospitality industry faces a range of ethical issues with respect to management and human resources; however, the marketing practices of tourism and hospitality providers have been singled out as facing the greatest challenges of all. In particular, issues of truth in representation haunt the activities of marketers. We identify that the core issue in many ethical situations is the competing sets of norms that ethical decision makers must choose between: personal, professional, organisational and wider societal norms of behaviour. In this sector it has been demonstrated that most decision-making processes are informed by personal experience and/or organisational norms. Mainstream marketing ethics frameworks, such as the General Theory of Marketing Ethics (Hunt and Vitell 1986) can be applied across many tourism and hospitality-related settings and can assist in resolving a range of ethical problems. While such frameworks are largely informed by deontology and teleology, alternative approaches such as virtue ethics and social contract theory may be of value within the sector.

Tourism labour practices provoke a number of issues, not least the ethical implications of the global division of labour and the division of labour within specific localities. The range of ethical issues and concerns in relation to the tourism labour market and labouring conditions for workers all hinge on how class, race; gender and country of origin are significant determinants of place within this hierarchy and industry. We focused on cruise liners as they provide a useful illustration of the emergent transnational working class in tourism and demonstrate how, in search of new tourist products and meeting the expectations of the growing middle classes in search of tourist consumption, the disadvantaged continue to be disadvantaged. Justice frameworks and egalitarianism are particularly useful when critically addressing ethical issues in relation to labour and the tourism labour market(s).

Finally, in Chapter 14, we have canvassed codes of ethics, documented their origins and contemporary development and the links to corporate responsibility. There are a range of criticisms directed at codes of ethics and their assumed relationship to ethical behaviour – these criticisms focus on the prescriptive nature of codes and the limitations of externally imposed sets of rules. Some advocate that a greater (utilitarian) focus on the consequences or outcomes of unethical conduct might result in greater adherence to codes. In addition, while codes might serve to highlight the need to behave in a certain manner, in the end it will only be through activities that 'good practice' becomes normative and in turn provides evidence of moral accountability.

15.2 AN ETHICAL TOURIST?

Throughout this book, through elaborating on a number of ethical frameworks, we suggest 'ways forward' to achieving better outcomes from tourism. Essentially we can condense these down into two requisite improvements: fostering ethics among tourists; fostering an ethical approach across tourist industry providers and relevant stakeholders. Codes of ethics and conduct have been identified, for example, as means of producing ethical or responsible behaviour in visitors – opening the eyes of tourists and other tourism stakeholders to the amalgam of behaviours that together constitute responsible or ethical tourism. This brings us back to the concept of the 'responsible tourist' (see Chapter 1) who has been compared with the 'new moral tourist' (Butcher 2003) and the 'ethical tourist' (Stanford 2008: 260).

However, an interesting question arises over what perspective should define our responsible tourist. Stanford conducted research in New Zealand, with a range of tourism industry participants, seeking to identify the essential characteristics of a responsible tourist. She notes that from the International Centre for Responsible Tourism (ICRT 2012) perspective, a responsible tourist may be a niche ecotourist, travelling lightly, spending time with the local community, engaging carefully with nature, and observing Māori protocol. In this sense, they are the antithesis to the packaged, culturally insensitive mass tourist. However, from a hard-nosed tourism industry perspective, the responsible tourist may not be the *desirable* tourist. As one of Stanford's research participants – a tourism attraction operator from the resort of Rotorua – commented, 'Our mass tourist in Rotorua is possibly not what Tourism New Zealand [the national tourism marketing organisation] thinks of as Mr Right, but Mr Wrong is one of the highest spenders' (2008: 270). So Mr Wrong, while not being 'ethical' or 'responsible' may indeed be tourism industry's ideal tourist (at least from a short-term, economic perspective).

Thus, defining the responsible, moral or ethical tourist is complex and multidimensional – how do we prioritise those dimensions, especially with industry stakeholders having a quite different view? Perhaps this is where we can draw upon initiatives developed more fully in other sectors, most notably, that of corporate social responsibility, to drive the tourism industry forward in a more ethical way.

CASE STUDY: FAIR TRADE TOURISM – *KARLA BOLUK*

The fair trade notion has emerged as a way to readdress the sustainability and inequality issues that exist within the tourism industry. Fair Trade Tourism (FTT) through applying fair trade principles provides a better deal for tourism producers and service providers in the Majority World. FTT prioritises those in host communities who are ready to engage with tourism, yet who (Tourism Concern 2009):

- Have not previously had a voice in the tourism decision-making process;
- Are economically and socially disadvantaged or discriminated against.

Cross-pollination between Fairtrade products and FTT is taking place, most commonly in the context of gastronomy tourism (Boluk 2011a). Coffee and tea tour programmes are in operation in several countries. For example, In Tanzania several coffee farmer communities have implemented a 'sustainable form of coffee-related tourism' (Goodwin and Boekhold 2010: 181) and locally owned and managed coffee tours return sizeable benefits to individuals, families and their communities. Another example of a community that practises FTT is Makaibari Tea Estates in India. Makaibari is a locally owned tea company that produces Fairtrade certified Darjeeling tea on site. As a way to accommodate the constant flow of visitors to Makaibari some villagers in 2005 offered their homes to paying guests. Currently, there are 21 families providing accommodation at a rate of $25USD per couple including meals. The profits have been regenerated into the community by way of creating a computer centre benefitting nearly 80 children, a scholarship fund to assist individuals in studying horticulture, the creation of a community loan fund – which has assisted 100 families with housing needs, medical needs, education, livestock and small business development (Makaibari Tea Estates 2011).

In addition to FTT emerging from tangible Fairtrade certified products, the philosophy of fair trade has influenced the development of many tourism businesses. In 2002 South Africa launched its trademark certification known as Fair Trade Tourism South Africa (FTTSA). The goal of FTTSA is to promote equitable and sustainable tourism development. FTTSA certification is based on quantifiable criteria regarding labour standards including wages, the treatment of people, local employment, procurement opportunities for families and communities, HIV/AIDS support, black empowerment and a number of environmental conservation practices (FTTSA 2011). FTTSA businesses are prioritising the needs of the poor: by including the poor in tourism decision making, creating employment opportunities and stimulating entrepreneurship and providing skilful opportunities in areas where people have had limited access to resources (Boluk 2011b). Such outcomes demonstrate a re-evaluation of priorities from the perspective of tourism businesses.

Discussion questions

1 In what ways has FTT benefited local communities in the Majority World?
2 How is the definition of FTT similar or different to other alternative forms of tourism?
3 To what extent, and how, does FTT align with the ethical approach to tourism espoused in this book?

References

Boluk, K. (2011a) 'In consideration of a *new* approach to tourism: A critical review of Fair Trade Tourism', *Journal of Tourism and Peace Research*, 2(1): 27–37.
—— (2011b) 'Fair Trade Tourism South Africa: A pragmatic poverty reduction mechanism?', *Tourism Planning and Development*, 8(3): 237–51.
Fair Trade Tourism South Africa (FTTSA) (2011) Available at: <http://www.fair tourismsa.org.za/fairtrade_insouthafrica.html> (Accessed 12 March 2009).
Goodwin, H. and Boekhold, H. (2010) 'Beyond fair trade: Enhancing the livelihoods of coffee farmers in Tanzania', in Jolliffe, L. *Coffee Culture, Destinations and Tourism*, Bristol: Channel View, pp.181–96.
Makaibari Tea Estates (2011) Available at <http://www.makaibari.com/stay.html> (Accessed 11 November 2011).
Tourism Concern (2009) *Fair Trade in Tourism*. Available at: <http://www.tourism concern.org.uk/index.php?page=news> (Accessed 9 January 2009).

15.3 AN ETHICAL INDUSTRY? – ETHICS AND CORPORATE SOCIAL RESPONSIBILITY

In search of tools that have more precision than sustainable development in terms of measurable outcomes, the business world has arrived at the concept of corporate social responsibility (CSR). Can CSR provide the basis for a more ethical tourism industry? Broadly speaking, CSR provides a 'triple bottom line' (economic, environmental, social) approach to evaluating the success of business. It is 'the management of a company's positive impact on society and the environment through its operations, products or services and through its interaction with key stakeholders such as employees, customers, investors and suppliers' (Business in the Community 2005).

The relationship between ethical, economic, legal and philanthropic responsibilities is depicted in Carroll's (1979, 1991) CSR pyramid (Figure 15.1). The model entails the simultaneous fulfilment of all four CSR components.

But what is the relationship between CSR and ethics, and is it adequate in discussions of a more ethical tourism industry to just defer to CSR as a guideline for ethical behaviour? Ethics concerns: 'the rules and standards of conduct related to rules of moral philosophy, [while] social responsibility concerns the social contract existing between business and the society in which it operates' (Hunt et al. 1990: 240). In tourism this social contract crosses societies and engages a range of stakeholders, not all of whom share an equal footing. This recognition of a 'contract' between business and society has been stressed from the outset by CSR proponents. Carroll (1979), for example, takes the perspective that businesses are responsible to society and should do what is expected from society. However, critics of CSR believe that businesses are not responsible to society but are only responsible to their stakeholders (and not all equally) (Holcomb et al. 2007). Most famously, economist Milton Friedman (1998: 251) argued that:

Be a good corporate citizen — Philanthropic — Desired

Be ethical — Ethical — Expected

Obey the law — Legal — Required

Be profitable — Economic — Required

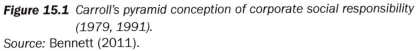

Figure 15.1 *Carroll's pyramid conception of corporate social responsibility (1979, 1991).*
Source: Bennett (2011).

> There is only one social responsibility of business – to use its resources and engage in activities designed to increase its profits so long as it stays within the rules of the game, which is to say, engages in open and free competition without deception or fraud.

Such a position, that 'the business of business is business', is hotly disputed. It has been pointed out that Friedman's view is the result of an 'inadequate' social philosophy, and that there must be some 'minimal moral codes that cannot be overlooked' (Lozano 2000: 58). Lozano believes that CSR is desirable from an ethical perspective because it is a form of 'enlightened selfishness', and it allows ethical criteria to take priority over economic criteria.

But can CSR replace an ethics approach, as a guide for tourism or business more broadly? As Carroll observes: 'The social responsibility of business encompasses the economic, legal, ethical and discretionary expectations that society has of organizations *at a given point of time*' (1979: 500 (emphasis added)). Thus social responsibility includes ethics, 'but only insofar that ethics is identified with the dominant moral values of a society to which its members are expected to adapt' (Lozano 2000: 66). What if the dominant moral values, at that particular point in time, are questionable? Conforming uncritically to dominant values (norms) is problematic, and indeed may end up being unethical. Thus, while CSR may be a useful tool in our striving for a more ethical tourism industry, it is necessary to acknowledge the limitations of CSR – especially considering the complex social and (cross)-cultural contexts in which tourism operates.

This book contributes to a growing debate in tourism scholarship on the need for the tourism industry to address ethics. As moral agents, students of tourism, tourism operators and tourists must be equipped to engage in critical reasoning and to habitually question touristic practice with a view to making informed ethical decisions. We think that current evidence demonstrates beyond doubt that the tourism industry cannot afford to 'turn a blind eye' to ethics. Nor can the industry afford to succumb to the hedonistic call to 'turn the other cheek' to the 'fun police'. 'Turning the other cheek' potentially undermines your own personal freedom and the freedom of others. If freedom is at the heart of your moral values and you have critically reflected on your learnt morality, then if and when this value is seriously threatened you will be better equipped to defend it. This book does not claim to solve all of the ethical dilemmas provoked by the tourism industry, but it is hoped that it will contribute to greater awareness of ethical concerns and issues. We also hope that various ethical frameworks and perspectives canvassed in this book will enable readers to apply ethics with a view to bringing about social change – in an industry that is undoubtedly one of the most significant social forces of the twenty-first century.

DISCUSSION POINT: ETHICAL TOURISM AND CORPORATE SOCIAL RESPONSIBILITY

In a study of CSR policies and practices in 10 international hotel groups, discrepancies were found between corporate CSR intent and actual practice (Font et al. 2012). And in that study, environmental performance was eco-savings driven; labour policies only aimed to comply with local legislation; socio-economic policies were inward looking with little acceptance of impacts on the destination; and customer engagement was limited. Mowforth and Munt (2003) believe that the tourism industry is well behind other industries in terms of CSR, and describe the absence of ethical leadership within the tourism industry as 'astounding'.

A critical question relates to the motivation for engaging in CSR. Tourism companies may be driven by a moral (intrinsic) motive, which holds that CSR is a moral duty of companies towards society, or by a strategic (extrinsic) motive which holds that CSR contributes to the financial success of the company in the long run. Studies have shown, however, that the moral (intrinsic) motive induces a stronger involvement in CSR than the strategic (extrinsic) motive (Ven van de and Graafland 2006).

Discussion questions

1 If the motivation for a tourism operator to engage in CSR is primarily on business grounds, can this be interpreted as ethical behaviour?
2 Some authors (e.g. Lantos 2002) argue that altruistic/philanthropic (intrinsically motivated) CSR by public corporations is actually unethical. This is because altruistic CSR unfairly involves 'confiscating stockholder wealth', and spending money for the general welfare at the possible expense of those the firm should be caring for, notably employees and customers. Do you agree or disagree and why? Is this different for a *private* company?
3 How does the cross-cultural nature of tourism challenge CSR as an ethical approach to tourism?

References

Font, X., Walmsley, A., Cogotti, S., McCombes, L. and Häusler, N. (2012) 'Corporate social responsibility: The disclosure-performance gap', *Tourism Management*, 33: 1544–53.
Lantos, G.P. (2002) 'The ethicality of altruistic corporate social responsibility', *Journal of Consumer Marketing*, 19(3): 205–232.
Mowforth, M. and Munt. I. (2003) *Tourism and Sustainability: Development and New Tourism in the Third World*, London: Routledge.
Ven van de, B. and Graafland, J.J. (2006) 'Strategic and moral motivation for corporate social responsibility', *Journal of Corporate Citizenship*, 22: 111–23.

Useful sources

Schwartz, M.S. (2011) *Corporate Social Responsibility: An Ethical Approach*, Peterborough, Canada: Broadview Press.
Visser,W., Matten,D., Pohl, M. and Tolhurst, N. (2010) *The A to Z of Corporate Social Responsibility*, Chichester: John Wiley.

SUMMARY OF KEY TERMS

Fair Trade Tourism Tourism that applies the principles of fair trade to address the social inequity and sustainability issues within the tourism industry.

Corporate Social Responsibility (CSR) Also known as social responsibility, corporate citizenship, and corporate sustainability. Broadly, it is a company's commitment to operating in an ethical way that takes into account society and the environment.

NOTES

a George Orwell (1903–50), British author and essayist. From *All Art is Propaganda* (first published 1941) Boston, MA: Houghton Mifflin Harcourt, 2008.

b John D. Rockefeller (1839–1937), American industrialist and philanthropist. As quoted in *The Forbes Book of Business Quotations* (2007) edited by Ted Goodman, p. 175.

REFERENCES

Bennett, A.J.W. (2011) 'Learning to be job ready: Strategies for greater social inclusion in public sector employment', *Journal of Business Ethics*, 104(3): 347–59.

Butcher, J. (2003) *The Moralisation of Tourism: Sun, Sand...and Saving the World?*, London: Routledge.

Business in the Community (2005) *Corporate Social Responsibility*. Available at <http://www.bitc.org.uk/resources/jargon_buster/crhtml> (Accessed 13 June 2012).

Carroll, A.B. (1979) 'A three-dimensional conceptual model of corporate social performance', *Academy of Management Review*, 4(4): 497–505.

Fennell, D.A. (2009) 'Ethics and tourism', in Tribe, J. (ed.) *Philosophical Issues in Tourism*, Bristol: Channel View, pp. 211–26.

Friedman, M. (1998) 'The social responsibility of business is to increase its profits', in Hartman, L. (ed.) *Perspectives in Business Ethics*, New York: Irwin McGraw-Hill, pp. 246–51.

Higgins-Desbiolles, F. (2010) 'Justifying tourism: Justice through tourism', in Cole, S. and Morgan, N. (eds) *Tourism and Inequality: Problems and Prospects*, Wallingford: CABI, pp. 194–210.

Holcomb, J.L., Upchurch, R.S. and Okumus, F. (2007) 'International Corporate Social Responsibility: what are top hotel companies reporting?', *Journal of Contemporary Hospitality Management*, 19(6): 461–75.

Hunt, S.D. and Vitell, S.D. (1986) 'A general theory of marketing', *Journal of Macromarketing*, 6: 5–15.

Hunt, S., Kiecker, P. and Chonko, L. (1990) 'Social responsibility and personal success: A research note', *Journal of Academy of Marketing Science*, 18: 239–44.

International Centre for Responsible Tourism (ICRT) (2012) *Responsible Tourism*. Available at <http://www.icrtourism.org/links/responsible-tourism-management-theory-and-practise/> (Accessed 14 July 2012).

Lozano, J.M. (2000) *Ethics and Organisations: Understanding Business Ethics as a Learning Process*, Dordrecht: Kluwer Academic.

Schumann, P.L. (2001) 'A moral principles framework for human resource management ethics', *Human Resource Management Review*, 11: 93–111.

Singer, P. (2000) *Writings on an Ethical Life*, New York: Harper Collins.

Smith, M. and Duffy, R. (2003) *The Ethics of Tourism Development*, London, New York: Routledge.

Stanford, D. (2008) '"Exceptional visitors": Dimensions of tourist responsibility in the context of New Zealand', *Journal of Sustainable Tourism*, 16(3): 258–75.

Vaughn, L. (2008) *Doing Ethics: Moral Reasoning and Contemporary Issues*, New York: W.W. Norton.

Index